FROM THE STONE AGE TO CHRISTIANITY

William Foxwell Albright, one of the world's foremost Orientalists, has been W. W. Spence Professor of Semitic Languages at Johns Hopkins University since 1929. He has lectured at universities and seminaries throughout the world and has also been Sometime Director of the American School of Oriental Research in Jerusalem, in addition to directing many archaeological expeditions in the Middle East. Dr. Albright is a member of the National Academy of Sciences (Washington), the American Philosophical Society (Philadelphia), the American Academy of Arts and Sciences (Cambridge), and the Royal Danish, Flemish, and Irish Academies, and is also a corresponding member of the Académie des Inscriptions et Belles Lettres and of the Austrian Academy of Sciences. He has received degrees from Yale, Georgetown, Trinity College (Dublin), Jewish Theological Seminary of America, Hebrew Union College, Jewish Institute of Religion, College of Jewish Studies, Utrecht, Uppsala, St. Andrews, Boston College, and Oslo. Among Dr. Albright's writings for the general reader are *Archaeology and the Religion of Israel* and *The Archaeology of Palestine*. He is now (1956–59) president of the International Organization of Old Testament scholars.

A hardcover edition of FROM THE STONE AGE TO CHRISTIANITY was first published in 1940 by The Johns Hopkins Press. The Second Edition (1946) is reprinted here with minor changes and a new introduction by the author.

FROM THE STONE AGE
TO CHRISTIANITY

Monotheism and the Historical Process

William Foxwell Albright
PH.D., LITT.D., D.H.L., LL.D., TH.D., DR.HON.CAUS.

Second Edition
With a New Introduction

Doubleday Anchor Books
Doubleday & Company, Inc.
Garden City, New York

COVER BY ANTONIO FRASCONI

TYPOGRAPHY BY EDWARD GOREY

Clothbound copies of *From the Stone Age to Christianity* are available from The Johns Hopkins Press, Baltimore 18, Maryland.

This book is published by agreement between Anchor Books and the Biblical Colloquium. The Biblical Colloquium is a scholarly society devoted to the analysis and discussion of biblical matters, and the preparation, publication, and distribution of informative literature about the Bible for the general reader as well as students.

Library of Congress Catalog Card Number 57–5562

CONTENTS

TITLES OF JOURNALS AND BOOKS ABBREVIATED IN THE FOOTNOTES

Altor. Texte = *Altorientalische Texte zum Alten Testament*, by H. Gressmann and others (Berlin, 1926).

Am. Jour. Arch. = *American Journal of Archaeology*.

Am. Jour. Sem. Lang. = *American Journal of Semitic Languages and Literatures* (Chicago).

Ann. Am. Sch. Or. Res. = *Annual of the American Schools of Oriental Research* (New Haven).

Ann. Arch. Anthr. = *Annals of Archaeology and Anthropology* (Liverpool).

Arch. Pal. Bib. = *Archaeology of Palestine and the Bible*, by W. F. Albright (New York, 1932-35).

Arch. Rel. = *Archiv für Religionsgeschichte* (Leipzig).

Arch. f. Orientf. = *Archiv für Orientforschung* (Berlin).

Bull. Am. Sch. Or. Res. = *Bulletin of the American Schools of Oriental Research* (Baltimore).

Bull. Inst. Fran. Arch. Or. = *Bulletin de l'Institut Français d'Archéologie Orientale du Caire*.

Harv. Theol. Rev. = *Harvard Theological Review* (Cambridge, Mass.).

Heb. Un. Col. Ann. = *Hebrew Union College Annual* (Cincinnati).

Jew. Quar. Rev. = *Jewish Quarterly Review* (Philadelphia).

Jour. Am. Or. Soc. = *Journal of the American Oriental Society*.

Jour. Bib. Lit. = *Journal of Biblical Literature and Exegesis*.

Jour. Bib. Rel. = *Journal of the Bible and Religion.*
Jour. Eg. Arch. = *Journal of Egyptian Archaeology* (London).
Jour. Pal. Or. Soc. = *Journal of the Palestine Oriental Society* (Jerusalem).
Jour. Roy. Asiat. Soc. = *Journal of the Royal Asiatic Society* (London).
Jour. Soc. Or. Res. = *Journal of the Society of Oriental Research* (edited by S. A. B. Mercer, but now extinct).
Jour. Theol. Stud. = *Journal of Theological Studies* (London).
Mitt. Altor. Ges. = *Mitteilungen der Altorientalischen Gesellschaft* (Berlin).
Mitt. Anthr. Ges. Wien = *Mitteilungen der Anthropologischen Gesellschaft in Wien.*
Mitt. Vord.(-aeg.) Ges. = *Mitteilungen der Vorderasiatisch (-aegyptischen) Gesellschaft* (Leipzig).
Nach. (Kön.) Ges. Wiss. = *Nachrichten der (Königlichen) Gesellschaft der Wissenschaften* (Göttingen).
Or. Lit.-zeit. = *Orientalistische Literaturzeitung* (Leipzig).
Pal. Expl. Fund Quar. State. = *Palestine Exploration Fund Quarterly Statement* (now continued by the following journal).
Pal. Expl. Quar. = *Palestine Exploration Quarterly* (London).
Proc. Am. Acad. Jew. Res. = *Proceedings of the American Academy of Jewish Research* (New York).
Proc. Am. Philos. Soc. = *Proceedings of the American Philosophical Society* (Philadelphia).
Rev. Bib. = *Revue Biblique* (Paris).
Rev. Hist. Philos. Rel. = *Revue d'Histoire et de Philosophie religieuses* (Strasbourg).
Rev. Hist. Rel. = *Revue de l'Histoire des Religions* (Paris).
Sitz. Bay. Akad. Wiss. = *Sitzungsberichte der Bayerischen Akademie der Wissenschaften* (Munich).
Sitz. Heid. Akad. Wiss. = *Sitzungsberichte der Heidelberger Akademie der Wissenschaften.*
Sitz. Preuss. Akad. Wiss. = *Sitzungsberichte der Preussischen Akademie der Wissenschaften* (Berlin).
Zeits. Äg. Spr. = *Zeitschrift für Ägyptische Sprache und Altertumskunde* (Leipzig).
Zeits. Alttest. Wiss. = *Zeitschrift für die Alttestamentliche Wissenschaft* (Giessen, now Berlin).
Zeits. f. Assyr. = *Zeitschrift für Assyriologie* (Leipzig and Berlin).
Zeits. Deutsch. Morg. Ges. = *Zeitschrift der Deutschen Morgenländischen Gesellschaft* (Leipzig).
Zeits. Deutsch. Pal. Ver. = *Zeitschrift des Deutschen Palästina-Vereins* (Leipzig).
Zeits. Neutest. Wiss. = *Zeitschrift für Neutestamentliche Wissenschaft* (Berlin).

INTRODUCTION TO THE ANCHOR EDITION

Since the first appearance of this book in 1940, it has been reprinted three times; on each occasion it was revised throughout as much as practicable without resetting more than a few consecutive lines or changing the pagination. Since 1946 there has been no further revision in English, but the German (1949), French (1951), and Hebrew (1953) translations have incorporated much revision and some enlargement of the text. In this introduction I will first describe the most important advances in the state of knowledge which affect the book as a whole and then take up each chapter in succession, indicating the kind of revision or expansion which I should like to incorporate in a rewritten text.

Since the Second World War came to an end in 1945, there has been progress in archaeological work all along the line. There have also been some utterly unexpected discoveries, such as that of the Dead Sea Scrolls, which revolutionize our knowledge of the text of the Old Testament and of the Jewish background, time of composition, and historical position of the New Testament. The discovery of the radiocarbon index to chronology (since 1948) is rapidly revolutionizing our understanding of prehistory. The reinterpretation of the history of biblical concepts and institutions by G. Ernest Wright, George E. Mendenhall, John Bright, Frank M. Cross, Jr., David Noel Freedman, and others of my students, has revitalized my own thinking, leading to progress all along the line. Since 1940 there has been an unprecedented rise of general interest in the philosophy of history, as well as in anthropological and historical method. Philosophers of religion have plunged into the arena, though too often from the direction of philosophical idealism, which is by its nature better suited for utilization of historical research than for contribution to it.

However, none of these discoveries has in any way

changed my attitude with regard to the basic positions taken in 1940 and maintained ever since. I still insist on the primacy of archaeology in the broad sense, including the interpretation of written documents recovered by archaeologists as well as the excavation and reconstruction of material culture. I continue to maintain, without reservation, that we must approach history, as the story of man's total past, with just as rigorous a method as is used by natural scientists, and that *within proper limits* we must follow the general principles of logical empiricism. I insist on the antiquity of higher culture, and distinguish sharply between the proto-logical stage of thinking (which governed religion, and to some extent art and literature, down roughly to the late second millennium B.C., and was characteristic of magic and mythology down to much later periods in the Near East), the empirico-logical stage (which characterized everyday life in all periods and gained ground in higher culture after the late third millennium), and the stage of formal logic (which was the contribution of Greek philosophers, from Thales to Aristotle, and was unknown in ancient Egypt and southwestern Asia before the fourth century B.C.).

Turning to Israel, I defend the substantial historicity of patriarchal tradition, without any appreciable change in my point of view, and insist, just as in 1940-46, on the primacy of oral tradition over written literature. I have not surrendered a single position with regard to early Israelite monotheism but, on the contrary, consider the Mosaic tradition as even more reliable than I did then. Without altering my general view of the growth of the social and political institutions of Israel, I now recognize that Israelite law and religious institutions tend to be older and more continuous than I had supposed—in other words, I have grown more conservative in my attitude to Mosaic tradition. In particular, thanks to the studies of G. E. Mendenhall and my own subsequent work (both of which remain largely unpublished), I recognize that the Covenant is not only fully as ancient as I had thought, but was much more pervasive in its effect on the religious and political life of Israel.

I have not changed my views on the origin and development of the prophetic movement in Israel, but have made further observations which confirm them. In particular, I now insist much more vigorously on the pattern of prophetic thinking which made the Prophets such successful predictors of the course of history. I continue to maintain the corollary of that pattern: the prophetic message was validated in part by the truth of its predictions, and there are very few biblical prophecies which failed to be confirmed. There seems to be hardly a single "prophecy after the event" in the whole extant prophetic literature of Israel, though it became common enough in eschatological literature after the Greek period had begun.

My approach to the Hellenistic and New Testament periods remains the same in all fundamentals, though the Dead Sea Scrolls have revolutionized details. I still insist on the basic character of the Greek revolution in higher culture, and deny the possibility of definition of concepts, logical classification of data, and deductive reasoning among the Hebrews before the third century B.C. I continue to insist that both the Sadducees and Pharisees had been hellenized in vital respects before the time of Christ. I still maintain that the original Essenes came from Mesopotamia in the second century B.C., and were less affected by Hellenism than were the larger Jewish sects. I still connect the beginnings of Christianity more closely with the Essenes and their congeners than with the larger sects, and insist on the early date of the Gospels, including John. On the other hand, I now lay more stress on the continuity of Old and New Testaments, and on the indissoluble bond between pre-Christian Judaism and early Christianity than ever before, thanks largely to the discovery of the Dead Sea Scrolls (since 1949). These priceless documents have brought a wealth of confirmation and illustration, at the same time that they have vastly widened our horizon and have made it possible to bring the whole New Testament into the picture in a way quite impossible in 1940-46.

CHAPTER I: NEW HORIZONS IN HISTORY

Since the resumption of excavations after the end of the Second World War, there has been great progress in discovery, in publication of results, and in general synthesis; cf. the compact surveys in my chapters in *The Old Testament and Modern Study* (Oxford, 1951, ed. H. H. Rowley) and the latest revised edition of my *Recent Discoveries in Bible Lands* (Pittsburgh, 1956). For Palestine see my Pelican *Archaeology of Palestine* (Harmondsworth, latest edition 1956), with the revised and enlarged French translation, *L'archéologie de la Palestine* (Paris, 1955). A fine synthesis of archaeological finds is being published in Hebrew by M. Avi-Yonah and S. Yeivin (*The Antiquities of Israel,* Vol. I [Tel-Aviv, 1955]). For Egypt, see particularly J. Vandier's *Manuel d'archéologie égyptienne,* several volumes of which have already appeared (Paris, since 1952). A. Parrot has undertaken a somewhat parallel manual for Mesopotamia, two volumes of which have been published as *Archéologie mésopotamienne* (Paris, since 1946). For Asia Minor and Persia we now have two good Pelican books: O. R. Gurney's *The Hittites* (Harmondsworth, 1952) and R. Ghirshman, *Iran* (Harmondsworth, 1954), and for India we have Stuart Piggott's admirable *Prehistoric India* (Harmondsworth, 1950).

There has been great progress also in interpretation and decipherment. The Erman-Grapow dictionary of Egyptian has been finished, with all the volumes of references to passages where words occur, and the Chicago *Assyrian Dictionary* has begun to appear (Vol. VI, 1956). With W. von Soden's great Assyro-Babylonian grammar (*Grundriss der akkadischen Grammatik* [Rome, 1952]) and Elmar Edel's grammar of Old Egyptian (*Altägyptische Grammatik* [Rome, 1955]), not to mention many other useful handbooks of hieroglyphic and cuneiform literature, the student is now much better equipped than he was in 1946. Even the minor languages are much better known: witness C. H. Gordon's *Ugaritic Manual* (Rome, 1955). Johannes

Friedrich has given us a splendid Hittite grammar and introduction in his *Hethitisches Elementarbuch* (Heidelberg, 1940-46), followed by his *Hethitisches Wörterbuch* (Heidelberg, 1952-54). To the same able scholar we owe our best Phoenician grammar (*Phönizisch-punische Grammatik* [Rome, 1951]). The advanced state of our knowledge is well illustrated by *Ancient Near Eastern Texts Relating to the Old Testament*, by a group of specialists under the editorship of James B. Pritchard (Princeton, 1950, 1955).

The most striking advance in decipherment is without doubt the decoding of the Minoan-Mycenaean Linear B script from Knossos, Pylos, Mycenae, and elsewhere in Crete and Mainland Greece. This brilliant feat of Michael Ventris, with the aid of John Chadwick, was accomplished in 1953. To the surprise of most scholars it turns out that the language of these tablets from the fourteenth and thirteenth centuries B.C. was an early form of Classical Greek, closely related to the somewhat composite dialect employed by Homer (whom I had dated in 1950 to the tenth century B.C.).

CHAPTER II: TOWARD AN ORGANISMIC PHILOSOPHY OF HISTORY

I should rewrite this chapter today—though I still adhere to the views expressed in it—because there are new considerations which demand priority. Arnold J. Toynbee's *Study of History* (London, 1934-54) is now completed in ten volumes and has achieved unprecedented popularity, its author being decried (often unfairly) by most professional historians and regarded as an oracle (also imprudently) by wide circles of the public. Thanks to Toynbee's Gifford Lectures on *An Historian's Approach to Religion* (1956), it has become even clearer just what Toynbee's underlying philosophical points of view are, since they are nowhere clearly explained in his ten-volume work. His world view is essentially pantheistic, in spite of occasional use of high church phraseology, oscillating between a kind of Platonic Christianity, a Hindu-Buddhist religious philosophy, and a quasi-Jungian psychologism. For practical purposes it would seem that this modern Gnosticism of Toynbee has increasingly displaced his early organismic approach through the definition of societies and the analysis of their individual history and their relation to one another. My criticisms remain valid as far as they go, but criticism of quite another and more penetrating sort is needed for the vast syntheses which he has now painted. It is particularly difficult to deal with Toynbee because of his surprisingly prejudiced attacks on ancient Israel and modern Jewry, accompanied by constant disparagement of their historical rôle. He makes repeated onslaughts on the alleged intolerance of ancient Israel, to which he traces the intolerance sometimes found in subsequent Christianity and Judaism. This assumed intolerance and the claim of uniqueness made by all the standard faiths which have arisen from Mosaic religion are regarded by Toynbee as an impious arrogation of special rights and privileges in contempt of God and the rest of humanity. Actually nearly all peoples, both primitive and sophisticated, claim uniqueness, while intolerance—which is only one facet of the basic human drive for power—is universally human.

Under "Current Aspects of Historical Determinism" I should now emphasize the growing popularity of various forms of anthropological determinism, especially the vogue of functionalism. This wave of anthropological thinking began with the work of Malinowski and Radcliffe-Brown, according to whom all closely associated or "essential" aspects of an integrated culture are functionally interrelated; if one element is dislocated the entire structure is thought to be in danger of collapse. In America it has been modified at the hands of anthropologists who are directly or indirectly affected by the teachings of Franz Boas, but the basic functionalist tendency has remained unaffected by these modifications in detail. There is a strong inclination to introduce functionalist theory into the treatment of ancient and modern higher cultures, with some very strange results. Actually, for instance, the national groupings of Europe are so closely linked by innumerable crosscurrents that it is folly to think that any single culture can be sharply distinguished from its neighbors in any functional sense. The ancient Near East was substantially comparable to modern Europe in this respect, and the position of J. A. Wilson, for example, who holds that the civilization of the Egyptians did not affect the higher culture of their neighbors and was not itself affected by them, is quite untenable in the extreme form in which he presents it. Yet it is obvious that one must study each civilization for and by itself before looking for interrelations. Since I have always insisted on this point, it is not necessary to qualify any of my 1940-46 positions, so far as I can see.

In dealing with "The Epistemology of History," I am no longer satisfied with the threefold classification of historical judgments which I first proposed in 1940-46. Since then I have continued reading both earlier and later historical literature, and it has become increasingly clear that no student of historical method has appreciated the importance of careful classification of the principal types of historical knowledge. My innovation, "judgments of typical occurrence," is of vital significance, since it covers a very large area of history which shares this class of "law" with natural science. To this class and to Maurice Mandelbaum's two basic classes of "judgments of fact" and "judgments of value" we should add at least one more class: "judgments of cause and contingency," which do not fall under any of the other categories. Doubtless such a heterogeneous class as "judgments of value" might be broken up advantageously, but in multiplying categories one does not necessarily increase clarity of understanding—often the reverse is true.

My classification of historic modes of thinking with reference to their logical constituents, first advanced in 1940, still holds. Here I have been widely misunderstood because of my own too concise statement of my case. I did indeed adopt Lévy-Bruhl's distinction between prelogical and logical thinking, but I modified it so drastically that it is not at all the same thing. Instead of Lévy-Bruhl's two phases,

I distinguished three, which I now label "proto-logical," "empirico-logical," and "logical." The second stage reflects the empirical logic characteristic of all ordinary human activity of material and social nature: it began at a very primitive stage and may, indeed, be traced back to animal reactions; it gained the upper hand in ancient Oriental science and wisdom literature and especially in the religion of Israel, where it achieved its finest results. Lévy-Bruhl's famous work left out this category entirely, and in 1938 when he abandoned his distinction between "prelogical" and "logical" (published posthumously in 1947) it was precisely because he found so much evidence of quite logical thinking in the ordinary affairs of life, even in the most primitive tribes of today. This logic born of experience preceded Greek formal logic by many millennia, but it was still incapable of formulating definitions of concepts, systematic classification of data, and deductive logic (see above). In the French translation of this book, *De l'Age de la Pierre à la Chrétienté* (Paris, 1951), pp. 86 ff., I have discussed Lévy-Bruhl's recantation and have pointed out that my classification is not affected by it in the least—quite the reverse. Proto-logical thinking refers primarily to the religion, art, and literature of ancient and modern primitives, and in some respects it is even more alive in the West today than it was three thousand years ago.

CHAPTER III: PRAEPARATIO

Our knowledge of human prehistory has been greatly enlarged and has become far more accurate in detail than it was in 1940-46 because of the great expansion of archaeological exploration and especially because of the extraordinary development of the new radiocarbon technique. My treatment of this material here and even in my *Archaeology of Palestine* (1949), will ultimately require considerable modification, but we are not yet ready for a comprehensive survey, owing to numerous basic uncertainties which continue to subsist. My cautious approach to such problems as the classification of prehistoric man into species and sub-species, as well as to absolute chronology, has paid dividends, and there is *so far* much less modification necessary than might reasonably be expected. Physical anthropologists are more conscious of the polymorphism of mankind and are in general less inclined to apply such terms as "species" or "sub-species" to the races of fossil toolmaking men. There is actually no longer good reason to deny any human maker of tools the appellation "Homo sapiens"—though the latter is no longer such a proudly worn title as it used to be.

Radiocarbon dating appears to be forcing a general reduction of dates, but it is not yet clear how it will affect our chronology of the Middle or Early Palaeolithic Age. The end of the last Ice Age (the last advance of the Würm in Europe and of the Wisconsin in America) can now be placed with confidence about 11,000 years ago; naturally this date is only a rough approximation, since there were minor oscillations and it may have taken centuries for the change to be completed. I see no reason any longer for refusing to connect the traditions of the Great Flood in most regions of Eurasia and America, including particularly Mesopotamia and Israel, with the tremendous floods accompanying and following the critical melting of the glaciers about 9000 B.C. It may not be accidental that there are no clear traditions of the Deluge in ancient Egypt, which must have escaped the worst of these floods. The beginning of the last Ice Age is placed by geologists working with radiocarbon experts in Washington somewhere near 35,000 B.C. It is already certain that the age of cave paintings (Late Aurignacian and Magdalenian) must be dated between about 15,000 and 9000 B.C.; it is by no means impossible that the entire Mousterian must be dated after 50,000 B.C. However, radiocarbon refuses to aid us after we reach the beginning of the Würm Ice Age, and one must avoid all extrapolation. So the date of our earliest human tools remains quite uncertain, though it is highly improbable that it goes back half a million years, as frequently asserted.

Our knowledge of the Neolithic, in both pre-pottery and pottery phases, is being greatly extended. Kathleen Kenyon's brilliant work at Jericho since 1953 has not only confirmed the existence of Garstang's pre-pottery Neolithic, but has also shown that it was a much richer and more important culture than had been guessed, with a depth of occupation exceeding thirty feet; Jericho was then a strongly fortified town, with elaborate cultic and funerary practices. Radiocarbon has proved that this phase of the Neolithic went far back into the sixth millennium and that pottery was not invented until somewhere in the first half of the fifth millennium. Braidwood's work has shown that the pre-pottery Neolithic was also found in Mesopotamia, and it may have had a very wide geographical extension. One thing is clear: we must still give priority to southwestern Asia, and we must assume a greater or smaller lag in culture as it was diffused in all directions, toward Europe, into Africa, and far into the great continent of Asia.

Our knowledge of the evolution of Mesopotamian and Egyptian civilization has been considerably deepened since the end of the Second World War. With assistance from scattered radiocarbon dates and better use of the comparative data providing cross-datings between the material cultures of different countries, the low chronology on which I have insisted since 1919 for Egypt and since 1938 for Babylonia has been confirmed as against the higher chronologies which were in vogue and are sometimes still defended. In this Anchor edition Babylonian dates before cir. 1500 are reduced by from 64 to 100 years, and now agree as a rule with those of F. Cornelius. In 1942 he and I independently dated the First Dynasty of Babylon cir. 1830-1530 B.C., placing Hammurapi about 1728–1686, 64 years after my date in 1940, which had agreed independently with that of Sidney Smith. Evidence for the general reliability of our new low chronology has been steadily accumulating; see Cornelius in *Archiv für Orientforschung*, XVIII (1956), and my own decisive stratigraphic proof from the data now published by Sir Leonard Woolley in his final report on the excavation of Alalakh in Syria (*Bulletin of the American Schools of Oriental Research*, No. 144 1956).

My succinct description of the religious life of the Early and Middle Bronze Ages might easily be expanded, but there would be no change in essentials. Above I have explained my "proto-logical" phase of thinking, which is emphatically true of the religion of the Egyptians and Sumerians in the third millennium; for a much more detailed treatment see the German translation of my *Archaeology and the Religion of Israel* by F. Cornelius (*Die Religion Israels im Lichte der archäologischen Ausgrabungen* [Munich, 1956], pp. 37 ff.). In spite of minor criticism, I do not think that the picture I have drawn of polytheism tending to become monotheism on the one hand and pantheism on the other is distorted. Of late much more attention has been paid to parallels in mythological thinking and quasi-metaphysical interpretation between the Near East, on the one hand, and India and China, on the other. I believe that careful study of this material, following patterns tentatively established by Siegfried Morenz and H. H. Rowley, will prove exceedingly illuminating.

CHAPTER IV: WHEN ISRAEL WAS A CHILD . . .

Our knowledge of the history and culture of southwestern Asia between the eighteenth and the thirteenth centuries B.C. has increased greatly since 1940-46. Many volumes of tablets from such key points as Mari on the Middle Euphrates, Ugarit and Alalakh in Syria have been published and analyzed, and we now know the life and politics of Mari in the eighteenth century B.C. better than we knew the corresponding state of affairs in seventh-century Assyria in 1940-46. Our knowledge of the Semites in Egypt and of the character and extent of the Egyptian empire in Asia has also been increased substantially by the publication of new Execration Texts from the nineteenth century B.C. and lists of Asiatic slaves in Egypt from the following century. We also know a good deal more about the flow of higher culture—art, literature, and religion—between Mesopotamia, the Hurrians, Hittites, Canaanites, and Egyptians, as well as about the westward stream of higher culture from the East into the lands of Greek culture (including Late Bronze Greece, Crete, and Cyprus) and conversely. There can no longer be any doubt that Canaan was then surrounded by countries with which it was in the closest cultural as well as political relations. Hundreds of Canaanite (Hebrew) loan-words are found in Egyptian of the New Kingdom, and Semitic religion was taken over almost bodily, with a score of Canaanite divinities mentioned in Egyptian inscriptions, and with many Canaanite myths quoted—sometimes in literal translation—in Egyptian magical books like the Leiden Papyrus. The influx of Egyptian words, ideas, and divinities into Palestine and Syria was somewhat less significant but was still substantial; Egyptian art completely saturated Canaanite craftmanship.

My description of ancient Near-Eastern polytheism in the second half of the second millennium B.C. and my emphasis on the cosmic nature of all the high gods, no matter how small might be their local shrine or how few the number of people who worshipped them under any given appellation, may now be illustrated by many new examples. For instance, the passage in the "Babylonian Job," asserting that Marduk (chief god of Babylon) must be worshipped by men wherever they live, "as far as the earth extends and heaven spreads and the sun shines and fire glows and water flows and the wind blows" (which I quote in this volume in connection with a later period) may now be safely dated with W. von Soden in the last centuries of the second millennium. It would be impossible to paint a more vivid picture of universal dominion! A hymn to the Hittite sun goddess of Arinna in Asia Minor addresses her as follows: "Within the circuit of heaven and earth thou . . . alone art the revered deity, and thou art the father and mother of every land." In another Hittite text the god Telipinus is implored to show special favor to the land of the Hittites, since he is worshipped nowhere else!

In the light of the now available data it is perfectly clear that the period between 1350 and 1250 B.C. was ideally suited to give birth to monotheism, since it covers precisely the century from the attempted suppression of the solar monotheism of Akhenaten to the middle of the reign of Ramesses II, the great amalgamator of Egyptian and Semitic culture. The debate about the nature of Atenism and the part played in it by Akhenaten still continues; it is absurd to deny the term "monotheism" to a faith which rejected all the gods except the solar disk, even though it was far from reaching the abstract level of Hebrew, Christian, or Muslim monotheism. I am still convinced that the Heretic King was only a tool in the hands of others. It is totally erroneous to suppose that the Aten heresy was completely extirpated by the priests of Amun. There are two large collections of hymns from the thirteenth century B.C. which are very close to the Aten hymns of Amarna in spirit, stressing the beneficent aspects of the god Amun-Re' and the universality of his power. He is called the "good shepherd" and the "nearest kinsman of mankind," god of nobles and paupers, of Mediterranean peoples as well as of Egyptians.

The historical foundations of early Israelite tradition are becoming more and more solidly established by the progress of archaeological discovery. In the first place, it is certain that the critical phase of the Israelite Conquest must be placed during the reign of Marniptah, successor of Ramesses II, about 1224-1216 B.C. (I now prefer M. B. Rowton's solidly established date for Ramesses, 1290-1224, to L. Borchardt's, 1301-1234) in view of the conclusive proof for the destruction of Hazor in Galilee, as well as of Lachish, Tell Beit Mirsim, and probably of Bethel and Jericho, about this time. This means that the Exodus cannot be placed later than about 1250 B.C. (assuming that "forty years" refers to a generation as elsewhere in the Bible and the ancient world), and that my preferred date early in the reign of Ramesses II, about 1290 B.C. (or, better, about 1280) remains the most plausible solution. In the second place, there has been striking confirmation of geographical and onomastic details connected with the life of Moses and the Exodus. For instance, both the names of the midwives said to have served Israelite women at the time of Moses' birth, Shiphrah and Puah, have been proved (1954) to be good Northwest-Semitic women's names in the second millennium B.C. This is a minor detail, but since some of the most eminent scholars have declared these names to be fic-

titious, it is significant. Again, our Sinai Expedition of
1947-48 was able to prove that the "southern" route of the
Exodus across Suez was impossible and that the only possible route is that described in Exodus and fixed by recent
finds, from the neighborhood of Tanis (Zoan, Raamses) to
the Wâdi Ṭumeilât (Pithom), and thence back to the coast
near Baal-zephon (Tahpanhes, Greek Daphne) and across
the Papyrus Lake (as the Egyptians called the Hebrew
"Lake of Papyrus" or Reed Sea) into the Peninsula of Sinai.

No less important than our archaeological confirmation
of the general tenor of Israelite tradition is the rapidly accumulating evidence for an ancient date of the archaic poems preserved in the Pentateuch and elsewhere. At the same
time it is clear that much prose tradition in the earlier historical books goes back to poetic originals which may still
be identified by stylistic survivals and by occasional quotations or reminiscences of the verse prototype. This evidence
comes chiefly from the far-reaching parallels which we
find in Ugaritic mythological poetry, originally composed in
Phoenicia and its hinterland before the fifteenth century B.C.
Work on this material was inaugurated by H. L. Ginsberg,
and I have continued it with the aid of my students, especially of Frank M. Cross, Jr., and D. N. Freedman. It
is true that we also find some parallels in very late biblical
poetry, but these parallels seldom contain archaic grammatical features, and the stylistic structure is as a rule radically different. For instance in the Psalms of Degrees we
find much repetition of words and phrases, but it is not at
all the same as the elaborately patterned repetition of Ugaritic and early Hebrew poetry; it is archaistic and not archaic. In Job we find many rare words and expressions
which are reminiscent of Ugaritic, but few, if any, archaic
grammatical features and no repetitive patterns. The Song
of Miriam in Ex. 15 and the Oracles of Balaam in Num.
23-24 are full of Ugaritic parallels, and almost certainly go
back to the thirteenth-twelfth centuries B.C.; they are thus
even older than the Song of Deborah (which resembles the
Song of Miriam closely in a number of respects). The Blessing of Jacob in Gen. 49 is also very old, as are a number of

Psalms, notably Psalm 68. Moreover, some of the same phenomena recur in such prose texts as Gen. 14, which probably goes back to an early poetic source.

There is further confirmation of the state of higher culture as pictured in the Mosaic tradition. Semites in Egyptian service in the mines of Sinai used our ancestral alphabet for funerary and other inscriptions in the fifteenth century B.C.; both my dating and general decipherment of 1948 are finding more and more support as new inscriptions are discovered in Syria and Palestine. We know from an Egyptian inscription that a name formed with *Shaddai*, said by biblical tradition to have been the patriarchal name of God before *Yahwê* came into use, was employed among the Semites living in Egypt before the Exodus. We now know that there were more law codes known in the second millennium than had been supposed; since 1946 the relatively complete Code of Eshnunna (nineteenth or eighteenth century B.C.) and the fragmentary Sumerian Codes of Lipit-Ishtar and (Z)ur-Nammu (between the twenty-first and the nineteenth centuries B.C.) have been published. These law codes all exhibit the same basic structure as the biblical Book of the Covenant, and since nothing like them has turned up at Ugarit or Alalakh in Syria, it is becoming increasingly probable that the laws of casuistic type preserved in the Pentateuch go back through Mosaic tradition to earlier Hebrew customary law.

However this may be, it is increasingly clear that Moses played a highly original rôle in sifting and organizing earlier Northwest-Semitic, and specifically Hebrew, concepts and practices. In particular it is now becoming evident that all recent attempts to explain the name *Yahwê* in various adventurous directions are fallacious. The name (which occurs as a place name or tribal name in a list of settlements in southern or eastern Palestine from the thirteenth century B.C.) can only be derived from the verbal stem *HWY* "to fall, become, come into existence" (as I have maintained all along). The name cannot be the ordinary imperfect (*qal*) of the verb, which in an archaic stative (intransitive) form would be *yíhwayu* (indicative), later becoming

*yihwê, whence yihyê (spelled in classical Hebrew YHYH). On the other hand, the causative (hif'îl) form corresponding to *yihwayu would be *yáhwiyu, whence the later indicative Yahwê (spelled YHWH) and the normal abbreviated (jussive) form Yáhû (spelled YHW). As D. N. Freedman and I pointed out some time ago, the formulas Yahwê ṣebā'ôt, Yahwê shālôm, and probably Yahwê yir'ā (not yir'ê) mean, respectively: "He (Who) Causes the Hosts (of Israel?) to Come into Existence, He (Who) Causes Peace to Exist, He (Who) Causes Worship to Exist." These are obviously quotations from ancient litanies of the supreme patriarchal deity, and the new name is thus derived from an abbreviation of a liturgical formula, just as I held in 1940-46 with regard to the words *Yahwê 'asher yihyê.

One point which I emphasized briefly in 1940-46 was the pre-Mosaic origin of the Covenant between God and His people, as illustrated by the word berît (berith) and its uses. Here, however, I failed to recognize that the concept of "covenant" dominates the entire religious life of Israel to such an extent that W. Eichrodt's apparently extreme position is fully justified. We cannot understand Israelite religion, political organization, or the institution of the Prophets without recognizing the importance of the "Covenant." The word itself appears as a Semitic loan-word in the fifteenth-twelfth centuries in Syria and Egypt and clearly goes back to the earliest times in Israel. G. E. Mendenhall has demonstrated that the description of the Covenant between Yahweh and Israel in the time of Joshua (Josh. 24) preserves a clear pattern which in no fewer than eight distinct points reflects the characteristic structure of Syro-Anatolian treaties of the fourteenth-thirteenth centuries B.C. which had been preserved in the Hittite archives at Boghazköy. The structure of half a dozen Assyrian, Aramaean, and Phoenician treaties which we know from the eighth century B.C. and later, is quite different. Since then I have discovered that the word which replaces berît in the Priestly Code, 'ēdût, reflects an older 'ādôt "covenant" (which appears also as 'ādîm in hitherto mis-

understood passages). In other words, there are some twice
as many references to the Covenant between Yahweh and
His people in the Hebrew Bible as we had supposed.

CHAPTER V: CHARISMA AND CATHARSIS

My analysis of the origin and development of the
prophetic movement in Israel was correct as far as it went,
but was not sufficiently penetrating, largely because I
failed to grasp the full significance of the Covenant principle. I hold even more tenaciously than ever to the interpretation of the word *nābî* as "the one who is called, who
has a vocation." Both Torczyner (Tur-Sinai) and I started
with the very old Accadian word, "to call," with the same
consonants. Now, however, we have lists of Northwest-
Semitic proper names from Mari (eighteenth century B.C.)
which contain several names formed with the same verb
in the same meaning—and this verb appears in West-Semitic, not in Accadian, form. There can, accordingly, be
no intelligent rejection of this obviously correct explanation
of the word for "prophet." Of course, the establishment of
its etymology does not fix the earliest date at which it was
used, much less its exact later connotations. That the
Prophets were not only dedicated men, but also predictors
of the future, is fully recognized in biblical tradition but
has been under-emphasized by modern biblical scholars,
including myself in 1940-46. Since then I have seen my
error and I now stress the predictive element again, though
perhaps from rather novel points of view. The dominant
pattern of prophecy, as found in the earliest rhapsodist
("writing") Prophets of the eighth century, is firm belief
in the validity of the ancient Covenant between God and
His people, according to whose terms Israel would be se-
verely punished for its sins, both moral and cultic, but
would ultimately be "restored" because of the mercy or
grace of God (*ḥésed*) which exceeded the formal terms of
the Covenant and thus made it more binding than it would
otherwise have been. At the same time this pattern of doom
and restoration was very ancient in the Near East, and the

Prophets simply modified it in keeping with the concepts of Yahwism.

This pattern was validated by the disheartening succession of political events in the eighth-seventh and seventh-sixth centuries B.C., which convinced pious Yahwists that ineluctable doom lay ahead of them—but a doom followed by ultimate restoration. It was this conviction which—historically speaking—brought Judah back in the first known event of the kind in history to the land from which it had been uprooted in 597-582 B.C. It was this same traditional conviction which has brought the Jewish people back to its ancient home in recent generations, thus proving twice in twenty-five centuries how tremendous was the momentum of the prophetic word of ancient Israel. It is wholly unnecessary to reckon with "prophecies after the event": we have exceedingly few cases of *vaticinium ex eventu* in the Hebrew Bible before the third or second century B.C. How perilous this type of reasoning may be can be shown in the case of Jeremiah's prophecies of a seventy-year desolation of Judah (25:12; 29:10, etc.). In several passages in the inscriptions of Esarhaddon, king of Assyria nearly a century before the fall of Jerusalem, he states that after Sennacherib's destruction of Babylon in 689, Marduk, chief god of Babylon, had intended to allow his city to remain in ruins for seventy years, but the merciful god changed his mind and turned the cuneiform writing of "seventy" upside down, when it automatically became "eleven" (vertical wedge + corner wedge becoming corner wedge + vertical wedge). That "eleven" was only approximately right did not disturb the Babylonian priests any more than the fact that "seventy" was an inexact estimate of the period during which Judah and Jerusalem lay waste worried the Jews. It thus follows that "seventy years" was a recognized pattern for the period of destruction of cities or countries whose gods still remained interested in their people.

It should be emphasized that fulfilment of prophecies was only one important element in the validation of a "true" Prophet, and that it was not always essential, as illustrated by the apparent failure of Haggai's prophecy against the

Persian Empire (2:21 f.). More important still was the moral and religious content of a Prophet's message. Moreover, the Prophets did not always follow a definite pattern; sometimes they undoubtedly shared in the capacity for intuitive grasp of wide fields of perception which has characterized certain figures of the last 250 years, at least in occasional moments of exaltation. We need refer only to the famous prophecies of the future of Germany and France by Heinrich Heine and Leon Bloy, or to the fantastic previsions of future technology by Jules Verne, or to the glimpses into the future on the part of Emanuel Swedenborg and Ellen White. It was no *vaticinium ex eventu* when Jules Verne described the giant submarine *Nautilus*, operated by solar power, ninety years before the launching of the U.S. submarine by the same name, powered by nuclear energy. On the other hand, it is no accident that logically trained specialists are seldom able to predict the future; this is notoriously true of physical scientists, historians, and other academic folk.

Chapter VI: In the Fulness of Time . . .

When I wrote the final chapter of this book it was quite impossible to foresee the discovery of the Dead Sea Scrolls. This totally unpredictable series of finds, which burst upon an unprepared world in 1948 and has been continuing ever since, has revolutionized our approach to the Jewish background of the New Testament. All attempts to present a synthesis of the subject are necessarily tentative, since only a fraction of the Qumran scrolls and fragments has yet been published and the contents of many of the most important recent finds are still unknown. This is not the place to survey the extensive Essene literature now known, much less the tremendous mass of publications which deal with it. I shall limit myself to the aspects of Essene literature which confirm or modify the point of view stated in Chapter VI.

The picture which I have drawn of the impact of Greek ways of thinking on the regions which belonged to the Achaemenian Empire before Alexander's conquest is in no

way exaggerated, but should rather be painted even more
vividly. For instance, Neugebauer's work seems to prove
that Schnabel and others were mistaken in supposing that
the Babylonian astronomers Naburianus and Cidenas flourished in the Persian period; actually both of them seem to
have done their work in the late fourth or third century
B.C., after Greek scientific method had fructified the empirical observations and elementary calculations of Babylonian scholars. Greek ways of thinking undoubtedly affected
Ecclesiastes about 300 B.C. or a little later; they also
affected Ben Sira about a century later. There is no trace
of them in the Book of Jubilees, probably because it goes
back to lost Jewish sources of higher antiquity; I now
accept L. Finkelstein's date of the book not far from 175
B.C. and also favor E. Bickermann's date about the same
time for the Testaments of the Twelve Patriarchs. (The recent attempt by De Jonge to attribute the Testaments to
Christian authorship has been partly disproved by the discovery of a closely related Aramaic recension of the Testament of Levi among the Qumran fragments; J. T. Milik's
compromise view that the Testament of Levi is pre-
Christian but that the other Testaments are Christian disre-
gards Charles's demonstration that Hebraisms are scattered
through all the Greek Testaments. Besides, the style and
point of view of the Testaments are far too homogeneous
to permit such an arbitrary division. It is quite true that
there are Essene as well as Christian interpolations which
are not consistent with the theology of the Testaments as a
whole.)

The theology of Sadducees and Pharisees reflects in
large measure different applications of Greek ways of
thinking to the Hebrew Bible. The latter mentions existence
after death, for instance, often without making clear what
is meant. The Sadducees adopted one alternative interpretation and denied life after death; the Pharisees adopted
a different method of exegesis, based on ancient tradition,
and insisted on the fact of bodily resurrection. Even among
the Essenes we find evidence of indirect Greek influence in
the clarity of the creedal statement in the Scroll of Discipline

and in a new emphasis on the distinction between "spirit" and "flesh" which goes far beyond anything in the Old Testament.

In general, however, the Essenes were much more strongly oriented toward the Iranian East than toward the Hellenistic West. Very significant new evidence may be brought from the Scrolls in support of my 1940-46 position that "the Essenes represent a sectarian Jewish group which had migrated from Mesopotamia to Palestine after the victory of the Maccabees." All my previous arguments remain cogent, but there are additional ones of even greater pertinence. In the first Isaiah Scroll, which differs in important respects from the standard pre-Massoretic text of this book, found in other manuscripts and fragments at Qumran, we have a number of absolutely correct spellings of Assyro-Babylonian names and words (where w is used to denote u or o), though the earlier Greek translation of Isaiah in the Septuagint and the official Jewish tradition in the Massorah both give erroneous vocalizations. This scroll —or more probably a scroll from which it was directly or indirectly copied—must have come from Babylonia, where cuneiform scholastic tradition was still alive as late as the end of the first century A.D. Furthermore, K. G. Kuhn, A. Dupont-Sommer, and H. Michaud have shown that the dualism of the Dead Sea Scrolls is definitely Iranian (Zoroastrian) in origin, and that it closely resembles the early Zervanite heresy, in which both the good and evil spirits were created by "Unending Time" (Zervan akarana). Zervanism was already known to the Greeks in the fourth century B.C., and by the middle of the first century A.D. it had been taken over in part by nascent Mithraism.

It is not necessary to suppose that Essenism as we know it in the Qumran literature was exclusively Eastern in origin; it doubtless drew many adherents from the same pietist circles which gave rise to the Pharisee movement. As is generally recognized, these pietists (hasîdîm) tended to reject the leadership of the Hasmonaeans once the latter had turned out to be worldly potentates instead of the pious

rulers they were expected to be. Some of them may have
united with Jewish immigrants from the East, both idealists
attracted to the new Jewish state and fugitives from the
Parthian invasion about 140 B.C. By about 100 B.C. (possibly a little earlier) the communal center at Qumran had
been founded (as we know from the evidence of coins),
presumably by the Teacher of Right (*môrê has-
sédeq*). The Essene literature now available to us seems to
have been composed during the last century B.C.

In 1940-46 it was impossible to foresee that "the
slight dualistic element . . . already present in Judaeo-
Hellenistic literature as a legacy from Iranian religion"
would prove to belong to the same Essene group through
which lustration by water passed into early Christianity.
The simple dualism of good and evil, light and darkness,
truth and falsehood, assigned to two spirits who were both
created by God to contend for the allegiance of men, came
through the Essenes from Zervanism or a related Iranian
system into Judaism and Christianity. While this point of
view is dominant in the Gospel and Epistles of John, it is
found all through the New Testament, including particularly the Pauline Epistles. The lists of parallel expressions
given by W. H. Brownlee, K. G. Kuhn, Raymond Brown,
Roland Murphy, T. H. Gaster, and others may easily be
extended; it is already certain that most, perhaps all, of the
books of the New Testament arose in an environment which
had been strongly under the influence of the Essenes and
related Jewish sectarians. It is now clear that St. Paul himself was also strongly influenced from this direction, in spite
of his immediate Pharisee background. Even a book like the
Apocalypse, which shows comparatively little such influence, will probably be found to have been profoundly
affected by the Essenes and their congeners, since we have
remains of books describing the "heavenly Jerusalem"
among the Qumran finds. The late R. H. Charles was correct in recognizing the Hebrew background of the Apocalypse, and C. C. Torrey is probably right in dating it about
68 A.D., shortly before the Fall of the Second Temple. Second Peter, which was not accepted by all the Church

Fathers and which is generally dated by critical scholars about the middle of the second century A.D., contains many reminiscences of the Qumran literature, including the true way, light in darkness, the final destruction by fire, etc. The repudiation of the Pastoral Epistles of Paul, now commonly assigned by critical scholars to the second quarter of the second century A.D., becomes rather absurd when we discover that the institution of overseers or superintendents (*episkopoi*, our bishops) in Timothy and Titus, as well as in the earliest extra-biblical Christian literature, is virtually identical with the Essene institution of *mebaqqerim* (sometimes awkwardly rendered as "censors").

In short, thanks to the Qumran discoveries, the New Testament proves to be in fact what it was formerly believed to be: the teaching of Christ and his immediate followers between cir. 25 and cir. 80 A.D. In the light of these finds the New Testament becomes more Jewish than we had thought—as truly Jewish as the Old Testament is Israelite. Yet both parts of our Bible are deeply indebted to the world in which they arose. The Old Testament arose in a world of Mesopotamian and Egyptian culture, and streams of influence from the entire civilized world of that day were to pour into it and to be transformed by the faith of Moses and the Prophets. The New Testament arose in a Jewish environment which had been enriched by Hellenic and Iranian elements. The non-Jewish streams which flowed through Judaism into nascent Christianity were transfigured by the Cross and given a spiritual depth which was to transform the world. Now again we see the religious world confronted by the imperious necessity of choosing between biblical theism and Eastern pantheism, which threatens to sweep away theistic faith as it is reinterpreted by neo-Gnostic religious thinkers of the contemporary West.

W. F. ALBRIGHT

December, 1956

Chapter I

NEW HORIZONS IN HISTORY

The light shed by the discoveries of modern archaeology on the history of civilization is apparent to all, but the bearing of these discoveries on the study of underlying historical processes is not yet generally understood. Few realize, even today, what a transformation in the matter, the scope, and the method of history has been effected by archaeological research. Moreover, the extraordinary progress of archaeology has been paralleled, though not equalled, by philology, linguistics, and anthropology, all of which furnish data of fundamental importance to the historian. Yet the latter is too often content to take the results of archaeological and philological research which are compiled for his use by the specialist, without attempting to familiarize himself with these fields or at least to control the methods employed by the specialist in obtaining his results. It is, accordingly, not surprising that scholars often fail to recognize the fundamental change brought about in the philosophy and especially in the epistemology of history by the use of modern archaeological and philological methods. The philosophy of history, like the philosophy of science, is now increasingly devoted to the analysis of historical data and of the methods by which they are obtained, as a necessary prelude to successful evaluation of historical phenomena. The question of method is, or should be, quite as important to the historian as to the scientist. Only by competent analysis of methods employed in obtaining factual data can one determine, for example, where these data stand in the hierarchy of probability, whether they may be considered certain, probable, possible, improbable, or impossible. Only where there is a sufficiently broad basis of critically sifted data can inductive reasoning lead to sound generalizations.

A. The Archaeological Revolution

Modern archaeological excavation may be said to have begun with the first organized work at Herculaneum (1738) and Pompeii (1748), and modern comparative archaeology may be dated from the epoch-making researches of J. J. Winckelmann (1717-68) in the history of Graeco-Roman art. It is interesting to note that the serious collection and interpretation of pre-Christian literature and inscriptions from the Near East began about the same time, with the remarkable expedition of the Dane, Carsten Niebuhr, in 1761-67 and the recovery of the principal works of Avestan literature by Anquetil-Duperron during the years 1755-71.

The systematic surface exploration of the Near East did not begin until the turn of the century.[1] In 1798 Napoleon's

[1] Among the more useful and reliable accounts of archaeological exploration and excavation in the Near East may be mentioned the following general treatments:

H. V. Hilprecht and others, *Explorations in Bible Lands during the 19th Century* (Philadelphia, 1903).—Best for the period covered.

Louis Speleers, *Les fouilles en Asie antérieure à partir de 1843* (Liége, 1928).—Most convenient synopsis, but has many mistakes.

W. F. Albright, *Recent Discoveries in Bible Lands* (New York, 1936; bound with Young's *Analytical Concordance*, 20th edition).—Compact.

James Baikie, *A Century of Excavation in the Land of the Pharaohs*, London (1923).—Popular.

R. W. Rogers, *A History of Babylonia and Assyria* (5th ed., New York, 1915), Vol. I.—Admirable for the period covered.

F. J. Bliss, *The Development of Palestine Exploration* (New York, 1906).—Excellent for the period covered.

scientific expedition began an elaborate exploration of the Nile Valley which was promptly made available to scholars in the stately volumes of the *Description de l'Egypte* (1809-13). The discovery of the Rosetta Stone in 1799 was followed by its decipherment through the combined efforts of Akerblad, Thomas Young, and especially of Champollion, who published his first correct results in 1822. Mesopotamia was systematically explored and described, with particular attention to its antiquities, by Rich and Porter from 1811 to 1836, when Rich's posthumous work appeared. In 1815 appeared the first publication of the results of Grotefend's decipherment of Persian cuneiform, which he had begun in 1802.

By the middle of the nineteenth century scientific exploration and excavation had been launched by competent scholars in Egypt, Mesopotamia, and Palestine. Richard Lepsius conducted a well organized and very successful expedition for the purpose of recording the monuments above ground in Egypt (1842-45). Mariette began a career of thirty years of excavation in Egypt with the discovery of the Serapeum in 1850. Paul Emile Botta commenced the excavation of Khorsabad, the ancient capital of Sargon of Assyria, in 1843 and A. H. Layard undertook the excavation of Nimrud (Calah) two years later. In Palestine the brilliant surface explorations of Edward Robinson, whose centenary we have just been celebrating (1938),[2] showed how ancient topography should be reconstructed. We shall survey the subsequent development of the Near Eastern field in section B.

W. F. Albright, *The Archaeology of Palestine and the Bible* (New York, 1935), chapter I.—Stresses the development of method in excavation.

J. Simons, *Opgravingen in Palestina* (Roermond, 1935).—Detailed.

L. Hennequin, "Fouilles et Champs de Fouilles en Palestine et en Phénicie," in *Supplément au Dictionnaire de la Bible* (Vigouroux), Vol. III, cols. 318-524 (Paris, 1936).—Very complete and comprehensive.

[2] See the papers collected in *Jour. Bib. Lit.*, LVIII (1939), pp. 355-87.

Work in the great field of prehistory, which was to yield some of its most remarkable discoveries in the Near East, began to be scientifically cultivated at the same time. Jacques Boucher de Perthes (1788-1868) began working in the Somme Valley of France in the thirties and in 1846 he published his first sensational account of finding human artifacts together with the bones of extinct animals. In 1860 Eduard Lartet began the excavation of palaeolithic caves, where he found the first clearly defined stratigraphic sequence, enabling Gabriel de Mortillet (after 1869) to arrange palaeolithic remains in the classical series Chellean-Mousterian-Aurignacian-Magdalenian.

Of late the greatest progress in the field of prehistory has been made in three directions. First we may place the extension of research by Dorothy Garrod and others to Asia and Africa, making it possible for Oswald Menghin to write a world-history of the Stone Age (*Weltgeschichte der Steinzeit,* 1931). Second we may put the development of geochronology by Count de Geer and others, among whom Friedrich Zeuner has been most active in the past few years.[3] Thanks to their study of glacial and pluvial varves (laminations in sediment), as well as to the correlation of successive phases of glaciation with corresponding phases of solar radiation, a new degree of precision in prehistoric chronology has been reached. As correlations between North European and Mediterranean river-terrace formations and similar phenomena are being set up this chronology becomes more and more solidly established. The results of Sandford and Arkell in the Nile Valley since 1926 can provisionally be correlated with corresponding material in Europe, but it is still too early to accept the theories of Leaky and others with regard to correlations between Europe, Egypt, and South Africa. There is so great a gap between Europe and geological deposits in China or

[3] See the account of his work up to 1937 published in the *First Annual Report* of the University of London Institute of Archaeology (London, 1938), pp. 29-46. On the likelihood of a pronounced lag between radiation minima and glaciations see Sir George Simpson, *Proc. Roy. Inst.,* XXX (1938), pp. 125 ff.

the East Indies that no safe correlations at all can yet be made. Third, we may list the sensational discoveries of fossil human and anthropoid remains since 1925. Palestine, with rich cranial and skeletal remains from Galilee and Carmel, has now replaced France as the focus of prehistoric research. Palaeanthropus Palestinus (sic!) exhibits just the mixture of archaic and of neanthropic features which might be expected from the crossing of Homo Mousteriensis (Neanderthalensis) with Homo sapiens, that is, of the human sub-species characteristic of Middle Palaeolithic with modern man. Palestine thus appears in Middle Palaeolithic as a bridge between the more advanced regions of Southern Asia and the more backward continent of Europe. The successive discoveries of Sinanthropus Pekinensis in China by Davidson Black and Teilhard de Chardin and of Homo Soloensis in Java by von Königswald have keyed the interest of physical anthropologists to the highest pitch, as was vividly illustrated by the crowded sessions of the International Symposium on Early Man, held in Philadelphia in February, 1937.[4] Further discoveries in Java, in India, and in South Africa have since reduced the gap between man and the anthropoids to a very narrow interval, which is practically bridged by a number of evolutionary series, the most striking of which is dentition.

While our interest is concentrated on the Near East in the present volume, a perspective in space is as necessary as one in time. It has well been emphasized by thinkers that no science can be regarded as solidly established while there is any serious gap in recording and interpreting accessible evidence. So it is with archaeology. Until within the past few years little had really been done outside of the classical fields of Europe and the Near East. After the World War local and regional archaeological work received a great impetus and there is now scarcely a corner of the earth's land surface where some excavation has not been

[4] The proceedings of the Symposium on Early Man were published in Philadelphia in 1937, edited by G. G. MacCurdy. See also the valuable correlation of the results so far achieved by H. de Terra, Scientific Monthly, 1940, pp. 112-24.

undertaken and where nothing is known about past cultures. It is quite certain now that no early civilizations worthy of the name ever arose outside of the Near East, India, China, Middle America, and western South America.

In 1921 the existence of a highly developed civilization in the early Indus Valley was discovered; subsequent excavation at Harappa, Mohenjo-daro, and Chanhu-daro by Sir John Marshall and Ernest Mackay has accumulated a mass of detail and has clarified the chronological picture, showing that the Indus culture culminated during the second half of the third millennium B.C. and disappeared well before the end of the same millennium.[5] Strictly speaking, this early civilization of India was no less dependent on the West than was the later Aryan culture, since there is close general parallelism and there are many specific points of identity between it and the contemporary culture of Mesopotamia and Susiana.

Since the First World War our direct archaeological knowledge of China before the first millennium B.C. has been carried back to the Chalcolithic by the discovery of painted-pottery cultures in northern China and to the second millennium B.C. by the excavations at An-yang in Honan.[6] It is still true that no actual written document can be dated with certainty before the twelfth century B.C., but the names of kings of the Shang-Yin Dynasty on the oracle bones from the site take us to the beginning of the dynasty, i. e., to about the middle of the second millennium. It is hardly likely that future finds will carry written records back before 2000 B.C. Comparative archaeological investigations have shown with increasing clearness that nearly all basic elements of Chinese civilization penetrated from the West at different periods, so that the eminent Sinologist, C.

---

[5] The latest synthesis is that of W. N. Brown in *Supplement to the Journal of the American Oriental Society*, Dec., 1939, pp. 17-31.

[6] For a recent discussion of the early Chinese cultures and their chronology see H. G. Creel, *Studies in Early Chinese Culture* (Baltimore, 1937).

W. Bishop, can justly call Chinese culture "a civilization by osmosis."[7]

It was formerly thought by amateurs like Rider Haggard that the extensive remains at Zimbabwe and elsewhere in Rhodesia proved the existence of an advanced culture in South Africa before the Christian era, but subsequent investigations by trained archaeologists have shown that these speculations were devoid of foundation; actually we must date the remains in question in late mediaeval and early modern times.[8]

In America stratigraphic methods of excavation have begun to be applied since the middle of the nineteen twenties and the relative chronology thus established has been translated into absolute dates by the brilliant work of A. E. Douglass on tree-rings. The resulting method of dendrochronology has now carried the earliest Pueblo towns back to about the seventh century A.D. and the oldest datable deposits of the primitive "Basket-makers" in New Mexico and Arizona back to about the third century A.D.[9] To about the Christian era belong the earliest datable glyphs on Mayan monuments, though an additional period of evolution must separate the oldest dated records from the earliest sedentary communities. Not a single demonstrable case of borrowing from the Old World can be shown in any pre-Columbian culture of the past two millennia in the Americas; in more remote times, but after the close of the last glacial period at the very earliest and probably within the past 20,000 years, there must have been wave after wave of migration across Bering Strait.[10] The predictions of A.

[7] See his article "A Civilization by Osmosis—Ancient China" in *The American Scholar*, V (1936), pp. 323-28, and his fuller treatment of the earlier cultural phases in *Supplement to Jour. Am. Or. Soc.*, Dec., 1939, pp. 45-61.

[8] Thanks to the work of Randall-MacIver, corroborated independently by Miss Caton-Thompson; cf. *Antiquity*, III (1929), pp. 424 ff.

[9] See the recent sketch by F. Martin Brown, *Antiquity*, XI (1937), pp. 409-26.

[10] The most recent competent treatment is that of J. G. D. Clark, *Antiquity*, XIV (1940), pp. 117-37.

Hrdlička promise to be fulfilled by more intensive explorations and excavations in eastern Siberia and northern China, where archaic racial stocks of Amerind appearance are already beginning to be discovered.

Archaeological research has thus established beyond doubt that there is no focus of civilization in the earth that can begin to compete in antiquity and activity with the basin of the Eastern Mediterranean and the region immediately to the east of it—Breasted's Fertile Crescent. Other civilizations of the Old World were all derived from this cultural center or were strongly influenced by it; only the New World was entirely independent. In tracing our Christian civilization of the West to its earliest sources we are, accordingly, restricted to the Egypto-Mesopotamian area. This historical situation provides an unanswerable reply to the frequent complaint that disproportionate attention is paid by archaeologists to the Near East.

B. THE DISCOVERY AND INTERPRETATION OF ANCIENT NEAR-EASTERN WRITTEN DOCUMENTS

Logically it might be more natural to discuss unwritten documents, i. e., human artifacts and uninscribed monuments, before taking up written documents, but the study of the latter came first in modern times, while the development of scientific method in dealing with strata and artifacts is, in general, very recent.

1. *Discovery and Interpretation: An Historical Sketch*

After 1850, when the first stage of exploration, excavation, and decipherment may be said to have closed, the progress of research and discovery became more and more rapid as the unparalleled value of the new historical and aesthetic treasure became clearer. Even World War I, though it brought a temporary set-back, was only the prelude to an extraordinary burst of activity in the study of the past. The international situation is now bringing about a material reduction in the amount of excavation and a corresponding shift in the personnel of scholarship which give us leisure to take our bearings and to consolidate the gains which we have made during the past two decades.

After the initial decipherment of Egyptian hieroglyphics by Champollion there was a temporary interval caused by his death. He was soon followed by a devoted little band of scholars, led by men of the calibre of Lepsius and Brugsch, Birch and Goodwin, de Rougé and Chabas. Lepsius' huge publication, *Denkmäler aus Aegypten und Nubien* (1849-56), provided a mass of material for philological study and Brugsch's *Hieroglyphisch-demotisches Wörterbuch* (1867-68, 1880-82) furnished an elaborate collection of words and meanings, which was not superseded for half a century. However, even in the eighties there was still no clear idea of the grammatical structure of Egyptian. Then came Adolf Erman, the founder of the so-called Berlin school of Egyptology, with a series of accurate and methodical grammars and dictionaries of selected periods in the long history of the hieroglyphic language. Employing a strictly inductive method, i. e., taking only passages whose meaning was reasonably clear and listing all occurrences of words, forms, and constructions in them, he built up a systematic picture of the language which was actually used by the Egyptians at different stages of their history, without importing extraneous or irrelevant data. Erman's first grammatical work was published in 1880 and his last in 1933; the great dictionary of Egyptian on which he had worked for decades began to appear in 1925 and is still in progress. The first half, containing words and meanings, was finished in 1931 and the second half, containing passages where the words occur, is already partly published. Thanks to Erman's brilliant pupils, K. Sethe and G. Steindorff, followed by B. Gunn and A. Gardiner, we can now read Egyptian with astonishingly little uncertainty as to the sense of words or the interpretation of passages. Even the vexed problem of vocalization, peculiarly difficult in a script where as a rule only consonants are written, has been partially solved by Sethe and the writer since 1923.[11] But Egyptologists have not stopped with the elucidation of the script and the language in which the Egyptians wrote: they have labored assiduously to collect and to systematize all the knowledge that can be derived from Egyptian literature, powerfully aided by mural paintings and artifacts. We thus have handbooks and monographs on all phases of Egyptian civilization: religion, administrative and economic life, arts and crafts, social and family life. The need of making this vast fund of information conveniently accessible and of combining it into a living picture has led to the brilliant syntheses of Erman-Ranke (1885-1923), of Wiedemann (1920), and especially of Kees (1933).[12]

When we turn to the cuneiform field we find a parallel situation. After Grotefend's successful beginning, the decipherment of Old Persian was completed by Henry Rawlinson in 1846. The Assyrian riddle proved more difficult to solve, but the efforts of Hincks, Rawlinson, and Oppert from 1846 to 1855 proved successful, though it was over twenty years before all competent scholars were convinced that Assyro-Babylonian cuneiform had really been deciphered and could be read with essential correctness. That they were not convinced was largely due to the lack of philological training and of scientific method on the part of most cuneiformists (with the brilliant exception of the Irishman, Edward Hincks, the importance of whose contributions was not fully appreciated until after his death). Rigid philological method was introduced into Assyriology, as it had been into Egyptology, by a German school, founded by E. Schrader and F. Delitzsch in the seventies and brought to full development by the latter and his pupils, especially Haupt, Zimmern, and Jensen. Delitzsch's first Assyr-

---

[11] See Sethe, *Zeits. Deutsch. Morg. Ges.*, LXXVII (1923), p. 207, and Albright, *Vocalization of the Egyptian Syllabic Orthography* (New Haven, 1934), for references to the literature.

[12] Erman-Ranke, *Aegypten und aegyptisches Leben im Altertum* (Tübingen, 1923); A. Wiedemann, *Das alte Aegypten* (Heidelberg, 1920); H. Kees, *Kulturgeschichte des Alten Orients: Agypten* (Munich, 1933).

ian grammar was published in 1889 and his epoch-making Assyrian dictionary appeared in 1896; in 1914 he accomplished for the older non-Semitic Sumerian what he had already done for Assyrian. After Delitzsch had placed knowledge of Assyrian on a solid scientific basis by combining meticulous accuracy with sound inductive method, a younger group of scholars, Ungnad, Landsberger, and their pupils, attacked the complex problems of historical grammar and dialectology with extraordinary success. Happily, vowels as well as consonants are expressed in cuneiform script, so Landsberger and his school have been able to raise our knowledge of the grammatical and lexical refinements of Accadian (Assyro-Babylonian) to a level above that of Biblical Hebrew and almost on a par with that of Greek or Latin. The Chicago Assyrian dictionary, now being prepared by Poebel and his assistants, will provide a mine of information to workers in the cuneiform field. Owing to the wealth of available material it is probable that very few passages in cuneiform literature will long resist the interpreter; in this respect the outlook is brighter than in Egyptian or indeed in Hebrew.

Cuneiform, unlike Egyptian, was not the medium for only one language (with a few unimportant exceptions); it was employed to write many different languages, mostly non-Semitic, in the course of its long history and wide diffusion. In fact, it was originally the script of the Sumerians, who spoke a tongue which has not yet been successfully related to any other language, ancient or modern. For at least a thousand years Sumerian was the sole written language of Mesopotamia (cir. 3500-2500 B.C.) and for some 2500 years more it remained the learned tongue of Western Asia, being at one time (about 1400 B.C.) taught in the schools of Syria and Asia Minor as well as in those of Mesopotamia and Susiana. Thanks to the many bilingual texts and word-lists left us by the Accadians, it has been possible to penetrate into the recesses of this mysterious speech, by far the oldest dead language in history. The efforts of Thureau-Dangin, Delitzsch, and especially Poebel, whose *Sumer-*

ische Grammatik appeared in 1923 and has already been antiquated in important respects by his subsequent work, have now solved all the main problems and Sumerian can be read with general accuracy, though the obscurity of its early religious literature provides us with plenty of work in interpretation.

Sumero-Accadian cuneiform was also used to write many other languages: Hittite (Nasian or Nesian), Horite (Hurrian), Luwian, Proto-Hittite (Khattic), Balaic (all in Asia Minor), Urartian (in Armenia), Cossaean, and Elamite (in the Zagros and Susiana). It was further used occasionally for a number of known languages, such as Indo-Iranian, Canaanite (Hebrew), Egyptian, Aramaic. Moreover, two independent scripts of alphabetic nature, North Canaanite (Ugaritic) and Old Persian, both use the wedge as the primary element in forming characters. The cuneiform languages of Asia Minor are known to us mainly from the excavations of Winckler and Bittel at Boghazköy, the ancient Hittite capital, east of modern Ankara. Hittite itself was deciphered by the Czech scholar B. Hrozný in 1915 and has been successfully interpreted by Forrer, Friedrich, Goetze, Sommer, and others; it is now quite as well known as Accadian was fifty years ago, owing partly to the fact that it is Indo-European. Hurrian is exceptionally interesting, not only because of its complex and enigmatic structure, which is equally different from Semitic, Indo-European, and Sumerian, but also because of the curious way in which it has survived: in a letter and in glosses in other cuneiform letters found in Egypt; in words, passages, and tablets scattered through the Hittite documents of Boghazköy; in tablets written in the cuneiform alphabet of Ugarit; in vocabularies and glosses in Accadian cuneiform literature; in words, constructions, and personal names in the business documents of Nuzi in eastern Mesopotamia; in fragmentary tablets excavated since 1935 at Mari, the ancient Amorite capital on the Middle Euphrates. Complex as has been the transmission of this material, it is rapidly yielding to the brilliant onslaughts of Friedrich, Goetze, and

Speiser.[13] There can be no doubt that it was the language which was originally spoken by the biblical Horites.[14]

What is true of Egyptology is also true of Assyriology. The wealth of data available in the scores of thousands of documents which have already been published (but which do not begin to exhaust the material in our museums) has spurred two generations of scholars to the task of analysis and synthesis. Such handbooks as Meissner's *Babylonien und Assyrien* (1920-26) and as the still incomplete *Reallexikon der Assyriologie* (1928-) are supplemented by numerous recent monographs on special subjects such as religion and magic, law, administrative and economic organization, society and family life, arts and crafts, etc. Owing to the much greater extent and variety of cuneiform sources, a great deal more is known about many aspects of Mesopotamian life than is true of Egypt, though correspondingly less is known about features of daily life which are now very well known in Egypt, thanks to mural paintings and the dryness of its soil.

Turning now from cuneiform to Semitic alphabetical literature, we find ourselves immeasurably poorer. Yet there are now thousands of inscriptions, nearly all on stone, written in Aramaic, in various dialects of Canaanite (Hebrew), in South Arabic, and in North Arabic; there is also an immensely valuable little corpus of clay tablets written in a Canaanite dialect and a cuneiform alphabet. The North-Semitic (Phoenician) alphabet was finally deciphered by W. Gesenius, whose great work on the subject appeared in 1837, and the South-Semitic (Minaeo-Sabaean) alphabet yielded its secrets almost simultaneously to Gesenius and to E. Rödiger in 1841. The earliest inscriptions in Phoenician or Aramaic known to Gesenius (aside from a few seals) belonged to the fifth century B.C.; one by one older inscrip-

[13] See especially E. A. Speiser, *A Hurrian Grammar and Chrestomathy* (*Annual Am. Sch. Or. Res.*, XX; New Haven, 1940).
[14] On this question see the writer's remark in *From the Pyramids to Paul* (G. L. Robinson Anniversary Volume; New York, 1935), pp. 9-26.

tions have since been found, pushing the date back to the ninth century (Mesha Stone, found in 1868), early tenth century (sarcophagus of Ahiram of Byblus, 1923), sixteenth or seventeenth (miscellaneous finds in Palestine since 1929).[15] Another early stage of the North-Semitic alphabet, which was the direct progenitor of our own, seems to be represented by the proto-Sinaitic inscriptions, first discovered by Petrie in 1905 and partially deciphered by Gardiner in 1916; their interpretation is handicapped by the scantiness of the material and none of the proposed decipherments can be considered as certain.[16] The recent discovery of the Ostraca of Samaria (published since 1924)[17] and the Lachish Letters (1935)[18] has been of very great value for biblical studies. The South-Arabic and North-Arabic inscriptions are less important, but they still form a unique body of material for the study of the pre-Islamic culture of Arabia and they frequently shed valuable light on the Old Testament. The foremost authorities on the two groups of proto-Arabic texts are, respectively, N. Rhodokanakis and F. V. Winnett. In spite of measureless exaggeration of the antiquity of the earliest South-Arabic inscriptions by Glaser and Hommel, it is now clear that none of them antedates the seventh or eighth century B.C., though earlier ones will probably be found in the future. The earli-

[15] For chronology and bibliography of these finds see J. W. Flight in Elihu Grant, *Haverford Symposium on Archaeology and the Bible* (New Haven, 1938), pp. 114 ff.

[16] Cf. the writer's attempt, *Bull. Am. Sch. Or. Res.*, No. 110 (1948), pp. 6-22, which remains the most recent serious effort.

[17] For the literature dealing with these ostraca see Diringer, *Le iscrizioni antico-ebraiche palestinesi* (Florence, 1934), pp. 21-74, and Albright, *Pal. Expl. Fund Quar. State.*, 1936, pp. 211 ff.; on their date see *Bull. Am. Sch. Or. Res.*, No. 73, p. 21 (the writer would now date them definitely to the reign of Jeroboam II, in the first quarter of the eighth century).

[18] See H. Torczyner and others, *The Lachish Letters* (London, 1938), and the relevant articles in *Bull. Am. Sch. Or. Res.*, Nos. 61-73. For the most recent treatment, with bibliography, see the writer, *Kirjath Sepher* (Jerusalem), XVI (1939/40), pp. 310 ff.; *Bull. Am. Sch. Or. Res.*, No. 82, pp. 18 ff.

est North-Arabic inscriptions are nearly, if not quite, as old, as has just been demonstrated by Winnett.[19]

During the past ten years a most important and entirely unexpected new script and literature have been discovered, deciphered, and made accessible. This is the North-Canaanite literature in a previously unknown cuneiform alphabet, which has come to light in C. F. A. Schaeffer's excavations at Ras esh-Shamrah, ancient Ugarit on the coast of northern Syria. The first documents were discovered in 1929 and published the following year. Almost immediately deciphered by H. Bauer and E. Dhorme, they have proved to be written in two languages, one a very archaic Canaanite dialect akin to pre-Mosaic Hebrew and the other a Hurrian dialect (see above). In eleven campaigns from 1929 to 1939 several hundred tablets and fragments in this script have been unearthed; a number of them belong to unusually large tablets with three or four columns on each side, containing originally several hundred lines. Nearly all the new alphabetic documents, which date mainly from the fourteenth century B.C., are of religious character and most of them belong to three mythological epics, which treat of the events connected with the death and resurrection of Baal, with the marriage of the demigod Keret, and with another demigod Daniel (Dan'el). The editor of these priceless documents, Ch. Virolleaud, has admirably commenced the task of interpreting this new material and many other scholars, among whom may be mentioned in particular R. Dussaud, H. L. Ginsberg, J. A. Montgomery and Z. S. Harris, A. Goetze, C. H. Gordon, and the writer, have contributed to its elucidation.[20] There is still much that is obscure and the historical-geographical views of Virolleaud

---

[19] See *Bull. Am. Sch. Or. Res.*, No. 73 (1939), pp. 3-9, and *The Moslem World*, April, 1940, p. 4, n. 8. Cf. also the writer's remarks, *Bull. Am. Sch. Or. Res.*, No. 66, p. 30.

[20] For the bibliography of this field see the lists and indices compiled by C. F. A. Schaeffer, *Ugaritica* (Paris, 1939), pp. 153-322. C. H. Gordon has just published a valuable *Ugaritic Grammar* in the *Analecta Orientalia* of the Pontifical Institute (Rome, 1940).

have not been accepted by most other scholars,[21] but owing to the wealth of material already available and to the resemblance of the language to Hebrew, most of the new texts can be translated with certainty or with reasonable confidence. In the present volume great care will be exercised not to draw on uncertain translations for evidence.

In addition to Egyptian hieroglyphics, Accadian and other cuneiform scripts, North-Semitic and South-Semitic alphabets, many other scripts have been recently discovered in the basin of the eastern Mediterranean. Here we shall list only the most important, in order to give some idea of the epigraphic riches being deciphered and still to be deciphered. First we may mention the Hittite "hieroglyphs," in which are written hundreds of inscriptions from Syria and Asia Minor, apparently all dating from between 1500 and 500 B.C. and mostly from the Iron Age, between 1200 and 700 B.C. First recognized and provisionally identified as "Hittite" in the seventies of the past century, decipherment was attempted by A. H. Sayce and P. Jensen, followed unsuccessfully by many others. Finally, in 1928, a new phase was opened by P. Meriggi, followed closely by E. Forrer, I. Gelb, H. Bossert, and especially by B. Hrozný;[22] scores of hieroglyphiform characters in this script can be certainly or plausibly read and the language has been associated to the satisfaction of specialists with the two proto-Indo-European languages of Asia Minor already known, Hittite and Luwian. It must be confessed that there is still a great deal to be done before philologically adequate translations of the inscriptions can be given. Very similar in origin, as well as apparently in structure, is the Aegean hieroglyphic script of the early second millennium, which developed about the

[21] Cf. the writer's observations, *Bull. Am. Sch. Or. Res.*, No. 71 (1938), pp. 35-40, and the detailed discussions of the controversy by A. Bea, *Biblica* (Rome), XIX (1938), pp. 435-53, and XX, pp. 436-53.

[22] Cf. the summary sketch of the history of decipherment given by the writer, *Bull. Am. Sch. Or. Res.*, No. 54, pp. 24-25, and the more detailed account now given by J. Friedrich, *Entzifferungsgeschichte der hethitischen Hieroglyphenschrift* (Stuttgart, 1939).

middle of the millennium into two linear derivatives, one of which is known from Bronze-Age Crete, Cyprus, and the Greek mainland. First discovered by (Sir) Arthur Evans in the nineties of the past century, the Cretan script is best illustrated by some 1600 clay tablets containing texts in the latest of its three phases, linear B, belonging to the fifteenth century B.C. Nearly forty years after this great find at Cnossus an additional one of six hundred tablets was made by Blegen at Nestor's ancient capital of Pylus in southwestern Greece (1939).[23] Many efforts have been made to decipher this script, which seems to have been used to write several languages, including Mycenaean Greek, but few generally accepted results have been obtained so far. When all the documents from Cnossus and Pylus have been published it will hardly take long to decipher them.[24] That there were still other hieroglyphiform syllabaries in use in the coastlands of the northeastern Mediterranean in the Bronze Age is indicated by such chance finds as the Phaestus Disk.

We have not begun to exhaust the list of undeciphered and partly deciphered scripts now known to have existed in the Near East in antiquity. The point of diminishing returns has not been reached and two new scripts seem to replace every script that is successfully interpreted. One of the latest and most interesting is the hieroglyphiform syllabary used at Byblus in Phoenicia toward the end of the third millennium B.C. One fragment of stone was published by the discoverer, M. Dunand, in 1930 and a number of similar texts on copper were described by him at the International Congress of Orientalists in Rome (1935).[25] Since this script appears to have been used to write a very early form of Canaanite (Hebrew) antedating the Patriarchal Age, we look forward eagerly to its decipherment.

[23] See *Am. Jour. Arch.*, XLIII (1939), pp. 564 ff.
[24] [Mycenaean linear B was deciphered in 1953 by M. Ventris.]
[25] Cf. *Bull. Am. Sch. Or. Res.*, No. 60, pp. 3 ff.

2. *Linguistic and Philological Method in the Interpretation of Written Documents*

The fundamental significance of sound method in decipherment and interpretation has been emphasized repeatedly in the preceding section. In conformity with our principle of stressing methodology, we shall now give a succinct analysis of linguistic and philological method in the interpretation of written documents. Following recent usage we define "linguistic" as relating to the scientific aspects of language as such, i. e., to the form, structure, vocabulary, and comparative treatment of individual languages. Similarly we define "philological" as relating to the scientific study of documents, written or orally transmitted. This point must be stressed, since the usage of the nineteenth century substituted "philological" for what we now prefer to call "linguistic," owing to the fact that the technical and comparative study of language had replaced the investigation of documents as the primary interest of philologians. We now revert to the eighteenth-century understanding of "philology" and apply the term "linguistics" to the subsequently developed technical part of the field. Of course a sharp distinction is not always possible, especially when we deal with the grammatical and lexicographical exegesis of a text.

The primary function of the linguist is to describe the phenomena of a given language or dialect as exactly and as comprehensively as possible. The utmost precision is here necessary in order to escape error in establishing the phonetic form of an oral or written document and in analyzing its grammatical structure. Of course, phonetic form in written documents is dependent on the accuracy and consistency of the orthography and may be quite a different thing from the original phonemic pattern of the document as read aloud. The analysis of the structure of a language follows the same logical principles whether the language is well known or is new, whether it is found in ancient documents or is taken down from the mouths of living men. The analysis must always follow the same logical sequence: induction, deduction, analogical reasoning. Since all language is rigidly bound by law—which operates as effectively when it originates in custom and imitation as when it arises from anatomical, physiological, psychological, or other sources —linguistic phenomena are capable of as scientific treatment as are any data of biological origin. The methodological triad, observation, experiment, induction, on which natural science is based, operates in a corresponding way in linguistics. We include the word "experiment" advisedly, since the linguist who studies a new language as spoken by living men must constantly test and correct his observations and his tentative hypotheses by devising suitable procedure for making such tests. The investigator of ancient languages employs the same logical method, though in a more restricted way, when he tests his observations and inductions by applying them to new or previously excluded written documents. Just as the linguistic anthropologist or the dialectologist restricts himself carefully to a given dialect or group of speakers, in order to avert confusion, so the up-to-date specialist in ancient languages is scrupulously careful to limit himself as far as feasible to a given geographical dialect or historical phase of a language. Thus the Assyriologist who wishes to specialize in Accadian grammar distinguishes sharply between such phases as the following: Old Accadian (cir. 25th-22nd century B.C.), Old Babylonian (cir. 20th-17th century B.C.), Middle Babylonian (cir. 15th-11th century B.C.), Neo-Babylonian (cir. 9th-5th century B.C.), Old Assyrian, Middle Assyrian, Neo-Assyrian, the Larsa dialect, the dialect of Mari, the dialect of Nuzi, etc. Sometimes different bodies of literature are written in different dialects, as in the case of the Accadian texts of the hymnal-epic class, which belong to the end of the third millennium and the beginning of the second. The prologue of the Code of Hammurabi (18th century B.C.) is composed in a more archaic and literary language than is the corpus of laws which follows it.

Since there is widespread vagueness as to the applicability of linguistic methods to the study of ancient historical sources and data, we shall list a few fields where such application is justifiable. Language may be used with caution to prove an original physical association between different groups of men. Of course, it is no longer necessary to emphasize the fact that a common linguistic inheritance does not necessarily carry with it a common racial origin, since language may be borrowed whereas physical inheritance cannot. But for the historian it is even more important to demonstrate linguistic relationship than it is to establish racial kinship, since the former has an intimate bearing on past cultural association while the latter may be quite devoid of concrete historical meaning (unless one is primarily interested in prehistory). The most important result of comparative linguistic science is the demonstration (now over a century old) that the various branches of the Indo-European family speak closely related languages which can all be traced back to a common ancestral tongue; linguistic methods make it possible to reconstruct the most essential phonetic and morphological features of the latter. It is increasingly probable that, as shown by Forrer and especially by Sturtevant, Proto-Indo-European is a sister or aunt, not the mother of the newly deciphered tongues of Asia Minor such as Hittite and Luwian. In the past few decades it has become certain that there is a similar genetic relationship between the Semitic tongues of Asia (Canaanite-Hebrew, Aramaic, Accadian, Arabic) and the Hamitic of North Africa, with Egyptian taking an intermediate position between them.[26] Here, however, the time which elapsed between the original diffusion of Hamito-Semitic peoples and the earliest available documents in the individual languages is much greater than in the case of Indo-European, so the difficulty of formulating the laws governing phonetic change as well as of reconstructing grammatical evolution is correspondingly greater. It must be said, most emphatically, that

[26] For the writer's latest statement of his position see *Archiv f. Orientf.*, XII (1937), pp. 72 f. and for the latest statement of the other recent theory, that of Zyhlarz, see H. Ranke in *Supplement to Jour. Am. Or. Soc.*, Dec., 1939, pp. 15 f. Zyhlarz's view is too complicated for the evidence which he adduces (much of which is misleading).

most efforts to prove linguistic relationship in opposition to the views of competent specialists are doomed to failure. In few fields of learning has more nonsense been perpetrated by amateurs, i. e., by enthusiasts who are unwilling to submit to the painfully rigid discipline of linguistic method.

Since observation and induction prove that each dialect and each phase of linguistic history has its own phonetic and other laws, which often overlap but seldom permit exceptions (themselves due to the operation of conflicting laws) inside of each dialect or phase, the greatest care is needed in applying linguistic law to the solution of specific philological or historical questions. E. g., in deciding whether a given form of a Canaanite name or word can be identified with a foreign name or word transcribed into Egyptian, we must determine the exact time of the document or documents in which the transcription is found, we must fix, if possible, the phonetic form which the given Canaanite word would have at that time or earlier, and must then see whether the resulting equations of Canaanite phonemes with Egyptian signs are in accordance with inductively established relationships of the same age and type. The procedure sounds complex and it must be rigorous. What results can be achieved may be illustrated by the following chain of recent investigations and discoveries. In 1923 K. Sethe and the writer independently established the phonetic laws governing the principal changes in the Egyptian vowel-system from Proto-Egyptian to Coptic, over a period of at least 4000 years.[27] This was accomplished mainly by a rigorous confrontation of the inner Egyptian principles of vocalism as inductively worked out by Steindorff and Sethe a quarter century before with cuneiform transcriptions of Egyptian names and words, going back to about 1400 B.C. Two years later a cuneiform vocabulary of Egyptian words from the 14th century B.C. was published—and the vocalic theories in question were confirmed throughout, as far as the new evidence went. In 1934 the writer published a reconstruction of the vocalic system which was employed by the Egyptians of the New Empire for writing

[27] See note 11, above, for references.

foreign names and words. In this work much use was made of reconstructed forms of Canaanite words and names, according to the evidence of comparative linguistics, checked by transcriptions into cuneiform in the Amarna Tablets and elsewhere. The method was criticized by scholars who were not linguists, but discoveries since 1934, especially from more intensive study of Ugaritic, have confirmed it most strikingly.[28]

Formerly the main special use of linguistic method was in determining the etymology and hence the primary meaning of a given word. Biblical handbooks are cluttered with false etymologies, as well as with correct etymologies from which erroneous or undemonstrable deductions have been made. Actually, no competent lexicographer in any language fixes the precise meaning of a word by its etymology but rather by collecting as many passages where the word occurs as possible or practicable and by listing all meanings and shades of meaning in them. Words change their meaning through use to such an extent that the etymological method of fixing significance is only employed as a last resort, where other evidence is inadequate. Wherever possible the combinatory method (i. e., the collection and comparison of all passages where a word occurs) has replaced the etymological one in decipherment and interpretation, at least among competent scholars.

A few illustrations of the importance of linguistic methodology for the biblical scholar will be more effective than further description. Many historians have thoughtlessly identified Zerah (Zrḥ) the Cushite (II Chron. 14:9) with the Bubastite pharaoh Osorkon I.[29] If, however, we examine all certain cases of transcription from Egyptian into Hebrew in the same general age and fix the approximate pronunciation of the consonants in question in both languages at that time, the identification is at once seen to be

---

[28] Cf. *Archiv f. Orientf.*, XII, pp. 384 f.
[29] So, for example, H. R. Hall, in *The Ancient History of the Near East* (5th ed., 1920), and *The People and the Book* (1925); A. T. Olmstead, *History of Palestine and Syria* (1931; cf. the writer, *Jew. Quar. Rev.*, XXIV, p. 370).

absurd—as it really is historically. The Hebrew word *shîr* "song, poem," was long ago connected etymologically with Arabic *shi'r* "poem," though the loss of the consonant *'ayin* could not be explained. Now we know that Hebrew *shîr* must be traced back through Canaanite to Old Babylonian *shîrum, shêrum* (with the nominative ending *um*), itself derived from parent Semitic *shi'rum*. Moreover, this derivation fits perfectly into the picture which we now have of the passage of cultural loan-words from Accadian to Canaanite, and the date of the borrowing may be fixed by comparative linguistic methods to before the sixteenth century B.C.[30] Again, Old Testament scholars have been inclined to make much of the fact that *kâhin*, the Arabic cognate of Hebrew *kôhēn* "priest," means "soothsayer, diviner." Unfortunately, however, the word is isolated in Arabic and may, therefore, like thousands of other cultural words in that language, be considered equally well as a loan-word from older Canaanite *kâhin* or from Aramaic *kâhnâ*, both meaning "priest"; should this be true we would have an indication of specialization in function among the Arabs and not of a supposed magical background of the Israelite priesthood.[31] Such examples can easily be multiplied.

In studying written documents from the ancient Near East there are four main stages: decipherment of the script, linguistic interpretation, philological analysis, and historical interpretation. Success in decipherment requires great ingenuity and usually demands erudition and industry. Grotefend, Bauer, and Dhorme, all three of whom were

---

[30] Cf. *Jour. Pal. Or. Soc.*, IV (1924), p. 210; *Beiträge z. Assyr.*, X, 2 (1927), pp. xvii f.

[31] Canaanite *kâhinu* "priest," is now established by the documents of Ugarit, where it appears frequently (15th-14th centuries B.C.). The view of Wellhausen that Heb. *kôhēn* is derived from Arab. *kâhin* has been rather uncritically accepted by many scholars; cf. T. J. Meek, *Hebrew Origins*, p. 127, who carries his deduction much too far. Nöldeke already recognized that the word was more probably an Arabic loan from the north; cf. the judicious remarks of G. B. Gray, *Sacrifice in the Old Testament* (1925), p. 183.

cipher experts, illustrate the necessity of ingenuity; Champollion and Hrozný illustrate the value of erudition. Many decipherers, like Grotefend, have been wholly unable to continue their work beyond the first stages, because of inadequate linguistic preparation. The linguistic interpretation of an inscription may follow strictly combinatory methods, as best illustrated by recent work in Egyptian and Sumerian, or it may avail itself of the assistance given by cognate languages, as in the decipherment of Assyrian and Ugaritic. Here, however, rigorous linguistic training is essential if the translation is not to descend to the level of guess-work, as is unhappily illustrated by many of the translations of Ugaritic texts offered by free-lances in England and America. Intuition is a very valuable heuristic aid when it is based on extended practice and knowledge, but even then it must be disregarded unless it can be otherwise controlled. The task of interpretation is, however, not finished when a document has been correctly translated. After the linguist has done all that he can, the philologist (in the narrow sense) must continue where he has left off and must determine the class to which the document belongs, investigate its verse-form or literary category, establish the text by methods of textual ("lower") criticism where it is corrupt, fix its date and authorship if possible, and draw conclusions which can be utilized directly by the historian. Finally, the historian attacks the documentary material, analyzing it for the purpose of reconstructing some phase of human history: political, social, religious, aesthetic, economic, legal, etc. It goes without saying that there is seldom such narrow specialization in the persons of interested scholars: the scholar is often decipherer, linguist, philologist, or philologist and historian; in rare instances he may be all four. As in all other fields of scholarship and science, the two most important essentials for success are precision and critical judgment. Without the strictest precision that is attainable a scholar's work may produce and transmit errors, often after they have been disproved by others; without severe critical method a scholar fails to avail himself of the aid which may be derived from the accumulated experience of his guild.

C. The Discovery and Interpretation of Unwritten Documents from the Ancient Near East

Until very recently there was a general tendency on the part of ancient historians and biblical scholars to neglect or even to despise the unwritten objects unearthed by archaeologists in increasing profusion. Sensational discoveries in prehistoric Egypt, Mesopotamia, the Aegean, and Palestine, together with the increasing interest taken by natural scientists in archaeology when divorced from written documents, have changed the prevailing attitude. It is now becoming hard to find a philologist who denies the value of anepigraphic archaeology (the science of unwritten documents), and the reverse has become fashionable in certain circles—with equally unfortunate results. To the real student of antiquity neither discipline is any longer adequate in itself; it is only by the union of philology with archaeology that we can make the ancient world live.

1. *Discovery and Methodology*

The discovery of the value of pottery, undecorated as well as painted, for chronological purposes lies at the foundation of modern archaeology. It is true that any other class of objects can also be employed for this purpose, but since whole vases and broken sherds outnumber all other artifacts in ancient Near-Eastern sites a hundred to one, since pottery styles changed as remorselessly as all other fashions, and since pottery was too breakable and once broken too unimportant to be preserved, it is incomparably the most useful class of object for dating.[32] The discovery of the chronological value of painted pottery was made in the

[32] See the writer's discussion of this subject in *So Live the Works of Men* (E. L. Hewett Anniversary Volume; Santa Fe, 1939), pp. 49-63.

nineteenth century by classical archaeologists, whose work culminated in the brilliant synthesis of Furtwängler (mainly in the eighties of the century). But the latter was primarily an historian of art, hence common, undecorated wares failed completely to interest him. It was reserved for a young Egyptian archaeologist, (Sir) Flinders Petrie, to discover that unpainted pottery might be just as good an instrument for dating as was painted, if the same attention were paid to it. This fact grew on him during his work in Egypt in the eighties of the past century, especially after working at Naucratis in 1885, but he failed to understand its full implications until he dug for six weeks on the scarp of a Palestinian mound, Tell el-Hesi (1890). Here he found over sixty feet of superimposed debris of occupation, covering (as we now know) more than two thousand years of history. This debris was, he found, clearly divided into strata, each characterized by its own types of pottery, though there was not, of course, strict correlation between periods of occupation and ceramic phases. Several strata he was able to synchronize with Egyptian dynasties, thanks to imported Syro-Palestinian pottery previously discovered in datable Egyptian tombs. In certain cases he was thus able to secure a nearly correct absolute chronology as well as an accurate relative chronology. That his absolute chronology was not correct throughout was due to the still primitive state of Egyptian archaeology itself.

Tell el-Hesi was not actually the first true mound, with stratified deposits of successive occupation, to be excavated; that honor falls to Hissarlik, ancient Troy in northwestern Asia Minor, where Heinrich Schliemann began to dig in 1870. But Schliemann remained a brilliant amateur, and though he recognized the implications of his work he was unable to develop a method of excavating or of dating the layers of a mound. Even the gifted Dörpfeld, who joined him at Troy in 1882 and resumed work there in 1892, after Schliemann's death, neglected pottery, though he developed a superior technique for accurate planning and recording of superimposed constructional remains. To Petrie and Dörpfeld we owe the elements of modern archaeological method in the Near East. Petrie's discovery of the importance of pottery for stratigraphy and chronology was unhappily not accepted by Dörpfeld, who even failed to keep pace with Furtwängler and became involved in an unfortunate controversy with him. Dörpfeld never surrendered his erroneous point of view about ceramic chronology, which still mars the pages of his *Alt-Olympia* (1935). Happily, all other Aegean archaeologists now follow the methods introduced by Petrie and employ pottery as the basis for their chronology of this region before the sixth century B.C.

Eleven years after his work at Tell el-Hesi, Petrie published an equally important ceramic discovery in his *Diospolis Parva* (1901). This discovery was that of the principle of sequence-dating. Seven years previously he had begun to find Egyptian remains antedating the Pyramid Age, which up to that time had marked the dawn of Egyptian monumental history. He and others attacked the new field of prehistoric archaeology with great enthusiasm and success, finding numerous and extensive cemeteries containing thousands of tombs and burials, most of which had been provided with vases of food when the original interments were made. Some of the tombs were dated to the First Dynasty by written objects found in them. The rest were mute and appeared at first sight quite undatable. But Petrie had already set up the principle that pottery could be used for chronological purposes and he was also familiar with the tendency of any kind of object to change its form after repeated imitation, i. e., after one form had been copied and the copy had been copied in its turn a sufficient number of times. One type, a large cylindrical jar with a wavy ledge-handle, showed a great many variations in the form of the handle, variations which could be arranged in an evolutionary series. Which end of the series came first, whether the wavy handle had developed from a rudimentary form or had been gradually reduced to a vestigial form, might have been hard to decide, but luckily one end—the vestigial one—terminated in dated tombs of the First Dynasty, so the other end had to begin in a more remote predynastic phase. By applying the same method to other series of pottery types which he found with the wavy-handled jars he was not only able to corroborate his results but also to prolong his sequence backward to a period long preceding the first appearance of the jars in question. At first Petrie's sequence-dating aroused the same skepticism and hostility that his earlier use of pottery for dating had stirred up, but subsequent discoveries have confirmed his method and his conclusions so often and so brilliantly that all competent archaeologists now take them for granted. It must, however, be remembered that sequence-dating is purely typological and often requires confirmation by stratigraphy before its results can be considered absolutely certain.

The most important contributions made since Petrie's original discoveries in the field of ceramic chronology have been technical and comparative. Petrie's technique in recording pottery was rough and ready; his drawings were generally only in outline and freehand; photography was seldom employed; descriptions were sketchy and wholly inadequate from our present point of view. Important details of form were neglected and only the scantiest information was given with regard to paste, finish, decoration, etc. G. A. Reisner and his pupils, especially C. S. Fisher, have introduced incomparably more precise methods. Virtually all competent excavators in the Near East now devote much, often most of their time to excavating, assembling, recording, classifying, and reproducing their pottery. The latest important forward step in dealing with pottery comes from the archaeological laboratories of New Mexico; it consists in minute petrographical analysis of the paste (composition) of pottery, with the aid of microphotographs and of chemical analyses. In this way significant details which escaped previous students can be detected and valuable conclusions for provenience and dating can be drawn.[33]

[33] The new microphotographic and petrographic methods were first systematically utilized by Kidder in his *Pottery of Pecos* (1931-36) and have been introduced into Near-Eastern

All other classes of objects made by human hand can now be treated in a comparable way, so that they may also be utilized for the purpose of chronology and the history of culture. Thanks to extreme care in clearing and describing the locus of objects (i. e., the place in which and the level at which they are found), as well as in describing and analyzing their composition, etc., their function and mode of manufacture may be reconstructed. Art objects are among the most valuable both for chronology and for the history of civilization, since so much attention has recently been paid to questions of technique and motif connected with them, and since they usually represent the greatest technical and aesthetic effort of ancient cultures. However, since such objects were often prized as heirlooms or were stored in temples and palaces for generations or even centuries, care must be taken in utilizing them for chronological purposes.

The systematic archaeologist is thus forced to employ two divergent principles at almost every step in his work: stratigraphy, or the study of the relation of objects to the layers or deposits in which they are found and the relation of these deposits to one another; typology, or the classification of objects according to types, following taxonomic methods, and the comparison of objects belonging to a type with one another, in order to determine chronological, geographical, and technical relationships. The principle of stratigraphy involves induction and experiment; that of typology is rather based on deduction and classification. The complementary character of the two principles in archaeology is somewhat like that of experiment and mathematical theory in physics. At an early stage of archaeological research in any given country, all the advantage is with

---

studies by Mrs. Ehrich in *Early Pottery of the Jebeleh Region* (Philadelphia, 1939). These methods are now being extended and refined by Vladimir Fewkes in the laboratories of the University of Pennsylvania Museum. New techniques of considerable importance are being developed by the ceramic department of the University of Pittsburgh, in collaboration with J. L. Kelso; see *Ann. Am. Sch. Or. Res.*, XXI-XXII, pp. 86-142.

the stratigrapher. At a later stage the typologist finds more and more to do and the trained typologist eventually acquires an advantage over the mechanical stratigrapher, except in dealing with undisturbed deposits. In the Aegean, for instance, typology has recently scored some signal victories over a stratigraphy which had become more refined than the technique of observation and recording warranted.

Recapitulating what we have said about the development of archaeological method, we must stress the fact that the stratigraphic method was first applied to archaeology in the Near East, but not until more than half a century after the beginning of archaeological excavation. In some circles it was not properly employed until within the past decade. Under these circumstances such progress as may be recorded was mainly typological and historical. Occasional control was furnished by the discovery of uninscribed objects in close conjunction with inscribed ones of known date, whether absolute or relative. Toward the end of the 19th century came the discovery that unpainted pottery could be used for dating and that the stratigraphic possibilities of ancient mounds were almost unlimited. Stratigraphy and typology then developed apace. In Egypt, where nearly all city mounds are still occupied by modern settlements and where tombs and temples attract almost all excavators, stratigraphy has only begun to be exploited in the past decade or so, whereas typology can be employed to great advantage because of the extraordinary number of intact, accurately datable tombs. Stratigraphy will always labor under a hopeless disadvantage in the Nile Valley, especially in the Delta, because the steady rise of the subterranean water level has flooded almost all early strata, often leaving nothing of pre-Ptolemaic date accessible to the spade without prohibitive expense. In southwestern Asia, on the other hand, a large proportion of the ancient mounds, especially in Babylonia, are now deserted; the change of the courses of Tigris and Euphrates in late pre-Christian times has left once fertile and densely peopled districts an arid wilderness, while other, formerly uninhabited tracts are now cultivated and are dotted with towns and villages. Stratigraphy flourishes most today in dealing with places and times where little intelligible writing is found, such as Palestine, Syria, Asia Minor, or the earlier phases of sedentary life in Mesopotamia and the Aegean.

The character and the direct value for history of what we have called anepigraphic archaeology may be illustrated by a brief sketch of its achievements in two directions: pre-Hellenistic Palestine, prehistoric Egypt and Mesopotamia.

As has already been emphasized, the history of modern archaeological research in Palestine goes back to Petrie's six weeks at Tell el-Hesi in 1890. In the following twenty years the British Palestine Exploration Fund organized excavations at some eight Palestinian sites, including especially five years of work at Gezer (between 1902 and 1909), directed by R. A. S. Macalister. The Germans and Austrians also dug at Taanach, Megiddo, and Jericho from 1901 to 1909 and an elaborately organized American expedition from Harvard University worked at Samaria from 1908 to 1910, under the admirable direction of G. A. Reisner. In spite of the quantity of objects and of data brought to light and made accessible to scholars (by 1913 virtually all pre-War excavations had been published), the results were disappointing and we have not yet entirely recovered from the disillusionment which their publication caused in philological and historical circles. This reaction was due not only to the extremely small proportion of written documents found by Palestinian excavators, but perhaps mainly to the vague and conflicting character of their conclusions. As a result of the first decade of work in Palestine, though few interesting objects and buildings had been found, Bliss had set up a roughly blocked out but substantially correct chronology going back to the early second millennium B.C. At Gezer, however, Macalister tried to arrange his chronology so as to cover a hiatus of several centuries (cir. 9th-6th centuries) in the history of the city and consequently reduced most of his dates between 1200 and 300 B.C. by several centuries. This erroneous telescoping of chronology was carried much farther by the Germans, misled by similar gaps at Jericho and by premature historical interpretation of their finds; in their case the error amounted at one point to about eight hundred years (cir. 1600-800 B.C.).[34] What a chaos ensued may be seen by examination of Handcock's systematic attempt at synthesis, *Archaeology of the Holy Land* (1916), where remains from the Bronze Age are mixed with others from the Iron Age, where "Israelite" objects are generally Canaanite, where "post-exilic" remains are likely to be pre-exilic, and where "cultural phases" are invariably crazy quilts composed of pieces of heterogeneous origin.

In 1920 the British administration in Palestine established a department of antiquities headed by a competent archaeologist, John Garstang, and did everything possible to encourage excavators. In 1921 the University of Pennsylvania Museum began its important work at Beth-shan; in 1922 the American School of Oriental Research in Jerusalem undertook the first in a long series of excavations, some of which were very important; in 1925 the University of Chicago began work at the great site of Megiddo; in 1926 and 1928 the excavations at Tell en-Nasbeh and Beth-shemesh, respectively, were launched; in 1927 the British School of Archaeology in Egypt (directed by Sir Flinders Petrie) commenced a series of excavations in the extreme south; in 1929 Garstang resumed the excavation of Jericho which had been begun by the Germans before the War; in 1930 the excavation of Teleilat el-Ghassul near Jericho was undertaken by the Pontifical Biblical Institute; in 1931 Harvard University resumed work at Samaria; in 1932 the Lachish expedition was launched; in 1933 Mme. Marquet-Krause undertook the excavation of Ai. This bald list mentions only the outstanding excavations in Palestinian mounds without attempting to exhaust the list. Thanks to this unprecedented concentration of activity in so small a country, we now have a remarkably precise and detailed knowledge of the chronology and char-

---

[34] The extent of their error was freely admitted by Watzinger in 1926 (*Zeits. Deutsch. Morg. Ges.*, LXXX, pp. 131-36), and has since been recognized by all specialists.

acter of successive periods of culture in Palestine back to neolithic times. By 1929 the data amassed before the First World War had been correlated with subsequent discoveries and the broad outlines of the history of civilization were clear back to the 17th century B.C., with no disagreement on chronology worth mentioning. In the past ten years innumerable details have been filled in and a series of remarkable undertakings has carried our knowledge back to the beginnings of sedentary occupation in the Neolithic Age, thus bridging the gap between archaeology in the narrow sense and prehistory. Moreover, the main stream of Palestinian culture has been correlated with that of Egypt and Mesopotamia back to the end of the fourth millennium, thus synchronizing the course of history in the two foci of culture in the Near East. Incidentally, the recent expansion of archaeological activity in Syria, with important undertakings at Byblus, Ugarit, Hamath, Mari, Rihaniyeh, Alalakh, etc., has not only brought quantities of written documents and art objects to light; it has also yielded a mass of stratigraphical evidence for the chronology of civilization in early Syria. Since there are so many close parallels and virtual identities between the cultures of Palestine and Syria in any one period, the archaeology of the two lands is intimately interrelated.

The second most important field annexed by anepigraphic archaeology is that of prehistoric Egypt and Mesopotamia.[35] This we may call one field because of the chronological parallelism of its two parts and the close similarity in their basic culture at any early period. The recovery of protodynastic and predynastic Egypt began in 1895 with the work of Amélineau, de Morgan, and Petrie in the oldest cemeteries, among which were found

[35] For the best account of this material from a broad point of view see V. Gordon Childe, *New Light on the Most Ancient East* (London, 1934). Thanks to cultural synchronisms it is now possible to establish far-reaching chronological parallelism between Egypt and Babylonia; cf. the latest syntheses by A. Scharff, *Zeits. Aeg. Sprache*, LXXI (1935), pp. 87-106, and *Historische Zeitschrift*, CLXI (1939), pp. 3-32, and Frankfort, *Am. Jour. Sem. Lang.*, LVIII, pp. 329 ff.

the tombs of the kings of the First Dynasty. In 1901 Petrie formulated his system of "sequence-dating" (see above), carrying back predynastic culture to S. D. 30; since 1924 a whole series of still earlier chalcolithic and neolithic cultures has been discovered, beginning with the Badarian and going back to the earliest sedentary culture now known to have existed in Egypt, the Faiyumian which, to judge from Palestinian parallels, is very early Neolithic. In Mesopotamia and Susiana the recovery of prehistoric sedentary cultures really began at Susa about 1898, soon after de Morgan had started excavating the great mound of the acropolis. Until de Morgan published his results in 1912 the world of scholars had no idea of the beauty of the pottery nor of the vast antiquity of this new culture. In Mesopotamia itself the culture was first discovered by Baron von Oppenheim at Tell Halaf, ancient Gozan in the extreme north, in 1911-13, but the significance of his finds did not become evident until after the First World War. In 1918 and 1919 Thompson and Hall discovered prehistoric painted pottery at two sites in southern Babylonia, and in 1928 the German excavators at Erech (Warka) in Babylonia secured the first stratigraphic evidence for the historical position of the painted-pottery cultures. The past decade has witnessed extraordinary activity in the study of Mesopotamian prehistory and the sequence of early cultures has now been worked out in detail, thanks particularly to the work of Speiser and Mallowan in the north. The last five years have shown that northern Syria and Cilicia passed through closely parallel phases of Neolithic, Chalcolithic, and Early Bronze.[36] Nowhere in the Near East outside of Palestine, however, has the gap between Palaeolithic and Neolithic been bridged.

2. The Historical Interpretation of Archaeological Data

It is advisable to enter into more detail in treating the historical exploitation of unwritten documents than in dis-

[36] See especially Garstang and Burkitt, *Ann. Arch. Anthr.,* XXVI (1939), pp. 38 ff., 51 ff.

cussing the use of written documents by historians, since methods and limitations are much less generally understood in the former case. It is true that interest in ancient architecture and art is nearly as old as that in literature, but it is equally true that the critical study of the latter goes back to Bentley and Porson in the late seventeenth century and was notably advanced by men like Friedrich Wolf and J. G. Eichhorn at the end of the eighteenth, whereas the corresponding stages in treating anepigraphical materials can hardly be said to have begun until the middle and the last quarter of the nineteenth century, respectively. Limitations of space prevent our dealing as fully with this topic as we should like; we shall restrict ourselves to two outstanding examples of the successful historical analysis of anepigraphic archaeological subjects, followed by brief discussions of the bearing of archaeology in the narrow sense on demography, sociology, race, civilization, and religion.

In 1919 the curator of the Egyptian section of the Berlin museums, Heinrich Schäfer, published an epoch-making book entitled *Von ägyptischer Kunst* ("Of Egyptian Art"). In the first two editions of this work he restricted himself to the analysis of line-drawing, but in the third (1930) he also included sculpture. As a result of an incisive examination of the ways in which Egyptian artists reproduced objects and landscapes in drawing and painting, Schäfer was able to go far beyond the point reached by E. Löwy and J. Lange in 1891-92, when they first described the law of frontality and symmetry in early Greek sculpture. Starting with the accepted distinction between conceptual and perceptual treatment of visual images he showed with a wealth of illustration from Egyptian art as well as from the drawings of children and savages, how dominant conceptual art was in Egypt and other lands in pre-Greek times. Analysis of various types of conceptual reproduction of images yielded important historical, aesthetic, and interpretative criteria. Turning to sculpture he showed that it developed directly from line art through the simple device of drawing five aspects of an object on five sides of a block of stone which was to be carved into sculpture. From this principle,

itself the result of Egyptian efforts to perpetuate accepted
canons of form and proportion, was inevitably derived a
strict law of frontality, later borrowed and modified by the
Greeks. Schäfer's principles have since been applied to
other ancient art and have profoundly influenced the whole
approach of historians of art. Though conceptual art tends
to sprout afresh in every period of artistic change, especially
in the past half-century, it was definitively replaced in
Greece by perceptual art and perspective during the age
of Pericles, and gradually penetrated even into China about
the middle of the first millennium A.D. An illustration of
inadmissible deduction is provided by W. Wolf's attempt
(1935) to explain Egyptian principles of line-drawing by
the pre-individualistic form of Egyptian society and its
strong group consciousness.[37] That the two principles were
roughly contemporary cannot be denied but that they
were not concomitant nor interdependent is shown by the
recent recrudescence of conceptual art in one of the most
individualistic periods and in some of the most individualistic circles in history.

Our second illustration lies in the field of architecture.
Here recent archaeologists and historians of architecture,
especially W. Andrae (*Das Gotteshaus*, 1930) and R.
Engelbach (*Ancient Egyptian Masonry*, 1930)[38] have
traced the origin, development, and modifications of the art
of building in the Near East so clearly and adequately as
to revolutionize all historical approach to this field. Their
treatment may not be quite so psychologically satisfying
as Schäfer's analysis of Egyptian art, but it is of considerably more direct value to the historian. Three underlying
principles have been recovered by analysis of the factual
material; they apply to all objects of human manufacture
but are peculiarly evident in architecture. These principles

[37] *Individuum und Gemeinschaft in der ägyptischen Kultur*
(Glückstadt, 1935); see the valuable criticism by R. Anthes,
Zeits. Deutsch. Morg. Ges., XCII (1938), pp. 421-40, and the
review by H. W. Müller, *Or. Lit.-zeit.*, 1935, cols. 674-78.

[38] Cf. now the excellent survey of the field by V. Müller,
Jour. Am. Or. Soc., LX (1940), pp. 151-80.

(which must be given here in our own formulation) may be stated as follows: 1. Skeuomorphism, where change of material is accompanied by minimal change of form; 2. Environmental displacement, where change of geographical or physiographical habitat involves inevitable change of form or material to suit local conditions; 3. Change of function, which carries with it some adaptation to new uses and purposes. The first principle is illustrated by Egyptian columns and capitals, going back to actual bundles of papyrus or lotus stalks, or to palm trunks; another illustration may be taken from the recessed niches which characterize the exterior of Babylonian and early Egyptian adobe buildings and which are also derived from building with reeds. The second is illustrated by the southward expansion of the northern hearth house (megaron, etc.) and the northward movement of the courtyard house (originally an enclosure for cattle with a hut), or by the evolution of the platform temple of early Babylonia into the temple-tower (*ziqqurat*). The third may be illustrated by the growth of typical synagogue architecture out of the private Graeco-Roman villa.[39]

Turning now to the bearing of archaeology on various branches of historical science, we may select first the subject of demography, or the state and movement of population. The best recent illustration of its applicability here is furnished by Nelson Glueck's work in Transjordan since 1933. In six years he has traversed all southern and central Transjordan repeatedly, recording all ancient sites and dating their occupation from surface remains, mainly potsherds. The dating of sherds, already known from previous work in Palestine and Transjordan, has been checked and corrected by several excavations in different parts of the country. Owing to the fact that there is hardly a true mound in the whole of Transjordan south of the Jabbok such surface exploration, if as carefully done as in this case,

[39] The principle of skeuomorphism is well illustrated in the field of the history of religion by the material collected by A. Bertholet, "Über kultische Motivverschiebungen" in *Sitz. Preuss. Akad.*, XVIII (1938), pp. 164-84.

yields entirely satisfactory results in the vast majority of
sites. In true mounds or in sites which have been continuously occupied for a long period, remains of earlier settlement are often completely buried under later strata, but the
discontinuity of sedentary occupation in Transjordan pre-
cluded the formation of true mounds, so that sherds from
earlier occupations, where they exist, are almost always to
be found scattered on the surface or the slopes below a site.
Several hundred pre-Byzantine sites have been studied and
proved to belong almost exclusively to three well-defined
ages, with yawning gaps between them. The first of these
ages covers the latter part of Early Bronze and the beginning of Middle Bronze, between 2400 and 1900 B.C.; the
second covers the Early Iron, from the twelfth (or thirteenth) to the seventh century B.C.; the third is Naba-
taean-Roman and begins about the second century B.C.
Occupation was still sparse in the first period, it increased
several times in density in the second (which corresponds
to the kingdoms of Edom, Moab, and Ammon in the Bible),
and became still denser in the third. Subsequent repopula-
tions have not equalled the density of population in early
Roman times. It would have been impossible to have deduced these facts from available written sources.

Archaeology has a direct and obvious bearing on questions of social and political organization, though great care
must be exercised not to generalize on insufficient basis.
Glueck's explorations prove directly that periods of agricultural occupation of Transjordan alternated with periods
of nomadism. The contrast between the ubiquitous fortifications of Canaanite age and the large proportion of
unwalled towns and villages in Israelite or later times shows
that there was marked improvement in public security,
evidently combined with more stable political organization.
Periods in Babylonia and Egypt where we find unusual activity in temple construction inevitably appear in written
documents as dominated by priestly systems. The coexistence of mansions and hovels in Bronze-Age towns of
Palestine demonstrates striking social inequality, which contemporary written documents show were due to an aristo-

cratic class system, where the normal population was divided into a patrician caste and an amorphous mass of serfs and slaves. The disproportionate space occupied by granaries (grain-pits or silos) inside Palestinian towns of Late Bronze and Iron I, when compared with towns of Middle Bronze and Iron II, indicates both a sparser population and greater insecurity, deductions which are justified by demographic and other evidence. The plan and organization of such a South-Judahite town as Tell Beit Mirsim (probably Kiriath-sepher) in Iron II, with striking homogeneity in plan and size of houses and with unusually numerous looms and dye-plants, suggests some sort of craft or guild organization, a deduction supported by documentary sources.

Archaeology has often, however, been expected to carry more than its weight. Excellent illustrations are found in the frequent attempts made to equate a given culture—even a ceramic culture—with a physically defined race or a linguistic group. Such deductions are based on the logical fallacy of concomitance where concomitant variation is not demonstrated. Race, culture, and language are heterogeneous entities; they tend to be associated, but exceptions are so numerous that no safe rule can be established. Other equally cogent illustrations come from efforts to define some still unknown aspect of civilization by a different aspect which is archaeologically known: e. g., to describe religion on the basis of pottery painting or mathematical attainments on the basis of empirical mastery of the art of building. Even more dangerous are the constantly recurring attempts to establish a correlation between line-painting and social organization, between architecture and literary genres, between peculiarities of material culture and the intellectual, aesthetic, or spiritual life of a people (see Chapter II). In the present work we shall strenuously resist all temptation to reconstruct the world of the spirit from fancied material analogies.

This warning does not mean that anepigraphic archaeology cannot throw important light on religion. The excavation of temples or outdoor places of worship, of idols, amulets, and cult-objects, of bones of sacrificial animals, etc., gives us a picture of the material, physical aspect of any religion which cannot be entirely replaced by written documents, though such finds cannot enable us to reconstruct details of priestly organization, of liturgy, or of mythology. Cultic scenes like those familiar in Egyptian temples and tombs or like the representations on the sarcophagus of Hagia Triada in Crete do replace mythological texts to a certain extent, and even such a plastic tableau as is found on a pottery cult-stand at Beth-shan gives some idea of the nature of Canaanite mythology—an idea confirmed rather strikingly by the mythological poems of Ugarit and other comparable data.

D. ORAL AND WRITTEN TRANSMISSION OF HISTORY

Though this is primarily a subject for the philologian and the folklorist, such brilliant illumination has been shed on many pertinent questions by archaeology that we are amply justified in including the following section in this chapter. As is well known, the pendulum of opinion has swung from one extreme to the other in determining the relative importance of history, mythology, and pure story-telling in a given poetic saga or folkloristic cycle. First, let us consider the characteristics of oral tradition as a medium for the transmission of literary and documentary matter.

1. *The Characteristics of Oral Tradition*

Strictly speaking, there is no hard and fast, or even reasonably clear line which can be drawn between oral and written transmission of records. As has often been emphasized by scholars, writing was used in antiquity largely as an aid or guide to memory, not as a substitute for it. It was so employed in classical antiquity, where pupils were expected to memorize Homer and Virgil, and it has been even more completely true in the East at all times. Even today Moslem boys learn the Qur'an by heart and use the printed text only to correct mistakes. The same is said to be true of

Hindu students of the Vedas to this day and the practice of committing the Chinese classics to memory only began to disappear in the past generation. Down to the World War Jewish students of the Bible and Talmud in Eastern Europe often memorized large parts—in extreme cases even the entire Bible or (*mirabile dictu!*) Talmud. It is a very well-known fact that the Mishnah and Gemara were both composed and transmitted orally, and there is no direct evidence that the Talmud had been reduced to writing before the Middle Ages, though it may be safely assumed that it was. Similarly, the Qur'an was transmitted by memory (in large part) from the time of its oral delivery at Mecca and Medina until some time after Mohammed's death. The case of the Rig-veda is by far the most striking of all, since its oral composition must be dated somewhere in the second millennium, probably before 1200 B.C., and it cannot have been reduced to writing until after the *brahmi* script had been adapted from a Persian Aramaic prototype about the fifth century B.C. The Vedas may not actually have been put into writing until the renaissance of Sanskrit literature which began in the fourth century A.D. It was not only the Rig-veda which was handed down for many centuries by word of mouth; the later Vedas and the Brahmanas were also transmitted orally and it is believed by many scholars that the great bulk of early Sanskrit liturgical and grammatical work was composed by word of mouth.[40]

A clear distinction must be made between different forms of oral composition, since the ease and success of transmission without the aid of writing depends largely upon

[40] For fuller recent discussions of the importance of oral tradition and its place in literary criticism see S. Gandz, "Oral Tradition in the Bible" (*Jewish Studies in Memory of George A. Kohut* [New York, 1935], pp. 248-69); H. S. Nyberg, *Studien zum Hoseabuche* (*Uppsala Universitetets Årsskrift,* 1935: 6), pp. 7 f.; H. S. Nyberg, *Die Religionen des alten Irans* (*Mitt. Vord.-aeg. Ges.,* XLIII [1938]), pp. 9 ff.; Harris Birkeland, *Zum hebräischen Traditionswesen* (*Avhandlinger . . . Norske Videnskaps-Akad.,* 1938 II, *Hist.-Fil. Kl.* [Oslo, 1939]), pp. 2 ff.

the stylistic medium. Here it is generally recognized that the verse form is much better adapted for oral transmission than is any kind of prose. The ease with which children learn poetry is well known; lists and recipes were formerly put into verse for mnemotechnic purposes. Historically this principle is illustrated by the simple fact that very few prose compositions are known to have been handed down by word of mouth, whereas this is certain of poetic works in all parts of the Old World. Aside from verse forms we also have prose legal and liturgical codes for which oral transmission is certain or probable. Here again we note the tendency to put legal corpora into formulaic style; this is illustrated by the Hebrew Book of the Covenant, the Ten Commandments, the Code of Hammurabi, the Sumerian, Hittite, and Assyrian laws, etc. This is equally true of other codes of law, such as the Laws of Manu in India. The Egyptian Negative Confession, the religious and cultic prescriptions of the Shurpu series in Mesopotamia, the cuneiform collections of omens, etc., all show the same tendency to stylistic uniformity. In the case of the Talmud we have something else; here individual opinions and stories are remembered separately and the association of ideas and content provides the connecting link. Moreover, the present uniformity of the Babylonian Talmud should not mislead one into assuming that talmudic literature always possessed it. That it did not is established by comparing parallel recensions of talmudic material such as are found in the Yerushalmi and the Bavli.

In practice the two forms of stylistic transmission cannot be sharply differentiated, since there must nearly always have been a short period of prose transmission before the traditions were put into verse form. In many cases we can show that our present prose form of an orally transmitted document is the result of a secondary adaptation or abstract. This secondary prose stage is found in many Graeco-Roman logographers and historians who narrate Homeric or other saga; it is found in Geoffrey of Monmouth and his successors down to Malory; it occurs in the Old Norse (Icelandic) "prose Edda," which gives a digest and account of older poetic sources (Edda); it is clearly present in the prose version of certain biblical stories which also occur wholly or partly in poetic form (e. g., the Song of Deborah).

Since the *Gestalt* psychologists have called attention to the demonstrable tendency of the mind to grasp selected composite forms and patterns as easily as it can grasp simple ones, as well as to the even more significant mental habit of impressing familiar patterns on groups of sensations and ideations, it is much easier for the folklorist to understand the mechanism of transmission of story motifs. Following the folkloristic atomism of investigators before the First War, a reaction set in and it became recognized that many units of story-telling were complex. Even when story motifs can be found in different contiguous lands, it is not safe to assume original relationship or borrowing except where the motif is complex, forming a pattern. An illustration of such a complex motif is the widespread myth of a goddess of fertility who seduces a young god or hero, who thereupon emasculates himself, leaving his testicles to form the commencement of a fertility cycle (the Adonis-Attis-Bitis cycle).[41] The contemporary British school of comparative religion, best represented by S. H. Hooke, is now applying the principle of patterns with great enthusiasm to the history of ancient Near-Eastern religions.[42] In dealing with mythology and cult-practices we can safely stress the psychological principle of *Gestalt*: the behavior of an element in a pattern is not determined so much by the class to which the element may belong as to the structure or

[41] Cf. the writer's treatment of a group of related cycles in *Jour. Bib. Lit.*, XXXVII (1918), pp. 111-31. This study needs extensive revision today, partly on the basis of further parallel material and partly by way of a more sober and critical treatment of the historical nuclei of the cycles in question.

[42] See Hooke, *Myth and Ritual* (London, 1933), *The Labyrinth* (London, 1935), and *The Origins of Early Semitic Ritual* (London, 1938). While the central idea is sound there is much that requires correction and change of emphasis in detail; cf. the writer's remarks, *Jour. Pal. Or. Soc.*, XIV (1934), pp. 152-56.

field (i. e., pattern) of which it forms part. Since General Smuts has popularized the philosophical doctrine of holism, no thinker can fail to grasp the obviousness and even the necessity of this principle. The demonstration that it really operates in human thinking has often been given experimentally in the past decade and a half by the adherents and friends of the *Gestalt* school.

A very important characteristic of oral transmission of literature and history is its didactic quality. This quality is largely responsible for oral transmission, especially in the field of law and liturgy, where there is little or no aesthetic pleasure in reciting or listening to recitation. Even in singing or chanting poetical compositions and in reciting prose tales, however, the didactic part is by no means absent, since such appeal to the senses and the emotions has always been recognized by teachers and preachers as essential to successful instruction in traditional ethics or social practice. Illustrations are innumerable; we may cite the poems of Hesiod, the didactic poems of Egypt, of Mesopotamia, and of Palestine, the fables of Aesop, the parables of Jesus, the *haggada* of the Rabbis. In judging orally transmitted literature we must also remember that the direct pedagogical complexion of this literature is indirectly increased by the selective character of transmission by word of mouth. Unnecessary and superfluous elements are dropped and only those elements are retained which have some positive appeal to the emotions or the intellect or which have clear pedagogical value.[43]

Historical narratives or data (aside from bodies of customary law or liturgy, etc.) are usually transmitted orally in the form of poetic saga, though prose tales and traditions of historical nature are also common. From what we have said above, it is reasonably clear that, as a rule, poetic sagas are preferable as historical sources to prose traditions concerning the same events, unless the latter are quite recent. However, saga is seldom labelled as such, but must be distinguished from myth and from *Märchen*.

[43] Cf. the writer's observations in *Arch. Pal. Bib.*, pp. 149-51.

There are no formal differences of language or style to indicate the distinction, which must therefore be based entirely on intrinsic evidence. We cannot propose a completely satisfactory solution of the problem, which has vexed scholars for nearly 2500 years, since Hecataeus of Miletus first rationalized mythology. However, the comparative history of religions, comparative folklore, and comparative mythology have made it possible to classify masses of ancient literary material as mythology or as folklore. We can dismiss narratives of definitely cosmogonic or cosmological nature at once, though we cannot deny the ultimate historicity of this or that figure who plays a rôle in them without careful critical study of the figure in question—and not always even then. We can also today dismiss narratives which are obviously associated with any one of a number of standard fertility myths.[44] But when we come to such epics as the Sumero-Accadian Gilgamesh or Lugalbanda and the Canaanite Keret or Dan'el it is not so easy, since they are superficially hard to distinguish from the Accadian epic of the King of Battle (*shar tamkhari*),[45] or from the Iliad and Odyssey, all of which swarm with mythological or marvellous episodes.

Until about forty years ago historians were divided into two schools, one of which denied any historicity or at least any appreciable historical value to mythically colored saga, while the other was inclined to minimize the mythical element and even to claim many demigods and "high" gods as originally human figures. The study of the process of myth-making by Hugo Winckler and others has shown that oral tradition inevitably carries with it the possibility of adding folkloristic elements, as illustrated by the legends —often of mythical origin—which have gathered around every notable monarch or sage. The nature of the mythical

---

[44] Cf. the writer's remarks, *Jour. Pal. Or. Soc.*, I (1921), pp. 51-53.

[45] On the folkloristic character of this epic see the writer's discussion, *Jour. Soc. Or. Res.*, VII (1923), pp. 12-20. The latest treatment of it is that of Güterbock, *Zeits. f. Assyr.*, XLII (1934), pp. 86 ff.

or folkloristic framework in which historical facts may be set by tradition, depends upon the suggestive power of the historical material in question. We need only refer to the treatment of such well known historical characters as Alexander the Great in the Roman-Byzantine age, as Virgil, Charlemagne in mediaeval Europe, as Solomon in early Islam and as Harun er-Rashid in more recent Islam. The ancient Orient provides many striking cases, brought to light by archaeological research in the past few decades. In Mesopotamia outstanding illustrations are the monarch Sargon of Accad (24th century B.C.), Queen Semiramis (9th century B.C.). Egypt yields such figures as Imuthes (Imhotep), originally a high official under king Djoser, first king of the Third Dynasty (not later than the 26th century B.C.); Amenophis the son of Paapis (cir. 1400 B.C.); the composite figure of king Sesostris; and many others. Syria yields the semi-mythical figure of the wise Dan'el, mentioned by Ezekiel and the central figure of a Canaanite epic text; much later we find that Queen Stratonice (third century B.C.) has been decked with a myth belonging to Astarte. Clearly, if we can remove the folkloristic accretions we shall find important nuclei of truth in popular descriptions of these figures and their deeds. Each case must be studied by itself; thanks to the evidence derivable from comparative mythology and folklore, from pertinent philological and linguistic analysis, and now from archaeological sources, we can often determine the boundary between legend and history.

In recent decades there has been a steady increase of the use of aetiology (the analysis of stories explaining ancient names or practices) to identify legendary accretions in orally transmitted material. The discovery and application of the method of form criticism, especially by H. Gunkel, M. Dibelius, and their followers, have given a great impetus to the utilization of the aetiological method, which has now reached a point where its leading exponents are inclined to deny the historicity of nearly all early stories of both the Old and the New Testament. This goes much too far. In the first place, the principle works both ways, like many other phenomena which are closely connected with social or psychological activity. The practice of giving explicit aetiological explanations originated as a mnemonic didactic aid, in accordance with the tendency which we have discussed above. When events of the recent past are mentioned, it is only natural to call attention to the place where they occurred, especially if there should be some striking natural phenomenon near by or if the event has given its name to the place, as very often happens. As a matter of fact the writer has found that Arab narrators of Dura in southern Palestine lay great stress on explaining just where events of recent traditional history have occurred, and they often bring in names or other peculiarities of the places in question.[46] The operation of the principle could hardly be reversed until it had been firmly established in the practice of narrators and teachers, as an obvious as well as a customary aid to memory, a kind of associational aid of the same basic nature as the *quipu* or as pictographs, but of much greater effectiveness. Intellectual curiosity grows by what it assimilates, even among relatively primitive folk; curiosity must be frequently aroused and satisfied before it can arise spontaneously. No one would think of asking why a place had a certain name unless his interest in the meaning of place-names had been somehow stimulated. The idea that a peculiar natural formation or a curious custom had some aetiological explanation would not occur to a man unless he had previously learned that such explanations existed in similar cases. The principle in question is particularly clear in the aetiology of liturgical practice, since the concocting of historical or mythological explanations for a given cultic act or series of acts necessarily follows the stage of symbolic mimesis or the dramatization of myths. Of course, myths themselves often result from the combination of a series of still more primitive cultic acts, usually of sympathetic or homoeopathic character. But such a primitive series of acts cannot be put into dramatic

[46] See the writer's discussion of the function of aetiology in historical tradition, *Bull. Am. Sch. Or. Res.*, No. 74 (1939), pp. 12-17.

form until they have been connected by a story sufficiently exciting to stimulate mimesis. In this connection it should be emphasized that recent discoveries in Egypt and Babylonia have demonstrated the great antiquity of mimetic rites and cultic dramas, previously assumed by many historians of religion but without adequate proof.[47]

We now come to the vexed question of the historicity of oral tradition. In preceding paragraphs it has been shown how dependent oral tradition is on form and on mnemonic aids. We may go a step farther and point out that the reliability of tradition is affected strongly by cultural and social forms. Where great stress is laid upon noble lineage and on the validation of claims of property or of prestige, as in either a patriarchal or a feudal society, genealogy and tribal or chivalric history flourish. The importance attached to traditional genealogy among the Hebrews, the Arabs of early Islamic times, the modern Sudanese, the Malagasy, and the Hawaiians, to give only selected cases, is well established. Many Bedouin or half-Bedouin Arab tribes still preserve their traditional genealogies by word of mouth. The men of Dura, for example, though partly sedentary, are organized in strictly tribal and clan forms and nearly all intelligent men or tribal heads know their ancestral trees back ten or eleven generations to the time of the conquest of the older Arab peasants by the Bedouin Abu Darahimah, and can give the more salient facts about tribal movements from the time when their ancestors left the Hejaz in Arabia. Moreover, it is very important to emphasize that a difference often exists between the reliability of oral tradition in regions or periods where writing was known, even though sparingly used, and where it was not in use at all. *Other things being equal*, the reliability of tradition is much greater in the former case, since the control exercised by

[47] Schroeder's classical treatment of the Hellenic and Indic materials in his *Mysterium und Mimus im Rigveda* (Leipzig, 1908) has been remarkably illustrated and in part confirmed by the work of H. Zimmern (especially in his study of texts relating to the "passion of Bel-Marduk"; cf. *Zeits. Morg. Ges.*, LXXVI, pp. 36-55) and K. Sethe (see his *Dramatische Texte zu altägyptischen Mysterienspielen* [Leipzig, 1928]).

written documents and by scribes or archivists, who must have had some preparation to use them, is by no means negligible, as archaeological research is now demonstrating more and more clearly.

Since this question is very important for our judgment of the early historical traditions of Israel, three parallels may be briefly treated: Homeric Greece, royal and early republican Rome, Arthurian England. We must emphasize the fact that early Israel seems to have a distinct advantage in this respect over the first parallel. In Greece the art of writing seems to have been neglected by the Greeks themselves between the end of the Mycenaean age in the twelfth century B.C. and the adoption of the Phoenician alphabet in the eighth. In other words, the Greeks may have been unable to write in the age which began soon after the events described in the Iliad and they did not cultivate writing again until the age of colonization and the beginning of the Olympiad chronology (776 B.C.).[48] The Iliad can hardly have been reduced to writing until the seventh century at the earliest and may not have been written down until the beginning of the sixth (under Pisistratus). Yet the Iliad, which records events belonging to the end of the Bronze Age and was perhaps put into epic form a century or two after the Fall of Troy, preserves the geography and the cultural life of the Mycenaean age with surprisingly few anachronisms, as shown most effectively by M. Nilsson in his *Homer and Mycenae* (1933). The principal towns of the Iliad, such as Mycenae, Argos, Orchomenus, and Pylus (where Blegen has just discovered

[48] The debate between Ullman and Carpenter must be decided in substantial favor of the latter; cf. the writer's provisional observations, *Pal. Expl. Fund Quar. State.*, 1936, p. 213, where the proposed date "in the ninth century" may be lowered to "about 800 B.C. or a little later." Mr. John V. Walsh is now engaged in preparing a detailed study of the problem. Ullman's arguments are both epigraphically and historically fallacious; Carpenter's essential arguments are correct, but we must substitute "current cursive" for "archaizing lapidary" script as the medium through which the borrowing took place.

a wealthy Mycenaean settlement of the 13th century with an archive of 600 clay tablets), prove to have been the chief Mycenaean centers, though they later lost their importance in many cases. Houses, clothing, arms and modes of warfare, etc., are generally Mycenaean rather than of the Iron Age. Ethnic, political, and international conditions are generally not suited to the Iron Age but reflect earlier conditions, after the fall of the Hittite empire and before the Dorian invasion and the beginning of Greek colonization. In other words, the burden of proof is increasingly on those scholars who deny the basic historicity of the Iliad.

Turning to royal and early republican Rome in the seventh, sixth, and early fifth centuries B.C., we find ourselves coming into a milieu where writing was known. The earliest Etruscan inscriptions go back to about the end of the seventh century, which is probably also the date of the earliest known Latin ones. But the Etruscans were a settled and civilized people from the late eighth century, at least, and Greek colonies were established in Campania about the same time. Excavations in Rome itself have demonstrated beyond cavil that it was a flourishing city with splendid public buildings in the seventh and sixth centuries B.C. Etruscan influence in the art of building is now just as clear to archaeologists as it is to philologists in the Roman language, religion, and political organization. All this warns against taking the nihilistic attitude toward early Roman historical traditions about the Etruscan dynasty and even the early Republic that was so common in the 19th century.[49]

Archaeology has also made great strides in England during the past few years and is increasingly able to throw light on the obscure and involved history of Great Britain in the fifth and sixth centuries A.D. Here writing was known and practiced by the Britons (Latin) and the Irish (Latin

---

[49] For the strong reaction against hypercriticism cf. Tenney Frank, *A History of Rome* (1923) and *Proc. Am. Philos. Soc.*, 1931, pp. 193 ff.; Hugh Last in *Cambridge Ancient History*, Vol. VII, Ch. XII (1928); Altheim, *Epochen der römischen Geschichte* (Frankfurt, 1934).

and oghams) as well as the English (runes), but there was so complete a displacement of population that a large proportion of the places mentioned in the Arthurian cycle and related British (Welsh) poetry fell into English hands long before the sagas were reduced to writing or were employed by extant historians as sources of history. However, thanks to the new control of tradition which archaeology affords in the hands of men like Collingwood, Wheeler, and Crawford, the fundamental historicity of the Arthurian cycle is becoming more and more evident, however much poetic fancy may have refracted and embellished the facts.[50]

When we compare the situation in early Israel or during the formation of the Gospel tradition with our three parallels, we find marked superiority in the former case and an almost entirely different situation in the latter (which we need not describe here). First of all, the Israelite traditions belong to a firmly established people, with strong tribal, family, and cultic ties, which require the existence of validating oral documentation. Secondly, writing was known all through the period and was used to an extent scarcely paralleled in early Rome or in Homeric Greece, to judge only from inscriptions on stone or other inorganic materials. Counting both published and recently discovered but not yet published inscriptions, we now possess over a score of inscriptions in the Phoenician (Canaanite) alphabet from Palestine, Syria, and Cyprus, all dating from between 1200 and 900 B.C.; four of them come from Israelite sites. This alphabet was already known to the Canaanites in the Late Bronze Age, as we know from half a dozen inscriptions, two of some length, belonging to the period between 1400 and 1200 B.C. What appears to be the same alphabet is known in a still earlier stage (between 1700 and 1500 B.C.) from

---

[50] See Collingwood and Myres, *Roman Britain and the English Settlements* (Oxford, 1936), Ch. XIX, especially pp. 320-24. Recent volumes of *Antiquity* bear eloquent testimony to the increasing seriousness with which literary tradition is being regarded in England, in spite of the obviously imaginative character of most of the Arthurian legends.

three or four inscriptions, all found in Palestine. That this alphabet was known to nomads as well as to sedentary Canaanites is certain from the proto-Sinaitic inscriptions, dating from the fifteenth century B.C.)[51] That it continued to be used by the nomads (or was reintroduced among them) is certain from the fact that the forms of alphabetic characters used among North Arabs and South Arabs in the seventh century B.C. go back to prototypes which must have diverged from corresponding Canaanite forms before 1400 B.C.[52] Moreover, quite aside from the proto-Canaanite script from which Phoenician is descended, we now know that the Canaanites of about 1400 B.C. also employed Accadian cuneiform, the Ugaritic cuneiform alphabet, and Egyptian hieroglyphics in order to write. We can hardly, therefore, be surprised to find archaeological discoveries confirming Israelite tradition almost always, *as far as they go*.

2. *The Transmission of Written Documents*

It is hardly necessary to discuss the familiar subjects of textual ("lower") and historico-literary ("higher") criticism, except when new light can be thrown upon them. The principles governing the reconstruction of written documents which have passed through many scribal hands are well known and need not be repeated here. The rules of external and internal evidence upon which documents may be dated or assigned to a given author or milieu are also well known. However, our new knowledge of the ancient Near East can contribute a great deal to the formal evaluation of biblical literature. We shall take up successively the principles of categories of composition (*Gattungsgeschichte*), of the authority of the written word, of scribal revision of orthography and grammar, with a few words about the analysis of sources.

The principle of *Gattungsgeschichte*, of the study of the

[51] See notes 15 and 16, above.
[52] Cf. the writer's remarks, *Bull. Am. Sch. Or. Res.*, No. 66, p. 30.

categories of literary style, was first recognized and applied to Graeco-Roman literature by the great classical scholar, Eduard Norden, in his *Antike Kunstprosa* (1898) and his *Agnostos Theos* (1913), in which he showed the bearing of his methods on the New Testament. In the same year H. Gunkel, who had been thinking and writing along somewhat converging lines, sketched a program for Old Testament literature which recognized Norden's principles as fundamental in all study of ancient literary forms. M. Dibelius has applied Gunkel's methods to New Testament research, going back beyond the present written text to find the pre-literary forms of discourse and of tradition. The student of the ancient Near East finds that the methods of Norden and Gunkel are not only applicable, but are the only ones that can be applied. In classical literature authorship is usually known, but modern tests of style and language must be employed with great care, since a single author might employ very different style and vocabulary in different types of composition, whereas different authors may converge in style and vocabulary when they imitate the same category of writing. In the Old Testament anonymity is more in evidence than in Graeco-Roman literature and the importance of categories of composition is correspondingly greater. In Egyptian and cuneiform literatures the author of a composition is seldom known, even when the narrative is couched in the first person, since anonymous scribes were responsible for the execution almost throughout. In these literatures the importance of categories of form is so great that it is a comparatively simple matter to distribute all known compositions among a limited number of categories, within which there is surprisingly little variation. These facts give sufficient warning against using canons of style and vocabulary too rigidly in trying to determine authorship of passages in the Old Testament. At this point, however, we must caution students against supposing that there was no originality in the ancient Near East. There undoubtedly were many gifted poets and narrators whose works made such an impression on their contemporaries that they were more or less slavishly imitated by others—until a new category of writing was established.

The principle of the authority of the written word is not really new, since it has long been recognized as obtaining in most periods and regions where the art of writing has been sufficiently practiced. However, biblical scholars have been misled by the analogy of Graeco-Roman antiquity into exaggerating the possibility of "pious fraud" in the fabrication of written records and documents beyond all analogy. Nearly every book and passage of the Old Testament has been stigmatized as a literary forgery by at least one scholar. Now it cannot be emphasized too strongly that there is hardly any evidence at all in the ancient Near East for documentary or literary fabrications. A few demonstrated ancient fabrications are known from Egypt: inscriptions which purport to go back to much more ancient times, such as the so-called Bentresh stela and the decree of Djoser on a cliff near Elephantine. Both, however, have been shown to belong to the Ptolemaic period; i. e., they belong to a time when the ethos of the ancient Orient had already disappeared for ever. Of course, there are historical romances where only intrinsic evidence can demonstrate the fact that they are novels and not historical documents. In such cases however, the script and language nearly always prove late date and the principle of categories of form nearly always shows at once what their nature is. Both Egypt and Babylonia are amply supplied with historical romances, mainly of folkloristic, not "literary" character.[53] The prolonged and intimate study of the many scores of thou-

---

[53] The Assyriologist B. Landsberger and his pupils have been inclined to exaggerate the amount of literary fabrication in early Babylonia. The admirable monograph by H. G. Güterbock, *Die historische Tradition . . . (Zeits. f. Assyr.,* XLII [1934], pp. 1-91) goes too far in this direction; for example, it is unlikely that the inscription of Lugal-anne-mundu of Adab is a later fabrication, and most of the supposed anachronisms vanish if we suppose that this king really lived in the late Accad or even the Guti period; cf. Th. Jacobsen, *The Sumerian King List* (Chicago, 1939), pp. 102, 138 ff. On the other hand, it is clear that many texts of the so-called *narû* type are essentially historical romances.

sands of pertinent documents from the ancient Near East proves that sacred and profane documents were copied with greater care than is true of scribal copying in Graeco-Roman times. Even documents which were never intended to be seen by other human eyes, such as mortuary texts, manuscripts of the Book of the Dead, and magical texts, are copied so that we can nearly always read them without difficulty if the state of preservation permits. Moreover, ancient Oriental historians and liturgiologists were accustomed to include the variants which had come down to them, so that their chronological lists show swelling regnal and dynastic totals: e. g., Hammurabi is correctly credited in one list with 43 years as king of Babylon and in another with 12 years (i. e., his last 12) as king of Larsa, so a later scribal scholar attributes 55 years to him. R. Weill and others have pointed out how this principle explains the abnormal swelling of Egyptian dynastic totals in Manetho.[54] Successive editions of the Egyptian mortuary texts known as the Book of the Dead illustrate this process of expansion by addition, especially when a given text can be traced from the Pyramids of the Sixth Dynasty through the Coffin Texts of the Twelfth to successive recensions of the Book of the Dead proper (from the Eighteenth Dynasty to the Hellenistic-Roman age). In such cases later recensions often contain commentaries and glosses to the original incantations and sometimes additional commentaries on commentaries.[55]

A principle which must never be lost sight of in dealing with documents of the ancient Near East is that instead of leaving obvious archaisms in spelling and grammar, as later became the fashion in Greece and Rome, the scribes generally revised ancient literary and other documents periodically. This practice was followed with particular regularity by cuneiform scribes. As a result scribes of the Middle-Babylonian age nearly always revise Old-Babylonian texts,

[54] Cf. *Jour. Asiat.*, 11th series, Vol. VI, pp. 101-17.
[55] The best illustration of this practice will be found in the elaborate critical edition of Ch. 17 of the Book of the Dead by H. Grapow, *Religiöse Urkunden*, I (1915).

substituting current grammatical forms and even contemporary phraseology. Neo-Babylonian recensions of the same texts are still farther modernized. The reverse is also found, and we have attempts to write Old Babylonian in Neo-Babylonian times, but the results are so indescribably confused that the modern cuneiformist can usually fix the true date after a single rapid perusal. That spelling was also modernized by biblical scribes we know now, thanks to Hebrew documents contemporary with different stages of biblical literature, such as the Lachish Letters. Here again scholars have frequently come to grief in trying to take the present Hebrew text as reflecting the orthography of its prototype.

Finally, a few facts may be pointed out which bear on the conventional methods of historico-literary criticism of the Bible. The tendency of ancient Oriental scribes and compilers to add rather than to subtract has a direct bearing on such questions as the method of compilation used by the ancient scholars to whom we owe the Pentateuch. This means that the divergences between narratives in the parallel documents J and E should not be considered as average variation, i. e., as typical of the differences between the documents, but rather as *maximum* variation; the real difference between the narratives of J and E was thus materially smaller than is commonly supposed. Some of the most striking variations may probably be due to divergent traditions which were both incorporated into either J or E, as the case may be. It also means that much of the expansion evident in legal and liturgic passages is not due to literary doublets but to the normal swelling of the text by the accretion of commentaries or of subsequent court decisions, etc.[56] Driver and Miles have shown that many of

[56] In this connection it may be interesting to note that the late H. M. Wiener, who was in his day one of the pillars of the Mosaic theory of pentateuchal origins, once told the writer that, in his opinion, not over one-third of the laws attributed to Moses actually came from him, the other two-thirds consisting of later commentary, glosses, and the results of court decisions.

the divergences between the Code of Hammurabi and the Assyrian laws of about 1100 B.C. may be explained in this way.[57] It further suggests a rational way of explaining some of the high biblical numbers. As critical study of the Bible is more and more influenced by the rich new material from the ancient Near East we shall see a steady rise in respect for the historical significance of now neglected or despised passages and details in the Old and New Testaments.

[57] *The Assyrian Laws* (Oxford, 1935), pp. 12-15 and *passim*. The formulation of the authors is too drastic; cf. San Nicoló, *Or. Lit.-zeit.*, 1936, cols. 514 f.

Chapter II

TOWARD AN ORGANISMIC PHILOSOPHY
OF HISTORY

It is not enough for the historian merely to accumulate a
great mass of facts, no matter how well tested they may
be as to their accuracy and how well selected with reference to their cogency and their representative character.
Unless long occupation with these facts has impressed on
him certain conclusions as to the pattern which they form
and the picture into which they fit, the accumulated mass
will never become history. This is not due, as is sometimes
supposed, to the fact that history arose as a prose form of
saga and thus possessed dramatic form and dramatic appeal
from the outset. It is rather due to the fact that human
life moves in patterns and configurations, whether we consider the life of an individual or the life of a nation, whether
we describe the movement of a culture or the development
of thought. It is the inner compulsion of the underlying
drama of history which has led nearly every great historian
of the past to write history in essentially dramatic terms,
whether we turn to Herodotus, to Thucydides, to Livy, to
Gibbon, or to Macaulay. Under the influence of the un-
consciously felt configuration of historical data Voltaire exclaimed, "Il faut écrire l'histoire en philosophe!" It is true
that he had a very definite propagandist purpose in writing
history, but he might have abandoned it in favor of natural
science if it had not been for the fact that his philosophical
spirit found congenial material in the world of history.

For some 2500 years most historians have been reading

their own world-view or their own partisan standpoint into history, until it has come to be doubted whether it is possible to write it impartially. Leading exponents of this relativistic position in America are C. A. Beard and C. L. Becker. On the other side is the great German "positivistic" school founded by L. von Ranke (1795-1886) and Th. Mommsen (1817-1903), and brought to a climax by the work of E. Meyer (1855-1930).[1] To members of this school, influenced both by the high ideals of accuracy set up by the German school of classical philologians and by the example of natural scientists, the task of the historian was to reconstruct as true as possible a picture of what actually happened in the past—"wie es eigentlich gewesen," to quote Ranke's famous phrase. Later historians of this school, dominated by evolutionary philosophy, often preferred to recast it as "wie es eigentlich geworden," feeling that it was even more important to know how a thing came to be than to know just what happened. It is obvious that, whatever happens to future history, scholars must always be profoundly grateful to the men who were the first to recognize the supreme importance of accuracy and completeness, both in defining facts and in explaining changes. However, it should also be rather obvious that the historian cannot limit himself forever to the accumulation of new facts and explanatory theories. If he should go on indefinitely without trying to interpret and classify his data, history would eventually collapse under its own weight. Natural science has only been able to maintain its effective life and to progress toward new triumphs by periodically ordering its house, simplifying the task of the scientist by

---

[1] The use of the term "positivistic" for this school is an extension of the original sense of the term, as used by Comte of his own philosophy; this extension has become general in current German writing (cf. the writer's observations in his presidential addresses, *Jour. Am. Or. Soc.*, LVI [1936], pp. 122 ff., and *Jour. Bib. Lit.*, LIX [1940], p. 97). Among philosophers generally there is a current tendency to employ the term with reference to the nineteenth-century rational-empiric attitude to reality; cf., e. g., C. H. Kaiser in the *Journal of Philosophy*, June 20, 1940, pp. 337 ff., *passim*.

classifying masses of heterogeneous data under inclusive rubrics—which we know as "natural laws." This also the historian must endeavor to do, though his task is far more difficult, owing to the vastly greater part which caprice and indeterminacy play in the domain of human affairs.

It is no longer possible to construct a philosophy of history without assuming some kind of evolution, whether it be the naturalistic progressivism of eighteenth-century rationalists, the metaphysical unfolding of Spirit which we find in Hegel, or nineteenth-century biological evolution. The combination of the evolutionary principle with positivistic historical research has given rise to a rather amorphous tendency to which the name "historicism" (*Historismus*) has been conventionally applied. Since the term was coined by critics of the historical method as a label for some skeptical and deterministic tendencies among modern historians, it has acquired a certain pejorative connotation. At its worst historicism leads, as pointed out by Troeltsch, to "relativistic skepticism regarding values and to doubts as to whether historical knowledge is attainable or is significant if attained" (*Gesammelte Schriften*, III, p. 108). In biblical research historicism has led to an exaggerated emphasis on the evolutionary principle in which unilinear schemes have become beds of Procrustes. All social, religious, or institutional phenomena must be made to fit into a given bed, regardless of the chronology or function which tradition accords them. If a phenomenon seems too advanced for its traditional phase it is assigned "on internal evidence" to a later stage; if it appears too primitive it is pushed back into an earlier phase, regardless of extrinsic evidence or lack of evidence. Against this exaggerated form of historicism vigorous protests have recently been made by men of such different backgrounds and viewpoints as the Swiss Old Testament scholar, W. Eichrodt,[2] and the American philosopher, Morris R. Cohen.[3]

---

[2] *Theologie des Alten Testaments,* Vol. I, p. 5; cf. the writer, *Jour. Bib. Lit.,* LIX, p. 96.

[3] *Reason and Nature* (New York, 1931), pp. 369-85. This chapter was, however, written in 1913 (p. 369, n. 1) and it

Our brief survey of the philosophy of history cannot be restricted to the field of religion in which we are here most interested, since the history of religion cannot be adequately understood except as a part of the history of culture. Moreover, the principles in which we are primarily interested apply to all branches of history alike, though not always to the same degree. The material from which the historian of religion selects his pertinent facts is the same as that from which every historian must draw; religion is an essential part of human cultural evolution—and much more important even to the positivist than some phases of culture which have been given factitious significance in our own day. At the same time, we shall draw most of our illustrations from the history of religion, and all our applications will bear primarily upon the religious history of the ancient Near East, in particular on biblical religion.

A. GENERAL TENDENCIES IN THE PHILOSOPHY OF HISTORY

In order not to be crushed by the weight of partly irrele-

---

reflects the anti-historical bias of contemporary American thinking, going so far as to say (p. 370), "the more developed a science is the less use it makes of history." He goes on to say: "Thus history has no applications in mathematical investigations, and next to none in physical researches." Of course not! Mathematics is simply a body of abstract and symbolical forms of logic, divorced as far as possible from non-mathematical considerations. By "physical researches" Cohen was undoubtedly thinking mainly of investigations in mathematical physics, where mathematics reigns supreme. On the other hand, the importance of the historical perspective to the scientist is being increasingly recognized and is practically illustrated by the rapid growth of attention to the history of the sciences in this country. Since "scientific method" is only the result of accumulated and systematized experience, it cannot be divorced from the history of that experience without fatal results. The innumerable references to facts derived from the history of science and philosophy in the body of Cohen's work form the best antidote for the statements just quoted. Cf. also his instructive analyses of Jewish philosophies of history in his article in *Jewish Social Studies*, I (1939), pp. 39-72.

vant material we shall limit ourselves to the period introduced by Hegel's *Philosophie der Geschichte* (begun 1825
but not fully published until 1837) and shall select only a
few outstanding phases of subsequent development. Owing
to the significance of the current encyclopaedic-classifica-
tory movement we shall devote special attention to it.

1. *From Hegel to the Sociologists*

The dominating concept of Hegel's philosophical thought
was, as known to all, his "dialectical" concept of three
stages in thought and nature: thesis, antithesis, and synthesis. This triad means that every concept or experience involves the existence of its opposite, which follows and re-
acts against its activity. The inevitable conflict is reconciled
by the synthesis, which comprehends and elevates thesis
and antithesis alike. Owing to Hegel's dominant interest in
fields related to man, such as political science, aesthetics,
and religion, he was able without difficulty to classify practically all phenomena on which he touched in triads, a plan
which gives his philosophy a strangely artificial appearance, at the same time that it imposes itself by its simplicity
and harmony. According to Hegel three main phases of history may be distinguished, both geographically and politi-
cally. The first stage is Asiatic and is illustrated by China,
India, and the Near East. In this stage, the thesis, the individual is absolutely subject to the will of the ruler and
the state is an absolute monarchy. Asia was the scene of
man's infancy, where he was still dominated by nature instead of spirit. The second stage is Mediterranean and is
represented by the classical civilization of Greece and
Rome. Here man grew to maturity, reacting against the
absolutism of Asia and developing some measure of individual freedom. Rome disciplined the culture of Greece and
taught the individual to retain his freedom while subjecting
his will to the needs of the state. In the third and final
stage comes synthesis, in which Germanic culture triumphs
and man becomes conscious of his freedom, but freely wills
the submergence of the individual in the universal idea.

This corresponds to old age, but Hegel emphasized that the old age of spirit is its strongest phase and that only nature becomes senescent. Hegel impressed his contemporaries and successors both with the originality and sweep of his philosophical conceptions and with the wealth of illustration from world-history which he gave to support them. The strongly nationalistic flavor of his philosophy of history prevented it for decades from exercising much influence outside of Germany, but there it had tremendous success. Even the violent reaction which set in against his teachings did not affect their triumphal advance, since his indirect influence on the past century has been incomparably greater than his direct impact.

The best illustration of the influence of Hegel in the field which interests us here primarily is F. C. Baur's work in New Testament history and theology, which began in 1831 and continued until his death in 1860. The Tübingen school which he founded, was very influential for several decades and has exerted a lasting effect on New Testament studies. Since Baur was an ardent Hegelian he carried out a thoroughgoing reconstruction of New Testament history according to Hegelian principles. To him the key to the beginnings of Christianity lay in the conflict between Jewish parochialism and universalism. Jesus and the first disciples, headed by Peter, were resolute champions of a Jewish gospel. The antithesis to this thesis was provided by Paul's universalism, followed in the second century by a synthesis of Judaizing and universalizing tendencies, a synthesis represented by the latest N. T. books and exemplified by the Catholic church of the early Christian centuries. All the books of the New Testament were arranged in historical order according to their relation to this controversy, beginning with the four Pauline epistles which were considered as authentic by Baur (the rest being of later origin), i. e., Galatians, Corinthians I-II, and Romans. Then came the Synoptic Gospels and finally the Gospel of John, which Baur dated about 160 A.D. or even a little later, accompanied by some minor epistles. Owing to the artificial and unilinear character of Baur's reconstruction and to the extreme lateness of his dates, his position is no longer held by any scholar of repute, though it enjoyed a temporary and partial rehabilitation in the work of the Dutch school around the turn of the century. However, the problems which he formulated still remain in the foreground of research and New Testament scholarship has never lost the Hegelian coloring which it received from Baur.

Somewhat less drastic in its application of Hegelian principles to the reconstruction of history and much more solidly established in detail was J. Wellhausen's brilliant formulation of a coherent system of the religious evolution of Israel, first presented in his famous *Prolegomena* (1878). In the introduction to this work Wellhausen freely acknowledged his debt to W. Vatke (1806-82), from whom he had "learned the most and the best." Vatke was an ardent Hegelian, who was one of the first and most untiring exponents of Hegel's system among the theologians of Germany; his most important book on biblical theology (1835) is saturated with Hegelian terminology. Wellhausen and his school, to which belonged in the last decade before the World War practically every Protestant Old Testament scholar of standing in the world, reflect their Hegelian background in various ways: in the division of O. T. religion into three phases, animism (polydemonism, etc.), the prophetic stage (henotheistic), the nomistic stage (monotheistic); in the chronological arrangement of Hebrew literature in the order, early poetry, prophetic writings, legal codes; in the unilateral theory of evolution and in the Hegelian view that the fully developed religion of Israel unfolded gradually from primitive naturalism to lofty ethical monotheism. In stressing the origin of these ideas we do not, of course, mean to refuse them any validity.

But for all the arbitrary and romantic elements in Hegel's philosophy of history, both philosophers and historians must remain forever in his debt. For the first time he brought together the data of history in a rational synthesis, exhibiting the progress of humanity from its Asiatic cradle to modern Western Europe and clearly recognizing the fact of cultural evolution. The connecting thread might be inadequate and the resulting construction badly lop-sided —yet an imperfect classification is better than no classification at all.

Over against the Hegelian and neo-Hegelian schools must be set the positivistic school, which was not nearly so original as that of Hegel and may be said to have emerged almost spontaneously from the spirit of the age, much as has been true of instrumentalism in more recent America. The initiator of the movement was Auguste Comte, a younger contemporary of Hegel, and its best known representatives were perhaps John Stuart Mill and Herbert Spencer. This movement was so closely identified with the scientific activity of the nineteenth century that it spread rapidly and is found, explicitly or implicitly, in nearly all historical and sociological theorizing of the past sixty years. In his great work, *Cours de philosophie positive* (1830–42), Comte presented an encyclopaedic system of thought, which he endeavored (often with signal lack of success) to base on scientific methods. Somewhat like Hegel, though quite independently, he based his system on a theory of three stages of mental activity: theological, metaphysical, and positivistic or scientific. All thinking begins with the first, passes through the second, and reaches its climax in the third stage. In the theological phase itself, again superficially like Hegel, he recognized three evolutionary stages, fetishism, polytheism, monotheism. Comte insisted at every opportunity that religion must be studied like any other natural phenomenon. Mill was even more rigidly rationalistic in his outlook than Comte. Spencer's immense synthesis exerted tremendous influence on his contemporaries, but is practically forgotten now. He seized on the discovery of biological evolution by Darwin and built up a most elaborate system, half speculative, half encyclopaedic, on the basis of the potent new clue to the sequence of phenomena.

A multitude of historians and philosophers now adopted the watchword "scientific method" and undertook to reconstruct historical thinking along essentially positivistic lines.

As long as they subordinated metaphysics (*pace* Comte) to the collection of historical data according to the methods of the great German school of Ranke and his successors, no serious harm was done by a little cheap rationalism, but the urge for systematization often carried them far beyond the limits of objective knowledge, as illustrated by E. Renan in France and many lesser men elsewhere. Through pragmatism the positivist path in philosophy led to John Dewey and American instrumentalism, where the philosophy of history becomes increasingly relativistic and history tends to become a means of liberal propaganda (C. A. Beard and others). Thus the very philosophic movement which was to emancipate history completely from the bonds of tradition and theology and which was to make it "truly scientific," has led to its almost complete dethronement from the place of honor among the social sciences. Positivists and instrumentalists have almost throughout based their system not on scientific method in the proper sense of the term, but rather on unwarranted analogies with the natural sciences. Since the philosophical system of mechanistic materialism *seemed* to suit the increasingly experimental and statistical methodology of the natural sciences, they have uncritically assumed the correspondence as proved and have then taken the resulting corollaries as postulates for their own systems. Curiously enough, the confidence of instrumentalists seems to have been more shaken by the internecine war between the statistical and the causal wings which has resulted from the discovery of the principle of indeterminacy in nuclear physics (W. Heisenberg since 1925) than by such devastating analysis of their position as that of A. O. Lovejoy in his *Revolt against Dualism* (1930).

Meanwhile the movement launched by Hegel was by no means doomed to sterility but continued to influence thinker after thinker, who in turn built up schools from which new branches sprang—until the wine of Hegelianism is sometimes extraordinarily watered. Marx and Engels converted Hegel's dialectical idealism into dialectic materialism and a whole army of lesser fry has tried to apply Marxianism to historical research, with the most fantastic results, since biblical and ancient Oriental facts are forcibly adapted to the Marxist pattern. A good illustration of the monstrosities of this method is found in one of the most serious monographs on the history of Israel which has emanated from the Marxist school: a study by M. Lurje (1927), who is said to have been subsequently "purged." In his effort to "prove" the existence of capitalism in the period of the Judges, for instance, Lurje assumes (without any proof, of course) that Heb. *raham* (maiden) in Jud. 5:30 means "prostitute" (in defiance of philological evidence and of common sense). If there were prostitutes there was proxenetism, which according to Marx is functionally dependent on the capitalistic system—hence there was already (in eleventh-century Israel!) a developed capitalistic system![4]

One result of the Hegelian revival during the past fifty years has been increasing emphasis in certain circles on the historical side of the historico-philosophical union of Hegel. Formally this development has had its extreme statement in the work of Benedetto Croce, for whom history and philosophy are theoretically one and the same: history *is* philosophy and philosophy is history. However, Croce's system remains too abstract and remote from the spirit of the times to exert much influence, except in the field of aesthetics. Oswald Spengler's grandiose work, *Der Untergang des Abendlandes* (partial appearance 1918, complete publication 1922), though fanciful and arbitrary to the highest degree, continues the Hegelian tradition in so direct a way and with so showy a façade that it has had and is still having a great effect on German thought. Spengler hardly mentions Hegel at all, yet his system is so saturated with Hegelian concepts and methods that it often appears as a caricature of Hegelianism. With a curious blend of Hegelian philosophy and Goethean romanticism as his foundation, Spengler constructed his system by combining ency-

[4] *Studien zur Geschichte der wirtschaftlichen und sozialen Verhältnisse* . . . (Giessen), pp. 2 f. For his liquidation in 1936 after the Zinoviev trial cf. G. Kagan, *Revue Historique*, CLXXXVII (1940), p. 29.

clopaedic range (including for the first time the ancient
Orient) with intuitive reasoning, where clever and occasionally almost brilliant *aperçus* replace inductive reasoning
and sober use of analogy. His basic idea is that chronology
and the concept of destiny are for the historian what mathematics and the principle of causality are for the natural
scientist. For Hegel's three stages of history he substitutes the designations "Magical" (i. e., Asiatic, including
Christianity and Eastern European culture), "Apollinian"
(Graeco-Roman), and "Faustian" (Germanic). Moreover,
these stages and the individual cultures which compose
them are living organisms, which are born, mature, decline,
and die. All human phenomena within their scope are integrated in them, so that every aspect of a given culture is
in organic relationship to every other. In Spengler's pessimistic mood inevitable fate is substituted for the advance
of spirit in the Hegelian system, which was founded on an
optimistic outlook on the future of Germanic culture. Some
of the outrageous extravagances of Spengler's treatment of
his "Magical Culture" have been pointed out by the late
C. H. Becker, one of the foremost specialists in Islamic culture of modern times.[5] It is not necessary to point out here
what a tremendous influence Spengler has exercised on the
growth of racist thought, with his intuitive racial and national mysticism and his fatalism, as well as his glorification of "Aryan" racial achievements. Indirectly, he has
helped materially to launch current tendencies in German
historical and biblical scholarship, much of which has recently been devoted to the task of demonstrating the alleged antithesis between all forms of "Jewish" life and
culture and corresponding forms of Germanism.

Historical and biblical studies have been increasingly influenced during the past fifty years by ethnology and sociology, particularly since the work of Robertson Smith and

[5] See *Zeits. Deutsch. Morg. Ges.*, LXXVII (1923), pp. 255-71.
For a more comprehensive criticism of Spengler's whole theory
of historical cycles by an accomplished philosopher-historian-
archaeologist see R. G. Collingwood, *Antiquity*, I (1927),
pp. 311 ff., 435 ff.

Sir James Frazer in England, of E. Durkheim in France, and of Max Weber in Germany. Robertson Smith (after 1885) correlated ethnological and Semitic data with great skill and learning; he introduced Tylor's concept of animism into the history of Semitic religion and tried unsuccessfully to acclimate totemism there; he interested Frazer and others in the task of extending the new method into other spheres of ancient history and religion. With the beginning of Frazer's monumental publication, *The Golden Bough*, in 1890, the anthropological method announced its extension to all antiquity. Following in the footsteps of the folklorist Mannhardt as well as of Robertson Smith, he built up an encyclopaedic collection of ethnographic data for the purpose of demonstrating the origin and development of many phenomena in the history of religion, such as fertility cults, rites of purgation, totemism, the belief in the after-life, etc. Unhappily his attempted explanations are invariably too narrow in their scope and too rigidly causal in their underlying motivation. Small wonder that in the preface to the third edition of his *Adonis, Attis and Osiris* (1914), he pessimistically exclaimed, "The longer I occupy myself with questions of ancient mythology the more diffident I become of success in dealing with them!" Frazer's influence on Anglo-Saxon (and to some extent on French) historians of religion has been very great, though more often as a source of ethnographic ideas and material than as a systematist, since Frazer's remoteness from philosophical speculation as such is characterized by the fact that he knew nothing of Hegel's work until nearly twenty years after his *Golden Bough* had begun to appear.[6]

E. Durkheim must be counted among the leading thinkers of modern times and he is often called "the father of scientific sociology." However this may be, there can be no doubt of the great importance of his work and of its profound influence on modern European—and more recently—American thought. His most significant work for our purposes is probably *Les formes élémentaires de la vie religieuse* (1912). Durkheim combined a strong philosophical

[6] Frazer, *The Magic Art* (1911), I, p. ix.

talent with a thoroughly objective ideal of precision in recording data. He insisted throughout his work on treating
the social group as the only independent element in sociology and history; all other social phenomena, including religion, are essentially functions of society. Social life must
be explained primarily from itself, not by bringing in such
external factors as environment and psychology (though he
did not, of course, deny the importance of these factors in
themselves). Social forms, social consciousness, and social
forces are, in his opinion, the central facts for both historian
and sociologist to consider. In pursuing the train of thought
begotten by his emphasis on the centrality of the social
group as such, he insisted that the collective mind exists
independently of the organic social group to which it belongs. Religion, in Durkheim's thought, is a valuable pre-
servative and cohesive force, which functions as the collective spirit of the group. In other words, the source of
religion is society and the idea of the sacred is only a reflection of hypostatized society itself. The great contribution
of religion has been in the creation and preservation of social
solidarity and it must, therefore, exist forever, in some form
or other.

The best illustration of the influence of the Durkheim
school on our field is perhaps the work of A. Causse, now
conveniently summarized in his book, *Du groupe ethnique
à la communauté religieuse* (1937). Causse's position,
which is carefully thought out and clearly presented, is a
very interesting illustration of the impact of sociological
conceptions on Hegelian Wellhausenism, with the remarkable result that Causse has unwittingly (as the writer learns
from a personal communication) become even more Hegelian in some respects than Wellhausen.[7] Following Durkheim, he makes the development of Israel's religion practically a function of its social evolution. Yahweh became
god of Israel with the covenant that united the tribes; He
became lord of the land and master of the state with the
establishment of the monarchy; He became universal God
with the destruction of the state and the emergence of the

[7] Cf. *Jour. Bib. Lit.*, LIX, p. 94, n. 11.

Diaspora. The evolution of the idea of God in Israel starts with a conception of the deity as the spirit of the tribe, apparently in very much the Durkheim sense, and ends with God as universal spirit (with strongly socialized definition of the term "spirit"), a development which reminds one of Hegel.

Max Weber (1864-1920) was probably the greatest sociologist yet to arise in Germany. Combining the breadth and accuracy of the trained historian with rare gifts of philosophic insight, he has produced several masterpieces of historical sociology, among which his book on *Das antike Judentum* (1920), planned to be the first volume of a great work on the social and economic ethics of the three world religions (Judaism, Christianity, and Islam), ranks deservedly high. Weber's special interest lay in the field of sociology of religion, and his contributions to this field are of lasting value, because of the sanity of his approach and the mass of carefully sifted data which he employed in all his work. According to Weber, economic, social, and religious factors influence one another so strongly that they may be said to be interdependent, yet none is a mere function of the others. A religion is never simply a form of social or economic activity, nor is the reverse any truer. However, in many cases, where sufficient data are available, it is quite possible to show that a given religious factor has profoundly influenced economics, or that a religious element is causally dependent on an economic or social one. It is quite impossible to do justice to Weber in a paragraph; we shall have occasion to mention specific contributions of his below. His work has strongly influenced contemporary German students of the history of Old Testament religion; A. Alt, the foremost recent historian of Israel, and his students show the effect of Weber's thinking in nearly all their work.

To the sociological school belongs essentially J. Pedersen, whose *Israel* (since 1920) is one of the most important contributions yet made to our understanding of Hebrew life and thought. His knowledge of the Semitic world and of the literature dealing with the subject is so vast and his use of ethnological and sociological data so objective that the work will have permanent value, regardless of shifting systems and theories. This does not mean, of course, that we can accept all his historical views.

2. The Encyclopaedic-Analytic Tendency in the Philosophy of History

Since 1934 a new movement has appeared on the horizon and has attracted such general interest, even among laymen, that we may safely predict extraordinary attention to the philosophy of history throughout intellectual circles in the coming generation. This is undoubtedly due in part to the crisis of international civilization through which we are passing, a crisis that urges thinking men to look for solutions, or at least to devise explanations and forecasts. Since 1934 Arnold J. Toynbee (born 1889) of the University of London has brought out the first six volumes of a great work, *A Study of History,* planned to include over a dozen volumes. In 1937 Pitirim A. Sorokin (born in the same year) of Harvard University published three still more massive volumes, followed by a fourth in 1941, entitled *Social and Cultural Dynamics.* Both works are of great importance to philosophers of history, dwarfing predecessors in this field by their volume and by the mass of data which they include. Both are products of the modern occidental method of providing a staff of research assistants and secretaries for a selected few distinguished scholars. It must be said that the outlay in money and time is more than justified in these two cases.

Toynbee began his career as a classical scholar (he is the son-in-law of Gilbert Murray), attaining some distinction in the fields of Greek and modern European history, as well as in international relations, before he undertook the task of reducing historical data to a comprehensive system. It is not easy to appraise an incomplete system which is developed in nearly 3000 pages, especially when the entire work is apparently intended to cover more than 5000 pages! It is even harder to condense an adequate account of his system into a few paragraphs. He has collected an immense body of material, making the collections of illustrative data by Hegel and his successors seem insignificant and futile by comparison. It must also be said that the data are seldom wrong in themselves, except where Toynbee has been misled by the specialists on whom he must rely, or when he has tried to "cut corners" in his simplification of complex processes. The work is admirably arranged, beautifully written, and is remarkably free from sloppiness in dealing with facts and citations.

Toynbee's philosophy of history is essentially organismic, recognizing the importance of treating history as the life of societal organisms. He divides historical mankind into twenty-one "societies," which he schematizes as "wholly unrelated, unrelated to earlier societies, infra-affiliated, affiliated I, affiliated II, and supra-affiliated." Of these societies over half are extinct and seven have been discovered and reconstructed by modern archaeology. For the first time, then, the results of archaeological labor here receive proportionate attention in a treatise on the philosophy of history. Analysis of the individual societies shows that they are in some cases independent of all other cultures, in some cases successive phases in the history of a single culture (Sumeric, Babylonic; Mayan, Yucatec, Mexic), and in some cases a congeries of different racial, national, and cultural groups of very dubious coherence (Syriac, Western, Orthodox Christian, Far Eastern). The task of distinguishing cultural groups of mankind is by no means a new one (Toynbee points to Count de Gobineau as an early predecessor) and it will probably go on for a long time to come. It is not unfair to say that such divisions really exist, but that they cross one another and change chronologically, geographically, and culturally to such an extent that they become rather useless as units of classification. The only sound method of broad classification is to employ the criterion of physical race for one category, that of linguistic grouping (in a very wide sense) for another, that of religion for a third, that of cultural facies for a fourth, and so on. An attempt to take a common material culture as the basis in one case and a common religious culture (Islamic, Christian) or even a racial background (as in dividing Islam into two separate modern societies, the Iranic and the Arabic) in another can only lead to confusion. The biologist has much more precise criteria at his command when he undertakes to divide living beings into families, genera, and species, but he does not employ the larger classifications as a rule except for taxonomic and phylogenetic purposes, limiting himself exclusively to the individual species (and often to an even smaller unit) for all experimental or comparative research. This principle is at least as true in human culture as in zoology and botany; we are helpless in trying to define cultures unless we limit them, so far as practicable, to relatively small units within a complex (which would correspond roughly to Toynbee's "society"). In other words, if we take Egyptian cultural history as such a complex we shall find some difficulty in setting up generalizations (except perhaps in physical race) which would be true of all its phases. We can only approach satisfactory results when we divide it into its successive chronological phases, Old Empire, Middle Empire, New Empire, Bubasto-Saite, etc., and take each of these phases as our unit. The larger division or complex retains its classificatory and historico-genetic significance, but must not be made the basis for detailed research. From the foregoing remarks it will be seen that we consider this side of Toynbee's investigation as relatively futile.

Unfortunately, the weakness of Toynbee's method does not end here. "The next step," he writes, "in a study of history is to put these twenty-one societies through their paces and compare their performances in their geneses and growths, their breakdowns and disintegrations, their universal states and universal churches and heroic ages, their contacts in Time and Space." In his first three volumes (we shall not deal here with Vols. IV-VI) he does not follow out this challenging program, but limits himself to studying various principles which bear on the genesis and growth of civilizations. Here his method is fundamentally sound, since his concrete illustrations are drawn from specific episodes and happenings in history. The number of examples is so great, they are so judiciously selected and so widely distributed among the twenty-one "societies," that the method may be fairly considered as inductive. It is true that he supplements his historical examples by drawing freely from a vast store of mythological and literary lore as well as from the biographies of great men. Since mythology and literature reflect the empirical observation of many generations of primitive men (who were by no means blind to what went on in the world around them) and many centuries of reflection on the part of thinkers and poets, they may be cautiously used to supplement historical examples, though Toynbee sometimes oversteps the bounds of prudence in drawing upon unhistorical sources. Sometimes one can hardly regard all his examples as serious, as when he gives an impressive list of great men, ending with Polybius, Clarendon, Ibn Khaldun, Confucius, Kant, Dante and—Hamlet.

The fundamental principles which he derives by his inductive methods are the following: "Challenge-and-Response" as a partial explanation of the genesis of civilizations; "Withdrawal-and-Return" as a partial explanation of the nature of their growth. Both principles are elaborately illustrated by examples. The former is divided into a series of special categories: *chalepà tà kalá* ("good things are hard"), the stimulus of hard countries, the stimulus of new ground, the stimulus of blows, the stimulus of pressures, and the stimulus of penalizations. He emphasizes, however, that while civilizations are born and progress by the aid of external stimuli, there is, none the less, a "golden mean." He further points out that a challenge or stimulus may be inadequate or it may be excessive. Aside from such points as the author's acceptance of Ellsworth Huntington's erroneous hypothesis of climatic change (see below), which seriously vitiate certain parts of his treatment, we can only praise its conception and execution. To be sure, there is nothing at all new about the idea of the value of the "hard way" in human life, but it has been so consistently disregarded or denied by modern writers and thinkers that it is a matter of the greatest importance to have it presented as clearly and convincingly as has been done by Toynbee. Similarly, the principle of the "conditioned reflex" is almost a matter of common sense and every-day experience, yet its demonstration by Pavlov must be considered as one of the greatest psychological discoveries of modern times.

Toynbee's principle of "Withdrawal-and-Return" is not quite as significant as the one just discussed, but it is also important. This principle he illustrates mainly from biographical sources, extending his treatment by analogy and confirmatory examples to the field of history. Great men, especially men of prophetic type, often exhibit periods of action separated from one another by phases of complete inactivity or withdrawal into seclusion, after which they emerge with fresh and "daemonic" energy. Sometimes nations, or cultures, instead of growing, reaching a climax, and declining for ever, show periods of curious inactivity, often accompanied by withdrawal from participation in the international scene, after which they emerge, apparently strong as ever, for a fresh career of activity. The sensational resurgence of German power since 1938 is a striking illustration. This idea is again not really new, but it has likewise been disregarded by recent writers, who prefer to stress the merits of active, as against contemplative life and to exalt the nervous energy of Europe at the expense of the quiescence of some other parts of the world. Toynbee thus appears in both approaches to the problem of history as an old-fashioned spirit, acquiring the reputation of a great innovator and even of a prophet because he presents old but neglected principles with elaborate logical proof of their salient reality. All honor to him for reinstating forgotten truths!

A violent onslaught on Arnold Toynbee's work was launched in 1936 by Lucien Febvre, the well-known collaborator of Henri Berr, under the informative title, "De Spengler à Toynbee: quelques philosophies opportunistes de l'histoire."[8] The collocation of Spengler and Toynbee has no apparent purpose except to show contempt for the lat-

[8] *Revue de Métaphysique et de Morale*, XLIII:4.

ter, to whom almost the entire essay is devoted. Perusal of Febvre's onslaught reveals no clear basis for his depreciation of Toynbee, except that of pique: Toynbee does not mention nor apparently recognize the existence of the Berr-Febvre school of historical synthesis. Emerging about 1901 with the creation of the *Revue de Synthèse historique*, followed by works on historical synthesis and by other periodicals and series of books devoted to the same subject, this school has had a great deal of influence on French and American historiography, as may be seen, for example, in the somewhat abortive effort of the so-called "new history" of Robinson and Beard.[9] The most concise statement of its methods and objectives has been given by Berr and Febvre in their joint article on "History" in the *Encyclopaedia of the Social Sciences* (1932). We have gone through the volumes of the *Revue* and other products of this school, and have tried to be fair to them, but it must be confessed that they are most disappointing. The epistemological foundation is weak (see below) and the plan to bring about a synthesis of the past life of man in all its multiform activities is superbly conceived but badly executed. Instead of a synthesis Berr and his colleagues have produced part of an historical encyclopaedia, characterized by many of the faults of a standard publisher's undertaking and by few of its virtues, since too many of the contributors are quite incompetent.[10]

Turning from Toynbee to Sorokin, we pass from a highly cultivated British humanist to a Russian sociologist with a varied record of administrative and scholarly achievement in his field. His thick book on *Contemporary Sociological Theories* (1929) shows his talents in a most favorable light. They include extraordinary control of sociological and philosophical literature in practically every European language, thorough independence and trained critical judgment, ex-

[9] On this school see the trenchant, though rather episodic criticisms of F. J. Teggart, *Theory of History* (New Haven, 1925), pp. 199 ff.

[10] For other weaknesses of the Berr school see Teggart, *op. cit.*, pp. 208-16.

ceptional ability in analyzing and characterizing systems of thought. On the debit side may be noted an omnivorous attitude to bibliography and a sloppy treatment of facts and citations, both of which stand in striking contrast to the fastidious standards of Toynbee. The first three volumes of *Social and Cultural Dynamics* also exhibit the foregoing merits, as well as a capacity for organizing and administering an elaborate project of research, involving a tremendous amount of statistical work of the most varied character. On the other hand, these volumes show a pronounced lack of ability to synthesize—a lack which can hardly be made up for entirely by the publication of the fourth volume, since it already appears too clearly in the introductory chapters of Vol. I, in which Sorokin develops his methodology and explains his purpose. Here again we are embarrassed by the difficulty of giving in a few paragraphs an adequate statement of material which covers more than 2000 closely printed pages! We shall compensate in part for the impossibility of doing Sorokin full justice by contrasting his approach and method with those of the British thinker.

In contrast to Toynbee's universal sweep, Sorokin restricts himself almost entirely to Europe in the past 2500 years, thus including only two and a half of the former's twenty-one "societies," and only half of his chronological scope. This plan has both merits and disadvantages. On the one hand it escapes the necessity of dealing with less familiar or less known regions and ages; on the other it leads the author to generalize from inadequate evidence and sometimes to show a striking myopia in his historical perspective. Moreover, as a philosopher rather than a historian, Sorokin is more interested in abstract types than in concrete phenomena, as is illustrated by his distinction between two pure types of integrated culture, ideational and sensate, in addition to which he lists two modified forms, idealistic and mixed. By "idealistic" he means "a balanced synthesis of both pure types." From the standpoint of anthropology, this classification can have little meaning, but as an interpretation of Western civilization from its emergence in the sixth century B.C. to the present time, in terms of its highest cultural manifestations, it has clear validity, though it is perhaps only one of several equally cogent clues.

Sorokin's epistemological approach is somewhat novel, and stands in striking opposition to that of the whole positivistic school of sociologists. He distinguishes between four main types of cultural "elements" (i. e., complexes or patterns): (1) spatial or mechanical adjacency (congeries), (2) association due to an external factor, (3) causal or functional integration, (4) internal or logico-meaningful unity. Only the two last are pertinent to sociological thought. He rejects the third type, which is employed by nearly all sociologists of recent times, and prefers the fourth. This substitution of subjective for "trans-subjective" (objective) methodology is very remarkable and threatens to relegate Sorokin's whole epistemological system to the sphere of intuitive metaphysics, taking it out of the world of causal-functional and statistical phenomena, which is the only one that we can control by scientific methods. Since this epistemological foundation does not seem to fit his statistical-analytical methods of research, we shall have to await the appearance of the fourth volume before making a detailed criticism. Meanwhile, some observations are in order. In "the logico-meaningful method of ordering chaos" Sorokin does not see any uniformity of relationship between the variable elements of a complex, but rather "identity of meaning or logical coalescence." "Hidden behind the empirically different, seemingly unrelated fragments" there is "an identity of meaning." He does not deny that there are causally or functionally related parts of cultural patterns, but insists that they are rare, or at least can seldom be proved by known methods to exist. Instead of wasting effort on making laborious and often questionable additions to the stock of such relations, he prefers to look for a "central principle which permeates all the components . . . and in this way makes cosmos out of a chaos of unintegrated fragments." To determine just what that "central principle" is in a given case, only experience and intuition can serve. In other words, "the proof of the pudding is the eating thereof," a principle which is very useful as long as the investigator remembers that the result must stand every logical and factual test but which becomes exceedingly precarious and even futile when he enters a domain where such tests become impracticable or even impossible.

One cannot deny that Sorokin has displayed his analytical talents to very good purpose in demonstrating the inadequacy of the causal-functional method as applied even by anthropologists of the high standing of Clark Wissler and the late Edward Sapir.[11] On the other hand, his approach is far more dangerous than theirs, since it is largely beyond the reach of scientific methods and thus lends itself to charlatanry. He has performed a real service in emphasizing certain epistemological aspects of sociological investigation, but the application of "logico-meaningful" terminology and methods belongs, as he frankly admits, to his own "ideational" horizon and is foreign to the "sensate" sphere in which productive scholarship has hitherto moved. It is misleading to use the word "logical" in this connection, since logic is scientifically useless unless it starts with axiomatic or demonstrated premises and postulates. Sorokin, however, begins with intuitively enunciated principles, on which he constructs a logical structure which is then made a frame of reference for elaborate statistical tables, from which he naturally makes deductions which agree with his principles—thus providing a beautiful example of a "logico-meaningful" *argumentum in circulo*. If a worker in the "sensate" sphere may be permitted to propose a sensate modification of his fourth type of cultural pattern, "empirico-adaptive" (a good sensate expression, according to Sorokin)[12] may be substituted for "logico-meaningful." The type is empirical, since it contains, in the main, elements which do not necessarily have any causal-functional relationship to one another, and it is adaptive, since the heterogeneous elements that go into the formation of a cultural pattern must often be modified in the process in order to coexist. In other words, they become, to quote Max Weber, interdependent but they are not functions of one another.

[11] Sorokin, I, pp. 31 ff.
[12] Sorokin, I, p. 69, n. 1.

Sorokin, with many other sociological theorists, does not reckon adequately with the fact that every cultural complex is itself a microcosm, in which opposing factors are constantly meeting and clashing, so that sometimes one, sometimes its opposite, prevails. Despite warnings which he himself utters, from time to time, against over-emphasizing the integration of cultures, he frequently falls into the trap and stresses it himself. However, it cannot be too strongly insisted that integration of a culture is not necessarily a good thing. Perfect integration of a personality leads to stagnation of that personality. Practically all great men, and certainly all geniuses have been very poorly integrated. It is precisely the friction and conflict between imperfectly balanced or harmonized elements in a man's mental make-up which may lead to innovations and discoveries. Real greatness often emerges from profound spiritual or intellectual travail. A placid, bovine mind may be exceedingly well integrated at a low level; a gifted demagogue may enjoy perfect nervous and mental health, with few conscientious scruples or intellectual struggles to prevent him from employing his talents to personal advantage and to public disaster—in other words, he is well integrated at a higher level. The same is true, *mutatis mutandis,* of groups and nations. A group may be so completely integrated that it exhibits little internal friction, a high degree of efficiency in accomplishing its purposes, together with self-sufficiency and smugness—but it will accomplish little of value for the world. The early Christians were certainly not well integrated as a group, since it required centuries for them to come to a temporary agreement on normative theological doctrines and social policies—yet few will dispute their potential capacities for good. Modern Jewish intellectual circles are generally as fine examples as can be found in history of lack of integration, yet they are producing an astonishingly high proportion of the significant intellectual achievements of our age. It is even possible that the greatest advances in any group are made when that group is in the highest state of excitation that can be attained without disaster to the group. All this obviously means that there is most likely to be progress within a group when that group contains an optimum number of polar elements, i. e., of elements standing in real or potential opposition to one another.

Nine-tenths of the bulk of Sorokin's work, as far as it has appeared, is devoted to the statistical and analytical survey of the fields of art (painting, sculpture, architecture, music, literature), the history of thought, science and technology, ethics and juridical theory, systems of social relationship, government and political theory, economic conditions, incidence of war and revolution, types of personality and behavior. He selects such concrete illustrations of his principles as the statistical relation in different periods between ideational (conceptual) and visual (perceptual) painting and the chronological incidence of nudity in art (to illustrate the sensate type). From elaborate statistical tables of such material he obtains data for constructing curves showing both the fluctuation of types in the past 2500 years and the tendency of various elements to vary concomitantly. In general Sorokin shows good judgment in selecting subjects for statistical treatment and his analysis of sources of error is often excellent. On the other hand, collection of the material has obviously been affected by many sources of error, some of them due to inexperience of the collector (often a student) and some due to onesidedness of the available material. However, it is probable that errors will cancel out so often that the results are not seriously vitiated. There can be no doubt that the results of this gigantic undertaking are very worth-while, whatever weaknesses there may be in detail—and these are many! Sorokin has statistically proved that Western civilization shows a fundamental tendency toward oscillation, an oscillation which is illustrated in hundreds of different ways. As he observes, however, this principle is not new, but was clearly enunciated by Vico over two centuries ago. Moreover, every thinking man is well aware of the constant oscillation between such phenomena as war and peace, prosperity and depression, conservatism and desire to change, mechanism and vitalism, rationalism and anti-rationalism. To be sure, the resulting picture is made very one-sided by Sorokin's careful selection of only those phenomena that show clear oscillation, leaving out the opposite ones—of which there are many. It is made much more misleading by failure to point out that the oscillations in question are in large part due to the fact that Western civilization has become a more and more composite thing, containing within itself so many opposing racial, national, religious, economic, and intellectual tendencies and movements that the resultant is much more likely *a priori* to show a pulsating curve than any other kind, unless one selects (as Sorokin has not done) factors which do shift in one general direction. In short, Sorokin, like Toynbee, has demonstrated the obvious, an achievement which is much more useful than it may sound when put so bluntly, since many historians and philosophers devote much of their energy to denying or minimizing the obvious.

B. Current Aspects of Historical Determinism

Innumerable efforts have been made to find a single key with which to unlock the mysteries of history. Some theorists have drawn on physics and mechanics, some on biology, some on geography, some on climatic change, others on racial, or physiological, or pathological, or economic, or societal, or psychological, or other decisive factors to explain the formation and differentiation of cultures. We have neither space nor need to dwell even briefly on all these hypotheses. Moreover, Sorokin has given an admirable detailed criticism of the various classes of historico-sociological determinism in his *Contemporary Sociological Theories* (1929), where he devotes over 750 pages to them, mentioning almost every scholar of the slightest importance who had maintained either a deterministic or an anti-deterministic position prior to that year. Thanks to him we can restrict ourselves here to a few observations on points which he has not treated at all or has not sufficiently elucidated for our purposes. Since we shall discuss the validity of mechanical and biological approaches to the philosophy of history briefly in section D, we need not deal with them here. We shall also dispense with any discussion of certain new but fantastic forms of biological determinism, such as the extraordinary development of racist theories since 1933, the attribution of fabulous powers to the endocrine glands as a result of underlying chemical or other factors, and the like. These speculations are either rejected by all competent and independent scientists or are too extravagant to be taken seriously. The interpretation of material cultures by their political or religious aspects is now so infrequent that we can disregard it, in spite of Max Weber's partly correct explanation of modern European capitalism as an outgrowth of Calvinistic culture. We shall select three types of determinism for brief discussion: geographical, climatic, and economic.

It is, of course, quite idle to deny the tremendous importance of geographical environment for human history. But the effect of such environment on peoples with different organization or cultural preparation is often entirely different. White Europeans have succeeded where American Indians failed over a test period of many thousand years. European Jews are now succeeding in the establishment of a flourishing agricultural population in the low-lying plains and river valleys of Palestine, where the Arabs, with inadequate organization and medical science, had failed completely over a period of more than a millennium. Arnold Toynbee's remarkable studies, to which we have referred above, have demonstrated with the utmost clarity that historical and cultural achievements are sometimes greatest where environmental conditions seem to be most unfavorable. The geographical factor, important as it is, can seldom be used alone as an explanation of cultural phenomena, but must usually be taken together with other factors—and it is a mathematical commonplace that results become more and more uncertain as the number of variables increases.

The climatic factor in history has received disproportionate attention during the past quarter-century, owing to the indefatigable efforts of Ellsworth Huntington. Since 1900 he has been busily engaged in geographical exploration in Asia Minor, Central Asia, Iran, Palestine, Central America, and elsewhere, supplementing it by statistical studies and investigations on climate and health, industry, achievement, etc. On the basis of this material he has developed an elaborate theory of cyclic changes in rainfall and temperature, ultimately supposed to be caused by variations in solar radiation and magnetic action. Owing to his great activity and industry, and to the enormous mass of data which he has accumulated in support of his theories, Huntington has exerted increasing influence on geographers, sociologists, and historians; and in many circles his views are regarded as authoritative. With the assistance of archaeology and dendro-chronology (tree-ring computations), he has built up an elaborate theory of climatic periodicity, with long and short variations in the amplitude of cycles. The short cycles are familiar to all students of weather reports and tree-ring graphs; the long ones are deduced mainly from historical and archaeological data. According to Huntington, regions which were once densely peopled and are now abandoned illustrate the cyclic theory: they were inhabited because they had heavier rainfall and they have been abandoned because the rainfall has been reduced for centuries. Great migrations of peoples are to be explained by progressive desiccation of semidesert regions; each successive period of drying up led to a nomadic eruption. Semitic scholars like L. Caetani have made a great deal of the supposed *inaridamento* of Arabia as an explanation for periodic migrations from the desert. According to Huntington and Caetani the Moslem conquest of southwestern Asia was primarily nothing but a result of progressive desiccation, which reached a point where Arabia had to disgorge its nomads into the surrounding fertile regions. In his *Palestine and its Transformation* (1912) Huntington made a great deal of the climatic cycle as a key to the history of Israel.

Unhappily for Huntington's elaborate conclusions, he has based his system throughout on false premises and on induction from wrongly observed facts. So far as the present writer knows, not a single competent scholar who is both archaeologist and historian has adopted his views. It is impossible to accept any of his many lines of evidence, mostly based on personal observations, which converge to demonstrate his thesis with respect to Palestine. He points to the Roman-Byzantine cities of the Negeb in southern Palestine, where there is not a single village today, as proof that there was then heavier rainfall than there is today. The excavations of the Colt Expedition since 1933 have shown that the cities of the Negeb flourished at different times during a period of nearly a millennium, so that there were apparently never more than one or two large towns at a time. Moreover, all these towns were built on important caravan routes, in an age when trade by land from Arabia to Palestine and Egypt was at its very height. Almost every house had one or two cisterns and there were reservoirs on every side, with dry dams at the head of every suitable valley near a town. Some of these considerations—and others—convinced Woolley and Lawrence in 1914[13] that Huntington's theory was wrong, but even they took for granted that the total population at one time must have been much larger than we now know to have been the case. At the oasis of Engedi, Huntington found many abandoned water channels which convinced him that there must have been much more water available in the Roman period. Competent investigation of the southern basin of the Dead Sea has since shown that the many abandoned water channels in all oases in this region are simply due to the fact that after several years of irrigation an irrigated section must be abandoned because of the formation of a crust of alkali over the surface of the soil. If the soil is left to itself for a generation or more the occasional winter rains will wash the alkali away and make further irrigation possible. Hence the rotation of irrigated terrains and with it the constant shifting of water channels. The same kind of superficial and erroneous observation is characteristic of all Huntington's work. At Jerash, for example, he regarded the stadium as an arena which could be flooded with water

[13] *The Wilderness of Zin* (new edition, 1936), pp. 51 ff.

for mimic naval combats (naumachy) and believed that the ancient inhabitants were entirely dependent on the water of the stream which flows through it. Actually the excavations there since 1928 have shown that the site is honeycombed by cisterns, constructed in order to supplement the supply of the Chrysorhoas.[14] In the Palmyrene he completely overlooked the existence of an elaborate system of subterranean aqueducts, called *fuqur* by the Arabs, which are found all over southwestern Asia in regions physically suited for them.

It has been amply demonstrated in recent years that Huntington's observations are equally misleading wherever they have been made: in Central Asia (where the rivers have changed their courses and where there are ruins of very elaborate irrigation works), in Central America (where he completely misunderstood the physiographic and archaeological situation), and elsewhere. Nor can a single really competent geographer be found who accepts his conclusions. In passing, however, it must be emphasized that his elaborate hypotheses have set scientists and historians to thinking, and have thus been of considerable heuristic value to science as a whole, in spite of their ephemeral character.

We should not take up economic determinism here at all, since it has been adequately dealt with by Sorokin. Above (p. 90) we have had occasion to mention the vagaries of the Marxist interpretation of ancient history. However, economic determinism has enjoyed such an unexampled vogue in recent American literature that a vigorous protest against it is necessary.[15] The importance of the economic factor is very great—just as great as that of the closely related geographical one—but it must not be overemphasized. The history of religious life in the Near East

---

[14] Cf. C. H. Kraeling and others, *Gerasa City of the Decapolis* (New Haven, 1938), p. 98.

[15] Peter Drucker's widely read book *The End of Economic Man* (London, 1939) has now made this protest most effectively, though a trifle too drastically. One may "throw out the baby with the bath."

is full of individuals and movements which challenge the principle. When the Israelites fled from Egypt into the desert they were not seeking food and comfort but freedom and opportunity to serve their God. Prophets like Elijah and Jeremiah were not looking for a chance to better their economic status. The Rechabites would doubtless have been much more prosperous, not to say comfortable, if they had abandoned their semi-nomadic way of life and had settled down and used their frugality and their high code of morals for economic self-improvement. Modern history is full of parallel examples.

As a counterpoise to these serious, though exaggerated, theories we may be pardoned for saying a word about a futile but widely read example of psychological determinism—Freud's *Moses and Monotheism* (1939). This book is simply the latest of a long train of books and papers on history and religion which have been issued by Freud himself and by other members of the psycho-analytical school during the past generation. Like them his new book is totally devoid of serious historical method and deals with historical data even more cavalierly than with the data of introspective and experimental psychology.[16]

C. The Epistemology of History

The problem of the source and validity of historical knowledge has been raised increasingly by philosophers and historians in the past generation. To what extent is historical knowledge basically distinct from scientific knowledge?[17] To what extent does history reflect opinion and propaganda rather than objective fact? There are two opposing schools of thought with regard to the answer

[16] For details cf. the able article by J. P. Hyatt, *Jour. Bib. Rel.*, VIII (1940), pp. 85 ff., with his references to the literature.

[17] For useful, though not very recent treatments of this subject see Teggart, *op. cit.*, pp. 44 ff., 153 ff., and Morris R. Cohen, *op. cit.*, pp. 13-15. A very interesting and instructive symposium on this subject appeared in *Mind*, XXI (1922), pp. 443-66.

brought to each question. Thanks to two important books which have recently appeared, Maurice Mandelbaum's *The Problem of Historical Knowledge* (1938) and Raymond Aron's study of German historical theory entitled *La philosophie critique de l'histoire* (also 1938), we are in a much more favorable position to discuss these elusive and complex questions than we were previously, since the extensive German literature on the subject is very difficult to cover without losing one's way.

The current opinion, held by most philosophers and historians, both relativists and positivists, is that there *is* a fundamental difference between historical and scientific knowledge. Henri Berr and Lucien Febvre say: "While physical phenomena would be known even without the intervention of someone to describe and classify them, the historical past exists only to the extent that there is an image of it—in other words, to the extent that it is recreated by the mind."[18] Mandelbaum is more logical: "The historian deals with specific events which once occurred in a certain place, and he seeks to delineate the nature of those events. The natural scientist, on the other hand, formulates judgments regarding 'typical' occurrences establishing the relation which those occurrences bear to certain of the conditions under which they appear."

The statement of Berr and Febvre is very strange and can hardly be defended by any epistemologist in the form in which it is put, which describes natural science from the standpoint of realism and history from that of nominalism. Physical phenomena doubtless *exist* without the intervention of some person to observe them, but they are certainly not *known* to man unless man is present when they transpire and is able to recognize them as they transpire. Moreover, past physical phenomena cannot be directly known either, but require the intervention of some indirect instrumentality of cognition. Exactly the same is true in principle of history: current historical phenomena are known to those who are in a position to recognize or to comprehend them;

[18] *Encyclopaedia of the Social Sciences*, VII (1932), p. 357 a.

the historical past can be known only through the intervention of an indirect instrumentality of cognition. Of course, it would be idle to deny that there is a real difference in practice, for the historian is generally interested in past historical events of specific character, while the scientist is usually searching for contemporary evidence on which to formulate natural laws of general application. But this intrinsic practical difference has led thinkers to postulate a drastic theoretical difference which simply does not exist, as we shall see.

Mandelbaum's definition of the difference between historical and scientific thinking is superior to the one just discussed, but it is also inadequate. Since the primary function of the historian is to collect as many facts as possible about the past—and present—of man (for the past cannot be understood without knowledge of the present), archaeological facts are entirely within the proper domain of the historian, even though he may have to leave their collection and part of their interpretation to the specialist. These facts, which cover the entire past of humanity, so far as it has been preserved and can be reconstructed, are tangible and contemporary, since they may be handled and can be verified by visits to museums and by examination of excavation reports and archaeological handbooks. The physical and material past of man can thus be recovered by substantially the same methods as are used in geology, palaeontology, palaeobotany, and related fields. From the epistemological point of view archaeological data are just as contemporary as are the facts gathered laboriously by astronomers through telescopes and spectroscopes, since the latter are also tangible records of events which transpired in the past—sometimes many millions of light-years ago. The historian of human culture is, moreover, just as much interested in discovering general laws as is the natural scientist, since every single phase of past—and present—culture has its own pattern of constituent elements. In a given group of sites or deposits from the same age and region, the archaeologist always recovers pottery and other human artifacts of the same types. There is some variation, of course, but the limits of variation are always subject to approximate definition—which is all that can be expected of most corresponding phenomena in the natural sciences. If we rise in the scale to mental phenomena, we find a given language or dialect in all documents belonging to a given region and period. This applies equally, as we have seen, to documents recovered by the archaeologist and to documents preserved in libraries. Furthermore, if we study these documents we find that each period and region or group has similar habits of thought, forms of organization, and types of economic and religious life, etc. The scientific historian is much more interested in establishing and defining these general laws than he is in fixing and relating individual facts, important as the latter are. If it is objected that the scientist endeavors to discover laws of more general applicability than the ones we have mentioned, one can only point out that the primary purpose of the botanist and zoologist, for example, is to establish the laws governing the life of individual species, of which there are millions. Similarly the chemist devotes much of his energy to discovering the principles governing the activity of each compound—of which there are untold millions. Astronomers must study individual phenomena in Mars or the Moon before they are justified in devoting themselves to astrophysical studies. There is, accordingly, no basic epistemological difference between *comparable* fields of history and of science.

The principal reason for the failure of philosophers to recognize this fact more fully is that they have limited the definition of history too sharply. The historian of man is as justified, however, in beginning his research with the fundamental facts of man's social life as the physicist is warranted in beginning with basic physical data, or as the biologist is in commencing with elementary phenomena of living organisms. Just as these data lead to a principle of universal validity, such as gravitation or unicellular life, so the historian arrives at the basic principle of human societal life, which is quite as immutable. As we ascend the hierarchic scale from plane to plane of variability, our laws become progressively less general and less binding or more uncertain—in both history and science—until we reach a plane where the number of variables makes prediction impossible, as far as the finite mind can tell. In the social sciences we reach this plane much more rapidly than in the physical sciences, but the basic modes of reasoning are the same. Mandelbaum has cogently distinguished between two types of historical judgments which he calls "judgments of fact" and "judgments of value." We would add a third type, "judgments of typical occurrence," where the data are, as a rule, quite as objectively ascertainable as they are in many fields of natural science. Illustrations of such typical occurrences in history have already been given above. If the objection be raised that some fields of natural science have a higher logical standard, since many of their laws can be stated in mathematical terms, we reply that there is only a relative, not an absolute difference, since statistics and chronology play a dominant rôle in many branches of physics and chemistry, just as they do in biology—and in history. It is again primarily a difference in the degree of variability and not in logical method.

Before we leave this subject, it may be well to stress the difference in historical certainty between the actions of groups and of individuals. Archaeology and the history of civilization have proved that the material, social, and mental characteristics of a given culture are relatively stable and can generally be fixed with a decreasing margin of error as social organization becomes more primitive and less self-conscious or sophisticated. On the other hand, there is no way of telling how an individual will react within the limits set by environment and education. It is, for example, impossible for men to judge the inner motives of any superior acquaintance. Consequently, biography is an art and not properly an historical discipline, though the conscientious biographer will spare no pains to make the external facts of his subject's life as accurate as possible. This principle has been very effectively stressed by the school of Strachey, Maurois, Nicolson, and Ludwig, though some members of the group seem to believe that they can closely approach absolute historical correctness by clever application of this or that system of psychology.[19] Moreover, the reaction of a group cannot be predicted if too many or too elusive variable factors are involved, or if a group is under the influence of a superior personality of unpredictable character. This is why a history of civilization, in any of its aspects, may possess scientific accuracy, whereas a narrative of past events may be colored by the opinions of past narrators and a causal-functional history of movements may be thoroughly misleading.

D. SOME FUNDAMENTAL PRINCIPLES UNDERLYING HISTORY

Without losing ourselves in detail we shall now undertake to point out the extent to which principles of mathematics, of the physical sciences, of biology, and of anthropology are applicable to history. Mathematical and mechanical principles may safely be assumed to have universal applicability within the limits of their operation, which is not so wide nor so rigorous as was believed before the discovery of relativity and of the character of mathematics as an indefinite number of frames of reference. Since these principles are merely forms of pure logic, such general applicability may be postulated with all reasonable confidence. The historical and sociological configurations, however, to which they are applied are less rigid than physical configurations; and consequently the application must, as a rule, be made in the form of analogy rather than of rigorous demonstration. "Every action is followed by an equal and opposite reaction," but the reaction becomes mechanically intangible unless it can be measured—and historical reactions can seldom be measured with any approach to precision. Yet the *fact* of a reaction is generally certain. Similarly, Vico's principle of *corsi e ricorsi* (fluxes and refluxes) is mechanically sound and has been adopted by Croce and Sorokin as normative to their systems. One is

[19] Cf. the writer's remarks, *Jour. Am. Or. Soc.*, LVI (1936), pp. 135 f.

justified in employing such terms as continuum, integration, frame of reference, orbit, centrifugal or tangential movement, operational method, etc., provided only that one fully recognizes the limitations of their use and does not attempt to deduce binding conclusions from their analogical application. In this connection it may be observed that Hegel's triad, "thesis, antithesis, synthesis," introduces an idea of limited mathematical and physical application, and has proved as miserable a failure in history as in natural science, in spite of its undoubted classificatory value.

Turning from mathematico-physical to biological principles of significance to the historian, we are immediately aware of the increasing rigor with which they can be employed, since man and society are both biologically controlled. We can safely use such ideas as organism, life cycle, and species, as long as we remember that society is not really an organism in Durkheim's sense, but that it merely acts as an organism under certain conditions. A societal organism is just as much an abstraction as a centrifugal tendency is. Similarly, every organized human group is born, grows, declines, and dies, as it must if it is an aggregation of individual living beings. Every known biological organism and cultural group of the past has died, so we are justified in expecting every similar organism and grouping of the future to die. Evolution and mutation are other exceedingly valuable biological concepts which may be applied to history, and both are illustrated by innumerable facts known largely as the result of archaeological investigation. Orthogenesis is a very fertile heuristic principle in history, illustrated by many cogent facts, such as the success of well-integrated movements which continue to develop in the direction of their early evolution and the corresponding failure of most sectarian offshoots, and by the abnormal results which indefinite evolution along a certain line may have (as in the Hindu caste system). Emergent evolution is another productive idea. In dealing with historical evolution there are many seductive errors of method into which historians have been beguiled by insufficient facts or by inadequate perspective. For example, the sequence of evolution is sometimes reversed and vestigial features are considered as rudimentary, as in certain studies of typological development in archaeology. Then, again, evolution may be telescoped into an impossibly brief period, as has been done by the Wellhausen school in reconstructing the development of the religion of Israel or by Breasted in dating the dawn of conscience. Evolution is not always homogeneous in human history— in fact the reverse is probably more common, as in the development of Egyptian civilization, for example. In general, it may perhaps be said that a homogeneous, evenly balanced evolution is just as likely in disturbed areas, as in ancient Palestine, where a given society is more open to outside influences and to equalizing currents, as in a relatively isolated land like Egypt.

When we come to consider the applicability of principles of anthropology we are in a different situation, since anthropology is simply one aspect of history (or the reverse). Here our most urgent problem is to determine the correctness of anthropological principles before applying them to history proper. Principles which have been ascertained by the physical anthropologist or the ethnologist to be true usually prove of great direct value to the historian, and particularly to the historian of antiquity, where conditions most closely parallel those of "primitive" peoples today. The reverse is equally true, since the anthropologist is faced with many problems of a general type which he cannot solve with his present data, as, for example, the question of the age of the belief in a supreme deity of abstract nature, the age and source of myths or other elements of culture. The old problem of cultural diffusion versus the principle of *Völkergedanken* (where both sides are partly right), the question of the primary or secondary character of totemism when compared to the socio-religious organization of Egypt in the fourth millennium, and many similar ones demand solution—and solution can only come through the joint efforts of the cultural anthropologist and the historian of antiquity. Is the modern savage degenerate or simply stagnant? Was primitive man more or less inventive than his modern representative? How far must puzzling cultural and social phenomena be traced to adaptation or skeuomorphism?—e. g., is the appearance of clothing in warm regions to be traced to the southward migration of northern peoples with the established custom of wearing some clothing as a protection against cold? To what extent can we speak of spontaneous "folklore," or is folklore in reality the residue of literature, systematic teachings, or miscellaneous information which has percolated down through society from the élite at the top?—as Norman Brown has shown to be the case with the allegedly popular oral literature of modern India.[20] It will be recognized at once that problems of this kind are most important for the correct understanding of antiquity, as well as of many phases of more recent history.

E. TOWARD AN ORGANISMIC PHILOSOPHY OF HISTORY

Having stated our approach to the epistemology of history and to the use of analogy from other scientific domains, we can sketch, with a clear conscience, our own attitude to certain basic questions of the philosophy of history—an attitude which will profoundly influence our interpretation of the meaning of the data contained in the following pages. The data themselves and their historical context are not affected by the interpretation which we may give them, since they have been scrupulously checked by the methods described and analyzed in Chapter I. But the interpretation of these data and contexts, as materials for the historical panorama which we reconstruct, is undoubtedly affected by our philosophy of history, just as is true of the work of every philosophically minded historian of the past.

To what extent is it possible to create a grandiose synthesis of history, in the fashion of Hegel, of Spengler, or in a sense of Sorokin? It is difficult to say, since the climax of human history remains in the hands of God, and interpre-

[20] *Jour. Am. Or. Soc.*, XXXIX (1919), pp. 4 ff.

tations of His will by theologians are quite as divergent as are similar interpretations of history by non-theologians. We know enough today, however, to be able fully to cover many features of human history in diagrammatic form. The following table will illustrate what can be done in a broad way, with reference to the relation between undifferentiated, differentiated, and integrated culture.

First Stage	Prehistoric Undifferentiated Culture	Early and Middle Palaeolithic
Second Stage	Prehist. Partially Differentiated Culture	Late Palaeolithic to Chalcolithic
Third Stage	Historic Differentiated Culture with Center in the Near East	Cir. 3000-400 B.C.
Fourth Stage	Historic Partially Integrated Culture with Center in the Mediterranean Basin	Cir. 400 B.C.—700 A.D.
Fifth Stage	Historic Differentiated Culture with Different Foci	Cir. 700-1500
Sixth Stage	Historic Differentiated Culture with Progressive World Sweep of West	Cir. 1500—

This classification is naturally arbitrary and no single stage is invulnerable to serious criticism. It is simply presented to illustrate the present writer's view of the possibilities. Will the next great stage be an integrated culture or will it be a return to prehistoric lack of differentiation between cultures? From the standpoint of the present study, this table reflects the writer's conviction that the Graeco-Roman civilization of the time of Christ represented the closest approach to a rational unified culture that the world has yet seen and may justly be taken as the culmination of a long period of relatively steady evolution. It was in the fifth century B.C. that we find the greatest single burst of intellectual and aesthetic activity that the world has ever known, with results unparalleled before or after, from the standpoint of the integral achievement of man as intellectual, aesthetic, and physical animal. Small wonder that such great geneticists as Galton and Bateson have expressed their conviction that the climax of human evolution was reached by the Attic Greeks in the fifth century B.C.! It was, moreover, about the same time that the religion of Israel reached its climactic expression in Deutero-Isaiah and Job, who represented a height beyond which pure ethical monotheism has never risen. The history of Israelite and Jewish religion from Moses to Jesus thus appears to stand on the pinnacle of biological evolution as represented in Homo sapiens, and recent progress in discovery and invention really reflects a cultural lag of over two millennia, a lag which is, to be sure, very small when compared to the hundreds of thousands of years during which man has been toiling up the steep slopes of evolution.

Another broad classification of human history may be made on the basis of man's mental achievement, as represented by the highest religious and literary accomplishments of his historic past, seen in the perspective of the modern contrast between primitive tribes and civilized nations. This progress begins at an unknown time in the Stone Age with prelogical, corporative thinking, to use Lévy-Bruhl's terminology (see below). With the Greeks in the fifth century B.C. we may say that the logical age of man begins, though it is quite true that the uneducated man often remains at bottom the same prelogical, corporative thinker as his remote forefathers and savage cousins. The intervening stage is represented by the ancient Near East from the third millennium to the fifth century B.C. Here men start, as we shall see, with a prelogical, corporative tradition and after the late third millennium progressively discard prelogical thought and enter the empirical stage of logical thinking, where the highest thought is quite logical as a rule, but draws its sanctions from the results of experience and not from formal canons of thinking. Almost simultaneously we see the individual beginning to receive formal recognition in religion and literature, with personal responsibility proclaimed for the first time in ethical teaching. Personalism tends to replace corporatism. It is significant that no fundamental change in man's highest achievement in modes of thought can be detected after the fifth century B.C. For the past 2500 years civilized man has thought in much the same fundamental ways, as is vividly illustrated by the oscillations between "ideational" and "sensate," or "mixed" types of culture which have been statistically and analytically established by Sorokin.

Turning from these broad horizons, where a single subjective dislocation can disorganize an historian's entire perspective, to firmer ground, we wish to state our conviction that an inductive organismic philosophy is the only proper way in which to approach the problem of the relation of historical contexts to one another. And this organismic basis must be, as we pointed out in discussing Toynbee's system, a modest one, not rising for operational purposes beyond the level of the culture-unit. By this we mean a geographically and chronologically limited horizon, in which there is a real homogeneity about the aspect of any element or factor, which ceases as soon as we cross these boundaries of space and time. Our European civilization is so complex and is so continuously modified in all directions by the influence of its many cultural centers that one who examines it too closely and exclusively, as is the case with Sorokin, fails clearly to grasp the real existence of sharply defined cultures in the ancient Orient as well as among more recent primitive peoples. To the archaeologist these cultures are tangible realities; to the linguist and anthropologist the same is true. The average historian, however, immersed in the study of complex higher cultures, often fails to see what seems so transparent to his colleagues. Actually, the historian of the West has just as adequate evidence of patterns and configurations of culture, though they are never as clear, owing to the complexity of the pattern of occidental civilization into which they are woven. When one culture yields to another there is nearly always (probably always under simple conditions) an abrupt change, a true mutation of culture, in which a generation may suffice for changes which might otherwise take a millennium to effect. In the ancient Orient, for example, a culture may last for centuries with only the slightest modification, after which there is a sudden interruption in its continuity, accompanied by changes so rapid that it is often hard for the archaeologist to distinguish the successive steps. The cultural revolution is then followed by a new culture or cultural phase, which may last again for centuries with little internal change. What is true of simple cultures is likewise true, *mutatis mutandis*, of patterns of nomistic religion, etc. There was an abrupt break between Judaism and Christianity in the first century A.D., followed by nearly two thousand years in which Judaism and Christianity themselves have changed but little, considering the magnitude of the original break between them. Protestantism is not a new religion, but simply an effort to return to early Christianity by discarding most of the results of nearly 1500 years of slow development; and all Protestant leaders were formerly convinced that their systems reflected early Christianity as closely as possible, given the changed environment of the West. Buddhism and Islam similarly represent abrupt breaks with the past, following which the standard forms of these faiths have changed but little, except for reformations like the Wahhabi movement, designed to restore primitive simplicity of faith and practice. It is the present writer's firm conviction, based on historical evidence which will be duly marshalled in Chapter IV, that Mosaism represents the same type of abrupt break with the past, of evolutionary mutation. Like Christianity and Islam, Mosaism changed slowly but surely in the following generations, until gradual evolution was violently interrupted by the prophetic movement, which may be compared to the Wahhabi movement or the Protestant Reformation with respect to the zeal of its protagonists and their desire to restore primitive Mosaism. It was partly successful in eliminating elements which it considered abuses and wholly successful in restoring Israelite piety, so it may well be compared with the Catholic Counter-reformation, which also succeeded in reforming numerous abuses without breaking up the Church.

It is, in the writer's judgment, a serious methodological error to assume that all the various elements of any "authentic" culture are linked together either in a causal-functional or in a "logico-meaningful" way, *à la* Sorokin. Of course, there are elements which are causally and functionally related to one another, but this is probably not true of all. Our standpoint is rather that a culture represents an empirico-adaptive system, in which elements have been brought together as a result of many quite dissimilar causes, but where they are adapted to one another by a process which reminds one of the unconscious ability of any man to make the products of his multifarious and often incongruous genes work together in tolerable harmony. These inner bonds are, in general, quite secondary and no amount of intuitive guessing is likely to reveal them. However, the more we can establish the existence of causal and functional as well as of purely empirical relationships, the better we shall understand history and sociology. In this respect we agree entirely with Max Weber.

In concluding these observations, it may be emphasized that organismic philosophy inevitably carries with it opposition, open or implicit, to monistic or atomistic speculations. Thinkers who deal habitually with patterns, configurations, and organisms cannot help but raise the question of entelechy, whatever form the question may take. If patterns and organisms have properties which none of the component units possesses, does not the Cosmos likewise have properties which raise it high above its most impressive constituent? If microcosmic man, who alone of created beings is able to think consciously and purposively, is forced by circumstances over which he may have little control to become one of a group which plays a definite rôle in a larger pattern, itself perhaps a unit in a still larger configuration, does not the human microcosm have its analogy in a macrocosmic thinker who is above these configurations of human societies? The student of natural science, where amoral law reigns supreme except where its rule is contested by the principle of indeterminacy, may answer in the negative. The student of modern history, mindful of its superficially meaningless oscillations and its frequent confusion of thought, may also answer in the negative. The sympathetic student of man's *entire* history can have but one reply: there *is* an Intelligence and a Will, expressed in both History and Nature[21]—for History and Nature are one.

[21] The philosophical contrasting of "History" and "Nature" seems to go back to J. G. Droysen (cf. E. Rothacker, *Historische Zeitschrift,* CLXI [1939], pp. 84-92). It has been ingeniously applied to Hebrew and Jewish history by S. W. Baron, *A Social and Religious History of the Jews,* especially Vol. I, pp. 3-32 (cf. the review by Canon H. Danby, *Jour. Bib. Lit.,* LVI [1937], 395 ff.). As we have tried to show, however, there is no such ontological dualism as History—Nature. It would be idle to deny that history and nature may often be advantageously contrasted, or that they frequently exhibit a real polarity, but aesthetic or adventitious dichotomies of this type cannot be made the framework for a systematic philosophy of history. —Since writing these lines I have read the illuminating article of R. Anthes in *Zeits. Deutsch. Morg. Ges.,* XCII (1938), pp. 421-40, in which the latter presents some very sound objections to the contrasting of "Nature" and "History" as done by W. Wolf in his *Wesen und Wert der Ägyptologie* (Leipzig, 1937). The point of view reflected by Anthes' paper is closely related to mine. My attitude to most of the philosophical tendencies criticized in this chapter is generally in accord with the neo-scholastic point of view as stated, e. g., by Ludovico D. Macnab (*El concepto escolastico de la historia* [Buenos Aires, 1940], especially pp. 83 ff.). However, there is no formal contact between my rational empiricism in dealing with historical problems and the methods of scholastic philosophy, which moves in a different sphere and deals with theological problems which lie beyond the scope of this book.

Chapter III

PRAEPARATIO

In this chapter we shall describe the cultural and religious evolution of the Near East from the earliest ages to about 1600 B.C. Since the purpose of the present work is not to recount political history except in so far as it throws direct light on the development of higher religious culture, we shall lay stress on the evolution of civilization through successive cultures, and especially on the unfolding of religious phenomena. Owing to the extraordinary progress in our knowledge of the most ancient Near East in the past ten years, we may advance beyond our predecessors and construct a fresh synthesis, based directly on archaeological material, both written and unwritten. We are forced by new discoveries to diverge farthest from previous historians in the reconstruction of the successive cultures of the Stone Age and the following transitional period, the Chalcolithic or Ceramolithic,[1] about which very little was known ten years ago. In dealing with the historical period from 3000 to 1600 B.C. our new knowledge is of special importance for chronology, and we can now fix dates and correlate the chronologies of Egypt and Mesopotamia with an approach

[1] The term "Ceramolithic" was suggested by the writer some years ago to designate the period when stone and pottery were used together (cf. G. E. Wright, *The Pottery of Palestine* . . . [New Haven, 1937], p. 4) and has had limited success, but it is better to adhere for the present to more generally recognized classifications.

to precision which was unknown a decade ago.[2] The
Sumerian age in Mesopotamia has been brightly illuminated by recent discoveries; the Dynasty of Accad has
become historically and culturally tangible; the age of
Amorite domination has emerged from obscurity into an
important place in history; Bronze-Age Palestine and Syria
are now better known than their Iron Age was a decade
ago.

A. The Evolution of Material Civilization in the Near East from the Earliest Times to the Seventeenth Century b.c.

1. *The Stone Age*

Thanks to the extraordinary progress of our knowledge
of the Stone Age in the Near East, as briefly described
above (pp. 28 f.), we can now present a correct chronological outline of the succession of human types and cultures, though there are still numerous minor gaps to be
filled and much fundamental knowledge of the earlier
phases is entirely wanting. No certain eolithic remains have
been discovered and the Early Palaeolithic remains obscure,
in spite of surface finds. Palestine and other highland regions of Western Asia have yielded surface stations of
Chellean and Acheulian type, but it is only in Egypt that
flint artifacts of these ages have been discovered in characteristic geological formations. In the Nile Valley there is
a series of high gravel terraces which roughly parallel the
present course of the Nile and which follow approximately
the same gradient as the modern river. In the highest of
them, the 100-foot terrace, the British archaeologists Sandford and Arkell, working on behalf of the Oriental Institute,
have collected a respectable number of Chellean flints. The
following, or 50-foot, terrace similarly yields Acheulian
flints. This geological sequence is confirmed by Fr. Bovier-
Lapierre's discovery of the same stratigraphical order in
gravel beds near Cairo; the lowest or Chellean deposits here

[2] See below, n. 16.

also contain characteristic early Pleistocene fossils. Owing to the extraordinary complexity of the observed phenomena, which seems to increase year by year, there is still no assured correlation between the successive glacial and inter-glacial phases of Central Europe, the raised beaches of the Mediterranean, the Nile terraces, and the pluvial phases of the Jordan Valley. While it is now certain that the former conservative dating of the Chellean of Europe in the third Interglacial (the Riss-Würm phase) was too low and that the Chellean must be dated back to the Second or even to the First Interglacial, with Breuil and others, a more precise relative chronology is still unattainable. The great advances made in the chronology of solar radiation since the World War (Milankovitch, Köppen, and others) have been so plausibly correlated with the glacial oscillations of the Pleistocene by F. Zeuner (since 1935) that we can be reasonably sure of the approximate absolute chronology, especially since his results coincide rather closely with the estimates previously made by Penck and Brückner on the basis of the rate of erosion.[3] That the magnitude of individual stages is roughly correct is also proved by Count de Geer's geochronological work in Sweden and by recent estimates of the time required to deposit the annual laminations of the Lisan terrace in the Jordan Valley (Blake: 40,000 years, Picard: materially less). We need not concern ourselves here with the latest objections to the Zeuner theory, based on the fact that increased solar radiation automatically increases the rate of evaporation, which raises the amount of water vapor in the atmosphere and reduces the effect of radiation, since this principle merely brings in a new factor of retardation in addition to those previously known. The important point for us to know is that the oldest stone artifacts so far found in the Near East, of characteristically Chellean type, cannot be less than 100,000 years old and may easily be much older. Very little is known about Near-Eastern man at this stage, since the earliest traces of cave-dwelling do not appear until later.

Toward the end of the Early Palaeolithic Age in the mid-

[3] Cf. Chap. I, n. 3.

dle or late Acheulian (Tayacian), perhaps about 60,000 years ago, appear the first cave deposits of human origin in Palestine. Deposits of this general age have been found by Dorothy Garrod and by R. Neuville in a number of caves in different parts of Palestine. At that time the severity of climatic conditions in the first phase of the Third Glacial Age (according to Breuil, whose view on the subject is generally accepted) forced Acheulian man to take refuge in caves and to make his abode in them. Having formed the habit he continued to live partly in caves even during warmer interglacial or interpluvial periods. In the early part of Middle Palaeolithic, many thousands of years after the beginning of the cave-dwelling age, when nearly forty feet of debris had accumulated during periods of living in the Mughâret et-Tabûn near Mount Carmel, the bodies of a dozen persons were left in this cave and a neighboring one. These remains have been carefully removed from the hard limestone matrix in which they were found imbedded, a task which has taken Sir Arthur Keith and T. D. McCown some five years of hard work; and since 1937 full accounts of the anthropological study of them have become available.[4] Like the Galilee skull, discovered by Turville-Petre in 1925, and like a group of four skulls discovered in Mughâret el-Qafzeh south of Nazareth in 1934 by R. Neuville, these skeletons belong to the earlier part of the Levalloiso-Mousterian, and must thus be at least 30,000 years old—perhaps much more. All of them belong to the extinct sub-species called Neanderthal man (Homo Neanderthalensis), like all known Mousterian skeletal remains from Europe and Siberia, but most of the skeletons found near Carmel show much more racial variation than do European skeletons of that age. Most important is the fact that the individuals from near Carmel show (with one exception) some strikingly modern anatomical features, characteristic of Homo sapiens from his earliest known appearance in the Aurignacian of Europe and found in all surviving races

[4] See now the definitive publication of these skeletons by Sir Arthur Keith and T. D. McCown, *The Stone Age of Mt. Carmel*, Vol. II (Oxford, 1939).

of man. This is usually interpreted to mean that the Near East was a stage in the journey of Homo sapiens from his supposed cradle in the Middle East to Europe; Palestine would thus illustrate the inevitable racial mixture that resulted from the meeting of Homo sapiens with Homo Neanderthalensis.

When these men lived human culture had advanced but little beyond the Chellean level; the principal material distinction lies in the increase both in the number of distinct kinds of stone artifacts which were used and the increased differentiation of types in different regions. In the Chellean there seems to have been very little difference between the artifacts of Egypt and Palestine and those of France. In the subsequent Tayacian, Acheulian, and Micoquian, all belonging to the Early Palaeolithic, this is still true, but in the Middle Palaeolithic there is for the first time a marked difference between the stone cultures of Europe and of Egypt and Palestine, though they may all be termed "Mousterian" in general terms. This tendency toward cultural differentiation increased steadily in the Late Palaeolithic. Palestine parted company from the Sebilian and Capsian of North Africa and joined the domain of Aurignacian culture which then held sway over most of Europe and the Highland Zone of Western Asia (Asia Minor, Armenia, and Western Iran). During the long-continued Aurignacian period there is no skeletal evidence from the Near East, where there is a probable gap between the latest cave deposits of Aurignacian type and the earliest of Mesolithic character. This gap is bridged in Europe by the Solutrean, Magdalenian, and such epi-palaeolithic cultures as the Azilian. Until we have more evidence in Egypt or in Western Asia it is not safe to make any inferences with respect to the development of human life and culture. To judge from European analogies the gap corresponds to a period of at least 6000 years (minimum date cir. 15,000-9000 B.C.) in the Near East, during which there was a remarkable improvement in the arts and crafts, from the flint artifact itself, which was now specialized in many directions, to the crafts of hunting, fishing, weaving of nets and mats, and even carving and painting.

Turning again to Europe for material to supplement our still inadequate observations from the Near East, we can say with reasonable confidence that the Mousterians had already begun to inter their dead. In the Aurignacian age regular burials became customary and corpses were often buried with ornaments of shells, teeth, and bone, as well as with flint tools and weapons and with red ochre for painting the body. Of much more direct importance for us is the discovery, in deposits of clear Aurignacian age, of stone, bone, and ivory reliefs and statuettes of nude women. All are alike in stressing only breasts, abdomen, navel, and hypogastric region, without any attempt to represent features or even in some cases to indicate feet and arms. The breasts are invariably heavy and pendulous and the abdomen protrudes in a way which can only indicate a woman in advanced pregnancy. This impression becomes a certainty when we examine the "Venus" of Willendorf and note the laterally distended navel, the exaggerated protrusion of the vulvar region, and the fact that the arms are placed over the breasts as though to press milk out (a proleptic touch), all of which remind us forcibly of later Halafian parallels in chalcolithic Mesopotamia. The nudity alone does not warrant any inference, since the Aurignacians had not yet learned how to sew leather, if we may judge from the absence of awls and needles, and presumably went naked when the temperature permitted. However, Halafian and later analogies, as well as the dynamistic parallels in Capsian and Magdalenian art, make it evident that these figurines were used as amulets or were at least somewhat comparable to the amulets of later ages, being used as sympathetic aids to fertility or to easy delivery or to both.[5]

[5] For recent general discussions of this subject see F. R. Lehmann, *Arch. Rel.*, XXXV (1938), pp. 304 ff., who discusses European literature; Mme. Luce Passemard, *Les statuettes féminines paléolithiques dites Vénus Stéatopyges* (Nimes, 1938), who covers the French literature and gives the best

In the gap between Aurignacian and Mesolithic in the Near East falls the Magdalenian culture of southwestern Europe, belonging to the physically superior branch of Homo sapiens which we call the Cro-Magnon race. Here the art of painting reached the highest point attained before the fifth millennium B.C., and in some respects the highest stage reached before the third millennium. The superb paintings of the walls of Altamira and other caves in France and Spain are so well known that no description is necessary; it is also a commonplace that the subjects chosen for execution, various details of treatment, and above all the extraordinary inaccessibility of many of the paintings, which are found in chambers and passages only reached with the greatest effort, must be explained dynamistically. In other words, the animals which are portrayed were objects of the chase, often represented in slightly later Capsian rock-drawings as being hunted by men, and the purpose of representing them was to give the hunter control over them. The technical excellence of the paintings is alone sufficient proof that there was a class of men who specialized in this form of sympathetic magic, which may better be called "dynamism," to use Bertholet's happy term. Prehistorians have explained the paintings and other objects of Magdalenian culture as illustrating still more developed religious and cultic practices, but most of their inferences remain quite uncertain.

Returning to the Near East, we find that the Mesolithic Age is more adequately represented than almost anywhere else in the world, thanks to Miss Garrod's discovery of the

graphic material; and G. A. Barton, *Proc. Am. Philos. Soc.,* LXXXII (1940), pp. 134 ff., who limits himself to Anglo-American literature. The authority of Schuchhardt, *Alteuropa* (2nd ed.; Berlin, 1926), pp. 27-31, inclines Lehmann to leave the question of religious or secular purpose open; Barton, on the other hand, decides without reserve for the religious interpretation, to which Mme. Passemard also inclines. Striking parallels from the later Near East, still unknown to these scholars, tip the balance definitively in favor of the latter; see especially Mallowan, *Iraq,* III, p. 20, and the writer, *Mélanges . . . Dussaud* (Paris, 1939), p. 119.

Natufian culture in 1928 and to subsequent finds.[6] The past ten years have brought a mass of evidence for this culture from several caves and settlements in Palestine. While it cannot be precisely dated as yet, we can hardly go wrong in placing its end long before 6000 B.C. A reasonable guess is that it was at its height about 10,000 years ago. According to R. Neuville, four phases of the Natufian can be distinguished, but there is some doubt about details as yet. The Natufians were a small, slender, long-headed people, markedly resembling the earliest predynastic Egyptians and the chalcolithic men of Byblus. In other words, they belonged to an historical race, probably to the same race from which the Hamites and Semites of later times descended.[7] The only marked difference is in stature and size of bones, which are notoriously dependent on nutritional and environmental factors, as is shown by recent biological and medical observations and experiments. The Natufians had already learned to grow cereals, presumably an early variety of millet or wheat, as we know from the discovery of flint sickles and sickle edges in considerable numbers. On the other hand, they had not reached the pottery-making stage and there are no ground edges on their microlithic implements. It is probable that they had learned to domesticate certain animals, though the evidence is still inconclusive. Artistically they had made considerable progress, since several carved statuettes of men and animals have been found; the best is a superb fawn carved from the end of a bone. They were also able to hollow out and shape stone basins and mortars, as well as to build simple constructions of stone. They buried their dead, laying the body on its side with legs drawn up, and in certain cases, at least, leaving ornaments in place.

Palestine has also yielded the first certain stratigraphic evidence in the Near East for the next important step forward in culture, the grinding of stone artifacts and the erection of massive stone structures. This stage has long

[6] See now D. A. E. Garrod and D. M. A. Bate, *The Stone Age of Mt. Carmel*, I (1937), pp. 29-41.

[7] See the writer in *Haverford Symposium* (1938), p. 7.

been known as the Neolithic in Western Europe, where it lasted much longer, and the term has often been erroneously applied to various relatively early cultures of the Near East, nearly all of which have subsequently turned out to be much later in date. The true Neolithic (see below, § 2) was first discovered in stratigraphic sequence by J. Garstang, in his excavation of the lowest occupied levels at Jericho in 1935-36. This culture, which must antedate the fifth millennium, exhibits two main stages, one before the invention of pottery, the other after it, being in this respect somewhat parallel to the Egyptian typological sequence Faiyumian-Merimdean. The explorations and soundings of R. Neuville have brought to light some of the cultural stages separating the Natufian of Carmel from the pre-ceramic Neolithic phase of Jericho, but it is not our purpose here to go into detail. Suffice it to say that the Tahunian I of Neuville is an intermediate culture which closely resembles the Natufian but exhibits the first arrow-heads; there are as yet no ground stone edges of true neolithic type.

The pre-ceramic Neolithic of Jericho is a culture of extraordinary interest. Here we find the oldest known permanent houses; we also find mud figurines of domestic animals and plastic statues of human beings. The latter occur in groups, each apparently containing a man, woman, and child; they were made by smearing limy marl paste on a kind of skeleton of reeds, and though of normal proportions *en face* are very thin in profile. The head which Garstang has published is nearly life-size. These curious groups must have a cultic significance, since they are otherwise inexplicable. The houses and supposed shrine are also very curious, since they are provided with carefully laid, levelled, lime-surfaced, painted, and *burnished* clay floors. In one place there are no fewer than seven superimposed floors of this type. Walls were of beaten earth (*pisé*) or of "plano-convex" adobe. A building of stratum XI (the third of the four early neolithic layers) contained a portico originally supported by six wooden posts, a wide antechamber, and a large inner chamber. In and around this building there were no clearly domestic objects, but there were numerous animal figurines, representing cattle, sheep, goats, and pigs, as well as plastic models of the male organs, small cones, etc. We thus find in this pre-ceramic culture, belonging to a very primitive agricultural and cattle-breeding folk, unmistakable indications of a rather developed religious cult. The implications of this situation will be discussed below.

The last great manifestation of the Stone Age in the Old World was the megalithic phase. Strictly speaking, there never was a "megalithic culture," since megaliths seem nearly always to have been burial monuments: dolmens, menhirs, and cromlechs, all built of huge, usually flat stones. Chronologically, most megalithic remains can now be shown to belong to the Neolithic Age, though they seem to have survived into the Chalcolithic in the Near East and they certainly lasted down into the late third millennium B.C. in northwestern Europe. The circle at Stonehenge (second millennium) was a temple. Megalithic burials appear in Palestine in their most archaic and simplest form, which may now be dated roughly to the fifth and sixth millennia B.C. The development of the art of building megalithic tombs lagged greatly in Western Europe, where it extended down to the close of the Neolithic. Burial chambers were still constructed according to the megalithic principle of arrangement, though of far smaller stones, in the early Chalcolithic of the Jordan Valley and there are vestiges of this tradition even in the Early Bronze of the southern Dead Sea district. True megalithic monuments are found in the Near East exclusively in the hill-country of Palestine, especially in Transjordan, and in the uplands of Syria, Asia Minor, Armenia, and Kurdistan. There can be no doubt that they belonged to pastoral peoples, who herded cattle, sheep, and goats, and who may have been members of many different races, since there is not a scrap of tangible evidence for the often inferred "megalithic race." Owing to the total absence of sculpture or carved ornament in megalithic tombs, as well as to the paucity of offerings found in those excavated, we have no basis for defining the religion of their builders, except to say that great emphasis was obviously laid on after-life. It has plausibly been suggested that the mastabas and pyramids of Egypt are ultimately derived from megalithic monuments, though we unfortunately lack all intermediate stages. On the other hand, the notion of the late Elliot Smith that the pyramids were the prototypes of megalithic monuments, has been thoroughly disproved by archaeologists.

2. *The Chalcolithic Age and the Irrigation Culture*

We shall now describe the earliest sedentary cultures of the Near East as a whole, from their beginning in the pottery-bearing levels of Late Neolithic to the displacement of stone by copper as the dominant material of tools and weapons, about 3000 B.C., or even a little earlier. A number of names have been proposed for this stage of human civilization; we have preferred "chalcolithic" because it is probably the one most commonly used, but "ceramolithic" is in many ways a more suitable term, since it refers to the coexistence of pottery with stone artifacts.[8] The boundary between true Neolithic and Chalcolithic is disputed, but there seems to be no reason why we should not follow Garstang's rehabilitation of the neolithic stage in the Near East, as a result of his work in 1935-36 at Jericho and in 1938-39 at Mersin in Cilicia. In the latter place he has discovered twenty feet of accumulated neolithic debris, with monochrome pottery and obsidian tools but apparently without metal. The stage of culture in neolithic Mersin corresponds roughly to that of late neolithic Jericho and also to that of the oldest layers of occupation in half a dozen recently excavated sites in northern Mesopotamia and Syria, all below the oldest "painted-pottery" strata. All settlements of this age which have been studied so far, are situated in large alluvial valleys or in low plains and small valleys in which sufficient running water is available for a developed system of irrigation.

The following stage, that of painted pottery, is extremely

[8] See n. 1, above.

widespread, since it is found almost all over Western Asia
and extends across Iran to Turkestan and the Indus Valley.
Moreover, similar types of prehistoric pottery have been
discovered in Mongolia and northern China. In Egypt and
Nubia we find a parallel, but apparently distinct stream of
ceramic tradition developing from the Neolithic of the
Faiyum and Merimdeh. Palestine and Southern Syria vary,
sometimes following the northern cultural tradition, sometimes the southern one. The main stream of culture then
flowed through Syria and Mesopotamia, since it is in those
lands that we find the greatest number of settlements, the
thickest deposits, and the highest cultural level, which is
not reached in any surrounding region at that time—except
possibly in the still little known East, Iran and the Indus
Valley.

In Mesopotamia and Syria the discoveries of the past few
decades (above, p. 57) have brought to light a succession
of highly developed chalcolithic cultures, each represented
by occupational deposits of great thickness. The oldest
seems to be the Halafian, which was well distributed
through northern Mesopotamia and Syria, with a surrounding zone which it influenced strongly. To judge from the
many strata by which it is represented at some sites, it must
have lasted for centuries (fourth millennium B.C.). The art
of building was well developed, including both houses with
prevailing rectangular plan and more massive buildings
with circular ground-plan (*tholoi*), superficially resembling the Pueblo *kivas*. That these circular buildings were
shrines has been well demonstrated by Mallowan, who excavated the first examples at Arpachiyah near Nineveh.
The earlier *tholoi* consist only of a simple circular building
on stone foundations and *pisé* superstructure; the later ones
are larger and have a rectangular antechamber before the
circular chamber. At Arpachiyah there was a marked concentration of figurines around the *tholoi*, a fact which suggests their cultic significance. Examination of the objects
themselves makes this inference certain, at least for the human figurines. The latter are almost all plastic representations of nude, painted females, with the head hardly in-

dicated, but with exaggerated portrayal of the breasts, abdomen, buttocks, and vulvar region, in keeping with the earlier Aurignacian practice. Most of these figurines, like numerous ones of the same general type found in other painted-pottery sites, are shown in a squatting position, with unmistakable indications of approaching delivery. In this connection it should be observed that squatting is the normal position for women in labor in the modern East, just as it was in the ancient Orient, as we know both from texts and from figurines and drawings. Animal figurines are also abundant; they nearly always represent cattle, sheep, pigs, and doves. Since the dove was so closely associated with the mother goddess in the later Near East, both in texts and in art, it is only reasonable to explain the dove here in the same way.

It was in the Halafian age, about 3800 B.C., that the highest stage in the early history of the decorative art was reached by vase-painters, probably in close imitation of skill already attained by basket-makers and rug-weavers. The intricate polychrome geometric and floral designs with which the Halafians decorated the inside of shallow bowls and platters have not been surpassed in beauty, at least from our modern viewpoint, at any subsequent time in history. That such decorative skill was not restricted to Mesopotamia is proved by its closely parallel development in the roughly contemporary Ghassulian of Palestine, where it serves to adorn fresco paintings. A site of about the same age near Persepolis in southwestern Iran, excavated recently by Herzfeld, shows almost equal beauty in vase-painting and the art of painting frescoes seems not to have lagged behind. In the same general horizon falls the marvellously delicate vase-painting of Susa I.

The Halafian was followed by the Samarran and especially the Obeidian, to which corresponds a stage known in Syria as Ugarit III, well illustrated by Ingholt's recent excavations at Hamath on the Orontes. The Obeidian is the earliest clearly defined culture of Babylonia, where we find its remains underlying nearly all the oldest cities of the country, such as Ur, Erech, Lagash, Eridu, etc. This proves that the occupation of the marsh-lands of Babylonia by human settlers came rather late in the history of the irrigation culture, probably not far from 3700 B.C. Babylonia rapidly distanced the older districts of the north, since men were by this time able to apply their acquired practice in draining marshes, digging canals, and building dams to great advantage in the rich alluvial plains of lower Mesopotamia. The civilization of Mesopotamia already began to assume, in the Obeidian age around 3500 B.C., the basic forms which it was to exhibit for more than three millennia thereafter. In a late Obeidian stratum (XIII) at Tepe Gawra in Assyria, Speiser has discovered (1936-37) well-built rectangular temples with symmetrical plans and with elaborately recessed niches inside and outside, forming part of a constructional scheme which served both to buttress and to decorate the building.[9] This new type of construction foreshadows a series of similar temples at Tepe Gawra in the late chalcolithic levels X-VIII, as well as the elaborate group of late chalcolithic temples excavated by the Germans at Erech in southern Babylonia. Recessed niches continued to be characteristic elements of temple planning down to the latest times in Mesopotamia.

After the Obeidian came the Warkan period in Babylonia, with parallel, though not identical, cultural phases in northern Mesopotamia and Syria. Now we witness an extraordinary burst of progress in the arts of civilization. This period is best represented by the archaic temples of Erech, under the later temples of Anu and Ishtar, the chief deities of the city. Here the German excavators have, in the past ten years, brought to light an artificial platform (for protection from the inundation) on which was built a cluster of elaborately planned and constructed temples. The objects from this age show that writing had been invented and had already passed the purely pictographic stage, though many signs still have the form of the object which they were meant to represent. Inventories and business documents were inscribed with a stylus on clay tablets. Ownership and business responsibility were fixed by impressing

[9] *Bull. Am. Sch. Or. Res.*, No. 66 (1937), pp. 2 ff.

seal cylinders, with exquisitely carved designs, on moist clay sealings and dockets. The designs on these seals show that even in the fourth quarter of the fourth millennium B.C. art had already passed far beyond any stage previously attained. Native skill, empirically developed by generations of artists and craftsmen, had reached the point where it became standardized, where canons of proportion were established, and where the prevailing motifs were processions of human and animal figures, temple façades, and fabulous monsters with interlaced necks and tails, etc. Standardization was thus accompanied by abstraction and symbolism. The archaic cuneiform inscriptions so far published are not entirely intelligible, but enough can be made out to indicate a complex economic life and an active cultic organization. The language of the country was Sumerian, as it probably had been for the whole of the Chalcolithic Age (though this is disputed and definitive evidence is lacking).

In the latest chalcolithic culture of southern Mesopotamia, named after the site of Jemdet Nasr in northern Babylonia where it was first identified, we have substantially only a continuation of the Warkan phase, with a considerable decrease of *élan*, as well as a corresponding artistic impoverishment, though coupled with technical development. This period is characterized by growing complexity in the arts of civilization, such as the increasing use of sculpture and of writing. The north was, of course, not so rich as Babylonia, but did not begin to lag appreciably in culture until later, as shown by the small, but symmetrically planned and well built temples of strata X to VIII at Tepe Gawra. To this age or a little later belongs the fantastic sculpture on the summit of Jebelet el-Beida in the extreme north of Mesopotamia, discovered in an ancient open-air shrine by Baron von Oppenheim.[10]

It is now possible roughly to synchronize the successive phases of the Egyptian Chalcolithic with Syria and Mesopotamia. Egypt remained much more restricted in its development and exhibits nothing comparable to the finest achievements of Halafian or Warkan Mesopotamia. The

[10] *Der Tell Halaf* (1931), pp. 199-220.

flowering of Egyptian culture was to come later. Owing to the irresistible movement of the Nile alluvium, which year by year rose in level and encroached farther on the arid zone which bounded it on both sides, the earliest villages and cemeteries are now buried deep under the mud. There is thus a gap between the neolithic cultures of the Faiyum and the earliest discernible cultures of the Nile Valley proper. Since 1924 Brunton's discoveries have carried the latter back by bringing to light the Tasian and the closely related Badarian which followed it. After the Badarian there is another lacuna, and then we come to the predynastic cultures of the fourth millennium which were distinguished by Petrie forty years ago and named by him much more recently: the Amratian, which was strongest in Upper Egypt, the Gerzean, which developed in Lower Egypt, and the Semainean, which ushers us into the Dynastic Age. Since only villages and cemeteries have hitherto been discovered, our knowledge of art and architecture is probably lop-sided, and architecture may have reached a much higher level than we can infer from our present material. However, it is now certain that the level of Egyptian culture remained considerably below that of Mesopotamia until the First Dynasty, when under strong indirect influence from the Euphrates Valley it forged ahead of the latter in a breath-taking spurt.

The chalcolithic cultures of Palestine have all been discovered since 1929 but it was not until 1937 that their sequence and relationship were adequately cleared up, thanks to stratigraphic excavations at Megiddo, Beth-shan, Jericho, 'Affuleh, and elsewhere.[11] The developed Early Chalcolithic of Palestine is known as the Ghassulian, from the site near Jericho where it was first discovered; it has

[11] For the best discussion of the chronology of these cultures see G. E. Wright, *The Pottery of Palestine from the Earliest Times to the End of the Early Bronze Age* (New Haven, 1937), and the table on p. 107. On the chronology of the Ghassulian, over which a bitter debate raged for a number of years, see now the observations of A. Bea and R. Koeppel in *Teleilat Ghassul* II (Rome, 1940), pp. v, 50, which show that there is now practical unanimity.

since been found or identified in numerous other sites in
different parts of Palestine. This culture, which must be
roughly contemporary with the Obeidian of Mesopotamia
and the Amratian of Egypt, was characteristically chalcolithic in type, with a highly developed flint industry, including polished axes, very well made pottery, and rectangular
houses of "plano-convex" adobe on stone foundations. E. L.
Sukenik has discovered models of Ghassulian houses which
were used as ossuaries to hold the bones of the deceased.[12]
The houses of this period were decorated inside and outside with fresco designs painted on a lime surface; a portion
of fresco recovered by A. Mallon shows an astonishingly
elaborate geometric pattern based on an eight-pointed star,
around which were fragmentary remains of an intricate field
of dragons and geometric figures. The whole must have
been a veritable phantasmagoria, showing that the artistic
imagination was abnormally active in Palestine nearly 5500
years ago. Another fresco, fortunately quite well preserved,
represents a bird, painted with a naturalistic precision and
an attention to detail which cannot be equalled in any subsequent period of Palestine, until the Greek period. The
most interesting and most enigmatic of all these mural frescoes is unfortunately very badly preserved and a number
of dubious interpretations have been offered.[13] All we can
see with certainty is a series of human legs and feet, all facing left except a smaller figure in front, belonging to the
lower part of a nude man facing right. Directly in front of
him are two pairs of somewhat geometrically drawn human feet (the first pair in embroidered shoes), each pair
on a four-legged footstool. Behind each stool are traces of
chairs. The position of the seated figures in this fresco is
naturally conceptual and the figures must be thought of as
seated side by side. From Canaanite mythological texts and
figured representations of the second millennium B.C. we
know that the gods were portrayed 2000 years later as sitting on thrones with their feet on stools, so we are war-

---

[12] *Jour. Pal. Or. Soc.*, XVII (1937), pp. 15-30.
[13] For previous explanations see especially L. H. Vincent,
Rev. Bib., XLIV (1935), pp. 100-102.

ranted in interpreting this scene in a similar way. As a matter of fact, interpreters agree in regarding it as clearly cultic, but some are inclined to go considerably farther than the fragment warrants. Suffice it to say that we have here evidence that the Ghassulians worshipped a goddess (in embroidered shoes) and a god, the former taking precedence. We also know that the dead were believed to pursue an existence somewhat parallel to that on earth, since they were carefully buried in stone-lined graves, with ornaments and pottery (originally containing food).[14] The Ghassulians of Khedheirah went farther, placing the bones of their deceased in house-urns, shaped like the houses of the living. This custom is also found in neolithic Europe, and reflects advanced conceptions of the after-life.

The Ghassulian was followed by a period of many centuries, during which we can discern a related, but definitely later series of cultures in different parts of Palestine; they are followed especially by the Esdraelon culture, which is best known from Megiddo and Beth-shan. The latter culture must be dated in the last quarter of the fourth millennium; it was roughly contemporary with the Warkan and the Jemdet Nasr phases of the Babylonian Chalcolithic. Mesopotamian influences are clear, especially in pottery and above all in the carved cylinder seals which were rolled over unbaked pottery in order to decorate it with floral and animal scenes in relief. The early cemetery of Byblus, recently excavated by M. Dunand, is characteristically Late Chalcolithic, showing that the coastland of southern Phoenicia then belonged to the cultural domain of Palestine, not to that of northern Syria.

At the beginning of this section we stressed the fact that the settlements of chalcolithic age are practically all located in river valleys and alluvial plains, where irrigation was possible. Chalcolithic culture may thus be justly called "irrigation culture," since its remarkable development would have been impossible without the powerful impetus given by the

[14] See M. Stekelis, *Les monuments mégalithiques de Palestine* (Paris, 1935), pp. 38 ff.

art of irrigation.[15] The monuments of the latest predynastic and the earliest dynastic Egypt agree entirely with those of Sumerian civilization in emphasizing the vast importance attached to the digging of canals and the building of dams. Thanks to irrigation it was possible to develop the arts of agriculture from their beginnings in the Mesolithic and their budding in the Neolithic of the Near East to their brilliant flowering in the Chalcolithic. By the fourth millennium B.C. wheat, barley, dhurah (a kind of millet), and other cereals were cultivated both in Egypt and in Mesopotamia; such fruit as dates, olives, figs, grapes, etc., were cultivated in different regions of the Near East; the Babylonians grew sesame for oil and the Egyptians grew flax both for oil and for cloth; many garden vegetables were known and used. It is probable that the domestication and development of garden vegetables belong to the most important accomplishments of the irrigation culture, since most of them cannot be cultivated in the Near East without an adequate supply of water. We know that the cultivation of onions and garlic, of lettuce and vegetable marrows, of melons, horse-beans and chick-peas, and of many other kinds of vegetables and condiments, goes back at least to the third and in part certainly to the fourth millennium in Mesopotamia and Egypt. The tremendous increase in the amount and the variety of available food is reflected in the striking rise of median human stature between the Mesolithic and the late Chalcolithic, especially in regions where the irrigation culture was really able to operate properly.

In order to dig canals and build dams, and especially in order to maintain the vital irrigating system after it had been finished, a coordinated state organization was imperatively necessary. Without supervision and compulsory labor the canals silted up, the dams broke, and the increasingly necessary dykes burst. Every unusually high seasonal inundation and every unexpected flood caused by violent rains in the upper watersheds meant wide-spread devastation,

[15] Cf. the writer's discussion, *Ann. Am. Sch. Or. Res.*, VI (1926), pp. 67-74, which is now out of date, but which has been proved strikingly correct in its main contentions.

which had to be repaired immediately lest famine and pestilence ensue. The perennial struggle with the river-floods was much more acute in Babylonia than in Egypt, where the rhythm of inundation is astonishingly regular. These three factors, the digging and dredging of canals, the building and repair of barrages and dykes, and the uninterrupted adjustment of disputes between town and town, between person and person about water-rights, made a stable and authoritative state a prerequisite to the maintenance of life itself. Small wonder that the oldest organized states which we find are in Mesopotamia and Egypt! First groups of villages had to coöperate; then, as longer canals and higher dams were undertaken, groups of district units. The same influence exerted itself in religion. Since it devolved upon the latter to uphold the moral standards of the state, the priests were forced to apply religious sanctions in cases of carelessness or lack of coöperation. The priests may sometimes, as in later periods, have taken over the upkeep of the irrigation system from a state which had demonstrated its weakness. Whatever may have happened in detail, the discoveries at Erech in Babylonia have proved that the temple-complex of Eanna was already before 3000 B.C. the center of an elaborate economic organization, whose records and accounts were kept on clay tablets, individual items frequently rising above 3600 in number (3600 was a round number in the sexagesimal system of the Sumerians). This is the age to which the Sumerian sagas of Gilgamesh and other heroes clearly refer, since he is credited with the construction of the wall of Erech, which according to archaeological investigations was actually first built in the Warkan period. To this general age must also be attributed the first union of Upper and Lower Egypt under one king, as recorded both on the Palermo Stone and in the Manethonian dynastic lists.

3. *The Early and Middle Bronze Ages: Mesopotamia*

The history of Mesopotamia between 3000 and 1600 B.C. may be divided into three main periods: 1. the classical

Sumerian age from the end of the Jemdet Nasr period to the triumph of Sargon of Accad about 2360 B.C.; 2. the Sumero-Accadian age from Sargon to the fall of the Third Dynasty of Ur, cir. 2360-1950 B.C.; 3. the period when Mesopotamia was dominated by Western Semites, from the rise of Isin and Larsa to the fall of the First Dynasty of Babylon (cir. 1530 B.C.). Our chronology follows the official Assyrian dates back to the 15th century B.C. and adjusts Babylonian chronology to them with the aid of the new Mari synchronisms between Assyria, Mari, and Babylonia, as pointed out by Sidney Smith and the writer.[16] There is perhaps a maximum error of fifty years back to about 2400 B.C.; the margin of error is less as we go down. Before 2500 B.C. we can only reckon in centuries, with a maximum error of one to two hundred years at the beginning of the third millennium.

Since 1928 the relative chronology of the classical Sumerian (often called "early dynastic") age has been firmly established by the stratigraphic work of Woolley at Ur, of Jordan, Nöldeke and Heinrich at Erech, and especially of Frankfort at Eshnunna and Khafajeh. This period may now be subdivided into three phases, each represented by adequate monumental data. To the first phase belong several hundred clay tablets from Ur, which have been published (1935) by the late E. Burrows. These are the oldest cuneiform documents which can really be read almost throughout at the present stage of investigation, and they may

---

[16] See Sidney Smith, *Alalakh and Chronology* (London, 1940), especially pp. 1 ff., 26 ff., 48 f.; the writer, *Bull. Am. Sch. Or. Res.*, No. 77, pp. 25-30, No. 78, p. 23, n. 1; A. Ungnad, *Arch. f. Orientf.*, XIII, pp. 145 f. The synchronism between Egypt and Babylonia by way of Byblus and Mari which the writer has pointed out, squares perfectly with the astronomical chronology set up by Smith and Sewell, on the basis of the Venus observations of the Babylonian king Ammisaduqa; Hammurabi would then have reigned 1792-1750 B.C. and the end of the First Dynasty of Babylon would fall about 1595. [Since this was written I have again lowered my chronology by ± 64 years, and the new dates are in the text; see above, p. 10.]

safely be dated about 2800 B.C. The third phase of the classical Sumerian age is very well known, thanks particularly to the famous Royal Tombs of Ur which belong to the early part of it, and to the monuments of Lagash, which illuminate its latter part. To the late second or the early third phase belong also the Shuruppak tablets, about 1000 of which have been discovered by a German expedition at the site of the traditional home of the Babylonian Noah, now called Tell Farah. These documents have been studied and partly published (1922-24) by A. Deimel; they yield extremely valuable information about cultural conditions and religious concepts at about the 26th century B.C. The Royal Tombs of Ur, which are a little later in date, are too well known to require description; their rich and varied contents illustrate both the great wealth of a city like Ur about 2500 B.C. and the primitive barbarity of its customs. Several thousand tablets from the Lagash period, mostly from the end of it in the 24th century B.C., have been discovered and a large part of them have been studied, mainly by A. Deimel and his students. The Lagash documents throw a flood of light on conditions in southern Babylonia at this time, and since nearly all of them are connected with the temple administration, they are of direct interest to the historian of religion. Of particular importance to us is also the group of inscriptions in which the last prince of this line, Urukagina (cir. 2350 B.C.), describes his administrative reforms, many of which relate to the exactions of the priests, who had become increasingly powerful and had finally displaced the civil heads of the state, a generation or two previously.

We now know that there were Semites (Accadians, to use the term applied to them later in Babylonia) in Mesopotamia long before Sargon of Accad. Kings with Semitic names appear in the Sumerian lists as reigning at Kish in northern Babylonia in three of the four pre-Sargonic dynasties of Kish, and Semitic names occur sporadically in the Shuruppak (Farah) tablets. Sumerian documents of the Lagash period already have Semitic loan-words. Moreover, at Mari on the Middle Euphrates we find a Semitic dynasty reigning about 2500 B.C., a century or two before Sargon of Accad. Since there do not appear to be any signs of profound Semitic influence on Sumerian language or culture, while the reverse is certain, and since many of the oldest names of towns and rivers in different parts of Mesopotamia are demonstrably Sumerian, whereas not one appears to be Semitic, we may be sure that the Semites did not precede the Sumerians there. It is probable that the Sumerians created the irrigation culture of chalcolithic Mesopotamia while the Semites were still in a semi-nomadic state. We shall point out below that the true nomadism of Arab camel-herds was impossible before the domestication of the camel in the late second millennium B.C.; earlier nomads were ass-herds, with vastly restricted scope of movement. However, the Semites must have begun to infiltrate into sedentary zones long before the end of the fourth millennium, and northern Babylonia was already dominantly Semitic before the time of Sargon, as we know from the fact that his predecessor, the Sumerian king Lugalzaggisi, had some of his inscriptions written in Accadian after his conquest of Kish.[17]

The Semitic Dynasty of Accad (cir. 2360-2180 B.C.) created an empire in the true sense for the first recorded time in history, though Sumerian tradition credits much earlier rulers with extensive conquests. Sargon and his successors, especially Rimush, Manishtusu, and Naram-Sin, ruled over a state which included the whole of Mesopotamia and intermittently extended its sway over Syria and Susiana (Elam), besides sending expeditions to southeastern Arabia and Asia Minor, if not farther. Until very recently, our knowledge of this dynasty was mainly derived from late sagas and from copies of its Semitic royal inscriptions made in later times for the use of the temple-schools, but we are now in a much more favorable position, thanks to discoveries at Nineveh, at Nuzi, and at Tell Ibraq, all in northern

[17] On the total absence of any evidence for serious racial hostility between Sumerians and Semites in early Babylonia see the excellent discussion by Th. Jacobsen, *Jour. Am. Or. Soc.*, LIX (1939), pp. 485-95.

Mesopotamia. The kings of Accad actually ruled northern Mesopotamia; business documents of the period, written in Accadian, are known from Chagar Bazar, Tell Ibraq, and Nuzi; Manishtusu built a temple of Ishtar at Nineveh and Naram-Sin built a great palace for himself at Tell Ibraq. In view of this new material we are no longer justified in denying the essential historicity of the epic called "The King of Battle" (*shar tamkhari*), according to which Sargon was persuaded by Accadian merchants trading in Asia Minor to invade that distant country.[18] As might be expected, there was also a remarkable artistic revival, which transformed and modernized the heavy Sumerian art of the Lagash period, long since standardized and unable to make further progress. Sargonic art, as shown by the triumphal stela of Naram-Sin from Susa and the bronze helmet from Nineveh,[19] as well as by superb examples of seal engraving, was not appreciably behind contemporary art in Egypt. However, while the Pyramid Age endured for nearly 400 years, the flowering of Sargonic culture hardly lasted more than a century. Long after the end of the Dynasty of Accad, its glories were remembered in saga both by the Accadians themselves and by the Hurrians and Hittites of the north.[20]

The empire of Accad crashed under the blows of Gutian barbarians from the Zagros Mountains (cir. 2180 B.C.) and Babylonia sank into a brief dark age, from which few records have survived. We know that Sumerian culture revived in the south, thanks to temporary freedom from Accadian overlordship, and a Sumerian renaissance began. Culturally this Sumerian revival was under the sign of Accad and its art was unmistakably influenced by the art of Accad. It has left us our most important document of Sumerian religion, the long inscriptions of Gudea, viceroy of Lagash under the Third Dynasty of Ur (cir. 2000 B.C.). This renascent Sumerian tradition was able to impose itself

[18] See Chap. I, n. 45.
[19] Now published in *Iraq*, III, pp. 104 ff.
[20] See Forrer, *Geschichtliche Texte aus Boghaz-köi* (1926), pp. 25* ff., and especially Güterbock, *Zeits. f. Assyr.*, XLIV (1938), pp. 45-83.

on the new Sumero-Accadian empire which was founded by Zur-Nammu of Ur and lasted over a century (the Third Dynasty of Ur, cir. 2060-1950 B.C.). The "kings of Sumer and Accad," as they called themselves in their official titulary, ruled over nearly as large a territory as the kings of Accad, but we seldom hear of wars—virtually never in the royal inscriptions. From this time on the old practice of both Sumerian and Accadian princes is altered and peace reigns undisturbed in later inscriptions of Babylonian kings, whatever the actual situation may have been. Only in the north of Mesopotamia was the Accadian tradition of celebrating martial exploits continued; in the south it remained "bad form" for nearly two millennia. The Sumerian renaissance which is documented by the inscriptions of Gudea continued through the Third Dynasty of Ur, but it is increasingly clear that the two linguistic groups lived together in harmony, while Semitic Accadian slowly, but irresistibly, gained ground as the language of the people. By the 18th century B.C. Hammurabi could speak of it as the language of the country and Sumerian seems no longer to have been actually used for personal names after his reign, though several kings of the following Dynasty of the Sea Lands took Sumerian throne-names in the 16th century B.C. The five hundred years from 2100 to 1600 were exceedingly active intellectually, and the material which has come into our hands from them, largely through the excavations of the University of Pennsylvania in the precincts of the temple of Ellil at Nippur, is of extraordinary importance.

The empire of Sumer and Accad collapsed in its turn, weakened by the obstinate encroachments of the nomadic Western Semites, who were called "Amorites" (that is, "Westerners") by the Babylonians.[21] The death-blow was

[21] The older literature on the Amorite question, including Clay's *Amurru* (1909) and *The Empire of the Amorites* (1919), is so completely out of date that it cannot be used at all. The new material from Mari now enables us to see the scattered data previously known in their true perspective. For general accounts, with full reference to the publications of Dossin, Jean, Thureau-Dangin, and others since 1935 see the writer's sketches in *Bull. Am. Sch. Or. Res.*, Nos. 67, 69, 77, and 78.

dealt by two former provinces of the empire, Elam and
Mari. According to Sumerian letters from the closing years
of the dynasty, Amorite mercenaries played a considerable
rôle in these wars, probably on all sides. The heritage of
the Third Dynasty of Ur was taken over by numerous
smaller states, the most important of which were Isin,
founded by the Accadian governor of Mari, and Larsa,
headed by an Amorite. Between 2100 and 1800 B.C. nearly
all these states passed under Amorite rule: Mari itself became Amorite in the course of the 20th century; Eshnunna
passed under Amorite domination a little later; Babylon became the center of an Amorite state about 1830; Assur, the
capital of Assyria, was occupied by an Amorite chieftain
about 1750. In Babylonia and Assyria proper, however, the
native Accadians continued to form the majority of the population and neither the Babylonian nor the Assyrian dialect
of later times shows any appreciable Amorite influence. The
Amorites were able to replace the Accadians only in northwestern Mesopotamia, from the frontiers of Babylonia up
the Euphrates to south of Carchemish, and eastward to the
Khabur basin, as we know from the new Mari documents,
discovered in 1935-38. North of Mons Masius and east of
the Tigris the population was dominantly Hurrian.

The Hurrians (biblical Horites) have only been known
to scholars for the past twenty years and most of our information about them is less than ten years old.[22] Since
they played a rôle in ancient Near-Eastern cultural history
fully as great as that of the Hittites and almost equal to
that of the Canaanites, a brief sketch of their history in the
light of our present knowledge is in order. Physically they
were prevailingly Armenoids of the brachycephalic type
still dominant among the Armenians; linguistically they
were certainly related to the Urartians of Iron-Age Armenia
and perhaps connected with the Caucasic peoples of later
times, such as the Georgians and Mingrelians. Their home-

---

[22] For accounts of the present state of our knowledge, with
bibliography, see especially the literature cited in Chap. I, nn.
13 & 14, as well as the convenient account by J. Friedrich, *Ex
Oriente Lux, Jaarbericht* No. 6 (Leiden, 1939), pp. 90 ff.

land was thus almost certainly the region south of the Caucasus, and they first appear in history about 2400 B.C. in the Zagros region. After the Gutian triumph over the last kings of Accad the Hurrians seem to have swarmed down from the Kurdish mountains into northern Mesopotamia, especially the East-Tigris country. Hurrian names were common even in southern Mesopotamia during the Third Dynasty of Ur and they continue to be fairly numerous under the First Dynasty of Babylon. Most interesting is the recent discovery of a number of fragmentary Hurrian tablets at Mari, where they must antedate the 18th century B.C. One of them contains an incantation against toothache (as known from the Accadian label). To this early phase of Hurrian literature (cir. 2400-1800 B.C.) belong some of the Hurrian religious texts found at the ancient Hittite capital of Khattusas (Boghazköy) in Asia Minor, as well as the lost Hurrian originals of several mythological texts which had been translated into Hittite. This we know from the fact that the gods are prevailingly Old Hurrian and from the status of Urkish, which appears in them as the chief Hurrian religious center, whereas we know from the inscription of Arishen that it was the capital of an important Hurrian state soon after the fall of Accad, about the 22nd century B.C. It is not yet clear whether the intensive Hurrian settlement of the East-Tigris country which we find in the 15th century B.C. goes back to this age or not, but it is already practically certain that the Hurrian occupation of Syria and parts of Palestine in the 15th century is the result of the Hyksos movement and does not in general antedate the 17th century. The Hurrians adopted the principal gods, heroes, and myths of the Sumero-Accadians, which they combined with their own, producing a most extraordinary syncretism. It was mainly through Hurrian mediation that Sumero-Accadian culture reached the Hittites and other Anatolian peoples.

A bright light is shed on the ethnic composition and culture of Northern Mesopotamia and Asia Minor about 1900 B.C. by the Cappadocian tablets, which consist of several thousand business documents and letters, written in Old As-

syrian and forming part of the commerical archives of the
Assyrian merchant colony at Kanish, modern Kültepe in
eastern Asia Minor. These documents have been intensively
studied by J. Lewy, thanks to whose work we can follow
the commercial and legal transactions of the Accadian colonists in Cappadocia and their relations with the native
"Hittite" population in great detail. The texts show that this
colony was, like scores of others, established in eastern Asia
Minor in the 20th century B.C. by a dynasty of Accadian
princes of Assur which rose to power after the fall of the
empire of Ur, cir. 1950 B.C., and lasted until displaced by
an Amorite chieftain (see above), about 1800 B.C. This
brief Assyrian commercial expansion was rendered possible
by the fact that the Amorite nomads had cut the old commercial route from Babylonia up the Euphrates by way of
Mari and Ibla and that the Assyrians had succeeded in developing a new one up the Tigris through Hurrian territory.

The 18th century B.C. is now one of the best known ages
of antiquity, thanks to the thousands of Babylonian documents from the time of Hammurabi (cir. 1728-1686) and
his immediate successors which have hitherto been published and to the discovery at Mari since 1935 of over 20,-
000 tablets, nearly all belonging to the latter half of the century. MM. Dossin, Jean, Thureau-Dangin, and others have
already described these documents so fully and accurately
that we can use them for historical purposes. Mari seems
then to have been the most important state in Western Asia,
whose power extended up the Euphrates from the frontier
of Babylonia proper to south of Carchemish, a distance of
over 300 miles in a straight line. The palace of its king
Zimri-Lim was one of the show-places of the world, as we
are expressly told in one of the letters; it was found by A.
Parrot to cover more than fifteen acres. In the palace were
mural paintings whose discovery has already revolutionized our idea of the development of Near-Eastern art in
the early second millennium B.C. Some 5000 of the tablets
are letters to the king from high officials and district officers
of Mari, as well as from scores of other Mesopotamian and
Syrian princes. The state of administrative efficiency was

remarkably high, as we see from the detailed instructions given and asked, and from the care paid to the irrigation system on which the prosperity of the land depended. How closely details were watched and what full records were kept appears, e. g., from two enormous tablets, each of which contains nearly a thousand names of craftsmen belonging to different guilds. Owing to the acute rivalry between the Amorite princes of Mesopotamia and Syria, as well as to the constant pressure of still unsettled nomadic groups of Amorite, Aramaean, or Hebrew origin, great attention was paid to defense and to public security. An elaborate system of fire signals, by which news might be flashed for hundreds of miles in a few hours, was maintained. The personal names of the people of Mari were nearly all Amorite, with a small proportion of Accadian and Hurrian names, and the tablets, though written in Accadian, are full of Amorite words, expressions, and grammatical peculiarities. Mari thus represents, as exactly as could possibly be expected, the result of the adoption of Accadian culture by a nomadic West-Semitic folk, speaking a tongue which must have been virtually identical with the ancestral Hebrew of the Patriarchs, as we shall see. The culture of northwestern Mesopotamia, the region around Harran, which often figures in these documents, was a mixture of Hurrian and Amorite elements, on a Sumero-Accadian foundation. The Cappadocian tablets, the Mari documents, the Code and archives of Hammurabi, and the Nuzi tablets of the 15th century B.C. are all important in defining and illustrating its various aspects.

With the victory of Hammurabi over Larsa, Eshnunna, and Mari, the ascendancy of Babylon began. The empire founded by Hammurabi covered about the same territory as had that of the Third Dynasty of Ur, and it lasted over a century and a half (cir. 1700-1550 B.C.), though with reduced territory; it was finally destroyed by a long-distance raid from Asia Minor, mentioned in both the Hittite and the Babylonian chronicles. Owing to the fact that the reigning dynasty was itself of Amorite origin and was solicitous to maintain its suzerainty over the west and northwest, as we know from several royal inscriptions, it was able to exert a disproportionate influence in the west. Babylon, which had been an insignificant town in previous centuries, suddenly rose to be the administrative and commercial center of a rich empire. Its buildings, now below the water-table of the Euphrates, must have been even more impressive than those of Mari, and its temple-tower, Etemenanki, "the House of the Foundation Platform of Heaven and Earth," was already one of the wonders of the world. In an Ugaritic saga of the fifteenth century King Pabel (for *Babel*) appears as a legendary figure of the past and in Hebrew tradition the Tower of Babel appears as the center from which men had dispersed to the four quarters of the earth. How completely it was destroyed by the Hittite king Mursilis, about 1530 B.C., appears from the fact that it lay in ruins for generations and that the earliest occupation levels found by the German excavators directly above the houses of the First Dynasty dated from about the 14th century B.C.

4. *The Early and Middle Bronze Ages: Egypt*

Egyptian history from about 3000 to the 18th century B.C. may be conveniently divided into four periods: 1. the Proto-dynastic (Thinite) Age, from the beginning of the First Dynasty to the end of the Second; 2. the Pyramid Age, covering the four Memphite dynasties from the Third to the Sixth; 3. the First Intermediate Age, from the late Sixth to the late Eleventh Dynasty; 4. the Middle Empire, from the late Eleventh to the Thirteenth Dynasty. Absolute chronology is fixed to within a decade back to about 2000 B.C., thanks to Borchardt's discoveries of datings of astronomical events in terms of the "vague" calendar and of a detailed genealogy of Memphite priests going back to the Eleventh Dynasty. The chronology of the third millennium is far from being settled in detail. However, careful examination of the Palermo Stone and its recently discovered Cairene fragment, as well as critical study of the famous Turin Papyrus (belonging to the 13th century B.C.) in the light of this stone and of contemporary datings and biographies of officials, makes it certain that all systems based on the Manethonian lists are much too high. Even the Turin Papyrus offers totals and regnal years which are often demonstrably excessive. Since Scharff's criticism of the Meyer-Breasted chronology in 1926 scholars have increasingly dated the accession of Menes, founder of the First Dynasty, about 3000 B.C. The latest possible date for Menes is about 2800 B.C.; we may safely adopt a tentative date about a half-century earlier.[23]

The close of the Predynastic Age and the beginning of the Thinite period witnessed a sudden burst of progress in the arts of civilization. This seems to have been connected in some way with an increase of cultural influence from Asia, since there are numerous exact parallels between Mesopotamian and Egyptian culture at this time, the former being demonstrably older and more original in nearly every instance.[24] This influence did not apparently affect language, script, or religious life; but it did bring new artistic motives, new artifacts such as the cylinder seal, and new industrial techniques. Since there is no evidence of an invasion of Egypt at that time by Asiatics, as has been rashly assumed, it is probable that this influence was brought into the land by the Egyptians themselves, who may already have established some kind of ascendancy over Palestine and Phoenicia, just as in the latter part of the First Dy-

[23] The most recent discussion of early Egyptian chronology by Scharff in the *Historische Zeitschrift,* CLXI (1939), pp. 3-32, covers the ground adequately from the Egyptian point of view. Farina's renewed study of the Turin Papyrus has demonstrated that Eduard Meyer was wrong in reading the length of the Eleventh Dynasty as 242 years (*Die ältere Chronologie Babyloniens, Assyriens und Ägyptens* [1925], pp. 63 ff.). The writer has become more and more convinced of the correctness of his estimate of the length of the period covered by the first eleven dynasties, which he published provisionally in *Ann. Am. Sch. Or. Res.,* VI (1926), pp. 72 f., according to which Menes would fall between 3000 and 2800 and may most safely be dated cir. 2850. [This is now held by many German scholars.]

[24] See especially the articles by Scharff cited in Chap. I, n. 35.

nasty. The wealth of the state under the first Thinite kings is vividly illustrated by successive tomb discoveries, especially those made by Emery at Saqqarah since 1936. While the order of kings is not absolutely certain, the work of Sethe and Reisner has practically demonstrated that the Horus kings Aha, Nar-mer, and Djer must be identified with Menes, Athothis I, and Athothis II of the later lists, respectively.[25] The first two completed the union of Upper and Lower Egypt by force of arms; the third king already invaded Asia, as recorded in the Cairo fragment of the Palermo Stone. In subsequent reigns we find increasing evidence of close relation with Asia; Usaphais claims to have smitten the Easterners; Semempses has left a triumphal representation carved on the rock above the copper-workings of Sinai; from the tombs of the latter kings of the dynasty come Syrian pottery and an ivory carving of an Asiatic Semite. In the Second Dynasty relations became still closer; its last ruler, Nebka (Horus Khasekhemwey),[26] sent votive offerings to Byblus, and he was presumably not the first pharaoh to do so. Byblus and Ai have yielded numerous Egyptian objects of the proto-dynastic period, showing that there was relatively considerable trade between Egypt and Syria-Palestine at that time. Since no temples of the age have been discovered and inscriptions are without exception very brief and stereotyped, we have little information about Egyptian religion. What we have comes mostly from the Palermo Stone, confirmed and illustrated by contemporary sources.

With the Memphite Third Dynasty commences the Pyramid Age (cir. 2600-2200 B.C.). It opens in a blaze of glory, since the founder, king Djoser, and his chief minister, Imhotep (Imuthes), have immortalized themselves by the constructions which the latter built for his master at Saqqarah. The step-pyramid of Djoser is the oldest of the pyr-

[25] This order has been demonstrated by G. A. Reisner, *Tomb Development* (1935), pp. 9 ff.

[26] On the basis of the writer's unpublished study of the Palermo Stone (cf. n. 23 above) the identity of Pharaoh Nebka with Horus Khasekhemwey appears to be certain.

amids and the beautiful mortuary temple at its foot (discovered in 1924 and since then excavated) is the oldest building of hewn stone known in the world. Imuthes became one of the heroes of Egyptian saga and was ultimately deified, but his historicity, long doubted by Egyptologists, has been effectually confirmed by an inscription found in the temple which he built. A generation after Djoser's death came Snefru, founder of the Fourth Dynasty (cir. 2550-2450 B.C.). The triumphs of architecture and of art which we associate with his successors Cheops, Chephren, and Mycerinus are known to all, especially since Reisner's excavations in the mortuary temple of Mycerinus. Egypt was then an absolute monarchy, in which the deified king was served by an army of officials and functionaries of various kinds. The entire power and wealth of the state were organized for the purpose of carrying out the tremendous building operations of each reign, culminating in the great pyramid of the pharaoh, which had to be finished in less than twenty years. What this meant may be realized when we recall that the Great Pyramid of Cheops contains over two million blocks of limestone, each averaging over two tons in weight—and yet the geometrical accuracy of the construction and the skill with which the limestone casing was finished still arouse the admiration of the ablest engineers. The most remarkable thing about the pyramids is, however, that we should have almost no knowledge whatever of the early history of the Egyptians if it were not for their faith in a glorious after-life for their kings!

Monumentally, the Fifth and Sixth Dynasties (cir. 2450-2200 B.C.) appear as pale reflections of the glories of the Fourth. Historically they are very much better known, since temples, tombs, and other remains are much more abundant and inscriptions are much more numerous and detailed. Egypt remained a wealthy and powerful country, and the abnormal concentration on building which had characterized the preceding dynasty was abandoned for healthier diversity of effort. The centralization of power in the hands of the king and his chief ministers was also replaced by a great increase of district autonomy under local nomarchs, whose semi-feudal office was generally transmitted by heredity. The Egyptian empire in Asia was maintained: Byblus, the emporium of the cedar trade, became virtually an Egyptian colony, to judge from the quantity of votive offerings sent to its temple by kings of these dynasties; campaigns in Palestine or Syria are described by their military commanders, one of whom gives us a list of captured towns with Canaanite names. The Fifth Dynasty continued to show great interest in the after-life of its pharaohs, who were descended from a priestly family and built superb temples to the sun-god at Abusir in Middle Egypt. The pyramid of Onnos, the last king of the dynasty, inaugurates a custom which was happily continued in the Sixth Dynasty: the walls of the interior chambers were covered with carefully carved and painted magical spells and hymns, all to be used by the spirit of the defunct king as he ascended to heaven to be united with the sun-god. These Pyramid Texts will hold our attention later, since they date from between 2400 and 2200 B.C. and are thus not only among the longest but also the oldest religious texts known; important additions to their contents have been made by recent discoveries. As we shall see they contain many texts which must go back to the Predynastic Age, and it is very unlikely that the corpus as a whole had been changed appreciably by oral transmission after the Thinite period, several centuries earlier. This impression of antiquity is confirmed by their archaic grammar and vocabulary, as well as by the predominantly phonetic writing, used to prevent the hieroglyphs from being read with wrong words and grammatical forms. Thanks to the admirable edition of them begun in 1908 by K. Sethe and still in progress since his death, they are now accessible to scholars generally.

In the course of the 23rd century B.C. (according to our minimal chronology) the power of the pharaohs was so reduced by the internal weakness of the state that several nomarchs were able to make themselves entirely independent of the throne. After the long reign (some 90 years) of Phiops II and the ephemeral ones of his successors, the unity of the state was entirely destroyed and for over a century rival Theban and Heracleopolitan kings contended for the supremacy. The union of the nation was not reëstablished until the reign of the Theban king Mentu-hotpe III, about the middle of the 21st century or a little later. During this dark age, known as the First Intermediate, little is known about the history of the land, and we are restricted mainly to the inscriptions of the local nomarchs for such information as we possess. Civil war was intermittent; the maintenance of public order was hardly even attempted; Asiatic invasions devastated parts of Lower Egypt. According to the careful analysis of literary texts from this period by J. Pirenne (1937),[27] it appears that the leading cities of the Delta made themselves independent of the state and set up local councils, like some of the Phoenician cities in later times. Under such conditions the irrigation works of Memphite times must have suffered great damage and the agricultural yield must have been greatly reduced. It is small wonder that the literary texts of the age, preserved in papyrus rolls of later centuries, exhibit profound pessimism, and begin to reflect in generalized terms on the place and worth of man in the scheme of things (see the detailed discussion below)!

The Middle Empire is much better known then preceding periods, though little information about external relations was available until Sethe's publication of the first execration texts in 1926 and the discovery of hundreds of additional ones in 1938. From these documents, supplementing what was already known, it is certain that the kings of Egypt controlled an extensive African and Asiatic empire, extending from south of the Second Cataract of the Nile to northern Phoenicia. The execration texts mention many towns and tribes of Palestine, southern Syria and northern Transjordan. Gold and spices came from Nubia; copper was mined in the Eastern Desert and Sinai; trade with Asia was extensive. For nearly three hundred years, from the reunion of Egypt in the 21st century to the breakdown of central authority in the 18th, Egypt was united and enjoyed an unprecedentedly high degree of prosperity.

[27] *Journal des Savants*, 1937, pp. 12-17.

For over two centuries of the Twelfth Dynasty (cir. 2000-1800 B.C.) successive pharaohs named Amenemmes or Sesostris, reigning an average of nearly thirty years apiece and connected by regencies with predecessors and successors, maintained peace and order in the land. Moreover, the kings did not exhaust the forces of their subjects in building great structures for their own glory, and the most impressive public works of which we know were concerned with the drainage and development of the Faiyum and the construction of a defensive wall across the Isthmus of Suez, in order to keep Semitic raiders out of Egypt. We cannot be surprised, therefore, to find that literature flourished as it never had before and never did again, and that mathematics, medicine, and other disciplines then reached the climax of their development in Egypt. The gradual breakdown of central power came in the Thirteenth Dynasty, which was brought to an end after about 1750 by successive waves of Asiatic invaders, whom the Egyptians called "Hyksos."

5. *The Early and Middle Bronze Ages: Palestine,*
Syria, Asia Minor

We have devoted what may have seemed disproportionate space to tracing the history of early Mesopotamia and Egypt in broad lines. Since Mesopotamia and Egypt were the foci of ancient Near-Eastern civilization and since recent discoveries have antiquated all existing handbooks, this has been necessary in order to provide the historical background for our main theme. The lands between them and adjoining them on the north need not be surveyed in such detail, but since recent discoveries have even more completely antiquated what is said about them in the latest handbooks, we shall devote ourselves mainly to correcting widespread misapprehensions about their culture and ethnic status between 3000 and 1600 B.C.

The cultural chronology of Palestine and southern Syria in the Early and Middle Bronze Ages has been practically settled by the archaeological work of the last ten years and has now been systematized by G. E. Wright (1937).[28] The Early Bronze may be divided into four phases which together lasted a thousand years, from before 3000 to about 2100 B.C. The cultural climax of this millennium was in its second quarter, as illustrated by the extensive ruins of the city of Beth-yeraḥ ("House of the Moon") at the southern end of the Sea of Galilee and by contemporary strata at Beth-shan and Megiddo. There is ample evidence now to show that the population of Palestine and southern Phoenicia was already Canaanite, i. e., that the spoken tongue was the "mother" or "aunt" of the South Canaanite of the Late Bronze Age, a millennium later. Canaanite civilization in the Early Bronze undoubtedly reached a high degree of development, illustrated by the fact that it employed its own system of writing, a syllabic script obviously patterned externally on Egyptian, to judge from recent discoveries of M. Dunand at Byblus.[29] The mythological poems of Ugarit may well go back in part to Old Canaanite prototypes of the Early Bronze.

The extent of Egyptian influence is vividly illustrated by recent discoveries at Byblus in Phoenicia and at Ai in central Palestine. After the middle of the third millennium occupation spread into southern Transjordan. About the 22nd century B.C., or even a little earlier, we find a break in the continuity of occupation; fewer and fewer towns were inhabited and such centers as Ai were destroyed and abandoned. This progressive depopulation of the country reached its extreme point about 2000 B.C., after which date the curve of occupation rises even more rapidly than it fell, except in southern Transjordan, where sedentary life ceased almost entirely for many centuries (cir. 19th-13th centuries B.C.).[30] This situation shows such remarkable synchronization with what we now know about the course of the Am-

[28] See n. 11, above.
[29] Cf. Chap. I, n. 25.
[30] Cf. the writer's observations, *Jour. Pal. Or. Soc.*, XV (1935), pp. 219 ff. and Glueck, *Ann. Am. Sch. Or. Res.*, XVIII-XIX (1939), p. 268 (where his latest summing-up of the results of his explorations is given).

orite movement in Mesopotamia (see above, p. 152) that it is difficult to separate it from the latter. That the two movements actually belong together is shown by the fact that the numerous personal names from Palestine and southern Syria which are found in the execration texts already published and which will be multiplied several times by those now in the course of publication, nearly all belong to precisely the same linguistic and onomastic type as the Amorite names in contemporary cuneiform texts from Mesopotamia and Syria. In the entire fertile crescent nomadic pressure seems to have reached its height in the period between 2200 and 2000, when it also penetrated into Egypt. From about 2000 B.C. on the nomads seem to have become more interested in settling down than in making fresh raids, so sedentary occupation began to expand, and with it the arts of civilization.

In this connection it is important to define the nature of "Amorite" nomadism at this time. As we have intimated above, the type of nomadic life then known in Western Asia was essentially different from the nomadism of true Arab Bedu during most of the past 3000 years. The latter is very well known to us from the pre-Islamic Arab poets and especially from the detailed accounts of men like Doughty and Musil, describing the life of the Bedu in the half-century before the First World War (since which conditions of life in Arabia have been radically changed). Arab nomadism is conditioned by the domestication of the camel, which makes it possible for Bedu to live entirely on their herds of camels, drinking their milk, eating camel curds and camel flesh, wandering through regions where only the camel can subsist and making rapid journeys of several days, if need be, through waterless deserts. The Assyrian accounts of campaigns in Arabia in the seventh century B.C. give an admirable idea of what the camel meant to the Arabs of that time. We do not know exactly when the camel was domesticated, though it is quite certain that wild camels were common in North Africa and Arabia in very early times. The camel first appears in cuneiform inscriptions and monumental representations about the eleventh century B.C. (inscription of the Broken Obelisk and earliest orthostates of Tell Halaf, biblical Gozan). From that time on it appears more and more frequently in cuneiform documents. It is interesting to note that the great irruption of camel-riding Midianites into Palestine also took place about 1100 B.C. or a little later.[31] Camels are never mentioned in Egyptian texts and they seldom appear in pictorial representations of historical times; camel bones do not appear ever to have been identified in Bronze-Age deposits in Palestine. In short, the effective domestication of the camel cannot antedate the outgoing Bronze Age, though partial and sporadic domestication *may* go back several centuries earlier. It is very significant that no mention of the camel has yet been reported from Middle-Bronze Mari, though it is situated on the edge of the Syrian Desert. It is interesting to note that the Amorites of the 18th century B.C. sacrificed the ass where the pagan Arabs of Byzantine times sacrificed the camel.

So far as their mode of life was concerned, the nomadic Amorites of about 2000 B.C. could not have been far removed from the modern Sleib of the Syrian Desert, except that the former were not travelling tinkers like the latter.[32] Their outward appearance may be reconstructed without difficulty from the mural paintings of Beni Hasan, which portray a nomadic chieftain named Absha with his clansmen and their families, 37 in all, about 1900 B.C. Asses are used for transportation. Both men and women are dressed in elaborately woven, many-colored woolen tunics; the men wear sandals and the women shoes. The men are armed with composite bows, heavy throw-sticks, and javelins. One of them carries an eight-stringed lyre. This tableau shows that we must not picture the Amorite nomads as too primitive, though they were doubtless wild and savage enough from the standpoint of the Egyptians and Accadians. In 1924 E. Chiera published an exceedingly interesting Su-

---

[31] See *Bull. Am. Sch. Or. Res.*, No. 78 (1940), pp. 8 f.
[32] On the Sleib see especially the monograph of W. Pieper in *Le Monde Orientale* (Uppsala), XVII (1923), pp. 1-75.

merian hymn to the god of the West, in which the following is said of the Amorites of the western hills:

> The weapon is (his) companion . . .
> Who knows no submission,
> Who eats uncooked flesh,
> Who has no house in his life-time,
> Who does not bury his dead companion.[33]

This is naturally a somewhat extreme description, but it
vividly illustrates the attitude of the sedentary folk of Babylonia at an undetermined period in the third millennium.
It may be added that the Arab peasants of Syria still call
the nomads *el-wuhûsh* "the wild beasts."

If we compare the nomadic Amorites with the true Bedu
of a generation ago, we shall thus find fundamental differences, because of the use of asses instead of camels for transport and the total lack of horses for swift movement. The
nomadic Amorites were dependent on pasturage for their
herds of cattle, sheep, goats, and asses and, apart from their
herds, on hunting game and raiding crops for food. They
could not, therefore, live in any part of the true desert except in the late winter and early spring. The rest of the year
they were obliged to live either in oases, on the outskirts of
zones of sedentary occupation, or in the hill-country of Palestine, Syria, and Mesopotamia. They could not make
dashes or long forced journeys without racing camels or
horses, and had to travel and attack on foot, depending on
ambush and darkness instead of on swift and unexpected
raids. In view of these facts, the difference in culture (as
distinct from mode of life) between settled Semites and the
nomadic Semites who lived cheek by jowl with them cannot have been appreciable, and the boundary between full
nomad and half-nomad must have been very much less apparent than among the Arabs today.

Turning to northern Syria and eastern Asia Minor, we
pass from Semitic territory to regions which have nearly
always been non-Semitic. The ethnic situation in Asia
Minor about 1900 B.C. is fairly clear, owing to the evi-

[33] *Sumerian Religious Texts*, pp. 20 f.

dence of the Cappadocian tablets (see above, p. 153) and especially of the later Hittite archives at Khattusas (Boghazköy). Eastern Asia Minor was still largely peopled by members of a linguistic stock known to themselves as the *Khatti* (Hittites), but termed by scholars "Proto-Hittites" in order to distinguish them from the later Hittites, whose official language was an Indo-European tongue which they themselves called *Nasi* or *Nesi*. The Nasians seem also to have settled in Cappadocia before 2000 B.C., but we do not yet know how long they had been in Asia Minor. Their language was related to that of another early Indo-European people known to the Hittites as *Luwi*. The Luwians occupied most of southern Asia Minor, entering probably not later than the early third millennium, if we may judge from the evidence of place-names; in the 18th century B.C. we find a Luwian dynasty ruling as far east as Carchemish on the Euphrates. The fact that a single linguistic group occupied the entire south of the peninsula was obviously of great importance for the diffusion of cultural elements from east to west, as well as from west to east after the flowering of Middle Minoan civilization in Crete about the 20th century B.C.

In the same general age the native states of Asia Minor first come into the scope of written history, thanks to the Cappadocian tablets and to the Hittite archives, sources from which we learn a good deal about their wars. It was not until the 17th century, however, that the Old Empire was established by the Hittites; its founder, Labarnas, gave his name to his successors as a royal title.[34] The progress of Hittite arms was rapid. Labarnas' son, Khattusilis, conquered most of eastern Asia Minor; his grandson, Mursilis, invaded northern Syria, capturing Aleppo, which had been a century and a half earlier the seat of an Amorite prince. Not content with this triumph, Mursilis sent an expeditionary force hundreds of miles farther and destroyed Babylon, putting an end to the First Dynasty (cir. 1550 B.C.). Soon

---

[34] This new low chronology is based on the corresponding reduction of Mesopotamian chronology in general, for which see above, n. 16.

afterwards the Hittite power declined, the nobles became occupied with palace intrigues and civil wars, and presently the Old Hittite Empire vanished from history.

B. The Religious Life of the Early and Middle Bronze Ages

Without succumbing to the temptation to enter into an elaborate discussion of comparative religion, we must first survey the situation in the field of primitive religion in order to see what light falls on the ancient Near East from this side. For pertinent questions of general method we may refer to Chapters I and II.

1. *The Nature and Evolution of Primitive Religion*

Thanks to the labors of many eminent ethnologists and historians of religion, we can see much more clearly in the difficult field of primitive religion than was possible even a decade ago. Certain conclusions emerge with high probability from their collections and their analyses, and certain general postulates justify themselves so consistently that we may accept them as binding. Recent progress has been mainly in two directions, in systematizing and clarifying our ideas of "primitive" and "savage" mentality, and in demonstrating the antiquity and the diffusion of belief in "high" gods. The first we owe largely to R. Lévy-Bruhl, whose two great books, *Les fonctions mentales dans les sociétés inférieures* (1910) and especially *La mentalité primitive* (1922), have crystallized opinion and have been increasingly influential during the past decade.[34a] Gathering a mass of ethnological data and analyzing it with the skill and experience of a trained psychologist, he has reached very important results, though many feel that he has somewhat exaggerated the difference between the thinking processes of "primitive" and "civilized" man— rather by neglecting to analyze the "primitive" thought-processes of unsophisticated modern man than by fail-

---

[34a] See the latest discussion of the problem by S. Hofstra, *Nieuw Theologisch Tijdschrift*, XXVIII (1939), pp. 331-62.

ing to understand those of the true savage. Lévy-Bruhl stresses the prelogical character of primitive thought, which fails to take account of contradictions, lacks any clear concept of causal relations, for which it substitutes simple explanation by sequence, or superficial concomitance, or accidental resemblance. Fundamental to primitive thinking are also impersonality and fluidity. The savage seldom or never thinks of the individual as having a distinct personality; all tends to be merged in collective or corporate personality, or is dissolved in factitious relationships between men, animals, plants, and cosmic or other inanimate objects and forces. There is a primitive power of abstraction which leads to a kind of elementary metaphysics, most characteristic of which is the long recognized idea of impersonal power or force (called "pre-animism" by Marett), which resides in unusual persons, objects, or phenomena, as well as in gods and spirits. This conception survives in early Near-Eastern religion and mythology, and remained dominant for millennia in magic. It is particularly the merit of K. Beth to have repeatedly emphasized the importance of the impersonal power, the *mana, orenda,* and *wakonda* of ethnologists, for the history of ancient Near-Eastern religion, as we shall see below.[35] A. Bertholet has recently coined the happy term "dynamism" to replace Marett's "pre-animism."[36]

[35] See his monograph "El und Neter" (*Zeits. Alttest. Wiss.* [1916], pp. 129-86), vigorously criticized by H. Grapow (*ibid.* [1917], pp. 199-208), to whom Beth replied (*ibid.* [1919], pp. 87-104). There can be no doubt that Beth went too far in his enthusiasm and introduced dynamistic conceptions into many expressions and passages where they do not belong. Grapow's criticism of his Egyptological competence was also quite justified. On the other hand, Grapow showed an amazing dogmatism and inability to see the nature of the problem with which Beth was grappling. In these investigations both philological competence and training in the history of religion and ethnology are needed; cf. the writer's observations about the successful collaboration of the two disciplines in another case (*Jour. Bib. Lit.* [1940], p. 96).

[36] See especially his monographs *Das Dynamistische im Alten Testament* (1926), *Das Wesen der Magie* (1927), *Dynamismus und Personalismus in der Seelenauffassung* (1930).

The second main development in recent study of the history of primitive religion is the recognition of the worship of "high" gods as well as of spirits. These high gods may be all-powerful and they may be credited with creation of the world; they are generally cosmic deities who often, perhaps usually, reside in heaven. These gods are found among savage peoples in all parts of the earth, including Africa, Australia, and South America. To have collected an immense body of data demonstrating the belief in high gods and to have classified pertinent ethnological phenomena as well as conceptions existing with respect to them is the merit of the great Catholic anthropologist, W. Schmidt, in his monumental work, *Der Ursprung der Gottesidee* (1912-36).[37] Fr. Schmidt believes that his data point to a primitive monotheism, which has gradually degenerated, leaving only widely scattered supreme beings and high gods to bear witness to it. He has also worked out an elaborate but subjective system according to which, he believes, primitive monotheism evolved into the various theological patterns found in primitive cultures of today. Among the most influential and independent historians of religion who have been strongly influenced in their views by Schmidt may be mentioned especially R. Pettazzoni and N. Söderblom, the latter of whom is followed by an increasing number of younger scholars, especially in Scandinavia.[38] German students of comparative religion, such as C. Clemen and F. Pfister, generally oppose Schmidt, though they have made many minor concessions to his position.[39] Mediating views are held by such authorities as

[37] For Schmidt's anthropological method see his *Handbuch der Methode der kulturhistorischen Ethnologie* (1937). His views are presented to English readers in *The Origin and Growth of Religion* (1931), *High Gods in North America* (1933), and *Primitive Revelation* (1939).

[38] See Pettazzoni, *Rev. Hist. Rel.*, LXXXVIII (1923), pp. 193-229; *Arch. Rel.*, XXIX (1931), pp. 108-29, 209-43; Söderblom, *Das Werden des Gottesglaubens* (Leipzig, 1916).

[39] See especially Clemen, *Arch. Rel.*, XXVII (1929), pp. 290-333; J. W. Hauer and F. Pfister, *Arch. Rel.*, XXXIII (1936), pp. 152-61. The latest attack on Schmidt's theory

G. van der Leeuw and K. Beth, both of whom emphasize
the dynamistic nature of primitive religion, which had previously found one of its chief exponents in Beth (see
above).[40] It has been particularly interesting to see the
reaction of American anthropologists, nearly all of whom
oppose Schmidt in his main thesis, though accepting many
of his ideas in detail. As a matter of fact, it is often very
difficult to distinguish sharply between dynamism and personalism, where a cosmic deity is concerned.

There can no longer be any doubt that Fr. Schmidt has
successfully disproved the simple evolutionary progression
first set up by the positivist Comte, fetishism—polytheism—
monotheism, or Tylor's animism—polytheism—monotheism.
Nor can Marett's correction to pre-animism (dynamism)
—animism—polytheism—monotheism escape radical modification. The simple fact is that religious phenomena are so
complex in origin and so fluid in nature that over-simplifi-
cation is more misleading in the field of religion than perhaps anywhere else. Moreover, as has been stressed above,
we must not forget the lapse of about 50,000 years since
the first Mousterian burials. During so long a period
many evolutionary tendencies undoubtedly completed their
cycles, returning to stages which were often superficially
like their starting points. Moreover, in Chapter I we have
already stressed the principles of imitation, adaptation,
and skeuomorphism, as a result of whose operation artifacts and institutions can be totally divorced from their primary function when they are borrowed by another people,
or when they continue in use among a given people after
environmental conditions have been radically altered.

Above (pp. 132 ff.) have been mentioned a number of
the principal phenomena of the Stone Age which bear on

---

from the standpoint of the ancient Near East has been made
by Th. J. Meek, *University of Toronto Quarterly*, VIII (1939),
pp. 181 ff. (reprinted in the *Review of Religion* [New York,
1940]).

[40] Van der Leeuw, *Arch. Rel.*, XXIX, pp. 79-107; *De primi-
tieve mensch en de religie* (Groningen, 1937); Beth, *Religion
und Magie bei den Naturvölkern* (Leipzig, 1914), and in the
articles cited above, n. 35.

religion. Thanks to the latest investigations of such men as Baron von Richthofen (1932),[41] F. R. Lehmann (1938)[42] and others, we are now in a good position to distinguish clearly between certain, probable, and doubtful deductions. It is certain that the belief in an after-life has a very long prehistory, going back in some form as far as the Neanderthal men of the Mousterian age. Moreover, this belief developed to an extraordinary degree in the Neolithic, as we know especially from the megalithic monuments of the Old World. Just what physiological and psychological sources it had, we can hardly demonstrate, though we may safely stress various contributory factors, such as empirically discovered sanitary requirements, fear of the spirit of the deceased (whose existence was inferred from dreams), affection for the dead, and general inability to distinguish sharply between dead and living men, so far as the dynamistic operation of their spirits was concerned.

We have also mentioned the evidence from Magdalenian and later ages for dynamistic conceptions. Among the hunters of the latest European Palaeolithic the flowering of imitative-aesthetic powers led to dynamistic practices such as the portrayal of the animals which they hunted, sometimes representing them with missiles sticking in their bodies, and of mimetic dances, where men put on animal masks. In the subsequent Neolithic and Chalcolithic of the Near East, we find plastic models of domesticated animals, phalli, and the like, sometimes in close connection with sanctuaries. The existence of such models can hardly be separated from the fact that the physical basis for existence had in the interim been shifted from hunting to animal husbandry. Since it is sometimes still insisted that small models of animals were already made for children's use as toys, it must be emphasized that the evidence from the early Near East is more and more strongly opposed to this interpretation, so far as the Bronze Age is concerned.[43] By

[41] *Mitt. Anthrop. Ges. Wien*, LXII (1932), pp. 110-44.

[42] *Arch. Rel.*, XXXV (1938), pp. 288-306.

[43] See Mrs. Van Buren, *Clay Figurines of Babylonia and Assyria* (New Haven, 1930), pp. xlviii ff., and the writer's comments *Jour. Am. Or. Soc.*, LI (1931), p. 176.

the Iron Age it is quite certain that many plastic models were only intended as toys and in Egypt we can demonstrate such use still earlier. Children doubtless played just as much in the Stone Age as in the Iron, but their toys remained simple, like those of savages today; the magical possibilities of models made them seem as dangerous for children as electric toys actually are today.

With the discovery of agriculture and animal husbandry in the Mesolithic and Neolithic periods religion became still more complex. The triad of plastic statues from the Neolithic of Jericho suggests that the divine triads of the ancient Near East, usually consisting of father, mother, and son,[44] were already known by the sixth millennium B.C., and that they were already worshipped with the aid of a shrine and rites of some sort. It was in this general age that the mythology and cultic symbolism which we associate with the gods of fertility must have been developed, since we find them full-grown in the early third millennium—though not so crystallized in form as they appear later in the Adonis-Attis-Osiris and similar cycles.

The decorative art of the Chalcolithic is very instructive when compared with Magdalenian and mesolithic art. The imitative-aesthetic capacity of palaeolithic man some 15,000 years ago was already highly evolved, though there is no need to suppose that the heights reached by Cro-Magnon man were equalled anywhere else by his contemporaries. The Natufian man of Palestine, many thousands of years later, was ahead of his Magdalenian precursor so far as art in the round was concerned. But in the chalcolithic cultures of Halaf, Susa, and Ghassul after 4000 B.C.

---

[44] The subject of divine triads in the ancient Near East, particularly Arabia and Syria, has been discussed repeatedly by D. Nielsen, especially in his books *Die altarabische Mondreligion* (1904), *Der dreieinige Gott in religionsgeschichtlicher Beleuchtung* (1922), and in his paper "Die altsemitische Muttergöttin," *Zeits. Deutsch. Morg. Ges.* (1938), pp. 526-51. Owing to Nielsen's strong tendency to over-schematize and to a certain onesidedness in dealing with the material, his work has been only moderately successful and must be used with great caution.

we find an extraordinary development of the imaginative-aesthetic powers of man, resulting in astonishingly complex geometrical designs and fantastic figures of dragons which carry us into the realm of phantasmagoria. It is very doubtful whether man's artistic capabilities are actually any higher today than they were in late prehistoric times, though the number of motifs, techniques, and media available to him now is, of course, immeasurably greater. When we bear in mind also that mythology must have been developed during the Late Palaeolithic, Mesolithic, Neolithic, and Chalcolithic Ages, as shown both by the intrinsic nature of mythology and by its distribution in history and geography, this flowering of man's imaginative powers becomes very significant. We can say with confidence that the amount of mythological lore current in the latest prehistoric age was far greater than the residue which was still known in the ancient Near East about 2000 B.C. Quite aside from all deductive evidence is the fact that a great many myths which are referred to in the Pyramid Texts and the Sumerian literature of the third millennium vanish without leaving any traces in later times. In other words, the same process of selection operated here as in other bodies of material which are orally transmitted.

To work out a chronological scheme for the origin and evolution of mythology is a thankless task and one which can probably never be satisfactorily accomplished in detail. Yet some things are already clear. Studied in the light of their geographical diffusion certain creation-myths and especially the myth of the Great Flood appear as among the oldest religious inheritances of mankind, since they are found among primitive tribes in both continents and as far from the foci of migration as southern South America. As is well known, recent ethnographical, geological, and archaeological research has proved that the prehistoric settlement of the New World proceeded by way of Alaska and was a long process, which began at the end of the Palaeolithic or in the early Mesolithic, and was finished many thousands of years ago, except possibly for the Eskimo migration. The story of the Great Flood must, therefore, go back like other American Indian cultural inheritances to an age preceding the Neolithic of Asia, and possibly antedating the Mesolithic.

Additional light on the antiquity of religious expression and thought is shed by linguistic science. We do not wish to return to the day, over two generations ago, when Max Müller declared that "mythology is a disease of language." However, the importance of linguistics for the history of religion is very great. What we have said about the pre-historic climax of creative mythology is closely paralleled by the facts of language. It is now quite certain that language had developed in prehistoric times to a degree of elaborateness which is seldom or never found among living languages. Thus we know that Proto-Indo-European was more complex in its structure than any of its living descendants, except possibly Lithuanian. We are also learning to-day, since the decipherment of Middle Canaanite and the development of comparative Hamito-Semitic philology, that this was also true of parent Semitic. The same phenomenon appears whenever we compare a living language with a known progenitor; cf. English, French, modern Arabic of any dialect, Hindi, etc. It is certain, for instance, that Sumerian had broken down phonetically to an extraordinary degree by the late third millennium B.C., just as has been shown by B. Karlgren to be true of modern Chinese.

Many of the clichés which have become popular in the past few decades with respect to language are false. It is, for example, not true that primitive man was incapable of abstraction. It is quite true that logical and philosophical abstraction were foreign to him. If we turn again, however, to the ancient Near East and study the situation in the earliest periods which we can reach through inscriptions or by linguistic methods, we find extended power of prelogical abstraction. The earliest known stages of the Egyptian, Sumerian, and Semitic languages show that general qualities, such as "goodness, truth, purity," could be abstracted from the related adjectives and identified as abstractions by some linguistic device such as suffix, prefix, or internal vowel change. Moreover, such formations were known before Egyptian separated from her Semitic sisters, i. e., at least 5000 B.C. Classificatory generalizations, such as "mankind," were equally familiar at just as remote an age. All the "proto-metaphysical" conceptions which are known to the cultural anthropologist from ethnological investigation are found in the earliest Near East. Tabu is represented by the Sumerian *nig-gig* and related conceptions elsewhere; the polar development of "holiness" and "abomination" from the concept of inviolability or untouchability is well attested.[45] The dynamistic power known to ethnologists by the term *mana*, etc., survives in traces and has been shown by Beth to inhere in the term *'el*, which means "god, God, divine power" in Semitic, and perhaps also in Egyptian *ntr* "god."[46] The external soul is represented in Egypt by the *ku'* ("ka").[47] A precursor of the Indo-Iranian *arta* and

[45] The close relation between the ideas of tabu and of holiness was shown in classical form by Robertson Smith, *The Religion of the Semites* (new ed., 1894), pp. 446-54. The best illustration of the interpenetration of these concepts is found in the various meanings of the stem *ḥrm* in Arabic, Aramaic, and Hebrew: Arabic *ḥaram* means "what is tabu," both because it is illicit or because it is particularly sacred; *ḥaram* and *ḥarim* mean also "sacred precincts"; *ḥarâm* means "illicit, improper," even "abominable." In Hebrew the denominative verb *heḥrim* means both "to devote something to destruction as abominable" and "to consecrate something to God as sacred." An excellent illustration is offered by the stem *w'b*, which means "to purify" in Egyptian whereas in Hebrew the derived noun *tô'ebah* means "negative tabu, abomination"; the original sense of the root may be preserved partly in Arabic *wa'aba* "to take (something) entirely," i. e., to have something intact or unsullied (Latin *intactus, integer*).

[46] See above, n. 35.

[47] For the pronunciation *ku'* see the writer's treatment in his book *The Vocalization of the Egyptian Syllabic Orthography* (New Haven, 1934), pp. 26, 61. The best discussion of the nature of the *ku'* from the standpoint of Egyptology is still the paper of Steindorff, *Zeits. Äg. Spr.*, XLVIII (1910), pp. 152-59; the best treatment from the point of view of comparative religion has been given by Van der Leeuw, *ibid.*, LIV (1918), pp. 56-64 (and in *Jour. Eg. Archaeol.*, V, p. 64). For the most recent expert statement see H. Kees, *Kulturgeschichte des Alten Orients: Ägypten* (Munich, 1933), pp. 319 f., where a bibliography of the pertinent literature will also be found.

even of the Platonic idea is found in the Sumerian *gish-khur*, the outline, plan, or pattern of things-which-are-to-be, designed by the gods at the creation of the world and fixed in heaven in order to determine the immutability of their creation.[48] The Sumerians also had substantially the same ideas about fate or destiny (*nam-tar*) which we later find among the Greeks.

Long before the fourth millennium men presumably applied to their religion the habits of thinking which we have described. By 3000 B.C. it is absolutely certain that they had. Using their native powers of abstracting and classifying, they had abstracted the idea of the "divine" from "divine being(s)," and they had associated this "divine" category with all qualities which they knew to be good in social relations. Similarly they had associated the "divine" category with power and with the act of creation. The empirical necessity of a single head for any complex organization had led them to infer a single power behind the complex manifestations of the universe. This power appears in various forms and with various limitations, but in each case a high god is head of the cosmos to his worshippers. So it is with the Egyptian Re‘, properly the sun-god; so it is with the Sumerian An, the god of heaven, at Erech, or En-lil, "lord of the storm," at Nippur and elsewhere; so it is with the contemporary *Dyeus-Patēr* "father sky," of the Indo-Europeans, from whom the daughter peoples derived their *Jupiter*, their *Zeus patēr*, and their *Dyaus pitā*.[49] Each of these high gods is the embodiment of good-

---

[48] See the writer's observations, *Jour. Bib. Lit.*, XXIX, pp. 150 f.; *Jour. Soc. Or. Res.*, VII, p. 79; *Jour. Am. Or. Soc.*, LIV, p. 121, n. 48. A thorough up-to-date study of this Sumero-Accadian conception is very much needed.

[49] For an admirable discussion of this figure and his original rôle as the head of the Indo-European pantheon see M. Nilsson, *Arch. Rel.*, XXXV (1938), pp. 156 ff. It is still uncertain whether the name *Dyeus* is ultimately the same as the common noun *deiwos (deus)* "god." If the words are identical we should have an excellent parallel to Semitic *el* "god," and *El* "head of the divine hierarchy." The root-meaning of the Indo-European words connects them with heaven through the con-

ness and power to his votaries—though we must remember that goodness was limited by its social connotations and that there might be rival aspirants for power.

2. *Egyptian Religion between 3000 and 1600 B.C.*

Just as Mesopotamia is unique in its importance for the history of ancient civilization, so Egypt stands alone in its significance for the study of ancient religion. The relative isolation of the Nile Valley and the conservatism that came from physical uniformity and the stability of institutions, combined to make Egypt the most conservative of countries in its religion. It has well been said that the Egyptians, like newly hatched chicks, carried their egg-shells around on their backs, i. e., they preserved outworn customs and beliefs long after they had become wholly incongruous in their new setting. This peculiarity, which differs rather strikingly from what we find in Mesopotamia, is illustrated in the Pyramid Texts (see above, p. 159); it is still present in the native religion of the Roman age. Our principal source for the earliest religion of dynastic Egypt is the corpus of Pyramid Texts, supplemented by miscellaneous data from a great many inscriptions, mostly of later date but incorporating older material. Thanks to the work of K. Sethe and others we can thread our way through the labyrinth of early Egyptian religion with steadily increasing confidence.

It must be emphasized strongly that all schematizations of the religion of the most ancient Egyptians are misleading.[50] It is clear that nothing quite like the types of totemism known from Australia, Africa, or America had ever existed in Egypt, though it possessed the raw materials out of which some form of totemism might have evolved.

---

cept of "light"; the original meaning of the Semitic word was undoubtedly "strong."

[50] This statement applies even to so careful and penetrating a study as that of K. Sethe, *Urgeschichte und älteste Religion der Ägypter* (Leipzig, 1930), which is a valuable corrective to the fantasies of earlier Egyptologists but goes much too far in correlating the evolution of Egyptian religion with the hypothetical development of Egyptian political organization.

Nearly all the local gods, each of whom was revered in a town or district (from which arose the later system of forty-two nomes) were represented in animal form, as we know from later idols, hieroglyphs, and allusions in Egyptian religious literature. Many of these divinities were believed to be incarnated in some special individual beast, such as the Apis bull which became so well known in later centuries. To many of these animal gods all representatives of their species were sacred, whence arose restrictions in food, of which we hear more and more in late times. But there does not appear to be a trace in early texts of specifically totemistic phenomena such as consanguinity, exogamy, and the like. Moreover, not all gods were specially connected with animals; some were conceived as trees, as human beings, or as inanimate objects, and some might be represented in a number of different ways, often quite contradictory from the standpoint of modern civilized man. It is a mistake to suppose that most, if not all, the Egyptian gods began as local numina, often as totems or fetishes. Before the Egyptians settled down as tillers of the soil in the Nile Valley, more than 7000 years ago, they must already have possessed complex religious beliefs, with high gods and lesser divinities, with elaborate mythologies and cult practices, like most of mankind, ancient and modern, in the neolithic stage of culture. This stage is reflected in Egypt by the fact that a single god may be worshipped at a number of different places, geographically far apart. It is also reflected by the wide diffusion of the cult of such cosmic deities as the sun-god Re', who can hardly have been originally a local god, since his very name means simply "sun, day." A striking characteristic of local Egyptian pantheons is the popularity of triads formed by father, mother, and son (as in neolithic Jericho), many of which were found in different parts of the country. The expansion of the triads to enneads, or groups of three triads, is in certain cases known to be very early, going back into predynastic times.

A remarkable link between primitive and sophisticated religious thought is provided by the so-called "monument of Memphite theology," copied by the Egyptians in later times, but which must go back to proto-dynastic times, as shown by Breasted, Erman, and Sethe.[51] According to this text, Ptah, the head of the Memphite ennead, is the creator and source of its other eight deities. From the union of the second and third of these successively created gods sprang Atum, the chief god of Heliopolis. Atum was the demiurge, through whose creative word everything was created: "and every divine word came into being through that which the heart thought and the tongue commanded"; and further, "when the eyes see and the ears hear and the nose breathes air, they carry (what they have received) to the heart (which decides what to do) and the tongue utters (the commands)." Ptah, moreover, is represented in this text as continuing to create, since whatever the other gods did they did as manifestations of him. "It came to pass that heart and tongue obtained the power over every member (of the body), teaching that (Ptah) was in every breast and in every mouth, of all gods, all men, all beasts, all creeping things, while he (Ptah) thinks and commands whatever he wishes." In this Memphite system from about 3000 B.C. we find primitive dynamism in the form of the creative word, primitive corporative psychology in the conflation of the personalities of the different gods, the conception of the impersonal high god in the figure of Ptah. At the same time there are very definite signs of theological speculation in the treatment of the ennead, in the fact that Ptah is made superior to the Heliopolitan Atum, as well as in numerous details of the text. We shall have occasion to say more later about the dynamistic and creative function of the word in the ancient Orient.

Cruder, but not necessarily more primitive, than the Memphite cosmogony is that of Heliopolis itself. The sungod Atum came into existence[52] in the primordial fresh-

---

[51] For the latest treatment see Breasted, *The Dawn of Conscience* (1933), pp. 29-42, where the most important literature is mentioned.

[52] The abstract terms "to come into existence" and "to cause to come into existence" are common in Egyptian religious literature from the Pyramid Texts on down and there is no

water ocean Nun (Hebrew *tehôm*), before heaven and earth had been created. In the Nun he found no place to stand, until he mounted a hill and ascended (as the sun) on the *bnbn* stone in Heliopolis. Then he found that he was alone and in order to create a companion he masturbated, whereupon he conceived and vomited forth the god Shu (air) and the goddess Tefnet, from whose marital intercourse were born Geb and Nut (earth and heaven), parents of the two pairs Osiris and Isis, Seth and Nephthys.

During the great Pyramid Age more and more attention was focussed on the person of the reigning monarch and on preparations for his future life as a god in heaven or in an elysium beneath the First Cataract of the Nile. This emphasis on the king's future is not surprising when we recall that the Egyptians already paid far more attention, relatively speaking, to their tombs and graves than did any other ancient people of historic times. In this respect they continued and exaggerated the neolithic tradition. Moreover, Pharaoh was the incarnation of the god Reʻ, of the falcon-god Horus (also a solar divinity), and in proto-historic times he became the incarnation of Osiris. Not least, he was head of one of the most absolute monarchies that the world has perhaps ever known—at least this was true in the early Memphite period, down to the end of the Fourth Dynasty. An equivalent royal attention to the hereafter meant, therefore, that the power of the state was concentrated on the building of the royal tomb and mortuary temple. Thanks to the fact that the last kings of the Memphite period inscribed the mortuary ritual of their predecessors on the walls of their tomb-chambers, we have an unequalled body of evidence for their beliefs (see above, p. 159). The standing theme, repeated over and over with innumerable variations, is that the king is not dead but still lives. In logical (but not prelogical) contradiction to the

---

reason to deny them a still greater antiquity. Moreover, it is hardly likely that these concepts possessed even an empirico-logical connotation in the Egyptian mind. In other words, they do not answer the question "how?" or "why?" but simply "what was the first thing to happen?"

solar traits of Pyramid mythology are the Osirian, since Osiris represented the vegetation of the Nile Valley, which dies in the early summer, when dead is submerged under the life-giving Nile inundation, and comes to life again as the inundation subsides. The home of Osiris is in the fresh-water ocean of the underworld, whence the Nile rose at the First Cataract, according to primitive Egyptian concep-tions. Therefore the king not only sets and rises again with Reʿ and Horus, but he also dies and comes to life again with Osiris. At the same time his living spirit emerges from the mouth of the tomb and flies straight to the never-dying (never-setting) circumpolar stars. One spell represents the king as flying to heaven as a heron, as a falcon, as a locust; another one has him climbing a celestial stairway, rising with the fragrance of incense, flying as a bird, riding in the solar bark as a dung-beetle. Cruder primitive ideas are re-called by an extraordinary hymn which exhibits the dead king as a gross cannibal, devouring the limbs of the gods as they are cooked for him in a pot in the northern heavens. In this archaic document the constellation Orion appears as the father of the gods. Countless myths are alluded to, but few are recited in detail, since the Pyramid Texts are not a series of mythological epics but of spells, incantations, and hymns. Through all there breathes the prelogical, dyna-mistic, corporative breath of primitive humanity. From Egyptian religious soil early in the third millennium B.C. might have arisen a Hindu pantheism like that of the pre-philosophical Brahmanas if corporative tendencies had pre-vailed, or a solar monotheism like that of the Aten, if in-dividualizing tendencies had won the victory. The latter ultimately triumphed for a brief interlude, more than a thousand years later, but the time had not yet come in the early third millennium, since primitive modes of thought were too strong and impersonal dynamism had to be effectively replaced by a more systematic and a more per-sonal stage of mentality in dominant circles before a true monotheism could arise.

When the darkness of the First Intermediate Age de-scended upon Egypt in the 22nd century B.C. high culture suffered temporary eclipse, old traditions were neglected, and the ancient customs fell into desuetude. As often again in the recorded history of man, it seemed to thinkers that all worth-while possessions of humanity had been lost in the general catastrophe of civilization, when art, literature, and religion were neglected and men lost interest in everything except their immediate needs and wants. But this rude and untutored age, this stirring and dramatic period of falling princes and rising commoners, of war, terror, and barbarian irruption, provided the needed catharsis through which civilization could be freed from its time-honored, but suffocating inheritance and start afresh. And the fresh start took place on a new plane of mental attainment, following a thousand years of organized and self-conscious historical life. As in contemporary Babylonia we emerge toward the end of the third millennium from a stage where prelogical, dynamistic thought held almost undisputed sway over priests and leaders of men into a stage where the best thought was essentially logical, though still empirical and pre-philosophical. From now on primitive logic and dynamism tended to be restricted increasingly to the realm of magic and folklore, from which they emerged at disconcerting intervals—as they still do—to warn men of the empirico-logical age that they could never quite lose the instinctive reactions of their savage ancestors.

Among the most significant literary documents of antiquity are the didactic and gnomic works of the outgoing Old and the Middle Empire. So far as preserved they begin with the Maxims of Ptah-hotpe, vizier of Izezi (Assa), which were composed not later than the 23rd century B.C., and they continue down to about the 19th century. The Maxims of Ptah-hotpe and another nearly contemporary work are characteristic in diction and attitude of the late Old Empire, where stability was traditional and where shrewd aphorisms and wise counsels were in constant demand on the part of persons ambitious for preferment. These aphorisms are often noble and always worldly: doing right and acting justly are necessary to success and will bring prosperity if combined with prudence. It is very significant that there is no mention of a god by name in Ptah-hotpe. The worldly and a bit cynical teacher may have recognized that gods and divine manifestations of the all-father Re' or Atum or Khnum were alike, so far as man's relation to them might be concerned. "The god" referred to by Ptah-hotpe may, however, always be the "great god" Horus, as Dr. K. C. Seele has suggested to me.

Next among dated works seems to be the Instruction for Merikere, a Heracleopolitan king who reigned about 2100 B.C. This work, whose date is certain, is invaluable for our knowledge of political, social, and religious life in the latter part of the First Intermediate of Egypt. The rules for a successful life remain, of course, approximately the same, but there is a very different spirit in important respects. The disillusionment produced by a long period of anarchy brings with it a loss of faith in the necessary connection between traditional religion and morality, on the one hand, and success, on the other. The god knows everything and punishes his enemies and those who rebel against his commands, at the same time that he rewards his friends and those who obey him. However, "the good conduct of the righteous man is more acceptable than the (sacrificial) ox of the evil-doer," an admonition that reminds one forcibly of the attitude of Isaiah and Jeremiah some fourteen centuries later. In contrast to this is a skeptical attitude toward the recompense of good in this world; divine service becomes rather a means to bring happiness in the next world than an instrument for ensuring immediate satisfaction in this one. Of unusual interest, showing how close to monotheism individual Egyptian thinkers must have come in the late third millennium, are the following words of the text: "One generation gives way to another and (the) god, who knows the natures (of things), conceals himself . . . Honor (the) god in his way, (honor) him who is made of precious stones and formed of copper, just as water takes the place of water. There is no stream that can be hidden; it breaks through the dyke by which it is hidden." These somewhat enigmatic sentences are clarified by the metaphor which closes them. The invisible, unknowable deity, who himself knows everything, acts as continuously as flowing water and as irresistibly as the Nile inundation. Divine cult and adoration of images are necessary, but they must not blind us to the reality behind the barriers of the senses. Here we find, possibly for the first time in our sources, conscious and explicit statement of the fluid concept of dynamism, which had previously been unconscious and implicit. In the process of clarifying the conception by analogy, the Egyptian thinker of 4000 years ago stood on the shifting boundary between dynamism, on the one hand, and pantheism or monotheism, on the other. One is vividly reminded of the part played by the principle of *Tao* in the system of Lao-tze, some fifteen hundred years later. A step in the direction of divine immanence would have led the Egyptian to the semi-pantheism of the apocryphal saying of Jesus from Oxyrhynchus (cir. 200 A.D.): ". . . Lift the stone and there shalt thou find Me; cleave the wood and there am I." A step in the direction of personalizing God might have led him to true monotheism.

To about the same time belong the pessimistic and misanthropic poems known as the Song of the Harper and the Dialogue of a Misanthrope with his Soul, both antedating the rise of the Middle Empire. The Song of the Harper is frankly cynical and hedonistic: the dead, both kings and commoners, rest in their tombs and none ever returns from beyond the grave; the wise man will, therefore, enjoy life to the full, not worrying about the day of death. The Dialogue of a Misanthrope with his Soul has been convincingly elucidated by A. Scharff (1937),[53] who has cleared away a number of ambiguities and uncertainties of previous interpreters. The author of this remarkable poem has well been called by Pieper "the first great poet of world-literature." Briefly stated, the poem contains a colloquy between a man who is so weary of life that he plans to commit suicide and his soul (Egyptian *bi'*), which tries to dissuade him from such a rash step. Alternately, each presents his case, the man painting the misery and suffering on earth and the bliss of life with the gods

[53] *Sitz. Bay. Akad. Wiss., Phil.-hist. Abt.*, 1937:9.

in the other world, and his soul pointing out that the afterlife is a vain hope and that the duty of man is to enjoy life on earth as fully as possible, since there is nothing after it. Finally the man convinces his soul that death is really better than life, whereupon his soul bids him throw himself into the fire in order that he may reach that bliss which the man has portrayed in such glowing colors. In keeping with the exaltation of the poet's spirit is the picture which he draws of life in the other world, where the deceased becomes a "living god" himself, punishing evil-doers, occupying the bark of the sun-god and helping to distribute its good things to earthly temples, engaging in unhindered conversation with Reʿ himself.

The so-called "Admonitions of an Egyptian Sage" also belongs to the First Intermediate period and is intermediate in type between the pessimistic compositions which we have described and the Prophecy of Nefer-rehu, from the Twelfth Dynasty. The sage, Ipu-wer, paints in drastic terms the terrible conditions existing in Egypt, where everything is in confusion, with contempt for and neglect of everything noble and good, accompanied by elevation of the ignoble and bad. After long enumerations of the evil things that have come upon the land during the reign of an aging king (whose name is not mentioned), he tells the latter that a good time will come, when the Egyptians, aided by Negroes and Hamitic tribes of the south, will drive out the Asiatics (evidently referring to the triumph of the Thebans over the north). Much of this important composition is so badly preserved that it is dangerous to make further deductions. Somewhat later is the prophecy of Nefer-rehu, which is extremely interesting as the oldest certain example of a *vaticinium ex eventu*, since it purports to date from the reign of Snefru of the Fourth Dynasty, but describes in some detail events from the reign of Ameni (Amenemmes), the founder of the Twelfth Dynasty, six centuries later. It also begins with a dismal portrayal of conditions before this dynasty, after which it predicts the coming of "a king from the south, named Ameni, the son of a Nubian woman . . . who will receive the crown of Upper Egypt and will assume the crown of Lower Egypt, who will unite the double crown . . ." It goes on to describe the principal events of his reign and to promise a return of justice and prosperity to the country.

Among the most striking results of the feudal age and the social upheaval of the First Intermediate Age is the extension of the future prerogatives of the king to nobles and the well-to-do generally.[54] The Coffin Texts of the Middle Empire contain many incantations and hymns from the Pyramid Texts, which are no longer applied solely to the king. At the same time there are interesting changes. The Osirianizing process which had already set in strongly in the Pyramid Age now tends to dominate the hereafter, though the conflation of the mythology and symbolism of Osiris with those of Re' leads to most incongruous results. The apparent contradiction did not disturb the ordinary Egyptian, who was doubtless equally happy to expect a blissful life with Re' in heaven or with Osiris in the nether world. Like the unthinking man of today, who is often promised just as conflicting things by the demagogue, so the Egyptian felt that the future would in any case be safer if there were more and better assurances. The Coffin Texts show another tendency which makes the increasing incongruity of mortuary theology easier to understand. When compared to the Pyramid Texts on the one hand and the Book of the Dead on the other, we note that they approach the latter more and more closely in reflecting the fears of the common people with respect to the traditional dangers of the journey to Elysium. More and more they become simple magical charms, with all the inner contradiction that magic usually exhibits. The prevailing dynamism of the Pyramid Texts becomes magic before our eyes, and it thus diverges increasingly from the route followed by the evolution of religion.

[54] See Breasted, *op. cit.*, pp. 223 ff., where we find the best and most recent account of this socio-religious revolution, based largely on the Coffin Texts, which are now being edited for the first time by the Oriental Institute of the University of Chicago.

Another and no less interesting result of the social upheaval of the First Intermediate, was a change and development in the ideals of social justice. There has been a
great deal of erroneous emphasis laid on the evolution of
social justice in the ancient world, suggesting that the idea
is comparatively recent, or even that it tended more and
more to replace religion in the proper sense. Actually no
community, primitive or modern, can long exist without a
body of customary law regulating the relations between its
members, or without a spirit of helpfulness and coöperation
which protects the weaker members of the group and
strengthens mutual loyalty. This characteristic of group
life strikes deep root in the animal world and is found
among all vigorous primitive societies of today. In the
Pyramid Age we find both tomb biographies and aphorisms
stressing the virtues of hospitality, kindness to inferiors, and
charity to the poor and helpless. Impartial justice is essential to kings and magistrates. In the First Intermediate and
the following Middle Empire there is an extraordinary increase in the attention paid to social justice, a fact that
again illustrates the profound catharsis which was effected
by the upheavals of the late third millennium in Egypt. As
a striking example of justice, we are referred to the vizier
Achthoes (Kheti), whose name shows that he belongs to
the First Intermediate, not to the Pyramid Age as supposed
by Breasted. Of him it was said in later times that he decided against his own kindred, even when justice was on
their side, in order that he might not be suspected of
partiality. This, later Egyptians consider as "more than justice." Among the many pleas for justice to the poor and
oppressed, none is so impressive as the story of the Eloquent
Peasant, referring to events of the Heracleopolitan period
and probably composed before the end of the First Intermediate Age. Here we read of a peasant who was arbi-
trarily and brutally robbed by an official but who went to
the court and so eloquently pled his case that the king
granted him justice. Both theme and rhetorical style were
so popular that the work was copied and recopied in later
times.

The foregoing pages have shown how religion and thought evolved in Egypt during a period of over a millennium. This evolution began in the age of dynamism and carried religion forward into a stage where it seemed to be on the point of developing into pantheism or into monotheism, but where polytheism and magic were still dominant among the masses. By the early second millennium both theology and ethics were being studied and expounded. Such branches of knowledge as mathematics,[55] surveying, and medicine were being logically formulated and systematized. The prelogical age was coming to a close.

3. *Mesopotamian Religion between 3000 and 1600 B.C.*

The history of early Mesopotamia was so disturbed and its cultural evolution was so complex when compared to Egypt that its religious development is neither so clear nor so instructive as that of the latter. The religion of the Sumerians was already much farther advanced on the whole than that of the Egyptians at the beginning of our period, and it remained in some respects more primitive at its end. Sumero-Accadian polytheism was much more clear-cut and consistent than was contemporary Egyptian and the dynamistic plane of thought was more sharply restricted to the domain of magic. The development of magic was also far advanced, and its association with embryonic science was so intimate as to make it virtually impossible to make a clear separation between them.

When we compare the politico-religious organization of Babylonia at the beginning of the third millennium with

[55] For the most recent light on the progress attained by Egyptian mathematics in the Middle Empire see S. Gandz, *Proc. Am. Acad. Jew. Res.*, IX (1939), pp. 13 f., on a remarkable text from the nineteenth century B.C. The great Rhind Papyrus was written in the seventeenth century but was copied, according to its colophon, from an original of the nineteenth century. On Egyptian mathematics, with full references to the work of Peet, Struve, and Neugebauer since 1920, see Kees, *op. cit.* (1933), pp. 291 ff.

that of proto-dynastic Egypt, a pronounced difference immediately appears. Whereas Egypt was broken up into dozens of districts, arranged end to end down the Nile, Babylonia was divided into a relatively small number of city-states, distributed not only along the two rivers but also located between them, thanks to several connecting water-courses. The country as a whole was, therefore, more compact and there was much less cultural and religious particularism. The gods worshipped in one place were generally also recognized in adjacent towns, and recur in the pantheons of towns in other parts of the country. At first blush, the total number of gods is alarming. The lists from Shuruppak (Tell Farah) in central Babylonia, copied about 2600 B.C., name over 700 gods and we have no assurance that we possess all of the lists. The vastly less complete material from the 29th or 28th century at Ur in southern Babylonia yields over forty names of deities.[56] Throughout Babylonia the Sumerians seem to have agreed on placing An (literally "heaven," originally "high") at the head of the pantheon with En-lil ("lord of the storm") next to him. In the archaic tablets from Erech, dating from before 3000 B.C. (see above, p. 141) we find, of course, the names of An and his consort Inanna (literally "mistress of heaven"), who were already the chief deities of the city, as they remained for over 3000 years, down to the abandonment of the site in Parthian times. In the slightly later tablets from Jemdet Nasr in northern Babylonia En-lil frequently appears. In Lagash, about 2400 B.C., a triumphal inscription of Entemena calls En-lil, "king of the lands (*kur* "foreign country," not *kalam* "land of Babylonia"), father of the gods," and calls Nin-girsu, the chief god of Lagash, "warrior of En-lil." From the earliest historical times En-lil's cult center, Nippur in central Babylonia, was regarded as a neutral, sacred city, which was never a dynastic center and to which votive offerings were sent from

---

[56] On this material see also Meek, *University of Toronto Quarterly*, VIII (1939), pp. 187 f. The Ur data, which Meek does not mention, were published by E. Burrows in his *Archaic Texts* (Philadelphia, 1935), pp. 19 ff.

different parts of the country. In later times the Babylonians were to identify Marduk, chief god of Babylon, with En-lil and still later the Assyrians were to equate him with their national deity, Assur. In fact the name became synonymous with *bêlu* "lord" (Canaanite *ba'al*).

Illustrations of the stability and relative homogeneity of the Sumerian pantheon may be multiplied with ease. The principal members of the divine hierarchy had their places already marked out almost as rigidly in early Sumerian times, as we know from the lists of Shuruppak and the inscriptions of Lagash, as they were in the early second millennium, from which date the great lists of gods, which remained canonical down to the end of Babylonian history. In this respect the early Babylonian pantheon reminds one strikingly of the Greek, with En-lil playing the rôle of Zeus and, like him, being considered as the father of gods and men and as ruler of the whole earth. Of course, in practice there was at least as much variation in function, genealogy, and mythology of the gods as there was in classical Greece. Yet it can hardly be denied that Babylonia and Greece came the closest of any known countries to setting up an organized polytheistic system. The influence of the Babylonian system upon the neighboring lands of Western Asia was very great, as we shall see.

When we turn to unilingual Sumerian religious texts from the late third millennium, chiefly from Nippur, we find that a large number of the divine names of the lists were simply liturgical appellations and that their bearers were not considered in general as distinct deities. This is very well illustrated in the Uttu myth, published in 1915 by S. H. Langdon, but not understood until more recently. Here the relations of the god En-ki ("lord of the earth" or "lord of the underworld") with a whole series of goddesses are described in such a way that the identity of the latter is certain. The names are fortunately all common and all transparent: Nin-sikilla is "the Lady of the Pure . . ."; Nin-tud is "the Lady who Gives Birth"; Damgal-nunna is "the Great Spouse of the Prince"; Nin-ghursag is "the Lady of the Mountain"; Nin-kurra is "the Lady of the Highland."

Other illustrations are provided in great numbers by the liturgies. This phenomenon certainly points to increasing syncretism and to a monolatrous tendency, where the worshipper concentrated his adoration on a single deity, with whom he identified all other gods of the same type, but S. H. Langdon was hardly justified in considering it as a close approach to monotheism.[57]

Tribal or national henotheism (on which see Chapter IV) does not seem to appear in any cuneiform religious sources from our age (3000-1600 B.C.). On the contrary, the cosmic gods of Mesopotamia were naïvely and unquestioningly believed to rule the entire world, each in his own designated sphere or function. The following excerpt from a Sumerian text extant in a copy of about the nineteenth century B.C. well illustrates the prevailing attitude, as it is expressed or taken for granted in thousands of documents:

> Unto En-lil do foreign lands raise their eyes
> (in adoration),
> Unto En-lil do foreign lands pay homage.
> The Four Quarters (of the earth) bloom like
> a garden for En-lil.

It would be hard to find more forcible statement of the universality of En-lil's dominion in a document of the empirico-logical age.[58]

Whereas in early Egypt, as we have seen, nearly all the gods are definitely associated with special animals or plants, there is hardly a single clear case in Sumerian Babylonia. To be sure, there are abundant signs of an older stage in which the boundary between animals, men, and gods was fluid: for example, there are a few gods who bear the name of an animal, such as Gud, the bull-god, Shaghan,

---

[57] Against Langdon's arguments see the trenchant observations of Meek, *ibid.*, pp. 186-89.

[58] See Langdon, *Oxford Editions of Cuneiform Inscriptions*, I (1923), p. 50. Langdon's translation of line 4 is grammatically impossible; the writer's changes follow the rules stated by A. Poebel, *Sumerische Grammatik* (1923), §§ 147, 626, and p. 302.

the serpent-god; there are numerous hymns in which a god is compared to some animal or animals, but they are generally clear similes, as when Nin-gizzida is addressed as a bull and a dragon in successive lines. Sumerian deities are nearly always anthropomorphic. On the other hand, where in Egypt there is generally a clear demarcation between the sexes of the gods (except in a few androgynous deities such as Hapi, the Nile), among the Sumerians the sex of the divinity is often a matter of secondary importance and a number of deities are alternately or simultaneously male and female. This is particularly true, as we shall see, of deities in the Tammuz cycle, but even the moon-god is addressed in successive lines of a very early hymn as "mighty young bull . . . with lapis-lazuli beard . . . fruit which begets itself . . . womb which bears everything." The cult of Tammuz undoubtedly goes back to the earliest Sumerian times, like the parallel cult of Osiris in Egypt. His full name was in Sumerian *Dumu-zid-abzu*, "the Faithful Son of the Subterranean (fresh-water) Ocean," but he is also called in late Sumerian liturgies *Nin-azu*, "Lord of Healing," *Sataran* (the serpent-goddess), *Ama-ushumgalanna*, "the Mother Python of Heaven," etc., etc. The father of Tammuz was named *Nin-gizzida*, "the Lord of the Faithful Tree," and his mother was called *Zertur*, apparently meaning "young maiden," or perhaps "virgin."[59] The Tammuz liturgies are nearly all composed in a late dialectic form of Sumerian which was spoken in northern Babylonia in the second half of the third millennium B.C. They deal at great length with the rape of Tammuz from his sister and wife, Geshtin-anna (literally, "Vine of Heaven") or Ninanna, later Inanna or Ninni (literally, "Mistress of Heaven"), identified with the Accadian Ishtar. Tammuz was carried away into the underworld and all life on earth —human, animal, and plant—languished and died. However, his sister penetrated into the nether world and succeeded in recovering him, after being imprisoned three

[59] See *Am. Jour. Sem. Lang.*, XXXVI (1920), p. 262. Unfortunately, no new evidence has become available during the past twenty years.

days and three nights.[60] There is a very interesting alternation in Babylonian mythological consciousness between the summer heat and the spring inundation as the cause of Tammuz' death; the inundation also brings him to life again. As a child he was said to lie in a sunken boat and as he grew he lay in the submerged grain; as a youth the flood carried him down into the subterranean ocean, whence he was later transported to heaven. We lack space to dwell on the cycle of Tammuz and to point out its many points of contact with other cycles of the dying god of fertility in the Near East, nor is it necessary, since excellent spade-work has been accomplished by Frazer, Baudissin, Langdon, and others.[61] Since these cycles must strike root into the Neolithic Age as far as animal husbandry is concerned and into the Chalcolithic in so far as they are connected with vegetation-spirits and the inundation, we can hardly be surprised to find kaleidoscopic variation in detail, together with an astonishing amount of similarity in general, between the Sumero-Accadian, Anatolian, Canaanite, and Egyptian myths of this type. It is also clear that conceptions which were originally associated with many different rites and deities have gradually been grouped around certain gods in each cultural region: Tammuz in Mesopotamia, Osiris in Egypt, Adonis in Syria and the later Hellenistic world, Attis in Asia Minor. This tendency of

---

[60] For the duration of the imprisonment of Inanna in the nether world see the new Sumerian text from Nippur published by S. Kramer in *Bull. Am. Sch. Or. Res.*, No. 79 (1940).

[61] Langdon's *Tammuz and Ishtar* (Oxford, 1914), though inaccurate in detail and now antiquated in many respects, remains the best account of the cult of Tammuz and related figures in Babylonia. Progress in the interpretation of the difficult dialectic Sumerian hymns and dirges belonging to the Tammuz cycle has not been very rapid, in spite of the efforts of Witzel and Frank; it is to be hoped that Poebel and his pupils will soon attack this important body of material. The writer's point of view, though slightly antiquated in detail, has not been appreciably modified since he wrote "The Goddess of Life and Wisdom" (*Am. Jour. Sem. Lang.*, XXXVI, pp. 258-94); cf. also *Jour. Bib. Lit.*, XXXVII, pp. 111 ff. and *Jour. Am. Or. Soc.*, XL, pp. 307-35.

myths to cluster around selected figures is clearly due to the dramatic quality of the cycles in question, which tended to spread and to oust or to absorb all rivals.

Before leaving the subject of Sumerian religion, it may be well to discuss a subject which will occupy us later and which has generally been misunderstood—the supposed Babylonian *logos*. Jensen, Langdon, and others have insisted on the high development of an alleged system of metaphysics in early Babylonia. We have already pointed out (p. 176) that one aspect of this "metaphysics," the *gish-khur* conception, belongs to the domain of primitive dynamistic thought, though it may be considered as a precursor of the Platonic idea. The second aspect is that of the *enem,* or "word," translated into Accadian as *awatu* "word." This *enem* is nearly always represented as the voice of the god En-lil, "lord of the storm," which sweeps destructively over cities and fields, over beasts and men. However, since *enem* is written with the same ideogram as *gu* "voice, thunder," it obviously meant primarily just that, as is established by its frequent alternation in the liturgies with *ud* "storm," defined as *enem Ud-gu-de* "the voice of the divine Thunderstorm."[62] There is a striking parallel (published in 1938) in slightly later Canaanite mythology, where Baal, the storm-god, creates the thunderbolt (*baraqu*) in order that men may hear his word or command (*hawatu* = Accadian *awatu*).[63] However, it is clear that the dynamistic conception of "creative word" is an essential part of the idea: thunder is the means by which the all-father makes his creative commands known to men. Sumerian *enem* is thus the most important ultimate source of the New Testament conception of the *logos,* as has justly been pointed out by the distinguished Catholic

---

[62] See the passage in Witzel's *Tammuzliturgien und Verwandtes* (Rome, 1935), p. 156, lines 6-7, where we have in succession "the 'word' of (the god) Storm which Gives Voice" and "the 'word' of (the god) Storm whose Voice Roars."

[63] *Bull. Am. Sch. Or. Res.,* No. 70 (1938), pp. 19 f.; cf. A. Bea, *Biblica* 1939, p. 447. Virolleaud's rendering of Canaanite *hwt* as "Verbe" (= *logos*) is impossible.

scholar, the late L. Dürr, in a recent work (1938).[64] The significant shift of idea must have taken place before the Semites translated *enem* by *awatu,* and before the Sumerians themselves extended the concept to Enzu, the moongod, and other gods who had nothing directly to do with the storm.

In general it is hard to point out elements in the composite Babylonian religion of about 2000 B.C. which are of Semitic, rather than of Sumerian origin. To be sure, many names of gods, such as *Ishtar, Shamash* (the sun-god), etc., are Semitic, but their appellations and myths are nearly always of demonstrably Sumerian origin, and the same is increasingly true of their rituals. The infiltration of the Accadians seems to have been too slow and the superiority of Sumerian culture too marked to permit any vital contribution—other than that of fresh and vigorous blood— from the Semitic side. It is, of course, easy to point out differences between the Sumerian religious literature of the third millennium and the Accadian literature written in the so-called hymnal-epic dialect, which seems to have been spoken in northern Babylonia in the second half of the third millennium, but we can never be sure whether these differences are attributable to a difference of race or simply to a new cultural age. At all events, it is certain that the Accadians borrowed Sumerian mythological cycles, such as that of Gilgamesh, Lugal-banda, the Creation and Deluge, the Descent of Ishtar, Agushaya, etc., and transformed them into real epics, with a dramatic movement quite foreign to the long-winded, liturgical compositions of the earlier Sumerians (some of which continued to be copied down to the end of the third millennium and in a few cases much later).

The union, stability, and prosperity brought to Babylonia by Hammurabi about 1700 B.C. made it possible for scholars to devote themselves to learned pursuits with a

[64] *Die Wertung des göttlichen Wortes* . . . (*Mitt. Vord.-aeg. Ges.,* XLII:1 [1938]). For minor differences between our points of view and a discussion of them see the writer's forthcoming review of Dürr's book in *Jour. Bib. Lit.*

singlemindedness and a continuity heretofore unknown. The following two centuries saw an extraordinary development of empirical scientific and scholarly interest, as is illustrated by many works on philology, lexicography, astronomy, mathematics, and numerous branches of magic and divination which were composed at that time, frequently in a form which remained canonical throughout later Mesopotamian history. While the Babylonians of this age did not equal their Egyptian contemporaries in their literary and rhetorical sophistication or in their knowledge of practical engineering and medicine, they surpassed them notably in less useful, but more intellectual pursuits. For example, they developed mathematics to the stage of being able to solve quadratic equations by the method of false position, employing a technique which was in some respects identical with that of the Greek algebraist Diophantus in the third century A.D.[65] In astronomy they produced the great canonical list of stars and constellations and interested themselves in the movements of the planets, as we know from the Venus tables and other sources.[66] They arranged cuneiform signs, Sumerian and Accadian words and grammatical forms in great lists and dictionaries which remained standard down to the latest times. They prepared elaborate compendia of various branches of divination and magic, such as prediction by omens of every conceivable kind (including astrology, hepatoscopy, lecanomancy, etc., etc.), and such as exorcism of evil spirits by incantatory rites. In theology the great list of the gods which was prepared by these early scholars also remained canonical. In short, they showed such taste and talent for collecting and systematizing all recognized knowledge that Mesopotamian learning nearly stagnated for a thousand years thereafter. Since the principles employed by these Babylonian

[65] See especially F. Thureau-Dangin, *Textes mathématiques babyloniens* (Leiden, 1938), pp. xix-xl, and his papers in *Rev. d'Assyr.*, XXXIV and XXXV; cf. also Neugebauer and Sachs, *Mathematical Cuneiform Texts* (New Haven, 1945).

[66] Cf. especially S. Langdon and J. K. Fotheringham, *The Venus Tablets of Ammizaduga* (London, 1928).

scholars were no longer prelogical, but were essentially logical, even though their logic was empirical and not analytical, the vast system produced by them exercised an extraordinary influence on succeeding generations, not only in Mesopotamia but also in the whole of Western Asia. Balaam, for example, was essentially a typical Mesopotamian diviner, as pointed out by S. Daiches.[67]

Sumero-Accadian morality and ethics were fundamentally much the same as Egyptian. Good and evil were recognized as individually and socially effective. The gods, especially the sun-god, are generally credited with higher standards than men. Urukagina of Lagash, in the 24th century B.C., undertook to reform the official corruption of his day and to check the oppression of the poor, thus reëstablishing the "righteous laws of Nin-girsu," which had been violated by evil-doers. Beginning with the Third Dynasty of Ur we find references to royal legislation, according to the "just laws of the sun-god." The lofty standards attained by this legislation may be inferred from the last codification which it received, the Code of Hammurabi, (cir. 1700 B.C.) which was, as we know now, only the continuation of a series of Sumerian codes with the same formulation and point of view.

The Babylonians had become so accustomed to change and civil disorder in the centuries from Sargon of Accad to Hammurabi, that we nowhere find the burst of disillusionment and misanthropy characteristic of Egypt after the 22nd century B.C. That stage was to come much later in Mesopotamia. The nearest approach to it in this period is the interest in various forms of primitivism, both chronological and cultural: in the former type we find emphasis laid on a more blissful life in hoary antiquity and in the latter we encounter a curious interest in a simpler way of contemporary life.[68] The former is best illustrated in the

---

[67] *Hilprecht Anniversary Volume* (Leipzig, 1909), pp. 60-70.

[68] See the writer's treatment of primitivism in early Babylonia in Lovejoy and Boas, *A Documentary History of Primitivism* (Baltimore, 1935), pp. 423 ff.

myths of antediluvian times, including the Uttu poem; the
second is remarkably developed in the Old-Babylonian recension of the Gilgamesh Epic. Babylonian thought became strongly centered on this world, owing to the lack of
any expectation of a joyous life in the next, such as was
created in Egypt by the extension of royal rights and prerogatives to commoners. More sophisticated thinkers, inclined to pessimism, stressed the impossibility of obtaining
eternal life. This idea is vividly expressed in the Accadian
Gilgamesh Epic, which in this respect seems to offer a striking contrast to the older and more primitive Sumerian version. After the death of the erstwhile wild man, Engidu,
who has meanwhile become his bosom friend, Gilgamesh
is overtaken by a morbid fear of death, which drives him
to strange adventures and unparalleled hardships in his
search for immortality—a search which is almost but not
quite successful. In this epic the gloomy future of man and
the hero's fear of death are portrayed in strong colors, and
a somewhat hedonistic way of life is inculcated. Thanks,
however, to the very fact that their concept of future life
was negatively conditioned, the Babylonians were driven in
later centuries to a much more profound consideration of
the problem of divine justice and human suffering than we
ever find in Egypt. In Babylonia after 2000 B.C. we also
find a pervasive idea of order and system in the universe,
resulting in large part from the tremendous effort devoted
to the systematization of knowledge and especially of divination (knowledge of the future), which surpasses anything found in Egypt.

Chapter IV

WHEN ISRAEL WAS A CHILD . . .

(Hosea 11:1)

In our analytical sketch of cultural and religious life in the Near East we have now reached the stage at which the historical memories of Israel begin to assume tangible form. According to the traditions preserved in the Priestly Document, Abraham left Mesopotamia on his way to Palestine some 645 years before the Israelites left Egypt, that is, in the late 20th century B.C. according to the most probable date of the Exodus. Unfortunately, there is no reliable test of the correctness of these chronological traditions, since they have no precise link with extra-biblical history. If we accept the probable hypothesis of some connection between the Hebrew entrance into Egypt and the Hyksos movement, and add three or four generations, we arrive at a date somewhere between 1900 and 1750 B.C. for Abraham's migration. The Patriarchal Age of Hebrew history would then fall somewhere in the latter part of the Middle Bronze Age in Palestine and during the late Middle Empire and the Hyksos period in Egypt. We shall see that this interpretation of Israelite tradition fits exceedingly well into the framework of external history.

A. THE ANCIENT ORIENTAL BACKGROUND OF ISRAELITE ORIGINS

After some twelve or thirteen centuries of practically continuous historical records in both Egypt and Babylonia, there is a virtually complete interruption in the contemporary records of Egypt and the lands of the Fertile Crescent. Thanks to the Mari documents we can now fix the approximate date of events in Mesopotamian history during the second millennium, with a maximum error of a generation or so.[1] The calendaric and astronomical researches of L. Borchardt have settled the chronology of Egypt after about 2000 B.C., with a maximum error of not over about seven years in the Middle Empire and almost complete precision in the New Empire.[2] In the past few years the discoveries of Borchardt and Farina have also fixed the approximate chronology of the Hyksos Age.[3] Contemporary Egyptian inscriptions almost vanish after about 1730 B.C. and do not resume their normal flow until about 1580; Babylonian inscriptions fail us entirely after the fall of Babylon (cir. 1530) and are almost completely lacking until after 1400 B.C.; Assyrian records cease about 1720 and do not begin again until after 1500 B.C. There are hardly any contemporary Hittite inscriptions of the Old Empire, but even later copies of early documents in the archives of Khattusas break off about 1480 and contemporary inscriptions do not begin until after 1400 B.C. In short, it is certain that there was a catastrophic interruption of the normal flow of ancient history. From later historical tradition and from a comparison of conditions before the blank period with conditions after it, combined with stratigraphic data and a few cuneiform texts from 1700-1500 in Syria, we are not badly off.

[1] See Chap. III, n. 16.
[2] Shortly before his death Borchardt collected all his results in his work, *Die Mittel zur zeitlichen Festlegung von Punkten der ägyptischen Geschichte und ihre Anwendung* (Cairo, 1935). For his most recent papers in the *Zeits. Äg. Spr.* see *Bull. Am. Sch. Or. Res.*, No. 58, p. 17, n. 24, and No. 68, p. 24, n. 8.
[3] Cf. G. Farina, *Il Papiro dei Re* (Rome, 1938) and the writer's remarks, *Haverford Symposium* (1938), pp. 44 f.

1. The Political and Cultural Background, 1600-1200 B.C.

In Egypt the strong Twelfth Dynasty was followed by a period of virtual anarchy, during which several groups or families of kings successively obtained the upper hand, all for ephemeral reigns. After about 1750 B.C. native Egyptian royal inscriptions cease almost entirely. Then comes a very obscure phase in which princes with West-Semitic (Amorite or Hebrew) names appear on scarabs. This phase was followed by the Fifteenth Dynasty, which consisted of Semitic invaders from Syria.[4] Thanks to G. Farina's reconstitution of the Turin Papyrus (1938) we know that it consisted of six kings and lasted 108 years (according to the best recension of Manetho it lasted 260 years!). The principal rulers of the Fifteenth Dynasty, Apophis I and Khayana, flourished in the 17th century; in the second half of the century the latter built up an ephemeral empire, the extent of which may be guessed by monuments of his which have turned up in places as far removed as Babylonia and Crete. The Fifteenth Dynasty was followed by a short but weak dynasty of foreign origin, under which the native Theban princes of Upper Egypt revolted, waging persistent war against the foreigners until their capital, Avaris (later called Tanis) in the northeastern Delta, was captured by Amosis I about 1560 B.C.[5] In later times the Egyptians applied the term *Hyksos*, literally "princes of the shepherds," to them, but this designation is probably a mistake for a

[4] For the relative chronology of this period see the writer's discussion, *Jour. Pal. Or. Soc.*, XV (1935), pp. 222 ff., especially p. 227. The discoveries at Mari, Alalakh, and Ugarit have now made it certain, contrary to previous indications, that the Hyksos royal names are either entirely or dominantly Northwest-Semitic, i. e., Canaanite or Amorite—probably the former. This question will be fully treated elsewhere in the near future.

[5] For the chronology of the reign of Amosis I cf. *Bull. Am. Sch. Or. Res.*, No. 68, p. 22, n. 2. On Avaris = Tanis see now H. Junker, *Zeits. Äg. Spr.*, LXXV, pp. 83 ff.

phrase with nearly identical pronunciation, meaning "foreign chiefs, chiefs of a foreign country," applied to Palestinian and Syrian chiefs and princes in the literature of the Middle Empire.

As a result of the Hyksos conquest of Egypt the Egyptian social and political organization was transformed and hardly any traces of the native feudalism of the Middle Empire remained. Military organization was entirely changed by the introduction of horse-drawn chariots and composite bows, and thenceforth both the Egyptian chariotry and bowmen became famous. A great many Canaanite (Hebrew) words entered Egypt during the Hyksos period and the following age, and with them came Canaanite deities and Asiatic wares and arts. Most significant of all is the fact that the Egyptians lost much of their old supercilious attitude to their Asiatic possessions, an attitude which was equally characteristic of both the Old and the Middle Empire. Thereafter they celebrated their Asiatic victories and the extent of their territory on every possible occasion. The pharaohs entered into active diplomatic correspondence with the kings and princes of Asia, presumably following a Hyksos precedent. To judge from the apparent total absence of letters from Egypt in the Mari correspondence of the 18th century B.C. such condescension had been unknown before.

Turning to Mesopotamia we find a much more complete interruption of normal life than in Egypt. Before the fall of Babylon about 1540 B.C., northern Babylonia was conquered by barbarian mountaineers from the southern Zagros mountains, called the *Kashshu*, or Cossaeans, who gradually extended their sway over all southern Mesopotamia and ruled for some 450 years.[6] The country was transformed into a feudal state of strongly military character; the warlike Cossaean nobles were little interested in literature and learning, which seem to have survived mainly in the south. It was not until the early 14th century that business returned to its old contractual basis, though with

[6] For the duration of the Third Dynasty of Babylon see the writer's observations, *Bull. Am. Sch. Or. Res.*, No. 77, p. 28.

sweeping changes in custom and practice. Assyria continued under native princes, but after cir. 1710 B.C. the empire of Shamshi-Adad shrank to an insignificant district and
we hear nothing more about its political history for over
three centuries, though the list of kings is preserved. It
would seem that the onslaught of northern barbarians,
about which we hear occasionally in Babylonia after Hammurabi, finally overwhelmed Assyria and the other Mesopotamian states, both Amorite and Hurrian.[7]

In northern Mesopotamia, when the Dark Age finally
came to a close about 1500 B.C., we find that there was a
powerful kingdom called Mitanni which controlled the
north from the Mediterranean to the Zagros—and this kingdom was ruled by a dynasty of kings with characteristic
Indo-Iranian names. Moreover, the royal gods were the
well-known Vedic deities Mithra, Indra, Varuna, and the
Nasatyas, and the national sport was chariot-racing, with
Indo-Iranian technical terms. There was an aristocracy of
chariot-warriors, called by the Vedic term *marya(nni)*, literally, "youth, young warrior(s)."[8] Extraordinary attention was paid to the horse, as we know from a Mitannian
treatise on horse-training which was translated into Hittite
about the 14th century B.C., and it must have fared much
better than the average peasant of the age. Sir Leonard
Woolley's discoveries at Alalakh (Tell 'Atshanah) in northern Syria since 1937 have yielded new historical data, carrying back the origin of the Mitannian state to before 1500
B.C. and giving valuable new information about conditions
in Syria a century before the Amarna Age. Schaeffer's excavations at Ugarit on the coast and du Mesnil's work at
Qatna (el-Mishrifeh), near Hamath on the Orontes, have
contributed very extensive additional data of historical im-
port, so that we now have an excellent idea of the state of
culture and the ethnic composition of Syria in the period
following the Hyksos Age. Excavations at such sites as
Megiddo, Shechem, Tell Beit Mirsim, Jericho, Tell el-'Aj-

[7] See *Bull. Am. Sch. Or. Res.*, No. 78, pp. 30 f.
[8] See the writer's discussion, *Arch. f. Orientf.*, VI (1931),
pp. 217-21.

jul, and Tell el-Far'ah in Palestine have clarified the sequence of cultural phases during the great Dark Age to an extent that has not been remotely approached elsewhere in the Near East, not even in Egypt. The Amarna tablets and several groups of cuneiform documents from Palestine and Syria, all dating between 1500 and 1300 B.C., have given us a good idea of the distribution of linguistic stocks. We can, therefore, compare the ethnic situation in Syria and Palestine after the Hyksos Age with what existed there in the period between 2000 and 1750, which we now know from new cuneiform and Egyptian sources. At that time there was not a single clear non-Semitic name to be found south of Carchemish; all names were Canaanite or Amorite. Three centuries later this is changed. Canaanite and Amorite names still occur and become commoner as we move southward, but both Syria and Palestine swarm with non-Semitic personal names distributed among Hurrians, Indo-Iranians, and a third still unidentified linguistic group.

It follows from the foregoing facts that there must have been a great barbarian irruption from the northeast into the Fertile Crescent in the course of the 18th century B.C. This migration, probably a part of the general movement which carried the Indo-Iranians into India and Iran, must have been unusually terrifying, since swift horse-drawn chariots were used by the invaders in battle.[9] The Cossaeans were forced from their mountains into Babylonia; the Hurrians were pushed considerably farther south in Mesopotamia and inundated Syria; a congeries of non-Semitic peoples of varied origin flooded Palestine. A. Hrdlička

---

[9] Cf. *loc. cit.*, also *Jour. Pal. Or. Soc.*, XV, pp. 223 f. Horses and chariots were not wholly unknown, however, as we now know from the Mari correspondence, which shows that horses were in demand for use in drawing chariots in the eighteenth century. However, negative evidence from Western-Asiatic sources makes it certain that they were still used very sparingly at that time. It is probable that chariots were still too cumbersome to be of much practical utility in warfare. By the sixteenth century all had changed and horse-drawn chariots dominated the military scene completely.

has determined (1938) that the dominant racial type at Megiddo also shifted about this time from long-headed Mediterranean to broad-headed people of Alpine affiliation.[10] Since many, perhaps most of the invaders had already been exposed to Syro-Mesopotamian culture, there was no appreciable decline of material civilization. On the contrary, the northern invaders built new towns and castles everywhere, raising the density of population in Palestine considerably. There was a great improvement in the art of fortification. After a brief interlude in which earthworks largely replaced stone walls, at least in some parts of the country,[11] massive cyclopean masonry with sloping glacis became the standard type of fortification. The patriarchal simplicity of social life in Amorite Palestine was replaced by a feudal system, in which there was increasing contrast between the houses of patricians and plebeians. At the same time the wealth of Syria and Palestine increased, owing in part to the fact that these lands had now become internationalized in culture and served more and more as manufacturing centers and as thoroughfares for trade. The new wealth was concentrated almost entirely in the hands of patricians, so that we find a great many rich tombs and houses, together with a remarkable development of art, never really surpassed and in some ways never equalled in any other pre-Hellenistic age in Palestine.

The Egyptian conquest of Palestine and Syria began immediately after the expulsion of the Hyksos by Amosis I, about 1560 B.C. or a little later, with the siege of Sharuhen (Tell el-Far'ah?). His son, Amenophis I (1546-1525, according to the new Borchardt-Edgerton chronology which we follow) presumably continued his father's conquests in Asia and the next king, Tuthmosis I, invaded northern Syria. From about 1550 to about 1225 B.C. Palestine remained an Egyptian province uninterruptedly except for

[10] See Guy and Engberg, *Megiddo Tombs* (Chicago, 1938), p. 192.

[11] For the latest discussion of this material, with bibliography, see *Ann. Am. Sch. Or. Res.*, XVII (1938), pp. 28 f., n. 2.

brief rebellions, such as one at the end of the reign of Queen
Hatshepsut and others in the time of Sethos I and Ramesses
II. It is very important to emphasize this fact, which has
often been misunderstood in recent literature. At first Egypt
simply took over the Hyksos feudal organization in Asia,
which was very different from the contemporary situation
in Egypt itself, where all obvious traces of the Hyksos ré-
gime had been eradicated. The local princes of Palestine
and Syria were permitted to govern their subjects as before,
and were not molested as long as they paid their tribute
properly and performed their part of the compulsory labor
for the crown (corvée). However, as time went on repeated
uprisings brought reprisals and fortresses were built by the
Egyptians in various parts of the country in order to exercise a more effective control. The Egyptian garrison at
Beth-shan was first established about 1450 B.C., to judge
from the most recent excavations there, but it was rebuilt
again and again before the final decline of the Egyptian
empire in Asia. Gaza and Joppa remained for a long time
provincial capitals, and they were probably not the only
ones. There was a curious double administration of government, which may have worked well under strong pharaohs
like Tuthmosis III and Harmais, but which undoubtedly
worked badly under a weak one like Akhenaten, as we learn
from the Amarna letters. This double system consisted of
the local feudal princes, each of whom was called "governor" (*khâziânu* in Accadian), on the one hand, and the
Egyptian commissioners, called "inspectors" (*râbiṣu* in Accadian), on the other. The native governors were supported
by local forces of patrician chariotry and plebeian footmen
(*khupshu*), with which they were even permitted to wage
internecine warfare, provided it did not interfere with tribute or reach dangerous dimensions. The Egyptian commissioners raised tribute, saw to the execution of work on the
roads and in the royal grain-lands of Jezreel or the forest-
reserves of Lebanon; they were supported by contingents of
Egyptian, Nubian, Bedouin, or Mediterranean slave-troops
and mercenaries, usually armed as bowmen. Since the
Egyptian bureaucracy was notoriously corrupt, as we know

from innumerable documentary allusions, the troops often failed to receive their wages or maintenance, whereupon they plundered the unlucky provincials. The native princes were allowed to correspond directly with the court, and employed for this purpose cuneiform tablets written in Accadian, which had become the *lingua franca* of Western Asia (see below).

Excavations in many Late-Bronze sites of Palestine have shown a progressive thinning out and impoverishment of the population which suggest that Egyptian domination was very oppressive. It is very significant in this connection that few new towns appear to have been founded in this age, to judge from excavations; in Transjordan Glueck's recent explorations have shown that there was little or no advance in the frontier of sedentary occupation until near the end of the Egyptian empire in Asia, in the 13th century B.C. The increasing poverty of tombs suggests that there was corresponding impoverishment of the upper classes, a deduction which is confirmed by the growing inferiority of patrician houses, of fortifications, and of art objects. To a certain extent this decline of Canaanite civilization may have been the result of inner weakness, but we must not underestimate the effect of two or three centuries of dishonest and rapacious administration by Egyptian bureaucrats. The great edict of Harmais (Haremhab) repeatedly alludes to the corruption and rapacity of Egyptian officials and soldiers about 1340 B.C.

The external history of Western Asia in this age centered around the political relations of the central state, Mitanni, with its neighbors. From the campaigns of Tuthmosis III (1490-1436 B.C.) in Syria to the time of Tuthmosis IV (1415-1406) Egypt was almost continuously engaged in war with Mitanni. At the end of this period the Hittites awoke from their sleep of two centuries and began to exert increasing pressure on Mitanni from the northwest. Naturally, therefore, the latter hastened to make peace with Egypt and for three successive reigns Mitannian princesses married pharaohs. About 1370 Suppiluliuma of Khatti conquered Mitanni, which he reduced to a tributary state, though it continued to exist for another century until its final subjugation by Shalmaneser I of Assyria (cir. 1264-1235 B.C.). From 1360 to after 1225 B.C. the Egyptian and Hittite empires were neighbors in Syria, the boundary between them standing roughly at the Eleutherus Valley on the coast and fluctuating in the interior. For the first fifty years (cir. 1360-1310 B.C.) each empire seems to have been too much occupied by internal affairs to interfere seriously in the affairs of its neighbor, and during much of this period the Hittites were kept busy by wars and rebellions in Asia Minor. The energetic kings of the Nineteenth Dynasty, Sethos I (1308-1290) and Ramesses II (1290-1224), resumed hostilities, which seem on the whole to have resulted unfavorably for Egypt, though the Hittites were too much weakened by disorders in the north and west to take advantage of their victories. In the year 1270 a formal peace was made by the two antagonists, who seem to have kept it more or less faithfully until the final collapse of the Hittite Empire before the blows of barbarian invaders from the north, in the late 13th century B.C.

2. The Background of Religion and Thought, 1600-1200 B.C.

The late J. H. Breasted happily applied the term "the First Internationalism" to the Late Bronze Age in the Near East. Thanks to the archives of Amarna and Boghazköy, supplemented by recent finds in Syria, we see a sharp contrast between this age and the Middle Bronze, which has been so brightly illuminated by the archives of Mari. It is true that the princes of Mesopotamia and Syria corresponded freely in the Middle Bronze, but they were all Accadians and Amorites, except for a very few Hurrian and other rulers who lived in regions where cuneiform had long been known. In the 15th-13th centuries, however, we find the Egyptians corresponding with Babylonians, Assyrians, Mitannians, Hittites, Arzawans (South Anatolians) and Cypriotes, writing exclusively (it would appear) in Accadian but receiving letters in various languages. Moreover, the Egyptian chancellery writes to its own Asiatic subjects in Accadian and expects to receive Accadian replies. So far does this custom go that about 1365 B.C. an Egyptian scribe writes ten letters from Tyre to the Egyptian court, all composed in Accadian, though the mistakes of the scribe and his lavish use of Egyptian words and ideas prove his Egyptian origin.[12] All the cuneiform letters written in Accadian from Egypt, Khatti, Mitanni, as well as from Canaanite and Hurrian subject states in Palestine and Syria, are written in types of Accadian which throughout betray the fact that their scribes were using an unfamiliar tongue learned in school. Thus the Egyptian scribes invariably reproduce Egyptian phonetic habits and idioms, the Canaanite scribes always show that they are translating their ideas from Hebrew into Accadian, the Hittite and Hurrian scribes reflect Hittite and Hurrian linguistic practice. The excavations at Amarna, Boghazköy, and Ugarit have brought to light ample evidence of the existence of scribal schools, where non-Accadians learned the *lingua franca* with the aid of vocabularies, unilingual, bilingual, and trilingual, of Accadian texts transcribed phonetically or otherwise, and of exercise tablets. Of course, we may safely assume that most of the instruction was given orally. It must also be remembered that the Accadian used in international correspondence and even in literary composition was not contemporary Babylonian, though it was influenced by it, but was a corrupt form of the standard Accadian language used throughout Mesopotamia in the 18th century B.C., as we know from the Mari archives. Moreover, there is such uniformity in the errors of the various national groups of scribes that there were evidently national schools which perpetuated "dialects" of Accadian that remind one of national forms of Low Latin in the Dark Ages of Europe.

In view of this situation and the extraordinary amount of reciprocal influence exerted by Egypt, Mesopotamia, and Syria in the Late Bronze Age on material civilization, it would indeed be extraordinary if there were not a consid-

[12] See the writer's analysis of the material in *Jour. Eg. Arch.*, XXIII (1937), pp. 196-203.

erable amount of exchange of higher culture. As a matter of fact we find that this was indeed the case. A few examples from the wealth of available material must suffice. Many literary works were translated from Accadian into Hurrian and Hittite, as well as from Hurrian into Hittite. About the 15th century B.C. we find a Hurrian hymn to the Babylonian goddess Nikkal translated into North Canaanite at Ugarit.[13] The Hittite treaty of 1270 B.C. was translated from Accadian into Egyptian. The Egyptian scribe at Tyre, of whom we have spoken, translated two Egyptian poems into Accadian. In the 13th century we find that the Canaanite myth of Astarte and the Sea, known from an Ugaritic fragment, had been put into Egyptian.[14] At Amarna were found a number of Accadian mythological texts, such as Nergal and Ereshkigal, Adapa and the South Wind, transcribed into special phonetic form for Egyptian students; we also find that the *Hittite* recension of the Accadian epic of the "King of Battle," dealing with the exploits of Sargon of Accad in Asia Minor, existed at Amarna in more than one copy, to judge from the number of fragments which have been found. Accadian astrological and divinatory texts have been discovered at Boghazköy in Asia Minor, at Alalakh and elsewhere in Syria, and were doubtless in great demand, to judge from Hittite and Hurrian translations of them. Egyptian and Babylonian scholars and professional men were prized in other lands, as we know from numerous allusions. About 1300 B.C., for instance, the Egyptian physician and architect (combining both professions, like Imuthes!) Pareamakhu, who seems to be the son of an Egyptian architect buried at Beth-shan in Palestine, was in demand in at least two Anatolian courts.[15] A little later a Babylonian physician named Raba-sha-Marduk sojourned at the Hittite court.

[13] See Ginsberg, *Orientalia*, VIII (1939), pp. 317-27.

[14] Published most recently by A. H. Gardiner, *Studies Presented to F. Ll. Griffith* (London, 1932), pp. 74-85. For its Asiatic origin see the writer's remarks, *Am. Jour. Sem. Lang.*, XXXVI, pp. 260 f., and *Jour. Pal. Or. Soc.*, XVI (1936), pp. 18 f.

[15] Cf. *Ann. Am. Sch. Or. Res.*, XVII, p. 77, n. 38.

The impact of this cultural internationalism on the religion of Western Asia was prodigious. The names and ideograms of Sumero-Accadian gods and goddesses were borrowed by Hurrians, Hittites, Amorites, and Canaanites alike. A good half of the known figures of the Hurrian pantheon in the second millennium B.C. is of Sumerian or Accadian origin. The principal deities of places like Aleppo, Qatna, and Kadesh on the Orontes bore Mesopotamian names or names written with cuneiform ideograms. The cult of Mesopotamian deities like Dagan penetrated into southern Palestine. Local Canaanite gods of Palestine were identified with such characteristically Mesopotamian figures as the war-god Ninurta. The cult of Ishtar of Nineveh was carried by Hurrians and Hittites into places as far removed from Assyria as Egypt and southwestern Asia Minor.[16] In slightly earlier (pre-Cossaean) cuneiform lists of gods we find the Hurrian Teshub (Teshup) and Shaushka and the Canaanite Addu (Hadad) and Ashtartu identified with Adad and Ishtar, respectively. Similarly the Canaanites of the Amarna letters identified the Egyptian Re' with their own sun-god, Shamash, while the Egyptians equated Canaanite Baal with their own Seth, Ba'alat Gubla ("the Lady of Byblus") with Hathor. The Egyptians of the New Empire adopted the Canaanite goddesses Astarte and Anath, as well as the gods Hauron and Rashap, etc., into their pantheon.

In view of the close parallelism in development, as well as of the interchange and cross-fertilization of cultural elements which we have been describing, it will be better to treat the outstanding phases of Late-Bronze religion, in so far as they are of special interest to us in the present study, thematically rather than geographically. We shall accordingly treat the following subjects: tendencies toward mono-

[16] Cf. Friedrich, *Der Alte Orient.*, XXV:2, pp. 20-22, for a long list of the residences in different parts of Western Asia from which she is summoned in a Hittite text from Boghazköy. Among these places are Ugarit, Alalakh, and Sidon in Syria, Cyprus, and southwestern Asia Minor (cf. *Jour. Bib. Lit.*, LIX, p. 105, n. 26).

theism; the growth of individual responsibility and emphasis on personality. We shall then sketch the religion of the Canaanites, as we know it today.

In the third millennium Mesopotamians and Egyptians had naïvely regarded their cosmic deities as universal, as we know from many passages in early religious literature. The sun-god of Egypt or Babylonia was the only sun, so far as both learned cosmology and instinctive reaction were concerned. Of course, there may already have been conscious identifications of Sumero-Accadian with Anatolian or Egyptian gods, but evidence is lacking. In the age of Hammurabi the homogeneity of culture in Mesopotamia, Syria, and eastern Asia Minor was so great that identification of deities began to become popular, as we have just seen. However, this was in itself no more decisive a tendency toward monotheism than was the corresponding process in Graeco-Roman times. The fact that there were many cultic forms of a national deity led to a certain movement in the direction of theological universalism. In Asia Minor and northwestern Mesopotamia we find that such divinities as Teshub and Ghepat were worshipped in many different places, after which the deities are named to distinguish them. This was equally true of Ishtar and Adad in Mesopotamia, and of Baal and Anath in Canaan. As a result of this phenomenon we find in Canaanite an increasing tendency to employ the plural 'Ashtarôt "Astartes," and 'Anatôt "Anaths," in the clear sense of "totality of manifestations of a deity." This is further illustrated by the frequent honorific greeting of Pharaoh in the Amarna letters as "my gods, my sun-god," which means, of course, that Pharaoh was extravagantly addressed as being the writer's whole pantheon. If the Canaanites were accustomed to use so grandiloquent an expression in addressing their Egyptian suzerain, referring (as we know from many passages) to the fact that he claimed to be the living incarnation of the sun-god, we may be confident that they had borrowed it from cultic phraseology, where they magnified one of their own gods in monolatrous fashion by addressing him as the totality of gods, i. e., as equivalent to the entire pantheon.

That this explanation is correct we know also from the fact that the Israelites took over the Canaanite plural, *elôhîm* "gods," in the sense of "God."

Belief in the universal dominion of a high god was the natural result of the slightest reflection about his cosmic functions, and was facilitated by the general identification of gods with similar functions. This belief is explicitly attested by many passages in the religious literature of our period, a number of which may be quoted. The most striking passages naturally come from Egypt, where our sources are much more extensive. Since the Aten heresy was a special development, which we shall describe briefly below, we shall restrict ourselves here to the great Egyptian Amun hymn of the 15th century (though most of the contexts are considerably older):

Thou far-traveller, thou prince of Upper Egypt, lord of the land of the Matoi (Eastern Desert of Nubia) and ruler of Punt (East Africa),

Thou greatest of heaven, thou oldest of the earth, lord of what exists . . .

Legitimate lord, father of the gods, who created man and made the animals . . .

Who made the upper ones and the lower ones, who illumines the two lands . . .

Whose sweet odor the gods love, as he comes from Punt, rich in fragrance as he comes from the land of the Matoi, with fair countenance as he comes from "God's Land" (Asia) . . .

Praise to thee who didst create the gods, who didst raise heaven and stretch out the earth!

. . . .

Thou art the only one, who created what there is; the unique one, who created what exists—thou from whose eyes came men and from whose mouth sprang the gods . . .

"Praise to thee!" (says) every wild animal, "Hail to thee!" (says) every foreign land, *as high as heaven and as wide as earth is and as deep as the sea is* . . .

Thou father of the fathers of all the gods, thou who didst

raise heaven and stretch out earth, thou who didst make
what is and create what exists . . .

Dweller on the horizon, Horus of the east! The foreign
land brings silver and gold to him and true lapis lazuli
(which came from Iran by way of Syria) because of its
love for him. Myrrh and incense (come) mixed out of the
land of the Matoi . . .[17]

Owing to the paucity of Mesopotamian religious texts of
comparable type which can be dated with certainty to the
period under discussion, we shall quote only from a prayer
of Tukulti-Ninurta I of Assyria (cir. 1234-1197). The attribution of this prayer to the first king of the name has now
been made certain by the discovery at Nineveh of extensive
portions of a triumphal poem of this king, referring to the
same situation and using almost identical language in
places.[18] The Assyrian king is represented as praying to Assur for help against the Cossaean king of Babylonia, Kash-
tiliash III, with whom he is at war. Assur is repeatedly called
"lord of lands" and "king of all the gods." His foes are described as rebels against his authority, as "trusting in their
own might and despising the name of God." One passage is
particularly instructive.

O lord, Assur, be gracious to thy land!

O Assur, great lord, king of the earth-gods, the land
(*mada* = Mesopotamia), O Assur, is thine!

O Assyrian En-lil, lord of the lands (*kur = foreign land*),
the land, O Assur, is thine![19]

An Accadian cuneiform text found at Nineveh and only
recently published, describes the power of the Babylonian
god Marduk in the following terms:

I am the great lord, Marduk;

[17] The best recent translations are those by A. Scharff,
Aegyptische Sonnenlieder (1921), and A. Erman, *Die Literatur
der Aegypter* (1923), pp. 350 ff.

[18] See E. Ebeling, *Mitt. Altor. Ges.*, XII: 2 (1938), pp. 3,
37 f.

[19] Translated by Ebeling in *Altor. Texte* (1926), pp. 263 ff.

I watch everything and traverse the mountains (beyond Mesopotamia) . . .

The one who traverses the lands, all of them, from sunrise to sunset, am I.

Marduk is then represented as saying that he went to the land of the Hittites and set up his throne there for twenty-four years, during which he advanced Babylonian interests in various ways.[20]

A very interesting passage from Canaanite literature has recently (1938) been published by Virolleaud.[21] In the mythological epic of Baal and Anath, which dates in its present form from about 1400 B.C. and probably reflects an earlier stage of mythopoeia, it is said of Koshar, who was identified with the Egyptian god Ptah of Memphis: "His is Caphtor, the throne on which he sits, and Egypt, the land of his inheritance." The word *Kptr*, biblical *Kaphtor* and Accadian *Kaptara*, certainly refers to Crete, and the term used for Egypt is the native name of Memphis, used in the same way in the Amarna tablets and later adopted by the Greeks as the designation of the Nile Valley.[22] Phoenician gods are not infrequently said to be enthroned on an island in the sea; cf. Ezekiel's words about the prince of Tyre (Ezek. 28:2), "I am a god; I sit on the throne of god in the midst of the seas." El appears in Ugaritic literature as dwelling "in the midst of the fountains of the two deeps," located at "the sources of the two rivers." To reach him it was necessary to journey through "a thousand plains, ten thousand fields."[23] The ancient Canaanites can scarcely have had any more difficulty in assuming the universality of a cosmic deity than the Homeric Greeks had. With the Greeks of the Mycenaean age, whose conceptions are reflected in the Iliad, the sun-god

[20] See H. G. Güterbock, *Zeits. f. Assyr.*, XLII, pp. 79 ff.

[21] *La déesse 'Anat* (Paris, 1938), pp. 85 ff. For translation and interpretation see H. L. Ginsberg, *Orientalia*, IX, pp. 39-44, and the writer, *Jour. Bib. Lit.*, LIX, pp. 107 f.

[22] See *Bull. Am. Sch. Or. Res.*, No. 70, p. 22, and Ginsberg, *loc. cit.*

[23] See R. de Vaux, *Rev. Bib.*, 1939, p. 597, and the writer, *Jour. Bib. Lit.*, LIX, p. 106.

is happiest when sojourning with the Aethiopians, Zeus is as much at home with the Trojans or Amazons as he is with the Greeks. No matter how far Odysseus wanders, he never gets beyond the jurisdiction of his enemy, Poseidon, or of his patroness, Athene. Another illustration of ideas in this general age may be drawn from the Report of Wen-amun, early in the 11th century B.C. Wen-amun is sent to Byblus to obtain cedars for the bark of Amun at Thebes. On the way he is robbed by the men of Dor, so he is handicapped in his negotiations, since Egyptian suzerainty over Phoenicia had long previously expired. Nevertheless, Wen-amun says to the Canaanite prince of Byblus, "There is no ship on the waters that does not belong to Amun, for his is the sea and his is Lebanon, of which thou sayest, 'It is mine!'" The Canaanite is then represented as admitting that Amun is supreme and as observing that he taught and equipped Egypt first, so that Egypt was able to instruct the Canaanites in the arts of civilization.

From the recognition that many different deities are simply manifestations of a single god and that the domain of a high god is universal, it was but a step, in a highly sophisticated and empirically logical age, to some form of practical monotheism. This stage is documented twice in Babylonian literature, and the composition of both texts may be referred with much confidence to the Cossaean period. The first has been known for more than forty years; its Cossaean date is established by the fact that the Cossaean god Shuqamuna and Tishpak, the chief god of Eshnunna, appear in it. In this tablet Marduk of Babylon is successively identified with a whole list of male deities: En-lil is a form of Marduk with reference to ruling and decision, Sin is Marduk as illuminer of the night, Shamash is Marduk as god of justice, etc. Since no goddess is mentioned, it is possible that the Babylonian theologian drew the line at amalgamating the sexes and limited his monotheistic evolution to a form of ditheism. The tendency, however, is unmistakable. The second document is of a somewhat different nature. It was first published by Ebeling over twenty years ago, but has escaped general attention.[24] Though the copy which we possess comes from Assur, the intrinsic evidence makes it Babylonian and dates it probably to the late second millennium B.C., when the cult of the war-god Ninurta became most popular. Here all the important deities are listed successively as parts of the body of Ninurta: e. g., his face is heaven; En-lil and Nin-lil are his two eyes; the protecting goddesses of his two eyes are Gula and Belili (Belit-ilani); his chin is Ishtar of the Stars; his lips are Anu and Antum; his tongue is Pabilsag; his gums are the vault of heaven and earth; his ears are Ea and Damkina; his skull is Adad; his forehead is Shala; his neck is Marduk; his throat is Sarpanitum; his breast is Nabu—and so on down to the lower extremities. In other words, Ninurta spans the whole cosmos and all the gods and goddesses may be symbolically equated with parts of his cosmic body. There can be little doubt that this remarkable conception goes back to dynamistic sacrificial ritual, where the virtue and the symbolic meaning of the animal to be sacrificed are extolled in hyperbolic terms. For instance, the black bull which was sacrificed in the ritual of the temple-musician (*kalû*) was symbolically designated as the great cosmic bull of heaven, companion of the god Nin-gizzida and decider of fate. The dynamistic conceptions involved are closely related to an Indic parallel in the ritual of the horse-sacrifice (*asvamedha*), where the horse is symbolically identified with the cosmos and parts of his body are treated as cosmic entities.[25] The idea of the cosmic body of Ninurta, taking root in dynamistic and corporative ideas, was definitely on the way to a pantheism of Brahmanic type. At the same time, there can be no doubt that this incorporation of all the gods and goddesses in one all-embracing deity is monotheistic to the extent that it deprives other deities of independent theological existence.

All of the monotheistic tendencies so far described remained partial or ineffective. It was reserved for an unknown Egyptian to take a long step toward true monothe-

---

[24] See his translation, *Altor. Texte* (1926), pp. 250 f.

[25] See the joint treatment by the writer and P. E. Dumont, *Jour. Am. Or. Soc.*, LIV (1934), pp. 107 ff., and p. 128, n. 69.

ism not later than about 1400 B.C. This step consisted in divorcing the figure of the supreme, universal sun-god, Amun-Re', from its mythological trappings, and in adoring the solar disk itself as the only god. It has often been maintained that this advance is due to the heretic-king, Akhenaten (Ikhnaton) himself, but the first traces of the new teaching date from the reign of his father Amenophis III (1406-1370 B.C.), where they even appear in a beautiful hymn to the sun-god found in the tomb of two brothers, Suti and Hor.[26] In the second strophe of this hymn the sun is addressed by the appellation *Aten* "solar disk," in words from which we may quote the following:

O creator of what the earth brings forth, Khnum and Amun of mankind! . . .
Excellent mother of gods and man, good creator who takes the greatest pains with his innumerable creatures . . .
He who reaches the ends of the lands every day and beholds those who walk there . . .
Every land adores him at his rising every day, in order to praise him.

Here the Aten is described as both father and mother of creation, as the lord of all lands and men, as identical with the creator-god Khnum of Elephantine. But in other strophes of this same hymn we find Amun-Re' appearing with the usual mythological trappings, so it is evident that the Aten cult had only obtained a precarious footing in certain quarters. As has been pointed out by Sethe, Breasted, and others, the Aten theology must have developed either in Heliopolitan circles or among priests familiar with the solar theology taught in them.[27]

In 1370 Amenophis IV, the future heretic-king, became

[26] See especially A. Erman, *Die Religion der Ägypter* (Berlin, 1934), pp. 107 f.
[27] See especially Sethe, *Nachr. Kön. Ges. Wiss. Göttingen, Phil.-hist. Klasse*, 1921:2, pp. 101 ff.; Breasted, *The Dawn of Conscience* (Chicago, 1933), pp. 272 ff., and Erman, *op. cit.*, pp. 107 ff.

pharaoh, though a weak, sickly lad of about eleven. His mummy was found in the tomb of his mother, Queen Teye, in 1907, and was examined by the famous anatomist and authority on Egyptian mummification, Elliot Smith. According to the latter's examination he was definitely pathological, with an abnormal pelvis and a peculiarly shaped skull; he was between 25 and 28 when he died. These facts agree with the evidence of art, which exhibits him with distended skull, protruding abdomen, and almost feminine build. The doubt first cast on the identification of the mummy has been largely removed by the discovery that the mummy of his nephew (?) Tut-ankh-amun exhibits almost identical physical characteristics, especially with respect to shape of the head.[28] The fact that he was not over 28 when he died and that he reigned 17 years would make him not over eleven at his accession. His eldest daughter, Meritaten,[29] cannot have been over twelve when she was married and she apparently bore no children; her youngest sister was married to Tut-ankh-amun, who cannot have been over thirteen when he became king. In view of these circumstances of age and physical health it is quite absurd to consider Akhenaten as the founder of the Aten cult, or even as the "first individual in history" (Breasted). He must, accordingly, have been the tool of others, either through his mother, Teye (who was still alive in the eleventh year of his reign), or his wife, Nefretete (who was probably older than he), or some unidentified favorite. Hence it was only the flattery of his courtiers which pictured him as the promulgator of a new "teaching."[30]

[28] See Howard Carter, *The Tomb of Tut.ankh.Amen,* II (1927), pp. 152-61. [But contrast now Engelbach, *Annales du Service,* XL (1940), pp. 151 f.]

[29] On this princess, who is mentioned in the Amarna Letters, see *Jour. Eg. Arch.,* XXIII (1937), pp. 191-94 (cf. *Bull. Am. Sch. Or. Res.,* No. 78, p. 24).

[30] For illustrations of the extensive use of the term "teaching, doctrine" by the followers of the Aten cult see Erman, *op. cit.,* pp. 121 f. The Egyptian word *sbâye(t),* Coptic *sbô,* has nearly the same connotations as Latin *doctrina* (from *doceo* "to teach") and *disciplina* (from *disco* "to learn"); it

Thanks to the ample documentation secured by successive excavators of the new capital, Akhetaten, built for himself by the young pharaoh when he was about 17, it is certain that the cult of the Aten did not attain its definitive form until after some eight years or more of vacillation. In its full, though brief, development it appears as a true solar monotheism, with the solar formula, "who rejoices on the horizon in his quality (literally 'name') as light which is in the solar disk." Adherents of the cult of the Aten were commanded to erase the name of Amun wherever it occurred; the names of all other deities were sporadically obliterated (especially at Karnak), showing clearly that the more fanatical monotheists regarded the solar disk as the only god. In the famous Hymn to the Aten, which has been reproduced so often that it is familiar to all, we find that the Aten is explicitly addressed as "the only god, beside whom there is no other," as maker and sustainer of Syria and Nubia as well as of Egypt, as creator of everything, lord of the universe, including the most distant lands. The Osirian mortuary ritual was modified with the disappearance of Osiris and his retinue. The sarcophagus of princess Meketaten substitutes the figure of the queen her mother for the protecting figures of discarded goddesses. In the official documents there is hardly a trace of the old mythology, except where it was consistent with the new ideas: i. e., the sun-god is still self-created, though we may safely conjecture that the Aten-worshippers abandoned the crude conceptions which more primitive times had associated with such creation.

While the Aten cult was, accordingly, a true monotheism, it was not suited to become the national religion of Egypt. In the first place, its atmosphere was much too rarified for the masses, and even for the upper classes. The extraordinary emphasis laid on "truth," which led the young king and his advisers to substitute more lifelike rep-

---

shares with the latter the two senses of "system of teachings" (e. g., *disciplina Etrusca* for the system of Etruscan divinatory lore) and "correction, punishment." Heb. *tôrah* has the same meaning; see below, note 96.

resentation for the standardized canons of proportion and the living language of the country for an extinct literary tongue, was good in itself, but it ended in materialistic hedonism. Moreover, the courtiers simply imitated the new fashions; now, for example, all royal retainers were represented with the abnormal head and limbs of the king! Only cheerful and pleasant things could be described in hymns or portrayed in art. The beautiful family life of the king, with his young queen and three little daughters, absorbed the whole attention of artists, and the duties of pharaoh as king and commander, as magistrate and administrator were disregarded. How little sexual ethics were reformed appears from the king's marriage to his own third daughter.[31] In another respect the new religion was materialistic in its tendencies. The king remained the incarnation of the sun-god on earth and was flattered and extolled by his courtiers (many of whom were upstarts, as we learn from their own inscriptions) to a slavish and otherwise unparalleled extent. In order, apparently, to develop a consistent theological system, moreover, the Aten was not infrequently represented as a hierarchic triad formed of the Aten proper, of "the living Aten in the temple of the Aten at Akhetaten," and of the king himself, who is said to be "the eternal son who has come out of the sun," and to be "born anew every morning, like the sun-god his father." The middle phase of the triad presumably linked the sun-god in heaven with his earthly incarnation by a hypostasis established permanently in the new temple. The new Aten theology had developed far from primitive dynamism or corporatism in the direction of empirical cultic theology. A third weakness of the Aten cult was that it nowhere seems to lay any stress on social justice or the well-being of the masses; the royal family and the courtiers were apparently quite without interest in the improvement of their subjects' lot, which must have been extremely hard, to judge from contemporary and slightly later documents. It is certain, at all events, that the Theban reaction came with a hatred and violence un-

[31] See H. Brunner, *Zeits. Äg. Spr.*, LXXIV (1938), p. 108.

paralleled in native Egyptian history, and the names of the heretic-king and his immediate successors were anathematized by priests and scribes down to the latest times. However, the Aten "doctrine" was well rooted in Heliopolitan theology and it had apparently been well diffused before the reign of Akhenaten, so it could hardly disappear overnight. We may confidently suppose that it continued to be taught for generations in Lower Egypt, long jealous of the ascendancy of Thebes. It is clear from our documentary sources that the priests of Thebes used their victory to enhance their own power, and the inevitable resentment felt in Lower Egypt may have been partly responsible for the return to Hyksos traditions and to the cult of the long despised god Seth, the enemy of Horus, which triumphed about 1310 B.C., with the accession of Ramesses I.[32]

The strength of this reaction was never clearly felt by scholars until P. Montet's excavations at Tanis in the northeastern Delta since 1930. Now it has become obvious, thanks to the wealth of new inscriptional data from Tanis, the old home of Seth. The Ramesside house actually traced its ancestry back to a Hyksos king whose era was fixed 400 years before the date commemorated in the "400-year Stela" of Tanis. The great-grandfather of Ramesses II evidently came from an old Tanite family, very possibly of Hyksos origin, since his name was Sethos (Suta). This Suta appears as a chief of archers who is mentioned several times in the Amarna tablets.[33] Ramesses II established his capital and residency at Tanis, which he named "House of Ramesses" and where he built a great temple of the old Tanite, later Hyksos god Seth (pronounced at that time

[32] On the relations between Upper and Lower Egypt at this time cf. H. Kees, *Nachr. Ges. Wiss. Göttingen, Phil.-hist. Klasse, Fachgr.* I, N. F., II:1 (1936), pp. 13 f., and H. Junker, *Zeits. Äg. Spr.* LXXV (1939), pp. 81 f.

[33] On this subject see a forthcoming paper by the writer. For previously known data concerning the origin of the Ramesside family see H. W. Helck, *Der Einfluss der Militärführer in der 18. ägyptischen Dynastie* (Leipzig, 1939), pp. 84 f.

Sûtekh).[34] Ramesses II also encouraged the cult of many other gods of the Delta, both Egyptian and Canaanite; he particularly worshipped Baal, who had already been identified with Seth by the Hyksos, and his sister and consort Anath, who received a special temple. Seth and Baal were recognized as the same divinity, who was the son of the goddess of heaven (Nut), lord of heaven and storm-god, for whose special use the thunder weapon was created. Even in iconography the Ramesside representations of Seth-Baal are practically indistinguishable, except in artistic technique, from those of the Canaanite Baal which have been found in considerable numbers during recent excavations in Palestine and Syria. In a similar way Anath was identified with Nephthys, the consort of Seth, and Astarte became Isis or Hathor, while the "great shepherd," Horon, was identified with Horus.[35] This thorough-going cultic amalgamation of Canaanite and Egyptian deities in the 13th century B.C., while hardly monotheistic, was undoubtedly the culmination of a long-existing process of internationalizing high gods. Moreover, it was an even longer step in the direction of monotheism when in such public documents as the treaty between Ramesses II and King Khattusilis of the Hittites the chief male deities of Syria and Asia Minor are all called "Seth" (Sûtekh). We are, accordingly, quite justified in insisting that the universalistic tendencies of the "First International Age" reached their climax in the thirteenth century B.C., where Egyptian gods are freely identified with the leading deities of Western Asia, and where the patron deity of the Egyptian king is also the chief god of Canaanites, Hittites, and Mesopotamians.

The development of personal religion and ethics, already

---

[34] For the cults of Tanis see the convenient summary by the excavator in *Rev. Bib.*, 1935, pp. 153-58. On the phonetic forms *Sûtaḥ* and *Sêth* see the writer's remarks, *Vocalization of the Egyptian Syllabic Orthography* (New Haven, 1934), pp. 56, XIV.D.3, 3a, and 17 f.

[35] See the writer, *Am. Jour. Sem. Lang.*, LIII (1936), pp. 1-12.

evident both in Egypt and in Mesopotamia during the early second millennium, as we have seen, attained new heights in both countries during the Late Bronze Age. Thanks to such material as the 125th chapter of the Book of the Dead, we are in an unusually favorable position to analyze and appraise the situation in Egypt at this time. In the New Empire the Book of the Dead takes the place of the Coffin Texts of the Middle Empire, which in their turn had replaced the Pyramid Texts. As will be recalled, the Coffin Texts contained much material from the Pyramid Texts, to which still more new material was added. The Book of the Dead includes many spells and selections from the Coffin Texts and a little of ultimately Pyramid origin. While there was no true "Book of the Dead" in the New Empire, the mortuary papyri of that age are generally parallel in arrangement and repeat so many of the then recognized stock of texts that it has been possible to establish a formal system of numbering "chapters." One of the longest of these chapters is the 125th, containing the so-called "Negative Confession" which was supposed to be made by the deceased at the court of Osiris before being admitted to life in the other world. Thanks to the studies of Breasted, E. Drioton, J. Spiegel, and others in the past few years, we now have a much clearer idea of the origin and nature of the "Negative Confession."[36] As Drioton first pointed out (1922), the document is composite, containing elements which go back in substantially their present form into the early Middle Empire and others which can hardly antedate the end of the same age. The oldest manuscripts containing this chapter belong to about the 15th century B.C. The composite origin of the document and the addition of variants from different recensions explain its repetitious character, which was not improved by a tendency to make the number of individual declarations equal

[36] See E. Drioton, *Recueil d'études égyptologiques dediées à . . . Champollion* (Paris, 1922), pp. 545-64; Breasted, *Dawn of Conscience,* pp. 250 ff.; J. Spiegel, *Die Idee vom Totengericht in der ägyptischen Religion* (Glückstadt, 1935); H. Moderau, *Arch. f. Orientf.,* XII (1938), pp. 258-68.

that of the 42 judges (one for each nome). In the standard form of the chapter there are three parts: first, a declaration that the deceased has not committed any one of a long list of sins; second, another longer declaration to the same effect; third, a short positive declaration, listing some of the good deeds of the deceased while on earth.

A careful analysis of the two negative declarations shows clearly that the first is older than the second, as might be inferred *a priori* from the more artificial form of the latter. In the first, sins against the gods are particularly emphasized, though they are still fewer than the sins against men. In the second one sins against the king and the local god are mentioned, and the catalogue of sins against men is considerably more detailed. Moreover, in the second there is a series of faults of character, such as lying, greed, eavesdropping, sudden anger, refusal to hear the truth, unseemly haste in acting, garrulousness, vanity, arrogance, prodigality, etc., none of which occurs in the first. The two lists include, between them, practically every important type of transgression against religious obligations and the rights of others. Attention has been called to the absence of any reference to honoring parents or authorities, but this is probably to be explained by the ultimately royal origin of the nucleus of the confession. Since the king was superior to all mankind, there could be no question of honoring any one beneath him in dignity; his duties to relatives and authorities were already covered by other declarations. Social justice was amply recognized by the inclusion of many references to just weights and balances, true surveying of fields, just use of water for irrigation, refraining from attempts to corrupt magistrates and from any oppression, as well as by both negative and positive assurances with respect to feeding the hungry, giving water to the thirsty, clothing the naked, and providing transport (across the Nile) for the one who had none. Compared with the Ten Commandments, the Negative Confession is unwieldy, repetitious, badly integrated, and lacking in any sense of balance between important and unimportant things. Yet there is not a single intelligible declaration which could not be conscientiously repeated by a member of the Society for Ethical Culture today—aside, of course, from some having exclusively to do with religious observances, and even these could hardly be rejected in principle, since breaking one of them would seriously offend a member of the religious group in question. When we recall that every Egyptian was supposed to submit to trial before Osiris and to strive for justification if he wished to enjoy a happy life in Elysium, the moral force of the Negative Confession becomes evident. On grave stelae of the New Empire there are many illustrations of individual efforts to realize these ideals or of claims to have fulfilled them. To be sure, in practice the ethical ideals of the ancient Egyptians hardly affected the life of the average man, who was either too ignorant or too eager for pleasure and gain to listen to admonition. Moreover, the ubiquitous sway of magic made both classes and masses sure of getting into Elysium, in view of the vast number and the reputed efficacy of the charms and spells which make up the bulk of the Book of the Dead. Many charms made extravagant claims which priests and magicians were not slow to exploit to their own advantage. In general we know that the Egyptians of the New Empire were excessively venal and corrupt, and that the efforts of a Tuthmosis III to raise standards of administrative honesty were transient in their results.

To the latter part of the New Empire belongs a remarkable series of devout sayings and prayers, most of which are preserved in graffiti and funeral stelae from the Thebaid, dating from 1300-1100 B.C. While some of the material which they contain may be shown to be older, much of it must be later than the Aten revolution. Thanks to the studies of Erman and Breasted, there can be no doubt that Egyptian religion here touches the highest point ever reached by any pre-Israelite faith with which we are acquainted.[37] In these intensely human documents we find a touching depth of simple piety. Take, for example, the prayer of Neb-re', a painter in the Theban necropolis under Ramesses II (1290-1224 B.C.):

[37] Breasted, *op. cit.*, pp. 312 ff.; Erman, *op. cit.*, pp. 139 ff.

Praise to Amun! I make hymns to his name!
I praise him to the height of heaven and the breadth of
     earth;
I tell of his might to him who saileth upstream and down-
     stream. . . .
Thou, O Amun, art the lord of the quiet (pious),
Who cometh at the cry of the poor.
When I cried to thee in my affliction thou didst come to
     save me,
In order to give breath to the feeble, to save me from
     bondage.
Thou, O Amun-Reʻ of Thebes, art he who saveth him who
     is in the underworld . . .
When men cry unto thee, thou art he who cometh from
     afar.

From the mass of material collected by Erman, we may
quote one other example, in a prayer to Thoth written
down in the late 13th century B.C., but composed somewhat earlier:

Thoth, thou sweet fountain for one who thirsteth in the
     desert!
It is sealed for one who talketh, but it is open for one who
     is quiet (pious)!
When the quiet one cometh, he findeth the fountain.

Turning to Mesopotamia we have our most important
data on conceptions of personal ethics and individual responsibility in the incantatory series *Shurpu,* especially in
the second and third tablets of the nine of which it was
composed. Just as in Egypt we find a new sense of individual responsibility arising after the eighteenth century
B.C. The *Shurpu* series is devoted to incantatory rituals by
which a sick or bewitched man was supposed to be cured
or freed from his state. Internal evidence points strongly
to the Cossaean period (between 1500 and 1150 B.C.)
as the date of its composition, as may be shown from the
divine names which it contains, from its language and

style (A. Schott, 1928),[38] and from other considerations (W. von Soden, 1935).[39] The first thing incumbent on the priest was to discover what the patient had done that was punishable by superior powers. Since this investigation was generally rather hopeless, all possible sins, violations of tabus, and acts which might have brought revenge from gods, men, or demons were scrupulously listed and the patient was freed from the effect of any one of them by the incantatory ritual which followed. It is obvious that this "shot-gun" method depended partly for its efficacy upon the completeness of the list of sins and tabus. We have no means of knowing how much stress, if any, was laid on the actual identification of a transgression on which the illness or other trouble of the patient might be blamed. In spite of the magical associations of the *Shurpu* list, it represents just as individual a relation between sin and punishment as the Egyptian Negative Confession. In the sins and faults listed we can easily detect a much stronger sense of social solidarity and patriarchal organization than in Egypt. No sins are stressed more often here than the breaking up of families and clans or the separation of father from son, of brother from brother, etc. Failure to honor parents, disinheritance of a legitimate heir, (trespassing) entrance into a neighbor's house, approach to a neighbor's wife, murder or robbery of a neighbor, and similar sins are listed in great detail. Transgressions against the gods are also emphasized. However, along with social and religious offenses are also listed, without any special order, acts of unkindness which might bring reprisals (e. g., to refuse the loan of irrigation water for a single day, to refuse the loan of a water jar, damming up a neighbor's irrigation ditch) and acts which were merely unpropitious, such as swearing by the sun-god at his rising, swearing an oath (by a god) with

---

[38] Cf. the abstract of his paper, *Zeits. Deutsch. Morg. Ges.*, LXXXII, p. lvii, which was based on a mass of stylistic material (on the general plan of his previous monograph, *Die Vergleiche in den akkadischen Königsinschriften* [Leipzig, 1926]).

[39] *Zeits. Deutsch. Morg. Ges.*, LXXXIX (1935), pp. 156-63, especially p. 157, n. 1.

unwashed hands, sitting in a seat facing the sun. Other acts, again, belong to the domain of empirically discovered hygienic tabus: e. g., urinating or vomiting into a stream, drinking from a water tap, etc. In short, *Shurpu* carries us into a different socio-cultural environment from what we find in contemporary Egypt. In Mesopotamia at this time the organization of society was more primitive than in Egypt, in part clearly as the result of reversion after a long period of feudal rule by the Cossaean barbarians, since the Code of Hammurabi and contemporary Old Babylonian literature reflect a definitely more complex state of society. At the same time magic played a greater rôle in daily life, whereas in Egypt it was at that time relegated in large part to preparation for the future life, a field which was virtually barred to it in Babylonia. The character of the individual was still of minor importance as compared to the stability of the group to which he belonged—yet the individual was now definitely accountable for his acts and he could not hope for a healthy or happy life in this world unless he lived circumspectly.

We can no longer adequately survey the religious background of early Israel without a brief sketch of the religion of the Canaanites of Phoenicia and Palestine as we now know it from the alphabetic texts of Ugarit, supplemented by sporadic archaeological finds. We have already described the discovery and decipherment of these invaluable documents (above, p. 39) and warned against uncritical use of the translations of any scholar. Happily there are now so many passages whose meaning is clear that we can give an adequate account without using questionable material. The mythological texts and rituals from Ugarit, the myths recorded by Philo Byblius on the authority of a Phoenician named Sanchuniathon (who seems to have flourished about the seventh century B.C.), and the scattered evidence from other sources agree so completely in all main aspects that there can no longer be any doubt that the Canaanites possessed just as sharply defined a religious and mythological system as did the Egyptians and the Sumero-Accadians, though it was much cruder as

well as more debased. From the names of Early-Bronze
towns in Palestine and Phoenicia we know that the Canaanites of the third millennium had the same gods as appear at
Ugarit and elsewhere later. It is highly probable that the
contents of the mythological poems of Ugarit are very early,
going back into the third millennium in substantially their
present form.

The head of the Canaanite (Phoenician) pantheon was
the god El (i. e., *the* god), just as among the Hebrews,
where he was early called *El 'Elyôn* "the Highest God,"
or *El Shaddai* (see below). El's consort was the goddess
Ashirat, the Asherah of the Bible, often called "Ashirat of
the Sea," meaning originally perhaps "She who Treads the
Sea." This goddess was also worshipped by South Arabians and Amorites; a votive inscription in Sumerian which
was erected to her by an Amorite of the 18th century B.C.
calls her "the bride of heaven." El is usually described in
the poems of Ugarit as residing in a distant cosmic spot
known as the "Source of the Two Deeps" ("deep" =
tehôm, as in Hebrew), from which "he causes the rivers
to flow." He plays a rather passive rôle as "the father of
years," receiving suppliants and sending his instructions by
his messengers. In this respect he resembles Egyptian Re'
and Accadian Anu. In one myth he is represented with
realistic imagery as seducing two unnamed women, who
duly give birth to the two "beautiful and gracious gods,"
Shahar (Dawn) and Shalim (the Perfect One). Philo reports also that El (Kronos) killed his son Sadidos and cut
his daughter's head off, "so that all the gods were struck
with fear of the caprice of Kronos."

The great active figure of the pantheon was Baal or
Haddu (Hadad), the storm-god and king of the gods (as
he is called both at Ugarit and by Philo). His common later
title among the Phoenicians was "lord of heaven" (*Ba'al
shamêm*), which has not yet been found at Ugarit, but
which was already applied to the Syrian storm-god in the
14th century B.C.[40] Baal was the son of Dagon, whose re-

[40] On Ba'al-shamem see now O. Eissfeldt, *Zeits. Alttest.
Wiss.*, LVII (1939), pp. 1-30.

lationship to El is not clear in the Ugaritic texts, but who
was one of three brothers of El according to Philo. Baal's
standing appellation in the epic literature of Ugarit is
Al'iyan, which seems to be a contraction of the formula "I
prevail (*'al'iyu*) over the champions who encounter me in
the land of battle," since this is explicitly given as his name
in a text published in 1938 by Virolleaud.[41] As Al'iyan,
Baal is the hero of a great mythological epic, extensive portions of which have been recovered from the ruins of 14th-
century Ugarit. Here the central theme is the glorification
of Baal, for whom a great temple is built and who is slain
by monsters and carried to the land of Death (*Môt*). Mot
is the son of El and Ashirat (Rhea) according to both the
early epic and Philo, who correctly renders his name as
"Death." After Baal's death all life on earth languishes, so
his sister, "the virgin" Anath, finds Mot, kills him in a terrible battle, after which she performs an interesting dynamistic ritual with his body:

She seized Mot, son of El;
> With the sword she cut him up, with the sieve she
>> winnowed him,
> In the fire she burned him, in the mill she ground
>> him,
> In the field she sowed him,
In order that the birds might eat their portion, in order
> that they might destroy the seed (?) . . .[42]

In no ancient mythology do we find such explicit identification of the body of a god with the grain, which is successively reaped and threshed, winnowed, baked as bread, and
ground to meal (these operations are transposed for greater
consistency of action), and finally sowed as grain in the
field. The purpose of this ritual was not to revive Mot but

---

[41] See the writer's observations, *Bull. Am. Sch. Or. Res.*,
No. 70, p. 19. The original reads *'al'iyu qurâdima qâriyêya
ba'arṣi malḥâmati;* the second word is Accadian *qurâdu* "warrior, hero," not Heb. *qardom* "axe."

[42] This rendering differs from those previously proposed only
at the end, where *npr* is identified with Accadian *nipru* "seed."

to revive Baal by sympathetic action. Considering the extraordinary fluidity and variation of these ideas, however, it is quite possible that Mot could also be treated as a form of Adonis.

Goddesses of fertility play a much greater rôle among the Canaanites than they do among any other ancient people. The two dominant figures are Astarte and Anath, who are called in an Egyptian text of the New Empire "the great goddesses who conceive but do not bear," i. e., who are always virginal but who are none the less fruitful. This somewhat sophisticated appellation was presumably an attempt to rationalize fluid Canaanite conceptions of goddesses of fertility, who were sometimes treated as virgins and sometimes as mothers and creatresses of all life. Thus Anath appears in almost the same breath as "virgin" and as "progenitress of the peoples."[43] Philo Byblius also emphasizes the virginity of Astarte and of Anath's sister, otherwise unknown. These Canaanite goddesses were nearly always represented in iconography as naked, as we know both from the many hundreds of "Astarte" plaques from the period 1700-1100 B.C. which have been discovered by excavators and from the fact that the Canaanite goddesses Astarte and Qudshu (or Qadesh)[44] always appear naked in Egyptian portrayals of this age, in striking contrast to the modestly garbed native Egyptian goddesses. Another dominant characteristic of the Canaanite goddesses in question was their savagery. In Egyptian sources Astarte and Anath are preëminently goddesses of war; a favorite type of representation shows the naked goddess astride a galloping horse and brandishing a weapon in her right hand. In a fragment of the Baal epic which has just been published (1938), Anath appears as incredibly sanguinary. For a reason not yet known she massacres mankind, young and old, from the sea-coast to the rising of the sun, causing heads and hands to fly in all directions. Then she ties heads to her back, hands to her girdle, and wades up to her knees—yes,

---

[43] See *Bull. Am. Sch. Or. Res.*, No. 77, pp. 6 f.
[44] Cf. the remarks in *Mélanges Dussaud*, I (1939), p. 118, n. 2.

up to her throat—in human gore.[45] The favorite animals of the Canaanite goddess were the lion, because of its ferocity, and the serpent and dove, because of their reputed fecundity.

Just as virginity and fertility appear side by side as characteristics of goddesses, so do emasculation and fecundity as contradictory features of gods. Emasculation appears often in the myths collected by Philo, Lucian, and others; even El castrates himself—though he appears as the father of the gods by numerous goddesses. El also castrates his own father, according to Philo. There can be no doubt that eunuchs played a leading rôle in the cult of Bronze-Age Syria and Asia Minor, and in certain periods even in Mesopotamia proper. The name applied to them by the Western Semites was *komer* (which already appears as *kumrum* in the cuneiform texts from **Capp**adocia in the 19th century B.C.), "gallus," as we may **confi**dently say after examining all early sources which mention this word.[46] That the term

---

[45] The text is given by Virolleaud in *La déesse 'Anat* (Paris, 1938), pp. 13 ff. The innovations in the writer's rendering are the following: *bmt* = "back" not "hill" (this is certain); *ḥbš* = "girdle" (Heb. *ḥbš* "to bind around," transposed *ḥéšeb* "girdle"); *hlq-m* = Arab *ḥalq, ḥulqûm* "throat."

[46] The writer has maintained this interpretation of the word *komer* for many years (cf. *Proc. Am. Philos. Soc.*, 1930, p. 450), but has never had occasion to defend it in detail. A few illustrations of the available evidence must suffice. In the Old-Assyrian tablets from Cappadocia the word is used constantly (*kumrum, kumra*) in the sense of "member of a class of priests" (J. Lewy, *Rev. Hist. Rel.*, CX [1934], pp. 46 f.). It is there used as synonym of Accadian *pašišu* (*UḪ-ME*), as shown by Lewy (*Archives d'Histoire de Droit Oriental*, II [1938], p. 124); *pašišu* is a regular appellation of Tammuz, notably in a passage where the latter appears particularly akin to Attis and Adonis (cf. *Am. Jour. Sem. Lang.*, XXXV, pp. 180 ff.), and may thus have some such meaning as "gallus." In the light of the certain connection between the cult of the goddess Kubaba(t) and the galli (Albright, *Arch. f. Orientf.*, V, pp. 230 f., *Bull. Am. Sch. Or. Res.*, No. 78, pp. 26 f., n. 21; Benveniste, *Mélanges Dussaud*, I, pp. 249 ff.), the *kumrum* of Kubabat (Lewy, *loc. cit.*) was presumably the prototype of Greek *kybēbos* "gallus." The fact that a *kumrum* might have

already designated "male prostitute" (biblical *qadesh*) as
well as "eunuch priest" (the meanings may have been practically interchangeable as in Graeco-Roman times) is clear
from the fact that *kumru* is found in an Egyptian text of
the late second millennium with the determinative "male
dancer."[47] The popularity of sacred prostitution of both
sexes among the later Syrians and Anatolians is well known.
In the late second millennium B.C. we find that one of the
most common forms of the Syrian goddess is that of a naked
woman holding symbols of fertility such as lily stalks and
serpents in her upraised hands—her name is "the holy one"!
A cult-stand of about the twelfth century B.C. from Beth-
shan shows a remarkable tableau in relief: a nude goddess
holds two doves in her arms as she sits with legs apart to
show her sex; below her are two male deities with arms in-
terlocked in a struggle(?), with a dove at the feet of one
of them; toward them from below creeps a serpent and from
one side advances a lion. This may be considered as a terse
epitome of the mythological symbolism of Canaanite religion at the end of the pre-Israelite age in Palestine.

Before leaving this subject, it must be emphasized that
there are many important parallels between Canaanite and
Israelite temple-service and sacrificial ritual, as we know
from such impeccable sources as the Marseilles Tariff,
whose story is confirmed for the Late Bronze Age in a number of respects by the ritual texts from Ugarit. A very interesting parallel from Lachish has been reported to the
"Times" by Sir Charles Marston (July 8, 1939). In the
13th-century temple were found many sacrificial bones, all

---

a son is no objection, since adoption was exceedingly common
at that time and parallels from Mesopotamia are easy to adduce. In the Amarna Letters the related word *kamiru* means
"eunuch" (*Jour. Am. Or. Soc.*, XXXV, p. 394). About 600 B.C.
two grave-stelae of priests of the moon-god Shahar at Neirab
in Syria exhibit the priests (called *kumrâ* in both cases) as
beardless, in striking contrast to the usual practice of the day
in representing men. In Syriac *kumrâ* acquires the sense of
"priest" in general.
[47] See Albright, *Vocalization of the Egyptian Syllabic Orthography* (New Haven, 1934), p. 60, XVII.C.5.

from the right front leg of the animal, just as in Mosaic ritual. The inference that this temple was Israelite is contradicted by the well-known fact that the same limb figures with equal insistence in the Assyro-Babylonian ritual, so that preference for it may safely be considered as general throughout ancient Western Asia. There are also numerous points of contact between Canaanite and *late* Israelite mythology and literature, as we shall see below. In view of the geographical situation and the close similarity in language, it is very remarkable that parallels and points of contact remain so few.

B. The Hebrew Background of Israelite Origins

1. *The Geographical and Ethnic Background*

The latest discoveries at Mari on the Middle Euphrates (see above, pp. 153 f.) have strikingly confirmed the Israelite traditions according to which their Hebrew forefathers came to Palestine from the region of Harran in northwestern Mesopotamia. The earlier migration from Ur of the Chaldees to Harran remains without archaeological illustration (aside from the excavation of the city itself) but the flight from Ur when that capital was destroyed by the Elamites about 1950 B.C. sounds like an excellent historical tradition. The original Hebrew text may have read, "Ur in the land of the Chaldees." Harran itself was a flourishing city in the 19th and 18th centuries B.C., as we know from frequent references in our cuneiform sources. In the time of Hammurabi it was under an Amorite prince. The city of Nahor, mentioned as the home of Rebekah's parents in Gen. 24:10, figures often as Nakhur in the Mari tablets as well as in more recent Middle-Assyrian documents; it seems to have been located below Harran in the Balikh valley, to judge from both the Mari references and the Assyrian records of the seventh century B.C., where Til-Nakhiri, "the Mound of Nakhuru," is the name of a town (with Assyrian vowel harmony) in the Harran district.[48] It was also ruled by an Amorite prince in the 18th century B.C. In addition to the certain location of the patriarchal cities Harran and Nahor in northwestern Mesopotamia, we have hardly less clear indications in the names of Abraham's forefathers which correspond to the names of towns near Harran: Serug (Assyrian Sarugi, Syriac Serug), Nahor, and Terah (Til Turakhi, "Mound of Terah," in Assyrian times, just as Nakhur had become Til-Nakhiri). Peleg and perhaps Reu also correspond to later names of towns in the Middle-Euphrates valley, but it is dangerous to push such comparisons too far.[49]

Besides these certain and probable geographical links between the Hebrew Patriarchs and their traditional home in Padan-Aram, "the Plain of Aram" (Aram. *paddânâ* = Heb. *sadêh* "field, plain"), we now have a wealth of other data pointing to an original home of the Hebrew people in northern Mesopotamia, where they were under mixed Accadian, Hurrian, and Amorite influence. Since the publication of the Nuzian documents of the 15th century B.C. it has become increasingly evident that the customary law reflected by the patriarchal stories of Genesis fits better into the framework of Nuzian social and legal practice than it does into that of later Israel or into that of the Babylonian laws and economic documents of the 19th century or the similar Assyrian material of the 12th century B.C. Many striking parallels have been pointed out by Sidney Smith, C. H. Gordon, E. A. Speiser, and others.[50] Moreover, the discovery of the Mari and related documents from the 18th century B.C. is now bringing even more striking parallels, especially in language and proper names: e. g., the tribe of Benjamin and the name "Jacob."[51] When the economic

[48] *Bull. Am. Sch. Or. Res.*, No. 67, p. 27, n. 6; No. 78, pp. 29 f.

[49] Cf. *Jour. Bib. Lit.*, XLIII (1924), pp. 385-88.

[50] See now the comprehensive discussion by C. H. Gordon, with full bibliography, in *The Biblical Archaeologist*, III (1940), No. 1.

[51] "Jacob" stands for *°Ya'qub-'el* "May El Protect," which occurs not only as a place-name in Palestine in the fifteenth century B.C. (Tuthmosis List), but also in the just published

tablets of Mari are published we shall doubtless find many
socio-legal similarities to the narratives of Genesis. The earlier cosmogonic and ethnogonic material of the first eleven
chapters of Genesis is mostly inexplicable unless we suppose
that it was brought from Mesopotamia to Palestine by the
Hebrews before the middle of the second millennium. Nothing like the matter contained in the pre-Priestly sources of
Genesis 1-11 is found in Canaanite sources, whether we pe-
ruse the mythological poems of Ugarit or the briefer but
very pertinent sketch given by Philo Byblius. Nor is there
any hint of it in our now fairly extensive miscellaneous evidence for Canaanite beliefs and legends. In spite of A. S.
Yahuda's imaginative researches, there is no close parallel
anywhere between Gen. 1-11 and Egyptian literature. On
the other hand, the Mesopotamian parallels are many and
striking, though they never suggest direct borrowing from
canonical Babylonian sources. It has been shown recently
in detail that the situation can be explained satisfactorily
throughout if we suppose that the story of creation in Gen.
2, the story of Eden, the accounts of the antediluvian Patriarchs, the Flood-story, and the story of the Tower of
Babel were all brought from northwestern Mesopotamia to
the West by the Hebrews before the middle of the second
millennium.[52]

The problem of the ethnic and linguistic background of
the Hebrew Patriarchs is hardly ripe for solution, since a
vast quantity of relevant documentary material remains to
be published and analyzed. However, a few cautious observations may be made. The Israelites themselves believed
in later times that they descended from a "fugitive Aramaean" ('Arammî 'ôbhēdh, Deut. 26:5), and their eastern
relatives, with whom they maintained connubium for several generations, are always called "Aramaean" in Genesis.
On the other hand, in the genealogical lists Eber, the an-

---

tablets of the early eighteenth century B.C. from Chagar
Bazar in northern Mesopotamia (C. J. Gadd, *Iraq*, 1940, p. 38,
n. 5) as *Ya-aḫ-qu-ub-il(um)*.
[52] *Jour. Bib. Lit.*, LVIII (1939), pp. 91-103.

cestor of the Hebrews, is sharply distinguished from Aram, whose brother Arphaxad (with a non-Semitic name!) appears as Eber's grandfather. Moreover, in the lists of Abraham's offspring by Hagar and Keturah we find North and South-Arabian tribes, some of which figure elsewhere as descendants of Eber through Joktan but not through Abraham's direct ancestor, Peleg. In one passage both Aramaean tribes and Chaldaeans are listed as descendants of Abraham's brother Nahor. The matter has been complicated in recent times by B. Moritz' discovery that most of the nomadic tribes of Babylonia which figure in the Assyrian inscriptions of the ninth-seventh centuries were really of Arab, not of Aramaean origin.[53] The nomadic Akhlamu who began to settle in Syria and Mesopotamia about the twelfth century B.C. may also have acquired both the name *Aram* and the Aramaic dialect from their precursors. Without going into further details, we can safely say that the Aramaean language sprang from a West-Semitic dialect spoken in northwestern Mesopotamia in the early second millennium B.C., a dialect which seems to have left clear traces in the Mari documents. The Hebrew Patriarchs presumably spoke this dialect before their settlement in Palestine, but there, at an uncertain period, they adopted a local Canaanite dialect which was not identical with the standard speech of sedentary Canaanites, as may be linguistically demonstrated. The genetic affiliations of the early Hebrews were probably so mixed that all the theories reflected in later Israelite tradition have some justification. The fact that the standard genealogy in Gen. 11 made Eber son of the non-Semitic Arphaxad and that the Hebrew migration from Mesopotamia to Canaan may have been roughly contemporary with the movements which formed the prelude to the Hyksos Age certainly suggests a composite ethnic origin, including Hurrian as well as Semitic elements.

More and more evidence has accumulated to suggest that the early Hebrews were connected in some way with

[53] *Paul Haupt Anniversary Volume* (Baltimore, 1926), pp. 184-211.

the 'Apiru (Khapiru),[54] who play a very curious rôle in cuneiform documents of the 19th and 18th centuries, as well as in Nuzian, Hittite, and Amarna documents of the 15th-14th centuries. In Mesopotamia and Syria they appear as landless soldiers, raiders, captives, and slaves of miscellaneous ethnic origins; in Palestine they are often mentioned in Canaanite letters of the early 14th century as raiders and as rebels against Egyptian authority, sometimes in alliance with Canaanite princes. Until recently most scholars accepted the equation of the Khapiru ("Habiri," etc.) with the Hebrews, and the opposition of such eminent scholars as E. Dhorme and B. Landsberger was based on etymologies now known to be erroneous. The discovery that the true form of the name was *Apiru* complicates matters again. However, Hebrew *'Ibhrî* may well stand for an older *'Iprî* (by a phonetic change common in that language and period), which may perfectly well reflect an adjectival form *'Apiru*, by linguistic processes of known validity in closely parallel circumstances.[55] Until the question is decided, we must content ourselves with saying that a Khapiru origin would square extraordinarily well with He-

---

[54] The name of this people in cuneiform was formerly read *Khabiru*, but since the sign *BI* also had the reading *pi* and since Semitic *'ayin* is generally transcribed as *ḥ* in cuneiform the reading *'Apiru* has been maintained by the writer since 1930; see *The Archaeology of Palestine and the Bible* (New York, 1932-35), pp. 206 f. Virolleaud's discovery that the name is written (plural) as *'prm* in Ugaritic (cf. *Bull. Am. Sch. Or. Res.*, No. 77, p. 32), combined with the recognition that the name appears as *'a-pi-ru* in Egyptian transcription (Albright, *Vocalization of the Egyptian Syllabic Orthography* [New Haven, 1934], p. 42, VII.B.4) makes this reading quite certain. The new material on this people from Nuzian and Marian sources is collected and discussed by J. Lewy, *Heb. Un. Col. Ann.*, XIV (1939), pp. 587-623; E. Dhorme, *Rev. Hist. Rel.*, CXVIII (1938), pp. 170-87, and A. Goetze, *Bull. Am. Sch. Or. Res.*, No. 79, pp. 32 f.

[55] Cf. the writer's observations about the phonetic processes involved in such a change (*Bull. Am. Sch. Or. Res.*, No. 77, p. 33); cf. also H. H. Rowley, *Pal. Expl. Quar.*, 1940, pp. 90-94.

brew traditional history and would clear up many details which seem otherwise inexplicable.

It is not our intention here to dwell on the history of the Patriarchal Age in Palestine. So many corroborations of details have been discovered in recent years that most competent scholars have given up the old critical theory according to which the stories of the Patriarchs are mostly retrojections from the time of the Dual Monarchy (9th-8th centuries B.C.). Conflicting versions of a given episode in the J and E documents warn us against depending too slavishly on the present form of the tradition. On the other hand they are altogether too close in form and content to be of distinct origin, especially when we remember that much close parallelism between them has presumably been eliminated by the redactor, who saw no purpose in unnecessary repetition (see above, p. 79). The most reasonable view is that of R. Kittel, that they reflect different recensions of an old national epic, based on poems which came down, like the lost source of Genesis 14, from the Patriarchal Age. The attempt of so great an authority on verse as E. Sievers to scan most of Genesis as poetry, at least illustrates its poetic flavor. A unitary background for J and E is also suggested by their remarkably homogeneous characterizations of the Patriarchs. The figures of Abraham, Isaac, Jacob, and Joseph appear before us as real personalities, each one of whom shows traits and qualities which suit his character but would not harmonize with the characters of the others. This is particularly true of Jacob and Joseph. The Joseph story does, indeed, exhibit distinctly folkloristic elements, some of which are essential features of the stories of Adonis, Attis, and Bitis, but the picture of Joseph which we get from them is not in the least mythological, so we must probably reckon with the universal human tendency to adjust elements of a story to a familiar pattern (see above, p. 67).[56]

The Egyptian sojourn of Israel is a vital part of early Israelite historical tradition, and cannot be eliminated with-

[56] See Chap. I, nn. 41-43.

out leaving an inexplicable gap. Moreover, we know from the Egyptian names of Moses and a number of the Aaronids that part of Israel must have lived for a long time in Egypt.[57] Then there are a great many correct local and antiquarian details which would be inexplicable as later inventions. Most striking is the obvious relation in which the Joseph story and the later history of Israel in Egypt stand to the Hyksos movement. The "king who knew not Joseph" and who oppressed the Israelites should be a pharaoh of the New Empire, after the expulsion of the hated Asiatics from Egypt. With this agrees the fact that the Israelites were settled around the Hyksos capital of Egypt, in the "plain of Tanis" (Zoan, Psalms 78:12,43). That there was a long Semitic occupation of the northeastern Delta before the New Empire is certain from the Canaanite place-names found there in the New Empire, which include Succoth, Baal-zephon, Migdol, Zilu (Sillo), and probably Goshen itself.[58] That there were a good many Semites among Hyksos officials is certain,[59] and it is also clear that most of the Hyksos chiefs bore Semitic names, among which is Ya'qob-har (literally, "May the Mountain-god Protect"), formed with the element "Jacob." It is impossible to separate the tradition quoted in Num. 13:22, according to which He-

[57] Cf. the most recent marshalling of the evidence by Th. J. Meek, *Am. Jour. Sem. Lang.*, LVI (1939), pp. 113-20. On the Israelites in Egypt see also H. H. Rowley, *Bull. John Rylands Library*, XXII, pp. 3-50.

[58] Cf. *Jour. Eg. Arch.*, X (1924), pp. 7 f. The writer has long planned to discuss the name "Goshen," which is non-Egyptian in form, since Eg. g (which is a voiceless-unaspirated stop, Worrell, *Coptic Sounds*, pp. 17 ff.) was heard by Semites as q; cf. Heb. qeseth "scribal palette," from Eg. gst' and qôph "baboon," from Eg. g'f. Suffice it to say that "Goshen" also reappears as a place-name in southern Palestine and that the element guš appears as the first part of a number of compound place-names in northern Palestine and Syria; its original meaning seems to have been "mound (of earth)," Heb. gûš, Arab. juthwah.

[59] Cf. such names as Naḥman, 'Abd, and Ḥûr (*Jour. Pal. Or. Soc.*, 1931, p. 114, n. 1; Steindorff, *Annales du Service des Antiquités de l'Égypte*, XXXVI, p. 171, Nos. 79-91).

bron was founded seven years before Tanis, from the Hyksos invasion of Egypt, and difficult to separate the Hyksos era of Tanis, according to which 400 years had elapsed at a time shortly before the accession of Ramesses I (1310 B.C.), from the 430 years assigned in Ex. 12:40 for the duration of the Israelite sojourn in the district of Tanis.[60] In short, it must be considered as practically certain that the ancestors of part of Israel, at least, had lived for several centuries in Egypt before migrating to Palestine.

2. *The Religious Background*

There are some relatively secure types of evidence for the pre-Mosaic religion of the Hebrews. The Israelites recognized that their ancestors, who lived beyond the Euphrates, had "served other gods" (Jos. 24:2). The chief god of the Patriarchs was believed to have been Shaddai, as we read again and again in the Priestly Code (confirmed by the evidence of personal names, three of which appear in Numbers while one, *Shaddai-'ammî*,[61] is attested by a contemporary Egyptian inscription), and several other divine names are reported. Later tradition recognized the deliberate choice of God by each successive patriarchal generation, and A. Alt (1929) has demonstrated the antiquity and importance of the principle.[62] There is some valuable material available in the personal names of the early Hebrews, including names from the first generation or two after the Exodus. Since this last body of evidence is the most objective from the standpoint of the historical critic we shall consider it first.

The early Hebrew onomasticon consists quite largely of

[60] See the discussion of this question, *Bull. Am. Sch. Or. Res.*, No. 58 (1935), p. 16.

[61] See Burchardt, *Die altkanaanäischen Fremdworte und Eigennamen im Ägyptischen*, II (Leipzig, 1910), p. 43, No. 826.

[62] See Alt, *Der Gott der Väter* (Leipzig, 1929); J. Lewy, *Rev. Hist. Rel.*, CX (1934), pp. 50 ff.; Albright, *Jour. Bib. Lit.*, LIV (1935), pp. 188 ff.

abbreviated names (hypocoristica) such as *Yiṣḥaq* (Isaac),
Ya'qobh (Jacob), *Yôseph* (Joseph), *Yehûdah* (Judah),
Gad, Dan, etc., which are of no direct value for our present
purpose. It also fortunately includes a large number of
names containing an appellation of deity: *el* "god"; *ṣûr*
"mountain" (Aram. *ṭûr*); *shaddai* "(god) of the moun-
tain(s)."[63] In addition there are many names containing
the elements *'amm* "kindred, family, folk"; *ab* "father";
akh "brother." There has been much discussion of the first
word, which has the meaning "paternal uncle" in Arabic,
especially since this sense can be shown to exist in South
Arabic at least as early as the seventh century B.C. However, since Heb. *'am* always means "kindred, folk, people,"
and since the Babylonian scholars of the second millennium
B.C. correctly translated this element (where it occurs in
Amorite names like *Hammurabi, Ammiṣaduqa*) as "family," we are certainly justified in adopting this meaning—
the only one which suits many of the names containing
it: e. g., *Reḥabh'am* (Rehoboam), "Let (my People be
Widened."[64] The terms of relationship which appear in
this group of names are nearly always interchangeable with
the word *el* "god," so it has been generally recognized by
recent students that they also refer to deity. Names of these
two types were already common in Semitic in the pre-
Accadian age, as we know from the fact that they are relatively abundant in Old Accadian documents (25th-23rd
centuries), and they became progressively less common as
time went on; they are also much more frequent in Old

[63] On the meaning of the name "Shaddai" see the writer's
discussion, *ibid.*, pp. 180-93, to which important additions
can now be made, rendering the philological explanation of
the name inexpugnable. We now know, for example, that the
adjectival-gentilic formation in question was common among
the Amorites of the Upper Euphrates valley in the early second
millennium. A number of good additional parallels to the formation of the name itself can also be adduced from Accadian.
E. Burrows' posthumous paper (*Jour. Theol. Stud.*, XLI [1940],
pp. 152-61) is antiquated.

[64] Cf. the writer's remarks, *Am. Jour. Sem. Lang.*, XXXVIII
(1922), pp. 140 f.

Assyrian records (20th-19th centuries) than later. In Amorite nomenclature of the period between 2100 and 1600 B.C. they abounded; in Canaanite they were much less common and the element *'amm* has not yet been identified in a definitely Canaanite milieu. In Israel both types of name were in common use until the tenth century, after which they went out of use rapidly and new names belonging to them ceased to be coined.

Since H. Ranke's convincing demonstration (1937)[65] that both Egyptian and Western-Asiatic sentence-names (i. e., names which form a sentence, as most unabbreviated Semitic names did in antiquity) represent utterances of a parent or person with authority at the birth of a child, it is easier to understand their connotation. Such names contain a vow or invocation to a god, or a statement of good omen connected in some way with a god. A name such as *Yishma'-'el* means "May El Hear"; *Eli-ṣûr* is "My God is (verily) a Mountain (in whom I can trust)"; *Pedâ-ṣûr* means "May the Mountain Redeem (me from suffering)"; *Shaddai-'or* (Shedeur) is "The One of the Mountain(s) Shines (shows favor to me)"; *Eli-'abh* means "My God is Father (to me)"; *'Ammi-'el* is "(the god of) my Kindred is God (to me)"; *Akhî-'ezer* means "My (divine) Brother is (my) Help," etc. In most abbreviated personal names, we must assume that the second element was originally a name or appellation of deity, usually *El:* e. g., *Ya'qobh* is an abbreviation of *Ya'qobh-'el,* "May El Protect," which actually appears as a personal name in northwestern Mesopotamia (18th century) and as a Palestinian place-name in an Egyptian list of the 15th century B.C.; *Yiṣhaq* stands for *Yiṣhaq-'el,* "May El Smile (favorably upon me in my distress)." These illustrations, which can easily be multiplied, throw much light on the pre-Mosaic religion of the Hebrews. Two facts emerge immediately. First, the principal deity of the pre-Mosaic Hebrews was a mountain god, or was invested with mountain imagery. This also appears, incidentally, in two names of early Hyksos chiefs, formed with the element *Har*, "Mountain-god." The mountain-deity in question is clearly the storm-god Hadad, generally called Baal (lord) by the Canaanites, and often addressed as "great mountain," or the like, in Accadian invocations to Amurru, the "Western One," i. e., the storm-god of the West. The second fact is that the Hebrews, like their no-madic Semitic forefathers, possessed a very keen sense of the relationship between a patriarchal group (clan or fam-ily) and its deity, who was therefore an actual member of the clan and could be addressed by a mortal kinsman as "father, brother," and even as "kindred." All the members of the clan were, accordingly, children, brethren, or kins-men of the god, who was the head of the house (family). Among the Amorites and Aramaeans of the late second and early first millennia the expressions "belonging to the house of" and "son of" are interchangeable, as we know from scores of examples in the Bible and especially in the Assyr-ian and Aramaean inscriptions. Consequently, the god who is considered as patron of a family or a dynasty was called "the lord of the house" among the Aramaeans of the ninth and eighth centuries B.C., as has just been pointed out by Euler (1939).[66] In the early first millennium the Ara-maeans are known to have named their children "Son of (god) Hadad," etc., and this custom later became very popular among the pagans of Syria and Mesopotamia in the early Christian age.[67]

There is no solid basis for the idea which is sometimes expressed that there was a kind of "El" monotheism among the early Western Semites and in particular among the

[66] *Zeits. Alttest. Wiss.*, LVI (1938), pp. 272-313.

[67] These names begin in the tenth century, according to our present information and become more and more popular, espe-cially in the first three centuries A.D., as may be illustrated by the following incomplete list: *Bar-Hadad, Bar-Ginai* (Ginai was the lion-god of Heliopolis in Syria), *Bar-Shamash, Bar-'Atte, Bar-Elâhâ, Bar-Nabû* (Barnabas), *Bar-Apaladad, Bar-Gaddâ, Bar-Adôn, Bar-Rabbâ* (Barabbas, which does not mean "Son of the Father," as universally supposed).

early Hebrews. It is true that very few specific names of gods appear among them during the nomadic or semi-nomadic stage and that the use of different appellations of gods in personal names seems to increase rapidly under sedentary conditions. However, there are too many divine names known to have been common to the ancestors of the various Semitic peoples, and there is too much evidence for polytheistic beliefs among the earliest South Arabians after the eighth century B.C. to warrant any such hypothesis. D. Nielsen has clarified the situation by showing that early South-Arabian pantheons were often organized in triads of father, mother, and son; he has also made it probable that the system of triads was proto-Semitic, though he has gone much too far in trying to carry it through Near-Eastern polytheism in general.[68] We pointed out above (p. 173) that such triads are archaeologically illustrated in neolithic Jericho, not later than the sixth millennium. Early Hebrew popular religion was presumably similar, with a father, El, a mother whose specific name or names must remain obscure (perhaps Elat or Anath), and a son who appears as the storm-god, probably named Shaddai, "the One of the Mountain(s)." It is only reasonable to suppose that there were also other minor divinities whose existence was recognized by different groups. Whether there was a sharp line of demarcation between El and Shaddai is questionable, in view of the fluidity of all known early Semitic pantheons. It is most unlikely that the element *el* in early Hebrew names refers exclusively to the all-father El; it may also have been a surrogate for another divine name (i. e., *the* god) or even in some cases a more fluid dynamistic expression for impersonal supernatural power.[69] It must similarly be emphasized that the fluid conception of the god of a clan as being its blood relative takes root in dynamistic and corporative ideas of great antiquity.

As Alt has pointed out (1929) there is no reason to doubt that the divine appellations of Genesis 14-35 formed with

[68] See Chap. III, n. 44.
[69] See Chap. III, n. 35.

the element El are pre-Israelite, since they are generally mentioned in connection with very early shrines.[70] This observation yields several important early Hebrew divine names, all of which were prefixed in Hebrew tradition by the generic name for "deity," which is grammatically very incongruous in one case (*el-Bêth'el* or even *ha'el-Bêth'el*). Four names are known: *'Elyôn* "the Lofty One"; *'Ôlam* "the Eternal One," literally "(God of) Eternity"; *Bêth'el* (Bethel), "the House of God"; *Ro'î*, possibly meaning "the One who Sees me." Since no fewer than three of these names occur as appellations of deity in Canaanite sources, it is clear that they are very ancient West-Semitic names for the all-father or the lord of heaven (the storm-god). Again they point to the nobility of early Hebrew conceptions of their high god or gods. Three of them recur in later Hebrew sources: two, *'Elyôn* and *'Ôlam* (usually in a genitive compound) in biblical literature, and one, *Bêth'el*, in the records of Elephantine.

As Alt has shown, biblical traditions with regard to the God of the Fathers are not of secondary origin, as has been rashly assumed by critical scholars, but actually reflect preMosaic Hebrew religious ideas. This is particularly true of the names applied to them in our earliest sources: the "God of Abraham"; the "Kinsman (*pahad*) of Isaac"; the "Champion (*abhîr*) of Jacob." Much difficulty has been caused by the current translation of the archaic appellation *pahad* as "terror," whereas it should probably be rendered "kindred, kinsman," as in later Palmyrene.[71] Each Patriarch is represented by Hebrew tradition as choosing his God for himself, and as selecting a different manifestation

---

[70] *Der Gott der Väter*, pp. 49 ff.

[71] Since the writer may not publish his treatment of this subject for some time, a few indications are called for. The word *pahid*, *pahd* originally meant "thigh, hip, loins," as shown by Hebrew, Aramaic, and Arabic cognates with this meaning. In Palmyrene *pahdâ* means "family, clan, tribe" and in Arabic *fahid* is said by the native lexicographers to mean "a small branch of a tribe consisting of a man's nearest kin"; in North Canaanite (Ugaritic) *phd* means "flock" (Dan'el, II, 5, lines 17, 23: *'emr b-phd* = "lamb from the flock").

of Yahweh, the later God of Israel. Alt has illustrated the practice of choosing one's god from Aramaic and Arabic paganism of the first Christian centuries, but closer parallels have been subsequently adduced by J. Lewy (1934) from the Old Assyrian inscriptions of the 20th century B.C., and by others from the Nuzian contracts of the 15th century and the Aramaic inscriptions of the eighth century. We can, accordingly, trace the existence among the early Hebrews of two conceptions, both characteristic of their environment: 1. a dynamistic belief in an undefined but real blood relationship between a family or clan and its god(s); 2. a recognition of the right of an independent man or founder of a clan to choose his own personal god, with whom he is expected to enter into a kind of contractual relationship. In combination, these ideas must have led to a form of tribal religion where both the collective and the personal aspects of deity were present, the former in tribal acts of religious nature and the latter in individual worship.

C. THE RELIGION OF MOSES

1. *The Documentary Sources*

In all three of the parallel pentateuchal documents (J,E,P) the figure of Moses dominates the early national life of Israel. The older sources, J and E, agree in the main with regard to the rôle of Moses and the leading events of his life. In view of the principle of adding differences and eliminating unnecessary repetition which was characteristic of ancient oriental compilers, we may be sure that the parallelism between J and E was originally much closer than appears in their present form. As we have seen in dealing with the account of the Patriarchs in Genesis, J and E must reflect two recensions of an original epic narrative, the nucleus of which had presumably been recited by Hebrew rhapsodists before the Exodus. It is possible that this epic included the story of Moses' early life and the Exodus, though the historical break between the Patriarchal Age and the time of Moses does not favor such a view. It is more likely that the whole story of Moses was added to the epic nucleus soon after the Conquest of Canaan and that the combined narrative (whether in verse or prose we can hardly say) was recited by Levites or rhapsodists until the break-up of the amphictyonic organization under Philistine blows in the eleventh century B.C. Thereafter, we may suppose, the two recensions J (in the south) and E (in the north) were separately transmitted, being written down not later than 750 B.C. and combined in the JE recension during the eighth or seventh century B.C.

It is not necessary to repeat the arguments which have convinced several generations of scholars that J is the oldest document, containing earlier and later elements (L or J_1 and J or J_2), which were put into substantially their present form between cir. 925 B.C. (Division of the Monarchy) and 750 B.C., and that J was particularly interested in Judah. The recent effort of Volz and Rudolph (1933-38) to show that E is not, after all, a primary source but simply represents supplementary material added to J, has convinced but few scholars and does not do justice to the homogeneity of these additions, nor to the principles according to which such compilations were made (see above). That E is later than J and represents a northern tradition is generally agreed. There has lately been a tendency to adopt lower dates than the standard ones held since Wellhausen's *Prolegomena,* according to which we must date J cir. 850, E cir. 750 B.C. This tendency may possibly be correct, as far as concerns the date when J and E were finally edited in substantially their present Massoretic form; it is emphatically wrong with respect to their first oral or written composition, since the discovery of the Lachish Letters (1935) has proved that such fine classical Hebrew as we find in the JE narrative must be considerably earlier than the end of the preëxilic Jewish state. Its close grammatical and stylistic resemblance to the account of David's later life in Samuel, which cannot have been written after the tenth century B.C., brings us to a date not too long after 925 B.C. So we come again to the accepted date between 925 and 750 B.C. for the original content of both J and E. S. A. Cook and others are certainly right in placing the date of the later elements in JE after the height of the Prophetic Age,[72] but we shall see that the latter must be dated in the ninth century, not in the eighth.

Since the date of the pentateuchal documents is a very important question, we may be pardoned for observing at this point that a reëxamination of JE's Table of Nations (Gen. 10), in the light of our latest information regarding geographical names and ethnic movements in the ancient Near East, points to a period preceding the eighth century B.C., since not a word is said about several important peoples and nations which then came into the limelight for the first time. Apparent exceptions, such as the mention of the Cimmerians and Scythians, are now being eliminated, since these peoples had certainly emerged upon the Syro-Phoenician horizon at a considerably earlier date than has often been supposed, judging only from cuneiform references.[73] It seems increasingly probable that Gen. 10 is derived largely from a document of the tenth century B.C.; the references to Assyria and Arabia fit this general period better than any other.[74]

It follows from the foregoing observations that J and E do not, as a rule, give independent traditions regarding the

[72] Cf. S. A. Cook, *Jour. Bib. Lit.*, LI (1932), p. 275 and n. 3.

[73] For the Cimmerians see the observations and references of J. Wiesner in *Der Alte Orient*, XXXVIII:2-4 (1939), p. 75; for the Scythians see J. Przyluski, "Nouveaux aspects de l'histoire des Scythes," *Revue de l'Université de Bruxelles*, 1937, p. 4.

[74] The tenth century B.C. is accidentally the date assigned by A. Hermann, in his fanciful book on *Die Erdkarte der Bibel* (Braunschweig, 1931; cf. H. Philipp in the *Philologische Wochenschrift*, 1932, cols. 175-80), to the "Phoenician" map of the world which is supposed to have become the nucleus of Hebrew cosmography. It is very significant that the Arab tribes listed in Gen. 10 are almost entirely different from the tribes known to us from the Assyrian inscriptions of the eighth and seventh centuries, as well as from the Sabaean and Minaean inscriptions of slightly later date. The writer formerly dated the bulk of the material in Gen. 10 about the end of the eighth century (cf. *Recent Discoveries in Bible Lands*, New York, 1936, p. 25), but the weight of the evidence is against so late a date.

life of Moses and the beginnings of Israel, but rather reflect the official version as it was known in the eleventh century B.C. However, it is highly improbable that substantial alterations were made in its form during the period of the Judges. We must naturally assume, as in other parallel cases, a short period during which traditions and legends were first told, were repeated, and were collected into some sort of standard form. Thereafter changes would be comparatively few, as long as the standard version continued to be recited. After it had been broken into two strands, J and E, changes would become much more frequent, but are subject to our control because of the two independent lines of tradition. Moreover, the story of Moses must have been too well known in the age of the prophets and too well controlled by written sources accessible to scribes to permit of much unauthorized variation from the standard form. Furthermore, as we shall see below, J and E are supplemented by P, which very often goes back to quite independent oral and written sources. Since many traditions imbedded in our three sources were actually formed and even phrased at different times, we have a staggered chronological relationship between them which greatly enhances their historical dependability. In spite of the four centuries or so during which stories of Moses' life were transmitted orally before being put into fixed form, they ought, accordingly, to be at least as historically reliable as the accounts of Zoroaster and Gautama (Buddha), which were transmitted much longer by oral tradition.

The Priestly Code is also important as an historical source for the Mosaic period. It is very different in character from the older J and E, but, in contrast to them, it belongs to a scribal circle which was interested in questions of chronology and topography, ritual and liturgy, and which unquestionably had access to early written documents. Moreover, it was also the result of a complex process of collecting and sifting tradition, as is clearly shown by the doublets in the description of the Tabernacle, etc. Its language and style are, in general, *older* than that of the writings of the Deuteronomic school, though its composition in its present form must be later and can hardly be preëxilic.[75] A warning against dating it too late is provided by such archaic documents as the list of tribal heads and their offerings in Num. 7, which can no longer be dismissed as fictitious.[76] A warning against dating it too early is furnished by the variant lists of the Israelite tribal census in Num. 2 and 26, which have been proved to be recensional doublets with a long manuscript tradition behind them. Since the original census must have belonged to the United Monarchy and probably to the time of David (II Sam. 24), we must allow considerable time for the differences in manuscript transmission to have arisen.[77] In brief, the material preserved in P is more heterogeneous both in date and content than that of JE, and consequently less reliable on the average. On the other hand, some of it, resting on early written sources, is perhaps more dependable for historical purposes than anything in JE. We must again emphasize the fact that alphabetic Hebrew writing was employed in Canaan and neighboring districts from the Patriarchal Age on, and that the rapidity with which forms of letters changed is clear evidence of common use. It is certain that the Hebrew alphabet was written with ink and

[75] H. L. Ginsberg has made a very interesting stylistic comparison between the Priestly Code and the oldest Aramaic papyrus from Egypt (515 B.C.); cf. *Jour. Bib. Lit.*, LIX (1940), p. x.

[76] G. B. Gray's careful study in his *Studies in Hebrew Proper Names* (London, 1896), pp. 190 f., has proved to be completely misleading, since his evidence was still almost exclusively biblical and there were few extra-biblical sources which might have enabled him to control his statistical deductions about the probability of early occurrence of certain types. F. Hommel's treatment in *Die altisraelitische Überlieferung* (Munich, 1897), pp. 298 ff., though much less critical, was based on original extra-biblical sources and has proved to be correct in principle, though wrong in many details. M. Noth takes a somewhat cautious intermediate position in *Die israelitischen Personennamen* (Stuttgart, 1928), pp. 7 f., but our material has increased greatly in the past twelve years and we need no longer be so cautious.

[77] See *Jour. Pal. Or. Soc.*, V (1925), pp. 20 ff.

used for every-day purposes in the 14th and 13th centuries B.C. (Lachish, Beth-shemesh, Megiddo), that quantities of papyrus were exported from Egypt to Phoenicia after 1100 B.C. (Wen-amun), that writing was practiced by a youth of Gideon's time (early eleventh century), that it was known in Shiloh before 1050 B.C., that several examples of writing from Iron I (cir. 1200-900 B.C.) have been found in Israelite Palestine, and that David had a staff of secretaries. In the light of these facts, hypercriticism with regard to the authenticity of much of the material preserved by P is distinctly unscholarly, and its independent attestation of facts given by J and E is a valuable guarantee of their historicity. It is even less likely that there is deliberate invention or "pious" forgery in P than in JE, in view of the well attested reverence which ancient Near-Eastern scribes had for the written tradition (see above, p. 77).

2. The Historical Foundations of Israelite Tradition

Steering as cautiously as possible between the Scylla of overreliance on tradition and the Charybdis of hypercriticism, we may confidently assume that Moses was a Hebrew who was born in Egypt and reared under strong Egyptian influence. This is independently attested by his clearly Egyptian name, supported by the Egyptian names current among his Aaronid kindred for two centuries. It is true that the sibilant in the name *Mosheh* (from the Egyptian abbreviated name *Mȃse,* pronounced *Mȏse* after the twelfth century B.C. and probably sounding very much like it in the Delta a century or two earlier) is differently treated from that in the name *Pinehas* (from Egyptian *Pi-nehase* "the Nubian"), but the spelling of the latter evidently rests on correct oral tradition, while that of the former reproduces orthographically the exact letter with which the name had to be written in Canaanite alphabetic characters in the 13th century B.C. (since *samekh* was then always used to transcribe an entirely distinct sound, *ts* or *tsh*). The name *Pineḥas,* of which we have just spoken, is interesting as providing an independent (and absolutely reliable) confirmation of the tradition that there was a Nubian element in the family of Moses (Num. 12:1).

The tradition in Ex. 1 that the Israelites were forced by the Egyptian corvée to take part in the construction of the store-cities Pithom and Raamses is also independently supported by the excavations at Tell Retabeh (Pithom, which is not Tell el-Maskhutah=Succoth, as formerly supposed) and Tanis, both of which were built (or rebuilt) by Ramesses II. Since Tanis was called *Per-Re'emasese* (The House of Ramesses) only for a couple of centuries (cir. 1300-1100), it is most improbable that the tradition could arise if it were spurious. With our present knowledge of the topography of the eastern Delta the account of the start of the Exodus given in Ex. 12:37 and 13:20 ff. is perfectly sound topographically, and Alan Gardiner, who long objected to its historicity on topographical grounds, has recently withdrawn his objections (1933).[78] Many additional pieces of evidence for the substantial historicity of the account of the Exodus and the wandering in the regions of Sinai, Midian, and Kadesh can easily be given, thanks to our greatly increased knowledge of topography and archaeology. We must content ourselves here with the assurance that there is no longer any room for the still dominant attitude of hypercriticism toward the early historical traditions of Israel. Even the long contested date of the Exodus can now be fixed within reasonable limits. In 1937 the discovery in the remains of the latest Canaanite Lachish of a hieratic inscription dated to the year 1221 B.C. (or possibly somewhat later, but in no case earlier) proved that the fall of this town into Israelite hands took place in or after that year. Moreover, the long known, but often misinterpreted, text of the Israel stele of Marniptah, which is dated in 1219 B.C., proves that Israel was already in Western Palestine in force (see below, p. 279), but had not yet settled down (the name is written with the determinative for "for-

[78] *Jour. Eg. Arch.*, XIX, pp. 127 f.; see also H. Junker, *Zeits. Äg. Spr.*, LXXV (1939), pp. 83 f.

eign people," instead of "foreign land").[79] If we allow the generation ("forty years") which Israelite tradition demands, we thus arrive at a date not later than cir. 1250 for the Exodus. However, it is very probable that we must allow a generation for the Israelite occupation of Eastern Palestine and advance westward in force, so a date in the early 13th century is safest for the Exodus. If we place it about 1280 B.C. we can hardly be far wrong, since the early years of Ramesses II (1290-1224) were largely occupied with building operations in the city to which he gave his name, the Raamses of Israelite tradition. The striking agreement between this date and that of 430 years given in Ex. 12:40, if we suppose that it belongs to the era of Tanis (cir. 1710 B.C.), may, of course, be purely accidental, but it is very remarkable.

Archaeological investigation has also shed some light on the situation in that general age in Sinai, Midian, and the Negeb of Palestine. There were as yet no towns or stationary camps, except probably in Edom, where Nelson Glueck has discovered a sedentary occupation going back to the 12th or 13th century. At the ancient site of Eziongeber or Elath near Aqabah, Glueck's recent excavations (1938-40) have proved that the first buildings were erected on virgin soil in the tenth century B.C. At Kadesh-barnea ('Ain el-Qudeirat), the oldest fortress belongs also to about the tenth century. In Sinai proper there were intermittently worked copper mines at Wadi Magharah and Serabit el-Khadem, but the former appear to have been virtually abandoned after the Middle Empire, whereas the latter were exploited on a large scale under nearly every pharaoh of the Nineteenth and Twentieth Dynasties, down to Ramesses VI (cir. 1125 B.C.); inscriptions of Ramesses II were particularly abundant in the temple there, which has been excavated by Petrie (1905) and Starr (1930). To judge from the potsherds picked up by Glueck around the copper mines of the 'Arabah, just west and south of Edom, intensive working began there in the Early Iron Age, but no

[79] See the writer's detailed discussion, *Bull. Am. Sch. Or. Res.*, No. 74 (1939), pp. 11-23.

exact date can be set. Since Midian (the region south and southeast of 'Aqabah) is much richer in copper ores than either Sinai or Edom, it is hardly possible that the Midianites of Moses' time had not begun to exploit them, especially since there were excellent customers close at hand in Egypt and Canaan. The marriage of Moses to the daughter of a Midianite priest, variously named Jethro and Reuel, is exceptionally well attested by Israelite tradition, since it appears repeatedly in different connections and since the family of Reuel's son Hobab, Moses' friend, became Israelite (Num. 10:29, Jud. 4:11). The clan in question, moreover, is repeatedly named "Kenite," i. e., "belonging to the coppersmith(s)"; cf. Gen. 4:22 and Arab. *qain,* Aram. *qaînâyâ* "smith." In short, Sinai and Midian were at that time far from being the domain of barbarous camel-nomads, but were actually occupied by semi-sedentary tribes which were connected by close ties of commerce and industry with Egypt and Canaan. It is interesting to note that camels are mentioned only once in the whole of the Pentateuch, aside from probably anachronistic allusions in a few passages in Genesis and from the mention of the camel among unclean animals (cf. p. 164 on the transition from ass-nomadism to camel-nomadism shortly before 1100 B.C.). The Israelites of the wilderness wanderings were, therefore, definitely ass-nomads and were, accordingly, restricted to just such a route as is marked out for them in Num. 33, where they were never far from oases or from the pasture lands of the Negeb and Transjordan.

3. *Moses and Monotheism*

We are handicapped in dealing with this subject by the fact that all our literary sources are relatively late, as we have seen, and that we must therefore depend upon a tradition which was long transmitted orally. Many scholars go so far as to deny the historian any right to use these sources to determine what the religion of Moses actually was. Under the circumstances we must content ourselves with establishing certain facts and some other probabilities. In the first place, it is absurd to deny that Moses was actually the founder of the Israelite commonwealth and the framer of Israel's religious system. This fact is emphasized so unanimously by tradition that it may be regarded as absolutely certain. Nowhere is there the slightest breath of doubt cast on this irrefragable fact by Israelite tradition. If we regard Zoroaster, Buddha, and Confucius as the founders of nomistic religions we cannot deny this right to Moses. In this case we are no more justified in insisting that the religion introduced by Moses was radically different from that of the Book of Exodus than we should be in trying to divorce the other higher religions which we have named from their founders. The Pentateuch reflects a series of traditions coming from circles in which the "law of Moses" was the ultimate standard. In order to determine the details of this law there had to be priests or scribes whose primary function it was to preserve and transmit them. As has recently been pointed out by S. Gandz (1935), there was a class of priests who are called by Jeremiah (2:8) "holders of the law" (*tôfesê hat-tôrah*), with name and function which remind us of the Moslem "holders" (*ḥuffâz*) of the Qur'an.[80] In many ways the transmission of the Torah must have resembled that of the Tradition (*ḥadîth*) in Islam; the apparent lack of the validating "chain" (*isnâd*) in Israel is presumably due to the anonymity of authors and scholars there (aside from the prophets of the eighth century and later).[81] In the course of time a great many laws and practices which can hardly have been Mosaic were introduced into Israel; their lateness is often established by comparison of the forms which they assume in JE, D, and P, which show a progressive development first adequately emphasized by Wellhausen.

There is absolute unanimity in our sources about the

---

[80] *Jewish Studies in Memory of George A. Kohut* (New York, 1935), pp. 257 ff.

[81] For an excellent account of the origin and development of the *ḥadîth* in Islam, together with a convincing demonstration of its essential authenticity, see J. Fück, *Zeits. Deutsch. Morg. Ges.*, XCIII (1939), pp. 1-32.

name given his God by Moses. The spelling *YHWH* (pronounced *Yahweh,* as we know from Greek transcriptions)
is always found in prose passages in the Hebrew Bible, as
well as in the Mesha Stone (ninth century) and the
Lachish Letters (cir. 589 B.C.). Beside this fuller form
there was also a normally abbreviated form *Yahu* (the jussive form of the imperfect causative which appears as
Yahweh),[82] which is found in all early personal names
(shortened in northern Israel to *-yau-* and after the Exile
to *-yah*). It has often been maintained in the past thirty
years that *Yahu* is more original than *Yahweh,* but all the
epigraphic and linguistic facts are utterly opposed to this
paradoxical view. It has also been insisted that this or that
earlier non-Israelite divine name or element in a personal
name shows the existence of the prototype of the Tetragrammaton before Moses. In itself this is not impossible,
but every single suggestion has been effectively disproved,
including the latest from Ugarit, where Virolleaud suggests
that a word *yw* is identical with *Yahweh.* Unfortunately,
the context does not lend itself in the least to such an interpretation, and the supposed *yw* should probably be
read *yr* "offspring," which suits the context well, so far as
it is preserved.[83] It is well known today that the most
plausible of the older suggestions, Accadian *yaum* in the
name *Yaum-ilu,* means simply "Mine (is the god)." Many
different meanings have been attributed to *Yahweh* by
scholars who recognized its relative antiquity, but only one
yields any suitable sense: "He causes to be." The other sug-

[82] See my discussions, *Jour. Bib. Lit.,* XLIII (1924), pp.
370-78; XLIV, pp. 158-62; XLVI, pp. 175 ff.; M. Noth, *Die
israelitischen Personennamen,* pp. 101-6.
[83] *La déesse 'Anat,* p. 97 f. (cf. A. Bea, *Biblica,* 1939, pp.
440 f.). The photograph given by Virolleaud in plate XIII
is not conclusive; the form is intermediate between those of
adjacent *w* and *r.* For the word *yr* "spawn, offspring" (Accad.
âru) see *Bull. Am. Sch. Or. Res.,* No. 63, p. 29, n. 36; No. 71,
p. 39, n. 38. The words *šm bny yr*(?) *'elt*(?)[ ] must be rendered, "The name of my son is 'Offspring(?) of the god-
dess(?)'[ ]." Note that in Keret, line 25, the word *yr* also
means "offspring (of a woman)."

gestions, "He blows, He fells, He loves, He is kindly," etc., are totally without parallel in ancient Near-Eastern onomastics.[84] It is objected that "to cause to be" is too abstract a meaning for so early a period. This again is erroneous, since Egyptian and Accadian texts of pre-Mosaic days swarm with illustrations of this idea, beginning with the Pyramid Texts. Linguistically the form *yahweh* can only be causative, and to judge from many analogies in Babylonia, Egypt, and Canaan, it is an abbreviation of a longer name or litanic formula. A few illustrations must suffice. In Sumerian Babylonia the name *Shagan* (later *Shakkan*), belonging to the god of animal husbandry, is an abbreviation of *Ama-shagan-gub* "He who Assists Bearing Mothers"; *Dumuzi* (later *Tammuz*) stands for *Dumu-zid-abzu; Asari* (a name of Marduk) represents the fuller *Asari-lu-dug; Gish* stands for *Gishbilgamesh* (later *Gilgamesh*), etc. Similar abbreviated formulae are common as divine names in later Accadian and Egyptian religion: cf. Accadian *Aṣûshu-namer, Uṣur-amatsa,* and Egyptian *Iusas,* etc. It is, indeed, probable that many Egyptian names of gods are just as abbreviated as the names of kings and commoners are known to be in all early periods; e. g., the name *Osiris*

---

[84] Among the latest ideas are Mowinckel's explanation as *yâ huwa,* (O He, O That One!) and A. Lukyn Williams' *Ya-hô* (supposed to be a solemn cry of some kind). Very extraordinary from the linguistic point of view is K. G. Kuhn's contention that the original form of the name was *Yaw* (*Orientalische Studien* [*Littmann Festschrift;* Leiden, 1935], pp. 25-42), with Littmann's own suggestion that the name is derived from Indo-European *Dyeus* (Zeus). There is much useful material for the history of the pronunciation of the Tetragrammaton in the article by O. Eissfeldt in *Zeits. Alttest. Wiss.,* LIII (1935), pp. 59-76, but it needs critical philological sifting. For example, it is quite certain that the Babylonian writing *ya-a-ma* reflects a pronunciation *yau* at the end of a theophorous compound; for the phonetic rules in question see C. H. Gordon, *Arch. f. Orientf.* XII (1938), p. 110, §§ 17-18, 20. Moreover, as C. H. Gordon has pointed out to me, the writing *Yhbyh* in the Jewish incantations of the seventh century A.D. means *YH-b-YH,* i. e., it is a kind of "exponential" strengthening of the Tetragrammaton.

is probably an abbreviation of the fuller *Osiris-onnophris*. A most remarkable illustration comes from the Canaanite religion of the 15th century B.C., where the standing appellation of the storm-god, Baal, usually given as *Al'iyan*, appears in its full form as "I prevail (*'al'iyu*) over the champions whom I meet in the land of battle."[85] The abbreviated name accordingly means simply "I will surely prevail." The enigmatic formula in Ex. 3:14, which in Biblical Hebrew means "I am what I am," if transposed into the form in the third person required by the causative *Yahweh*, can only become *Yahweh asher yihweh* (later *yihyeh*), "He Causes to be what Comes into Existence." Later this formula was modified, presumably because the old causative was no longer used in later Hebrew. In the dialect of Moses the formula may even have been *Yahweh zê-yihweh*, employing the *zê* which appears as a relative preposition in Canaanite and poetic Hebrew as well as in the appellation of Yahweh in Jud. 5:5, *Zê-Sinai* "the One of Sinai" (as first pointed out by H. Grimme, in accordance with widespread West-Semitic usage).[86] If the restored formula were isolated, one would be justified despite the evidence in suspecting its correctness, but we have it again and again in Egyptian texts of the second millennium B.C.: "(a god) who causes to be (or who creates) what comes into existence" (e. g., repeatedly in the great hymn to Amun from the 15th century B.C.). Even if this view should prove to be wrong, there is ample evidence in the Bible that the Israelites had always regarded Yahweh as Creator of All.

Another original characteristic of the Israelite God was that He stood alone, without any family connections, whether consort, son, or daughter. The nearest approach to attributing a family to Him that we meet before the Exile is the term *benê El* or *benê ha-'elôhîm* "sons of God," employed for the angels, but this expression which was bor-

[85] See above, n. 41.

[86] *Zeits. Deutsch. Morg. Ges.*, L, p. 573, n. 1; Albright, *Jour. Bib. Lit.*, LIV (1935), p. 204; *Bull. Am. Sch. Or. Res.*, No. 63, p. 10, n. 7.

rowed, as we shall see, from Canaanite does not necessarily have any more concrete meaning than does the frequent reference to the Israelites as children of God; both angels and Israelites were created by God and consequently might be poetically called His "children."

Still another equally original characteristic of Yahweh is that He is not restricted to any special abode. As the lord of all cosmic forces, controlling sun, moon, and storm but not identified with any of them, His normal dwelling-place is in heaven, from which He may come down, either to a lofty mountain like Sinai, to a shrine like the Tabernacle, or to any spot which He may choose. It is very significant that early Israelite poetry refers in only the most general terms to Mount Seir and Edom (Song of Deborah), to Teman and Mount Paran (the hymn imbedded in Habakkuk 3), to Sinai, Seir, and Paran (Deut. 33). The early Israelites laid so little stress on the exact spot that even the name of the mountain varies in our prose sources (Sinai or Horeb). This does not mean that it was not a sacred spot, but that there was no special cult associated with it, so the precise name and location were unimportant. The same situation is found in the early Christian church with reference to the location of the inn where Jesus was born and the tomb in which He was buried. The frequently stated view that Sinai must have been a volcano, a view popularized by A. Musil and Ed. Meyer, is without any solid basis. J. Morgenstern has effectively shown that the biblical theophany of Yahweh in Ex. 19 must be explained through the Hebrew imagery connected with the Glory of Yahweh (*kebhôdh YHWH*).[87] There is no volcano, active or extinct, in all Sinai or Midian proper. However, in adjacent regions of Hauran and Arabia there are many volcanoes which must have been active within the past few thousands of years. It is, therefore, quite possible that the sublime picture of the theophany in Exodus 19 was ultimately influenced by folk memories of volcanic eruptions (preserved in myth or metaphor), combined with more recent recollec-

[87] *Zeits. f. Assyr.*, XXV, pp. 139-93; XXVIII (1913), pp. 15 ff.

tions of terrific thunder-storms in the mountains of north-western Arabia or Syria. In other words, the sublime description of the theophany may owe certain features to the two most majestic spectacles vouchsafed to mankind: a sub-tropical thunder-storm and a volcanic eruption. We cannot emphasize too strongly that the principle of skeuo-morphism (above, pp. 61, 120) operates even more frequently in the world of ideas than it does in that of objects.[88] Many ideas whose origin cannot be explained from the culture or the environment in which they are found, have been taken over from an entirely different cultural environment where they have a perfectly logical explanation.

Just as there is nothing in the Mosaic tradition which demands a derivation of Yahweh from an original volcanic deity or storm-god, so there is nothing which requires us to explain Him as a modified moon-god. It is improbable that the name *Sînai* is derived from that of Sumerian *Zen* (older *Zu-en*), Accadian *Sin*, the moon-god worshipped at Ur (in his form Nannar) and at Harran, since there is no indication that the name *Sin* was ever employed by the Canaanites or the Semitic nomads of Palestine.[89] It is much more likely that the name *Sînai* is connected with the place-name *Sîn*, which belongs to a desert plain in Sinai as well as to a Canaanite city in Syria and perhaps to a city in the north-eastern Delta of Egypt. It has also long been recognized that it may somehow be connected with *seneh* (Aram. *sanyâ*), the name of a kind of bush where Moses is said to have first witnessed the theophany of Yahweh. The usual aetiological explanation is inadequate, though possible.

[88] See especially A. Bertholet, *Über kultische Motivver-schiebungen* (*Sitz. Preuss, Akad. Wiss., Phil.-hist. Klasse,* 1938, pp. 164 ff.).

[89] The writer must retract occasional statements to the contrary (e. g., *Jour. Soc. Or. Res.,* X, p. 259 and n. 58); cf. *Bull. Am. Sch. Or. Res.,* No. 71, p. 39, n. 42. The constantly swelling material from Syria and northwestern Mesopotamia in the eighteenth century, from Ugarit and other sites some centuries later, from new documents such as the Egyptian Execration Texts, etc., yield no clear examples of the name *Sin;* the Canaanite name of this god was *Yeraḥ,* not *Sin.*

Fundamental to early Israelite religion and profoundly rooted in Mosaic tradition is the anthropomorphic conception of Yahweh. Among the Egyptians, Mesopotamians, and Canaanites we find tendencies in this direction, but the concept of deity remained fluid and subject to extraordinary variation. Without considering the primitive dynamistic and corporative elements inherent in the concept of deity in the ancient Near East, we have only to glance at the mythologies, the iconographies, and the litanies to see that Near-Eastern gods shifted in disconcerting fashion from astral form to zoomorphic, dendromorphic, and composite manifestations. Yahweh, on the other hand, is virtually always referred to in the earlier sources in a way which suggests His human form though His body was usually hidden in a refulgent envelope called His Glory (*kabhôdh*). The most drastic and at the same time the clearest and presumably the most archaic illustration is the passage Ex. 33:23, where by special grace Moses sees Yahweh's back but not His face, "for there shall no man see Me and live." In the same way He appears in the early sources as having traits of human psychology, such as capacity for love and hatred, joy and sorrow, revenge and remorse, though always on a heroic plane.[90]

There has been a great deal of futile writing about the anthropomorphism of early Israel. First of all, we must be very cautious in using material from the stories of Genesis 1-11, since most of this goes back to the Patriarchal Age, sometimes perhaps in its very wording (e. g., Gen. 6:1-4). To be sure, some of these stories are more recent and they have nearly all been more or less influenced by later monotheistic conceptions (so for example in the Story of the Flood when compared with the cuneiform version). Simi-

---

[90] Cf. the discussion of biblical anthropomorphism by W. Eichrodt, *Theologie des Alten Testaments*, Vol. II (Leipzig, 1935), pp. 4 f., and by L. Köhler, *Theologie des Alten Testaments* (Tübingen, 1936), pp. 4-6. Neither scholar considers the problem in wide enough perspective; cf. the instructive treatment of the limits of biblical anthropomorphism by J. Hempel, *Zeits. Alttest. Wiss.*, LVII (1939), pp. 75 ff.

larly, we must be careful not to make uncritical deductions as to Mosaic or later Israelite religion from the narratives of the Patriarchs (Gen. 12-50), most of which come down, as we have seen, in substantially their present form from pre-Mosaic days. Thus the appearances of God in Gen. 18-19 are to be explained from pre-Mosaic polytheism, though the narratives have been revised in such a way as not to offend later Israelite, or for that matter Jewish or Christian readers.

Secondly, it cannot be emphasized too strongly that the anthropomorphic conception of Yahweh was absolutely necessary if the God of Israel was to remain a God of the individual Israelite as well as of the people as a whole. For the limited few who are natural mystics or have learned to employ certain methods to attain ecstatic state, the theological concepts attached to deity matter relatively little; there is a striking parallelism between the psychology of mysticism in Judaism, Islam, Buddhism, and Christianity. For the average worshipper, however, it is very essential that his god be a divinity who can sympathize with his human feelings and emotions, a being whom he can love and fear alternately, and to whom he can transfer the holiest emotions connected with memories of father and mother and friend. In other words, it was precisely the anthropomorphism of Yahweh which was essential to the initial success of Israel's religion. Like man at his noblest the God of Israel might be in form and affective reactions, but there was in Him none of the human frailties that make the Olympian deities of Greece such charming poetic figures and such unedifying examples. All the human characteristics of Israel's deity were exalted; they were projected against a cosmic screen and they served to interpret the cosmic process as the expression of God's creative word and eternally active will.

Equally vital to Mosaic religion was the aniconic character of Yahweh, who could not be represented in any visual or tangible form. In spite of the unanimous testimony of Israelite tradition, scholars have made repeated efforts to prove the existence of representations of deity in early

Israel. Every effort of this kind has been based on subjective arguments and on arbitrary assumptions which have won only the most limited acceptance even in friendly circles.[91] Of course, it would be equally unscholarly to deny the *possibility* of such images or portrayals in material form. But the testimony of our written sources, plus the completely negative results of excavation, should be evidence enough to prove that Yahwism was essentially aniconic and that material representations were foreign to its spirit from the beginning. We shall show below that there is no basis whatever for the idea that Yahweh was worshipped in bull form by the northern tribes at Bethel and Dan. The golden calf simply formed the pedestal on which the invisible Yahweh stood, just as in the Temple of Solomon the invisible Glory of God was enthroned above the cherubim; conceptually the two ideas are virtually identical.

After the demonstration by R. Hartmann and especially by H. Lammens of nomadic Arab parallels to the portable Tabernacle and Ark of the Covenant, some of them going far back into pre-Islamic times,[92] it is captious to refuse them Mosaic date, since they were completely foreign to sedentary Canaanite practice and since they are known to have persisted for some time after the Conquest of Palestine. The archaeologist no longer has any difficulty in proving the antiquity of many details in the description which is given in the Priestly Code.

The uniform testimony of our sources with respect to the existence of some kind of sacrificial ritual in earliest Israel can hardly be erroneous, though the constant reaction of the prophets against the formalism and externality of sac-

[91] See especially the sound remarks of R. H. Pfeiffer, *Jour. Bib. Lit.*, XLV (1926), pp. 211-22, and of J. Hempel, *Gott und Mensch im Alten Testament* (second ed., Stuttgart, 1936), pp. 264 ff.

[92] See particularly J. Morgenstern, *Heb. Un. Col. Ann.*, V (1928), pp. 81 ff., and the important monograph (overlooked by Morgenstern and other recent students) by H. Lammens, *Le culte des bétyles et les processions réligieuses chez les Arabes préislamiques*, in *Bull. Inst. Fran., Arch. Or.*, XVII (Cairo, 1919), pp. 39-101.

rificial cult hardly suggests that undue emphasis was laid upon it in the Mosaic system. The sacrifice of domesticated animals, such as cattle, sheep, goats, and doves, goes back to hoary antiquity and was common to all Western-Asiatic religions from the third millennium B.C. on down; it might thus have passed into Israelite religion in the Mosaic period or later, with numerous other elements borrowed from the sedentary peoples of Palestine. However the part played by animal sacrifice in Semitic religion was so vital that it may be doubted whether Moses could have omitted it from his system without seriously weakening its appeal to worshippers. Among the Semites of antiquity sacrifice was a means of bringing gifts to the deity and of paying him homage which was valid both for a single worshipper and for a group; it served to solemnize every important occasion in the life of a group; and as shown by Bertholet it brought the deity into dynamistic relationship to his worshippers, who became united in flesh and spirit with him by jointly partaking of the sacrificial flesh. Both the substitutional sacrifice, where an animal replaced a more primitive human sacrifice, and the ceremony of the scape-goat (found also in related form in Mesopotamia) emphasized a vital religious concept, that of vicarious atonement for moral transgressions which would otherwise have to be physically expiated by the people.

The problem of the origin of the ethical, civil, and ceremonial laws attributed in later Israel to Moses has been profoundly affected by the appearance of A. Alt's monograph, *Die Ursprünge des israelitischen Rechts* (1934). In this epochal study the gifted Leipzig scholar has distinguished sharply between two main types of pentateuchal legislation: apodictic law and casuistic law. The latter is found primarily in the Book of the Covenant (Ex. 21-23), which is a fragmentary legal code of the same class as the Code of Hammurabi (cir. 1700 B.C.), the Hittite Laws (cir. 14th century B.C.) and the Assyrian laws (12th century B.C.).[93] All these codes go back in their basic formula-

[93] For the date of the Code of Hammurabi, formerly placed from five to two centuries too early, see above, Chap. III, n.

tion (provided that . . . then) to the Sumerian jurisprudence of the third millennium (cf. above, p. 198). The
Book of the Covenant represents the form which the more-
or-less common corpus of older customary laws and court
decisions took under the special conditions existing in Canaan, and it may have passed into Israelite hands during the
period of the Judges. In the form which it takes in the Book
of the Covenant it can hardly be dated before the ninth
century. However, it is unlikely that the ninth-century form
differed much from its Northwest-Semitic prototype many
centuries earlier, in view of numerous archaisms in practice
and terminology which have older Mesopotamian parallels.[94] The formulation and spirit of the apodictic laws are
unique and original in Israel; those of the casuistic laws are
at home throughout Western Asia. Besides the Ten Commandments, which best illustrate the spirit of the apodictic
laws, we have many other examples, such as the old list
of curses imbedded in Deut. 27 and miscellaneous warnings
that certain sins must be punished by death, in different
parts of the Pentateuch. The most striking thing about the
apodictic laws is their categorical character, which stands
in sharp contrast to their nearest extra-Israelite parallels,
the Egyptian Negative Confession and the Babylonian
Shurpu; the Israelites are commanded *not* to commit sin,
because Yahweh so wills.

Of course, we cannot say how many of the apodictic
laws actually emanate directly from Moses, but the fact that
they cannot be paralleled in this form outside of Israel and
that they were believed by different schools of traditional
thought in Israel to go back to the time of Moses is sufficient
indication that they are in accord with the movement which
bears his name. Again we must stress the fact that oral
transmission of tradition is inherently more consistent and
logical in its results than written transmission, since it sifts

---

16; for the correct date of the Assyrian laws in their present
form see E. F. Weidner, *Arch. f. Orientf.*, XII (1937), pp.
46 ff.
[94] See *Jour. Bib. Lit.*, LV (1936), pp. 164-68, for the
writer's discussion of this subject.

and refines, modifying whatever does not fit into the spirit of the main body of tradition (cf. above, p. 68). In general it subjects detail to mass scrutiny instead of to the examination of a few who may be mentally superior but who are bound to deviate more frequently from accepted standards. The apodictic law of Israel was not so refined nor so all-inclusive as the Negative Confession of the Egyptians about 1500 B.C., nor did it lay so much stress on social solidarity as the Babylonian *Shurpu* of somewhat later date; on the other hand, it reflects a much more advanced standard of conduct in many respects. Vicious religious customs, such as child sacrifice, necromancy, and sodomy (which formed part of certain religious ceremonies in the ancient Near East), are forbidden; work on the sabbath, which endangered the physical and mental health of workers (as we know from the recent experience of occidental nations), was prohibited;[95] the worship of all gods save Yahweh and the careless use of His name were banned. As Alt has pointed out, there is nothing in this legislation that conflicts with conditions in Israel under Moses. In this respect it is very different from the Book of the Covenant, which presupposes organized sedentary society. As he has shown, an independent and very important testimony to the antiquity of the apodictic code is provided by the fact that it was annually recited in connection with the Feast of Tabernacles at Shechem.

Having sketched the certain or probable content of the Mosaic system, let us consider possible sources of its teaching. That it was a true "teaching" (*doctrina,* in the empirical, not in the philosophical sense, of course) may be con-

---

[95] It is true that many scholars date the introduction of the seventh-day rest into Israel much later, but their evidence is most unsatisfactory. Quite aside from the Neo-Assyrian and Babylonian seventh-day tabus, which have been frequently discussed in recent years, is the undoubted fact that the Egyptians divided the month into four parts, each of which was named *djn't*, literally "part," from the Pyramid Age on down. Moreover, the tabu against travelling on certain lunar feasts goes back to a very early age in Israel, as will be shown by one of my pupils.

sidered as virtually certain, in view of its traditional name *tôrah,* its traditional content, and the fact that the slightly earlier system of Akhenaten was also known as the "teaching" *(sbâyet).*[96] Since Moses bore an Egyptian name and according to tradition had reached a place of considerable social importance in Egypt in his early life, his original *tôrah* may well have contained Egyptian elements which later disappeared before the impact of native Hebrew conceptions. Some of these elements seem still to persist, though we cannot be absolutely sure of any one case, owing to the absence of direct documentation or of complex borrowings from Egyptian sources. Among such possible Egyptian influences may be mentioned: 1. The concept of the god who is sole creator of everything and the formula from which his name, *Yahweh,* was derived (cf. Amun-Re' and his litany in the New Empire); 2. The concept of a single god and the establishment of a doctrine based on monotheism (cf. the Aten); 3. Recognition of the necessarily international, cosmic dominion of the reigning deity (cf. Sutekh-Baal under the early Ramessides). On the negative side it is clear that the religion of Israel revolted against virtually every external aspect of Egyptian religion, including the complex and grotesque iconography, the dominion of daily life in the Nineteenth Dynasty by magic, the materialistic absorption in preparing for a selfish existence in the hereafter.

Turning to assess the influence exerted by native Hebrew religion on Moses, we are faced with the difficulty of determining just what the latter accepted and what was introduced into Yahwism after his death from the older Hebrew stock. Leaving the second alternative aside for the moment, since it has been partly stressed above and will be emphasized again in other respects below, we can distinguish a number of clear Hebrew factors—and they are what

[96] See above, n. 30. On the etymology of Heb. *tôrah* and the denominative origin of *hôrâ* "to teach," see *Jour. Bib. Lit.,* XLVI (1927), pp. 182 ff. Some details of my demonstration must now be modified, but these changes do not affect my thesis at all.

gave Yahwism much of its vital power over the hearts and minds of Israel: 1. The close association between god and worshipper(s), illustrated by the giving of personal names and by sacrificial rites; 2. The contractual relationship between the deity of a tribe and his people, as illustrated by the constant use of the word *berîth* "covenant," in early Israel (specific forms of this contractual relationship may be later); 3. The association of terrestrial manifestations of deity with storms and mountains, and the identification of Yahweh with Shaddai, "The One of the Mountain(s)"; the adoption of the stories of the Fathers as part of Israel's inheritance, and the identification of Yahweh with the God of the Fathers; specific appellations of deity and perhaps the nucleus of the cosmogony of Genesis, though the latter may again have been developed later from the native stock of myths and legends.

There is no clear trace of any West-Semitic influence of characteristically Canaanite type on the earliest religion of Israel. After the occupation of Palestine, however, this influence became more and more significant, as we shall see below. How remote early Hebrew tradition was from Canaanite influences may be illustrated by the total absence from it of any story of the conflict between the creator and the dragon at the beginning of world-history. After the seventh century B.C. we find such references becoming more and more frequent and the myth of the victory of Yahweh over Leviathan ultimately obtained wide popularity in rabbinic literature.[97]

In bringing this chapter to a close we have yet one question to answer: Was Moses a true monotheist? If by "monotheist" is meant a thinker with views specifically like those of Philo Judaeus or Rabbi Aqiba, of St. Paul or St. Augustine, of Mohammed or Maimonides, of St. Thomas or Calvin, of Mordecai Kaplan or H. N. Wieman, Moses was not one. If, on the other hand, the term "monotheist" means

---

[97] It is, of course, by no means unlikely that the triumph of Yahweh over the dragon was known in early Israel; our point is that it did not become part of the normative doctrine of Yahwism until later times.

one who teaches the existence of only one God, the creator of everything, the source of justice, who is equally powerful in Egypt, in the desert, and in Palestine, who has no sexuality and no mythology, who is human in form but cannot be seen by human eye and cannot be represented in any form—then the founder of Yahwism was certainly a monotheist.[98]

[98] For some further observations which are pertinent in this connection see the writer's remarks, *Jour. Bib. Lit.*, LIX (1940), pp. 91-96 and 110-12, especially p. 112. The latest study of Israelite monotheism, Bruno Ballscheit's *Alter und Aufkommen des Monotheismus in der israelitischen Religion* (Berlin, 1938) is very disappointing, though he has some excellent observations on the use of such terms as "henotheism," not to mention "practical monotheism" and "monolatry" (pp. 10 f.) as well as on the character of later Israelite monotheism. However, he completely fails to understand the nature of ancient Near-Eastern, especially Canaanite, conceptions with regard to the nature and scope of their deities. The first scholar (aside perhaps from the present writer) to recognize the nature of Canaanite religion in this respect is O. Eissfeldt (*Zeits. Alttest. Wiss.*, 1939, pp. 14 ff., especially p. 15).

Chapter V

CHARISMA AND CATHARSIS

Our documentary sources for the history of Israel from the late thirteenth to the early fourth century B.C. are, in general, remarkably reliable. Among them are first-hand memoirs, written down by the author himself or an amanuensis, such as the Book of Nehemiah and part of the Book of Jeremiah. They also include the priceless historical account of the last years of David (II Sam. 9-20, I Kings 1-2), which cannot have been written down later than the reign of Solomon. Most of the matter in Kings is singularly accurate from the standpoint of the modern historian, as has been shown by repeated archaeological and epigraphic discoveries: e. g., Hezekiah's tribute, II Kings 18:14, amounts to 30 talents of gold and 300 of silver in the Hebrew text, whereas the cuneiform inscriptions of Sennacherib list the amount as 30 talents of gold and 800 talents of silver, which is almost certainly exaggerated. This is not the only passage where Kings is more accurate than contemporary cuneiform records. The work of the Chronicler contains some matter of preëxilic documentary origin which is not in Kings; this additional matter was formerly discounted by historians, but it has repeatedly been shown to be original and important (especially by A. Alt and members of his school). The post-exilic matter in Chronicles and Ezra-Nehemiah has been regarded by a number of scholars (notably by C. C. Torrey) as largely apocryphal, but recent discoveries and investigations have strikingly discredited this extreme position and have shown that E. Meyer's brilliant defense of its authenticity in 1897 was not only fully justified as far as it went but was not sufficiently comprehensive.

Besides these documents and records of written origin there is much traditional matter, some of which may have been orally transmitted for several centuries before being reduced to writing. To this category belong most—perhaps all—of the narratives of Joshua and Judges, much in Samuel, especially in the first part of the book, such material as the Elijah-Elisha pericope in Kings, and most of the matter contained in the prophetic books. Some of this has probably been handed down with exemplary accuracy, as may safely be inferred in the case of the Song of Deborah and of most original poetic oracles and sermons in such books as Amos, Hosea, Isaiah. In these cases the poetic form of the document ensured its reasonably correct transmission by word of mouth for generations and even for centuries (see Chapter I). M. Noth and K. Möhlenbrink have recently made a vigorous attack on the historical reliability of the stories of the Conquest in Joshua, on various literary and aetiological grounds, but they have been opposed with equal vigor by the writer (1939);[1] archaeological discoveries of the past few years have proved that their attack far overshoots the mark (see above, pp. 38 ff., for our criticism of the aetiological method when it is not supported by external evidence). The stories in Judges contain matter of very different historical value, ranging from the high level of the

---

[1] See Noth, *Palästinajahrbuch*, XXXIV (1938), pp. 7-22; Möhlenbrink, *Zeits. Alttest. Wiss.*, LVI (1938), pp. 238-68; Albright, *Bull. Am. Sch. Or. Res.*, No. 74, pp. 11-23. On the other hand, the writer's proposed reconstruction (1935) has been criticized by Vincent (*Rev. Bib.*, 1935, p. 605) and Rowley (*Bull. John Rylands Library*, 1938, pp. 32 ff.); cf. also the discussion by Hempel, *Zeits. Alttest. Wiss.*, 1935, p. 202. The probability is that the actual course of events was closer to the biblical tradition than any of our critical reconstructions have been, and that some vital clues still elude our search.

Gideon and Abimelech narratives (Jud. 6-9) to the low level of the pericope of Samson, which contains much folklore. Many of the stories in Joshua and Judges were certainly handed down as poetic sagas or triumphal poems;[2] the best examples are the accounts of the battle of Gibeon (Jos. 10) and of the Kishon in Jud. 4-5 where the same events are described in both verse and prose. In their present form the Books of Joshua and Judges clearly belong to the seventh century B.C. (cf. Jud. 18:30), but some of their contents must have been put into writing as early as the tenth century.

As is increasingly recognized by competent scholars, most of the prophetic books may more correctly be called "anthologies of oracles and sermons," since their contents are seldom in correct chronological order. In other words, oracles and sermons attributed by common consent to a given prophet circulated under his name for many years— sometimes perhaps for generations—and were then gathered from miscellaneous sources, written and oral, by later collectors, much as was true of the first edition of the Qur'an, over a millennium later. As already noted, Jeremiah is in part an exception, though even here some of the material in the last chapters was evidently collected later and may contain wrongly attributed poems. The most remarkable case of erroneous attribution is Isaiah, which contains at least one, perhaps two, and possibly three bodies of poems from the exilic age or even in part later (Isa. 40 ff., and a number of preceding chapters). In most cases, thanks to historical and other allusions, it is relatively easy to distinguish oracles which fit into the original prophet's environment from those which do not. Our greatest difficulty in interpreting the Prophets is not the fact that extraneous material has been included in their anthologies, but the fact

---

[2] For the latest treatment of the poetic sagas reflected by the citations from the "Book of Jashar," etc., see S. Mowinckel, *Zeits. Alttest. Wiss.*, LIII (1935), pp. 130-52. As usual Mowinckel offers some original and helpful suggestions, but his date for the collected material (after the Assyrian invasion of 738 B.C.) and his attempts to relate it to J and E are not acceptable.

that the Hebrew text is often in such a hopeless state of preservation that nothing can be made of it without highly subjective emendation. Sometimes the Greek translation enables us to correct the Hebrew, but more often it fails us and we must be content to allow the text to remain unintelligible. It is unfortunate that commentators have so often tried to explain all difficulties instead of limiting their exposition to passages whose sense is clear.

A. The Charismatic Age of Israel

According to the standard tradition in the Book of Joshua, Palestine was occupied by the Israelites in the following stages: Gilead and Bashan in Transjordan (before Moses' death), south-central Palestine, southern Palestine, northern Palestine (all under Joshua's leadership). Careful analysis of the narratives in Joshua by Alt and his pupils, applying the methods of Gunkel (p. 77) has led to some important conclusions with regard to the relative age and literary character of the matter which they contain, though they have gone much too far in unwarranted use of the principle of aetiology (see above). Fortunately, a number of quite independent traditions, dating in their present form from about the tenth century b.c., are preserved in Jud. 1, so we can check our standard tradition from several directions. It follows, for example, that the rôle of Joshua has been expanded by tradition and that he had less to do with the conquest of Judah and Galilee than would appear from superficial reading of the narratives of the book which bears his name. However, the school of Alt is not justified in considering Joshua as only an insignificant local chieftain, nor in denying the historicity of Israelite traditions of the Conquest, just because various minor modifications must certainly be made (e. g., in the stories of Jericho and Ai) and still others may have to be introduced into the traditional picture.

A very important addition may be made to the records in Joshua and Judges 1 from other biblical sources. In Joshua there is a remarkable reticence with reference to the conquest of north-central Palestine, about which nothing is said except in the list of conquered towns in chap. 12. In Gen. 34, 48:22, I Chron. 7:20 ff. (cir. 400 B.C.), Jubilees 34 (cir. third century B.C.),[3] and elsewhere in still later sources there are allusions to, as well as circumstantial accounts of, the wars of the sons of Jacob in central Palestine, which must rest in part on very old tradition, though the post-biblical narratives are presumably full of legendary details.[4] In all these sources the conquest of central Palestine is referred back to the late Patriarchal Age. With this agrees, as has been recognized, the curious silence of the Amarna Tablets about towns in central Palestine, especially as contrasted with the many references to places in the south and north. It follows that not all the Hebrews from whom later Israel sprang, had participated in the Exodus under Moses; some of them must have occupied and have settled certain parts of Palestine before the Israelite invasion under Moses and Joshua. Judging from the references in the Amarna Tablets to the Khapiru, it is very likely that the latter, then in intermittent conflict with the Canaanite princes of the hill-country, represent a pre-Israelite phase of the Hebrew occupation of Palestine.[5] With this would agree an Egyptian reference, from a stela of Sethos I found at Beth-shan (cir. 1300 B.C.), to the 'Apiru of a mountain district with a Semitic name.[6] Both from the re-

---

[3] See Chap. VI, pp. 266 f., for the date of the Book of Jubilees.

[4] For the writer's view see *Bull. Am. Sch. Or. Res.*, No. 35 (1929), p. 6, and against it see Abel, *Rev. Bib.*, 1925, pp. 208 ff., 1936, pp. 106 f.; S. Klein, *Zeits. Deutsch. Pal. Ver.*, 1934, pp. 7 ff. Abel and Klein defend the theory that the stories preserved in Jubilees refer to the Maccabaean wars—which date a century or more after the probable time at which the Book of Jubilees was written!

[5] See Chap. IV, n. 54.

[6] See the writer, *Ann. Am. Sch. Or. Res.*, VI (1926), pp. 35 f. and n. 73; A. Rowe, *The Topography and History of Beth-shan* (Philadelphia, 1930), pp. 29 f. In the years 1924-25 the writer spent many hours before the stela, trying to determine its exact reading in line 10, but the surface is too weathered for certainty. The signs ' and *py* are clear; the

sults of archaeological surveys and from early records we
know that the Canaanite occupation was heavily concentrated in the plains and the low hill-country of Western
Palestine, and that much of the higher hill-country of both
Western and Eastern Palestine was not occupied at all by
a sedentary population until about the beginning of the
Iron Age, in the twelfth century B.C. It was, therefore, in
these regions where the Hebrews first settled down in late
patriarchal times and where they were first joined by the
Israelites proper in the thirteenth century.

The Israelites, however, proceeded without loss of time
to destroy and occupy Canaanite towns all over the country.[7] Bethel may have been one of the first to fall, as might
be expected from its exposed situation; it was taken at some
time in the thirteenth century B.C. and burned to the
ground, as shown by the indications of an unusually devastating conflagration which were found in the excavation
of 1934. Lachish fell about 1220 B.C. or a little later, as
is proved by a hieratic inscription on a bowl which was
found in 1937 in the debris of the destruction of the latest
Canaanite city. Kirjath-sepher (if correctly identified with
Tell Beit Mirsim) was destroyed by fire about the same
time. The Egyptians themselves were greatly impressed by
the Israelite advance, which they took ineffectual meas-
ures to check, as we may infer from a couplet in the triumphal poem of Marniptah, dated 1219 B.C.:

| The people Israel is desolate, | it has no offspring; |
| Palestine has become | a widow for Egypt! |

---

final *rw* (Rowe: *r*) is probable; the determinatives are clear.
In the following groups we can be certain of the words "of
the mountain of Y[ ]" and of the following determinative; it
is probable that the third sign of the name is *d* but Rowe's
Yrd[*n*] can hardly be correct. It is certain that the name
'A-pi-ru (or *'-pi-r*) is phonetically identical with the name
formerly read "Khabiru," as noted above; see already the
writer, *Vocalization of the Egyptian Syllabic Orthography*
(New Haven, 1934), p. 42, VII. B. 4.

[7] For details see especially *Bull. Am. Sch. Or. Res.*, No. 74
(1939), pp. 15-23.

Archaeological excavation and exploration are throwing increasing light on the character of the earliest Israelite occupation, about 1200 B.C. First it is important to note that the new inhabitants settled in towns like Bethel and Tell Beit Mirsim only a short time after their destruction. The Israelites were thus far from being characteristic nomads or even semi-nomads, but had reached a stage where they were ready to settle down, tilling the soil and dwelling in stone houses. A second main point is that the new Israelite occupation was incomparably more intensive than was the preceding Canaanite one. All over the hill-country we find remains of Iron-Age (12th century—) villages which had not been inhabited in the Late Bronze Age (15th-13th centuries) and many of which had never been occupied previously. Thanks to the rapidly increasing diffusion of cisterns, which were lined with true lime plaster (previously not used), the area of settlement was vastly extended and the Israelites began cutting down forests and settling in previously inaccessible districts (cf. Jos. 17:15).

The population of early Israelite Palestine was mainly composed of three groups: pre-Israelite Hebrews, Israelites proper, and Canaanites of miscellaneous origin. The Hebrews coalesced so rapidly with their Israelite kindred that hardly any references to this distinction have survived in biblical literature and the few apparent allusions are doubtful. The Canaanites were brought into the Israelite fold by treaty, conquest, or gradual absorption. The four towns of the Gibeonite confederacy were added to Israel by treaty, according to explicit tradition; the Bene Hamor (Sons of the Ass) of Shechem were also incorporated in some such way, to judge from various early references to them and to their god Baal-berith (Lord of the Covenant—note that the sacrifice of an ass was an essential feature of a treaty among the Amorites of the Mari period). Several towns appear both as autonomous Canaanite cities and as names of "clans" in the tribal genealogies: Shechem, Hepher, Tirzah, perhaps Zaphon, etc. The standard tradition correctly emphasizes the part played by the *herem* (devotion to death) in the Israelite Conquest. The practice of devoting a recalcitrant foe to destruction as a kind of gigantic holocaust to the national deity was apparently universal among the early Semites. In the Mesha Stone, from the ninth century B.C., a Moabite king describes how he massacred all the Israelite population of Ataroth as "satisfaction for the blood-lust" of Chemosh and Moab. In the same inscription he says, "I captured (Nebo) and killed everybody, seven thousand men, boys, women, girls, and maidens, because I had devoted it to (the god) Ashtar-Chemosh."

Strictly speaking this Semitic custom was no worse, from the humanitarian point of view, than the reciprocal massacres of Protestants and Catholics in the seventeenth century (e. g., Magdeburg, Drogheda), or than the massacre of Armenians by Turks and of Kirghiz by Russians during the First World War, or than the recent slaughter of non-combatants in Spain by both sides. It is questionable whether a strictly detached observer would consider it as bad as the starvation of helpless Germany after the armistice in 1918 or the bombing of Rotterdam in 1940. In those days warfare was total, just as it is again becoming after the lapse of over three millennia. And we Americans have perhaps less right than most modern nations, in spite of our genuine humanitarianism, to sit in judgment on the Israelites of the thirteenth century B.C., since we have, intentionally or otherwise, exterminated scores of thousands of Indians in every corner of our great nation and have crowded the rest into great concentration camps. The fact that this was probably inevitable does not make it more edifying to the Americans of today. It is significant that after the first phase of the Israelite Conquest we hear no more about "devoting" the population of Canaanite towns, but only of driving them out or putting them to tribute (Jud. 1, *passim*). From the impartial standpoint of a philosopher of history, it often seems necessary that a people of markedly inferior type should vanish before a people of superior potentialities, since there is a point beyond which racial mixture cannot go without disaster. When such a process takes place—as at present in Australia—there is generally little that can be done by the humanitarian—though every deed of brutality and injustice is infallibly visited upon the aggressor.

It was fortunate for the future of monotheism that the Israelites of the Conquest were a wild folk, endowed with primitive energy and ruthless will to exist, since the resulting decimation of the Canaanites prevented the complete fusion of the two kindred folk which would almost inevitably have depressed Yahwistic standards to a point where recovery was impossible. Thus the Canaanites, with their orgiastic nature-worship, their cult of fertility in the form of serpent symbols and sensuous nudity, and their gross mythology, were replaced by Israel, with its pastoral simplicity and purity of life, its lofty monotheism, and its severe code of ethics. In a not altogether dissimilar way, a millennium later, the African Canaanites, as they still called themselves, or the Carthaginians, as we call them, with the gross Phoenician mythology which we know from Ugarit and Philo Byblius, with human sacrifices and the cult of sex, were crushed by the immensely superior Romans, whose stern code of morals and singularly elevated paganism remind us in many ways of early Israel.

The social and political system of the new nation was exceedingly simple. Socially, it was divided into a number of clan-groups which are known to us as "tribes"; in Hebrew two designations are employed, both meaning "staff." The number and identity of these tribes vary somewhat in our lists; in theory there were twelve of them, whose organization went back to Moses and Joshua. Tradition uniformly emphasizes both the religious character of the bond between the tribes and the existence of a central sanctuary at Shiloh, to which the tribes could send representatives (Jos. 18:1, 21:2, Jud. 21:12, I Sam. 1-4, Jer. 7:12 and *passim*). A. Alt and his pupils have correctly stressed the amphictyonic nature of this system, which has a number of extraordinarily close parallels in the Mediterranean basin during the early centuries of the first millennium B.C.[8] When we add the force of this analogy to the consistent

[8] See M. Noth, *Das System der zwölf Stämme Israels* (Stuttgart, 1930).

Israelite tradition, the soundness of the latter becomes evident. As a matter of fact, the only reason why the school of Wellhausen has consistently disregarded or even rejected the straight-forward biblical account of the central Tabernacle at Shiloh is that it does not fit into the postulated, but never demonstrated, theory of progressive centralization of cult. Here we may safely trust to our documents and assume an oscillatory movement rather than unilateral evolution. The Tabernacle and the Ark were under the charge of the Levitic priesthood, who perpetuated their Egyptian traditions as late as the early eleventh century, when the two sons of Eli are called Hophni and Phinehas, both Egyptian names. At the head of the priesthood stood the chief priest, called in our earliest sources simply "the priest," since early Israel seems to have consistently eschewed honorific titles. That he was *de facto* head of the priestly system is obvious from the narratives where he is mentioned, and any other organization would hardly have been workable. Moreover, we know from the inscriptions of Ugarit that the head of the local priesthood was called *rabbu kâhinîma* "chief of the priests," as early as the 14th century B.C.[9]

It is not, however, correct to speak of Israel in the premonarchic age as a theocratic state in the sense that the head of the religious organization was also head of the state, as was to be true for a time in the fourth and third centuries B.C. The Israelites were too fond of freedom and too particularistic to follow a typical priestly leader—and only the exceptional head of a priestly system can also become the leader of his people in war and peace. Our traditions credit only two of the early chief priests with being

---

[9] In view of the continuous influence exerted by Egyptian culture and organization on Palestine in these centuries, as long emphasized by Alt and his pupils (see now also R. de Vaux, *Rev. Bib.*, 1939, pp. 394-405, who stresses it for the tenth century B.C.) it would scarcely be surprising to find that the triumph of the high-priests of Amun and the establishment of their "theocracy" about 1065 B.C. had repercussions in Israel. On the nature of Hrihor's victory and the attendant circumstances see especially H. Kees, *Herihor und die Aufrichtung des thebanischen Gottesstaates* (Göttingen, 1936).

military leaders. Nor did the tribal head or *nasi'* have any real power beyond his tribe. It is significant that none of the early narratives mentions a *nasi'*; it is only in the administrative lists which are incorporated into the Priestly Code and the Book of Chronicles that we find any reference to tribal chieftains.[10] The tribes were too jealous of their prerogatives to submit under normal conditions to the head of another tribe, even briefly. Neither Gideon nor Abimelech was able to extend his *political* power beyond the bounds of his native tribe of Manasseh.

Yet there had to be leaders whose direction would be accepted by Israel in times of crisis or danger, and there had to be magistrates whose decision in civil cases would provide a court of appeal for tribesmen who felt themselves oppressed. And leaders arose, heads of clans like Othniel, military leaders of humbler origin like Ehud, Barak, and Gideon, men of wealth like Jair, Ibzan, and Abdon, bastard adventurers like Jephthah, priests like Eli, prophets like Samuel, and even Canaanite chieftains like Shamgar of Beth-anath (cf. Jud. 5:6).[11] Among them later narrators included such semi-legendary figures as the strong man, Samson, and the woman Deborah (cf. Jud. 4:5 with Gen. 35:8), but their inclusion helps materially to explain the nature of the "office." Max Weber, followed by A. Alt, has happily applied the term "charismatic" to the Israelite leaders of the time of the Judges. The "judges" were respected and followed, regardless of tribal affiliations, because there was some special power about them which was believed to represent the direct outpouring of divine grace (*charisma*). A popular military hero was most likely to be considered as a charismatic "judge," but a man renowned for his wisdom and justice might also be placed on a level

[10] On the character and antiquity of the office of *nasi'* see especially Noth, *op. cit.*, pp. 151-62.

[11] See the writer's original observation, *Jour. Pal. Or. Soc.*, I, p. 55, n. 1, accepted by A. Alt (e. g., *Palästinajahrbuch*, 1926, p. 56, n. 2). This observation has been independently repeated by M. Noth, *Die israelitischen Personennamen* (1928), p. 123, n. 1.

with the hero, as far as recognition of his divinely granted superiority went. The name *shôphet* "judge," is an old Canaanite word, found later among the Carthaginians in the sense of "magistrate, civic leader" (*suffete*); it must have developed the charismatic sense somewhat as follows:— Local personages became distinguished far and wide for their wisdom and their honesty, and men came to them from increasing distances for adjudication of disputes. But a judge had to have a measure of special divine favor in order to employ the trial by ordeal, which was discontinued in later Israel but which undoubtedly played an important part in earlier times (cf. the story of Gideon). Hence his fame for wisdom and honesty was supplemented by a reputation as a special agent of divine power. The judge Samuel was even considered a diviner (seer). Samson was a Nazirite from birth, i. e., he was dedicated by special rites and ascetic practices to a life of exceptional austerity. Since Samson's character otherwise belies this tradition, it presumably illustrates the common attitude toward the charismatic leader rather than any phase of the hero's life.

A. Alt has effectively directed attention to the possible significance of the institution of "judges" (especially as seen in the Minor Judges) as a channel through which the casuistic North-Semitic law, best known from the fragments preserved in the Book of the Covenant (see above, p. 267, reached Israel.[12] As will be recalled, this law is much older than the time of the Judges and goes back in its ultimate formulation to Sumerian jurisprudence. During the second millennium it developed in various ways in different countries, through the constant reciprocal influence of legal codes and bodies of customary law, altered from time to time by the addition of new court decisions or the impact of some entirely new social, cultural, or religious situation.

Since Israelite culture was in many respects a *tabula rasa* when the Israelites invaded Palestine, we might expect them to have been influenced strongly by the culture of

[12] *Die Ursprünge des israelitischen Rechts* (Leipzig, 1934), pp. 31 ff.

their Canaanite predecessors. Yet excavations show a most abrupt break between the culture of the Canaanite Late Bronze Age and that of the Israelite Early Iron Age in the hill-country of Palestine. Early Israelite strata show no signs of the concentration of wealth and power in the hands of a few; the palaces of Canaanite towns are replaced by large and small rustic enclosures and huts. Massive Canaanite fortifications are replaced by thin walls of the new casemate type. The corvée was obviously unknown in Israel at that time, except when imposed briefly by foreign conquerors. The word which means "feudal serf" in Canaanite documents (Amarna, Ugarit, etc.) comes to signify "freeman" (*ḥophshî*), presumably because the peasant, to whom the word was commonly applied, had ceased to be a Canaanite serf and had become a freeborn Israelite.[13]

Passing over other illustrations of the cultural relation between Canaanites and Israelites and of the effect of the impact of the two peoples upon the latter, let us turn to the field of religion which interests us particularly here. Owing to lack of specific data for the time of the Judges, we shall postpone consideration of the cultic aspect of Canaanite-Israelite religious syncretism until we reach the Monarchy. However, it is quite possible to gain an approximate idea of the influence of the cult of Baal upon Yahwism as a religion during the age of the Judges. The proportion of names formed with "Baal" seems to increase rather steadily as we approach the end of the period, since there are no examples from the time of the Exodus or the Wanderings, and the number becomes considerable at the time of Saul and David. Furthermore, there is a detailed account of the conflict between Yahwism and Baalism in the story of Gid-

---

[13] The writer expects to discuss this word and its cognates fully in the near future. Meanwhile we may refer to partial treatments, *Jour. Pal. Or. Soc.*, VI (1926), pp. 106 ff., XIV, p. 131, n. 162; *Bull. Am. Sch. Or. Res.*, No. 63 (1936), p. 29, n. 32. The root is now known to have been *ḥpṯ*, with which the writer has compared Arab. *ḥbṯ* "be base, vile," and the partially assimilated *ḫbṯ* "be low, lowly, humble"; Can. *ḥpṯ* represents a very common type of partial assimilation of the middle voiced to the adjacent voiceless consonants.

eon, whose father, Joash (with a Yahwistic name) called his son Jerub-baal and erected an altar to Baal. The home of Gideon, Ophrah of Abiezer, has never been located with certainty, but all hypotheses place it in districts on the periphery of Manasseh, i. e., in territory which had probably been Hebrew even before the Conquest, and had remained peculiarly exposed to Canaanite influence.[14] Since Yahweh and Baal were both lords of heaven and senders of rain, were both storm-gods and givers of fertility, it is only natural that they should have been assimilated, especially in northern Israel where the pagan pre-Mosaic religion of the land remained dormant, constantly awaking and impelling men to adapt elements of Baalism to the worship of Yahweh. While we have no certain knowledge, it is only reasonable to suppose that the Levites were most active in maintaining the claims of Yahwism against Baal, or rather in defending Yahweh-Baal (Lord Yahweh) against the Canaanite Baal. As we shall see below, the invasion of the Tyrian Baal and his votaries in the ninth century led to a violent reaction against the whole dangerous practice of applying the title "Baal" to Yahweh.

Meanwhile the constant struggle between the Israelites and the surrounding peoples was slowly but surely hammering them into national unity. Hardly had they conquered most of the Canaanite towns of the hill-country than they were exposed to new enemies of greater vigor and potential menace. In the last half of the twelfth century came the Philistines and the Tsikal from the regions of the Aegean, bringing a rude barbaric energy from the north as well as exotic culture of Mycenaean type. Before the end of the century they were menacing Israel seriously, and about 1050 B.C. they defeated the Israelites in a great battle in the Plain of Sharon and destroyed Shiloh and its Tabernacle, taking the Ark of the Covenant into captiv-

---

[14] On the site of Ophrah see most recently the writer, *Jour. Pal. Or. Soc.*, XI, pp. 248-51, and Abel, *Jour. Pal. Or. Soc.*, XVII, pp. 31-44. Both views, however divergent they may be in detail, place Ophrah in districts peculiarly exposed to Canaanite influences.

ity. About the same time[15] came a never-forgotten irruption of the Midianites, who had learned how to use the recently domesticated camel with terrifying effectiveness in long-range raids.[16] Then there was intermittent fighting with the Canaanite city-states, with the Moabites and Ammonites on the east, and with Aramaean tribes from the Syrian Desert. Last, but not least, there was bloody civil strife between tribe and tribe, or between all Israel and a single tribe. As shown by the writer's excavations, Bethel was destroyed four times between 1200 and 1000 B.C. One can hardly be surprised if under such conditions Israel became martially minded and Israel's God became "Yahweh, God of (the) Hosts (of Israel)," one of whose primary functions was to defend His people against foes whose only aim seemed to be to destroy it utterly and to devote it to their impure gods. In an early triumphal poem, celebrating the first victory of Israel over its foes, we read for example (Ex. 15:3, 6):

Yahweh is a man of war	Yahweh is his name!
. . . .	. . . .
Thy right arm, O Yahweh,	is majestic in power;
Thy right arm, O Yahweh,	shatters the foe!

In the couplet just quoted is found the Canaanite poetical device in which two successive lines of verse have the scheme abc-abd, which has been shown by H. L. Ginsberg (1935) to be characteristic of Ugaritic poetry.[17] Yahweh here replaces "Baal" of the Canaanite prototype. The same device also occurs repeatedly in the Song of Deborah, though subordinated there to the device of climactic parallelism, which has not yet been identified in Ugaritic literature.

---

[15] On the chronology of this period see now the writer's observations, *Bull. Am. Sch. Or. Res.*, No. 78 (1940), pp. 8 f.

[16] See above, p. 257.

[17] The metric scheme in question, first outlined by Ginsberg in a paper presented at the Oriental Congress in Rome, was described by him in his paper on "The Rebellion and Death of Ba'lu," *Orientalia*, V (1936), pp. 180 f.

It is highly improbable that dominant circles in Israel were then tribal or territorial henotheists, since the spirit of Moses and his influence were still alive and victories over the Canaanites were too recent and too impressive to permit them to subordinate Yahweh to the Canaanite cosmic lord of heaven, especially since the latter was worshipped all over the Semitic Near East. Moreover, we see from the Song of Deborah that Yahweh was believed to be particularly at home in regions which were definitely outside of Israelite control and far beyond the immediate purview of the northern tribes. The ignorant or moronic are often polytheists or henotheists in an age of monotheism, as every experienced priest or pastor or orthodox rabbi knows. Many backward Catholics are polytheists, many ignorant Protestants are tritheists, and unthinking Jews express henotheistic ideas. The parade example of early Israelite henotheism is singularly weak. In a speech to the king of the Ammonites Jephthah is represented as saying (Jud. 11:24), "Wilt thou not possess what Chemosh thy god giveth thee to possess?" It is generally recognized that this speech, which cannot be older than JE, was originally addressed to a king of the Moabites; in any event it probably belongs to the seventh century and cannot be older than the eighth century B.C. It does not, therefore, in any case prove henotheism in the time of the Judges. However, it is quite unnecessary to suppose that it proves henotheism at any period, since the objectivity of the approach *ad hominem* is entirely characteristic of Hebrew thought and literature before the Exile. Patriarchs, national heroes, and religious leaders are described with the most impartial portrayal of faults and sins as well as of virtues. Israel's defeats are mentioned as often as are her triumphs. When the Egyptians speak of the Israelites they call them "Hebrews," not "Israelites." When Israelites address foreigners they use language suitable to their horizon and capable of producing a friendly reaction. There is nothing "modern" about this principle, which must have been a commonplace in the ancient Orient—though no other known people of antiquity can approach the objectivity of the Israelites in such matters, to judge from their literature.

B. The United Monarchy and the Beginnings of the Prophetic Movement

As A. Alt has pointed out, there was a striking difference in political organization between the various peoples in Palestine and southern Syria in the eleventh century B.C.[18] While the Israelites maintained their loose confederation on the amphictyonic principle, depending for guidance on spontaneously arising leadership, the surrounding nations were all highly organized. Edomites, Moabites, and Ammonites all had kings who were much more than tribal emirs, as we know from such monuments as the Balu'ah stela of the twelfth century and the Mesha Stone of the ninth, which confirm and illustrate the biblical data. The Philistines had their *seranîm* "lords," who seem to have been tyrants after the Aegean model. The Canaanites of Phoenicia were still organized in city-states according to the Bronze-Age prototype, but freedom from foreign domination and the great expansion of their commerce in the Early Iron Age had made Tyre, Sidon, and Byblus powerful nations with authority centralized in the hands of the king, as we know from Egyptian and biblical sources, supplemented by native inscriptions. No help against these potent adversaries could be expected from the ancient empires of the Near East. Egypt had ceased to maintain effective rule in Asia after the reign of Ramesses III (1175-1144 B.C.), though half-hearted efforts were made by several of his ephemeral successors, down to about 1125, to support Egyptian garrisons. The Assyrian Empire, after controlling Mesopotamia as far west as the Euphrates for over two centuries (cir. 1300-1100 B.C.) had, under Tiglath-pileser I (1115-1076 B.C.), conquered northern Syria and made the Phoenician states briefly tributary, but his successors were too weak to maintain the supremacy of Assyria over Syria,

[18] *Die Staatenbildung der Israeliten in Palästina* (Leipzig, 1930), pp. 31-36.

and the Assyrian border was kept in the Euphrates Valley.

The advance of the Philistines after the destruction of Shiloh (an event known from the Danish excavations there) threatened to reduce Israel to hopeless servitude, and the Philistines neglected no effort to assure their domination, if we may judge by their ruthless control of the manufacture of iron tools and weapons (I Sam. 13:19-21). Iron was just coming into general use in Palestine in the eleventh century B.C., as we know from excavations,[19] and the iron monopoly was not only a powerful aid to Philistine superiority in arms, but also a valuable commercial privilege, as the Hittites had found two centuries previously. The leaders of Israel, in particular the aging Samuel, had no recourse but to find a king, and it can hardly be accidental that their choice fell on Saul, who was not only famous for his stature and prowess, but was also a member of the weakest and most central tribe, that of Benjamin. In a confederacy where tribal jealousy ran high, it was of great importance that the new king should not excite particularistic friction from the start.

Though Toynbee seems to have overlooked the case of the Israelites between 1200 and 900 B.C., it would be difficult to find a better illustration of his principle of "Challenge-and-Response under the stimulus of blows." Under this stimulus the Israelites attained national unity in spite of the centrifugal forces operating to break up the confederation. Saul (cir. 1020-1000) was unable, it is true, to advance beyond a loose political confederacy, mainly, as would appear from our sources, because of innate weakness of character. But his successor, David (cir. 1000-960) who was the last of the great charismatic figures in Israelite political life, effected a true unity, cementing it by a victory over a palace revolt in the later years of his reign. David made no attempt, so far as we know, to establish a centralized state; the needs of his personal and official treasury were presumably met by the spoils of war and by regular

---

[19] On the date of the introduction of iron into common use in Palestine see G. E. Wright, *Am. Jour. Arch.*, XLIII (1939), pp. 458-63.

levies from the conquered Canaanites of Esdraelon, Sharon, and Galilee, from the subjugated Hebrew border-states of Edom, Moab, and Ammon, and from the tributary Philistines and Aramaeans. The prototype of the census-lists in Numbers probably dates from his reign (see II Sam. 24), especially since the total of about 600,000 suits the demographic requirements for Israelite population at that time exceedingly well, if we suppose that it originally included both sexes and all ages.[20] His son Solomon (cir. 960-922) soon found himself in a difficult position, since he undertook a series of most elaborate building operations throughout the country and also established a powerful standing army of chariotry, both of which occur for the first time in the history of Israel. It is true that scholars used to belittle the tradition preserved in Kings, to say nothing of the obviously exaggerated form which is given by the Chronicler, and reduce his building operations to very modest dimensions. However, archaeological discovery at Megiddo since 1929 has shown that Solomon's building activities in a single one of his "chariot-cities" (I Kings 9:15-19, 10:26) included well-constructed stables with cement floors for at least 400, and perhaps many more horses. At Hazor and Tell el-Hesi similar installations from the Solomonic age have also been found. Moreover, Nelson Glueck's work at Ezion-geber on the Red Sea since 1938 has demonstrated that Solomon built an elaborate copper refinery there, covering an acre and a half and surrounded by a strong brick wall. Nothing like it is otherwise known from the ancient Near East—yet it was so relatively insignificant an enterprise that it is not even mentioned in our sources. The expense of his extensive and costly building operations and of his relatively huge military establishment was not diminished by his elaborate mercantile and industrial enterprises, such as caravan trade in the desert, naval expeditions in the Red Sea and the Mediterranean, and copper mining and refining in the Arabah (of which nothing was known before Glueck's recent ex-

[20] See *Jour. Pal. Or. Soc.*, V (1925), pp. 20 ff.; Olmstead, *History of Palestine and Syria*, p. 330.

plorations and excavations). Moreover, the scale of his personal life appears to have been proverbially lavish. Solomon was, therefore, compelled to resort to the corvée (I Kings 5:13 ff.) and to reorganize the fiscal administration of the entire tribal confederacy, substituting twelve new districts (I Kings 4:7 ff.) for the former tribal units and placing royal officers over each one.[21] It is hardly surprising, therefore, that his death was immediately followed by a general rebellion of the northern tribes and the Division of the Monarchy (cir. 922 B.C.).

During this period of nearly a century of national unity Israelite culture must have made progress comparable to the cultural advance which we see in Egypt from Nebka to Cheops and in Babylonia from Sargon I to Naram-Sin. Israelite life had remained at a low cultural level during the preceding two centuries, as excavations have conclusively demonstrated. Even Saul was only a rustic chieftain, as far as architecture and the amenities of life were concerned; a clear idea of his cultural status is given by the writer's excavation of his citadel at Gibeah. Not a single building nor object from Palestinian soil can yet be attributed with confidence to David; probably the so-called "Jebusite" revetment of the recently excavated city-wall of early Jerusalem dates in part from his time. On the other hand archaeology is beginning, as we have seen, to shed a vivid light on the cultural achievements of the reign of Solomon. Moreover, comparative archaeological investigations can now clarify many details of the construction and decoration of the Temple and palace of the king, by comparison with similar remains excavated in other nearly contemporary sites of Syria and Palestine. The glowing accounts of the Book of Kings

[21] On the subject of Solomon's district organization and the differences in point of view between Alt and the writer see provisionally Alt, *Alttestamentliche Studien Rudolf Kittel gewidmet* (Leipzig, 1913), pp. 1-19; Albright, *Jour. Pal. Or. Soc.*, V (1925), pp. 25-37; Alt, *Palästinajahrbuch*, XXI (1925), pp. 100 ff.; Albright, *Jour. Pal. Or. Soc.*, XI, p. 251. The writer hopes to treat the question again in the near future.

may be slightly over-drawn, but when we compare the tangible illustrations brought to light by excavations with what we have from earlier—and later—Israel, it must be confessed that they are relatively correct.

The advance of material civilization was evidently accompanied by progress in higher culture, especially in literature. David was himself a musician and poet of note, according to a persistent tradition which can hardly be erroneous, since musical and poetic accomplishments were not considered as any more virile by the ancient Orientals, especially in a warlike age, than they are today. Solomon is also said to have been a most productive author of verse and gnomic literature. Unhappily nothing seems to have been directly preserved of this mass of literary production, so we may possibly infer that it was more prolific than inspired. Nor must we forget that literary works had to be extremely good to pass muster in Israel, if we may judge from the average level of literary composition in the Bible, even when seen through a text corrupted by many centuries of scribal transmission. The remarkable level to which prose literature could aspire under Solomon is shown by the brilliant narrative in II Sam. 9-20, written in flawless classical Hebrew. Though we may go perhaps a little too far in calling the age of Solomon "the Golden Age of Hebrew literature," it may be affirmed with confidence that during his reign Hebrew prose took the literary form which remained classical in the subsequent history of Judah. That the Hebrew of Solomon's court was the dialect of northern Judah and Benjamin might be expected from David's own background and history, and appears almost certain after recent epigraphic discoveries in various parts of Palestine.

In the absence of adequate direct records of Israelite religion under Solomon, we must draw our conclusions from such sources as the account of the construction and equipment of the Temple. Here the process of Canaanization appears to reach a climax. The Temple was not intended primarily to be a public place of worship for all Israel, but rather, as has been conclusively demonstrated by Alt,

Möhlenbrink, and Scott (1939),[22] to be a royal chapel into which the palladium of Israel was brought as a sign that the worship of Yahweh was thereafter to be under the special protection of the king. It was built by a Canaanite architect from Tyre, undoubtedly following Phoenician models, since there was none in Israel to follow. The closest parallels in plan, details of arrangement and furnishing, and nomenclature come from Phoenicia (Cyprus), Syria, and Mesopotamia. The Temple received a new, Canaanite name, *hêkhal* (a word originally borrowed by the Canaanites from the Sumerians before 2500 B.C., as shown by A. Poebel). The pillars of Jachin and Boaz, the Sea, the portable lavers, the great altar, the decoration of walls and objects with figures of cherubim (winged sphinxes), lions, bulls, palmettes and lilies, etc., are all of contemporary Canaanite inspiration. However, Yahweh Himself remained invisible, enthroned in majesty above the cherubim of the cella, which was called "the Holy of Holies."

The process of Canaanizing sacrificial practice and ritual probably began much earlier, and its roots doubtless go back through Moses to the Patriarchal Age. Yet it is at this time that it may have reached its culmination, and most of the ritual preserved in the Priestly Code must reflect the practice of the Temple of Solomon. R. Dussaud has shown (1921) the close relation existing between the terminology of the Priestly Code and much later Phoenician sacrificial practice, as we know it from Carthaginian sacrificial tariffs of about the fourth century B.C.[23] Recent discoveries at Beth-shan and especially at Lachish (1939) have proved that there was even greater similarity between the sacrificial materials of Canaanite cult in the thirteenth century B.C. and those of the Priestly Code than existed between the latter and the Carthaginian system. This is particularly evi-

[22] Cf. especially K. Möhlenbrink, *Der Tempel Salomos* (Stuttgart, 1932), and quite independently R. B. Y. Scott, *Jour. Bib. Lit.*, LVIII (1939), pp. 143-49.

[23] *Les origines cananéennes du sacrifice israelite* (Paris, 1921); cf. A. Lods, *Rev. Hist. Philos. Rel.*, VIII (1928), pp. 399 ff.

dent in the extensive use of the right front leg of a sacrificial animal (which is also characteristic of Mesopotamian practice).[24] On the other hand, there were such far-reaching differences between the Egyptian and the Canaanite-Hebrew sacrificial systems that any appreciable influence from the former upon the latter is excluded. In this connection it is curious to note that the Egyptians of the late second millennium B.C. borrowed the practice of offering holocausts (burnt offerings), to which they applied the Canaanite-Hebrew word *kalîl* (Egyptian *chelîl*).[25]

There is no indication that the Israelite idea of God was permanently influenced by Canaanite conceptions in this age. But it is clear that the doctrine of angels began to receive certain modifications which eventually developed into the elaborate Judaeo-Christian angelic hierarchy of Graeco-Roman times. Owing to the difficulty of dating our scattered references precisely, it is hard to define the early Yahwistic conception, but we may safely infer that it was not very different from what we find in the Pentateuch (outside of Genesis) and other prose narratives dating in their present form from the early monarchic age. The subject is exceedingly complex and obscure, and there were certainly many diverging tendencies and fluctuations in Israelite thought in different periods and circles. Yahweh was believed to have created astral as well as terrestrial beings, and the former were popularly called "the host of heaven" or "the sons of God" (*benê 'El* or *benê ha-'Elôhîm*). This meant simply "gods" in Canaanite, as is clear from numerous passages in Ugaritic literature, illustrated by many parallel Semitic expressions. In Gen. 6:1 ff., for example, we have an original myth in which the (astral) gods had intercourse with mortal women, who gave birth to heroes

[24] See above, Chap. IV, p. 236.
[25] For the fullest discussion of this question see Dussaud, *op. cit.*, pp. 159 ff. (with a contribution by I. Lévy). It should be added that the word *qrr* seems first to appear in the Twentieth Dynasty (Sethe *apud* Burchardt, *Altkanaanäische Fremdworte, ad voc.*), though it remained rare until much later, and that the word has been adapted to the native Egyptian verbal stem *qrr* "to burn," known since the Pyramid Age.

(literally, "meteors," *nephîlîm*), an idea that may often be illustrated from Babylonian and Greek mythology.[26] But the Israelite who heard this section recited, unquestionably thought of intercourse between angels and women (like later Jews and Christians); the passage would presumably have been eliminated by later editors if it had not been interpreted in some less objectionable way by verbal exegesis.[27] In Job (fifth century B.C.) the expression is still employed in the sense of "angels."

A very interesting and instructive passage, which has been misused, is Deut. 32:8 f., from the Song of Moses, which apparently belongs to the tenth century B.C., where we read (with the Greek translators of the third century B.C.):

When the Most High gave the nations their heritage,
    When He divided mankind,
(Then) He fixed the territories of the peoples
    According to the number of the sons of God;
But Yahweh's share was His people,
    Jacob was His inherited possession.

The third and fourth hemistichs have been rendered as follows by T. J. Meek (1939),[28] in an effort to demonstrate Yahweh's rank below the Most High: "He assigned the realms of the nations to the various deities"(!). What the passage really means, however, is clear from Job 38:7,

When the morning stars rejoiced together
    And all the sons of God shouted with joy.

There are many passages in the Old Testament where the

---

[26] See now J. Morgenstern, *Heb. Un. Col. Ann.*, XIV (1939), pp. 76-126, and the writer's comments, *Jour. Bib. Lit.*, 1940, p. 300.

[27] There was undoubtedly much more exegesis of the Hebrew text in preëxilic times than we often realize. Sometimes we can follow the operation of exegetical considerations in our text, e. g., in Gen. 3:1 ff. (see F. M. Th. Böhl, *Genesis*, I [Groningen, 1923], pp. 68 f.).

[28] *Univ. Toronto Quar.*, VIII (1939), p. 196; see Budde, *Jour. Bib. Lit.*, XL (1921), pp. 41 f.

stars serve as a simile for "multitude"; specific references
to "counting" the stars are found in Gen. 15:5 and Psalms
147:4. We must, accordingly, explain the fourth hemistich
in the passage quoted from Deut. 32 as meaning simply
"according to the number of the stars," i. e., God created
and assigned abodes to a multitude of different nations, but
of them all he chose Israel as his special charge. It may be
added that this passage, like a number of others in this
poem, is full of Canaanite literary reminiscences, as we
know from Ugaritic literature, so we need not take any single simile or poetic phrase too literally. The monotheistic
standpoint of the author of Deut. 32 is clear from a number
of passages: pagan deities are "evil spirits" (*shedîm*, v. 17),
"not divine" (v. 21); "I am I (so!) and there is no God
beside Me" (v. 39).[29]

It is generally recognized by scholars that only part of
the early prose passages which mention "messengers (angels) of God" or "the messenger of Yahweh" reflect their

---

[29] There is no question that this was also the later exegesis
of the First Commandment (Greek: *plēn emū*, Targum: *bar
minni* "except me"), but since this use of *'al panai* was unique,
not all exegetes agreed, as shown by Jerome's *coram me*, followed by the English Bible: "before me." The original sense
was, however, more concrete: "Thou shalt not prefer other
gods to me." This rendering agrees with the clear sense of
'al panai in several other passages (e. g., Ex. 20:20; Job 6:
28; and especially Deut. 21:16 and Gen. 16:12). Since Yahweh had no pantheon, no other deities could be associated
with him anyway, but a rebellious Israelite might deliberately
choose to worship another god. Jews and Christians have recited this commandment for twenty-five centuries without supposing that there actually were other gods in existence as rivals
of God, and there is no more reason to credit the Israelites
with henotheistic or monolatrous ideas when *they* recited it.
The emphasis is laid on the legalistic aspect of the Commandment, which concerns itself with what men may do, not on the
ontological aspect, which requires development beyond the
empirico-logical stage of thought. [In the 1946 edition, p. 367,
I pointed out that the Phoenician use of *'lt pn* (Marseilles Tariff,
lines 3,6) in the sense "besides, in addition to" supports the
Greek and Aramaic of Ex. 20:3. These renderings also agree
better with the parallel command, Ex. 34:14, as D.N. Freedman
points out.]

original sense. In some places, as in the patriarchal narratives (e. g., Gen. 18:2; 19:1), the original pre-Mosaic tradition referred to early Hebrew deities or demigods. In some later passages the term "angel of Yahweh" has clearly been substituted for "Yahweh." In the post-patriarchal period there is remarkable fluctuation: e. g., in Ex. 33 different strands of JE represent Yahweh himself, or his angel, or his Presence (*panîm*) as going before Israel to guide it through the desert. In this case it is safe to say that the earliest post-Mosaic version represented Yahweh Himself as leading Israel; the replacement of God Himself by His messenger is orthodox Israelite doctrine, but the use of the term "Presence" reminds one strongly of the late Canaanite (Carthaginian) idea that Tanit was the "presence (power) of Baal" (*Tanit penê Ba'al*) and may have been felt by orthodox Israelite theologians to verge perilously on pagan hypostatizations of deity. At all events it does not seem to appear elsewhere in biblical literature until the seventh century B.C. (Deut. 4:37; for later occurrences see below, p. 267). It is very clear that standard Israelite thinking in early preëxilic times insisted on the ideal anthropomorphic character of Yahweh, who was a personal God and not an impersonal manifestation of deity. While prophetic theology had not yet been reduced to "logical" terms, it was undoubtedly acutely conscious of divagations which might lead to disastrous practical results. In other words, it had reached an advanced stage of empirico-logical development.

C. The Divided Monarchy and the Charismatic Prophets

1. *The Age of the Ecstatic Prophets*

The first effect of the Division of the Monarchy (cir. 922 B.C.) was to implement the popular reaction against the process of centralization of government, both in secular and in religious spheres. In order to weaken the possible appeal of the Temple of Solomon to Israelites who were moved by the fact that it contained the Ark of the Covenant and was

thus the heir of the Tabernacle at Shiloh, Jeroboam I built
two new sanctuaries of Yahweh at Bethel and Dan. Both
of them claimed to represent the true Levitic priestly tradition of Moses and Aaron: the ancestor of the later priestly
line at Dan was said to be a certain Jonathan of the family
of Gershom, son of Moses (so with the original Massoretic
text, the Alexandrine Greek, and the Vulgate); the priestly
line at Bethel is said by the hostile Deuteronomic editor
(I Kings 12:31) to have been of non-Levitic origin, which
implies that it had claimed falsely to be Levitic, and the
originality of this claim is confirmed by the Ephraimitic tradition in Ex. 32, according to which Aaron himself made the
prototypic golden calf. Moreover, in presumable reaction
against the representation of Yahweh in the Temple of Solomon as an invisible deity enthroned above the two cherubim (winged sphinxes), which is now known to have
been influenced by contemporary Canaanite iconography
(where kings and gods are shown sitting on thrones supported by two cherubs), Jeroboam represented Yahweh as
an invisible figure standing on a young bull of gold. It is
true that the "golden calves" have been assumed by most
scholars to have been direct representations of Yahweh as
bull-god, but this gross conception is not only otherwise unparalleled in biblical tradition, but is contrary to all that
we know of Syro-Palestinian iconography in the second and
early first millennia B.C. Among Canaanites, Aramaeans,
and Hittites we find the gods nearly always represented as
standing on the back of an animal or as seated on a throne
borne by animals—but never as themselves in animal form.
It is true that the Hurrians considered the two bulls Sheri
and Khurri, who supported the throne of the storm-god
Teshub, as minor deities, but they were not identified with
the great storm-god! It was, therefore, pointed out by K.
Th. Obbink in 1929 that the "golden calf" must have been
the visible pedestal on which the invisible Yahweh stood.[30]

[30] *Zeits. Alttest. Wiss.*, XLVII, pp. 264-74; cf. J. Hempel, *Gott
und Mensch im Alten Testament* (second ed., Stuttgart, 1936),
pp. 265 f., and especially W. Eichrodt, *Theologie des Alten
Testaments*, I (1933), pp. 52 f.

In 1938 the writer showed that no other interpretation can be squared with the known facts.[31] The storm-god of Mesopotamia is actually represented on seal-cylinders of the second millennium B.C. as a schematic bolt of lightning set upright on the back of a bull, and this iconographic device may go back to Sumerian seals showing the bull who was the central figure in the ritual of consecration of a sacred drum with the winged shrine of music (so labelled!) on his back.[32] The bull on which the storm-god stood is sometimes clearly represented as a bullock of two or three years, just at the prime of life and vigor, so the term 'egel, which is also applied in Biblical Hebrew to a three-year old animal, is entirely suitable.[33] Conceptually there is, of course, no essential difference between representing the invisible deity as enthroned on the cherubim or as standing on a bull. We may safely assume, in the light of the conflate tradition preserved in Ex. 32, which probably has a very early nucleus, that the pre-Mosaic Hebrews had also been accustomed to thinking of their chief god, the storm-god Shaddai,

---

[31] In an illustrated lecture before the British Society for Old Testament Study at its Oxford meeting in September, 1938 (see also the abstract in *Jour. Bib. Lit.*, LVII [1938], p. xviii).

[32] These seals, to which C. H. Gordon has called my attention, belong mainly to the period of Accad and Ur III (cir. 24th-22nd centuries), and are well represented in the collections of the Iraq Museum of Antiquities. One of the unpublished seals contains the characters (LÙ) UŠ-KU, i. e., *gala* (Accad. *kalû*), "temple musician," written vertically in the winged shrine. For the bull of Lumkha (Ea as god of musicians) see *Jour. Am. Or. Soc.*, LIV (1934), pp. 118 ff., 122 ff.

[33] For Heb. 'egel in the sense of "young bull" see the excellent discussion by A. R. S. Kennedy in Hastings' *Dictionary of the Bible*, I, pp. 340 ff. That the bull on which the god Hadad stood was also supposed to be a young bull of two or three years has been pointed out by S. A. Cook, *The Religion of Ancient Palestine in the Light of Archaeology* (London, 1930), p. 141, n. 4. Both among Canaanites and Israelites three-year-old bulls were sacrificed as particularly pleasing to deity; cf. A. Rowe, *The Topography and History of Beth-shan* (Philadelphia, 1930), p. 13, and E. A. Speiser, *Bull. Am. Sch. Or. Res.*, No. 72, pp. 15-17.

as standing on a bull, and the pre-Israelite Hebrews of central Palestine almost certainly shared ideas of this kind with their Canaanite neighbors, who portrayed Baal in the same way. So Jeroboam may well have been harking back to early Israelite traditional practice when he made the "golden calves." It is hardly necessary to point out that it was a dangerous revival, since the taurine associations of Baal, lord of heaven, were too closely bound up with the fertility cult in its more insidious aspects to be safe. The cherubim, being mythical animals, served to enhance the majesty of Yahweh, "who rides on a cherub" (II Sam. 22:11) or "who thrones on the cherubim" (II Kings 19:15, etc.), but the young bulls of Bethel and Dan could only debase His cult. Like Solomon Jeroboam took the cult of Yahweh under his direct protection, and the sanctuary at Bethel was said by its chief priest to be "a royal chapel and a dynastic temple" (Amos 7:13).

At this dangerous moment in the history of Yahwism, when its pristine purity threatened to be violated by the Canaanizing encroachments of temple-cult, in both South and North, came the prophetic movement like a refreshing west wind, blowing from the sea and dispersing the stagnant air of the sirocco. Since the phenomenon of prophetism is of paramount significance for proper understanding of the development of Israelite religion, we must devote some attention to its nature and history before analyzing its function in ninth-century Yahwism.

It has repeatedly been emphasized since the work of G. Hölscher (1914) that the prophetic movement takes root in group-ecstaticism, i. e., in dances or other physical motions repeated so often by the members of a group that they finally succumb to a kind of hypnotic suggestion, under the influence of which they may remain unconscious for hours.[34] In this state the subconsciousness may be abnormally active, and persons of a certain psychological type may have visions and mystic experiences which thereafter control, or at least affect their entire life. This phenomenon

[34] *Die Profeten* (Leipzig, 1914), pp. 129-43.

is universal among mankind, being found among savages, in antiquity, and among the highest religions of today, as all students of the subject know from such parallels as the Moslem dervishes, the Jewish Hasidim, and Evangelical Protestant movements among Quakers, Methodists, Pentecostalists, and others. To primitive man, however, as shown by L. Lévy-Bruhl in his important work, *L'expérience mystique et les symboles chez les primitifs* (1938), certain aspects of mysticism, such as the consciousness of direct communion with invisible beings, are almost every-day matters, whereas modern man has relegated them to the background—often to his great loss. Mass activity is not essential to the mystic experience in modern man, since it can be attained through a long course of special ascetic training, as in the Hindu *yoga* or the somewhat parallel methods of the Hesychast monks of the late Byzantine age, or through concentrated meditation and prayer, as in the case of Christian mystics of mediaeval and modern times. However, there can be no doubt that the desired results come much more rapidly and with less effort of will when the individual is a member of a group, all engaged in the same exercises. Moreover, many so-called prophetic phenomena are not mystical at all, in the proper sense, but pathological. To this category probably belong most cases of hypnotic and clairvoyant subjects. The Hebrew seer (*rô'eh*) was perhaps a clairvoyant, but more probably an offshoot of the general class of diviners, which originated in Mesopotamia and spread in all directions as early as the middle of the second millennium B.C. (see above, p. 211).[35] Balaam (thirteenth century B.C.) was a diviner, not a prophet, though he played a rôle somewhat like that of later prophets.[36]

[35] A. Guillaume, in his *Prophecy and Divination* (London, 1938) has stressed the relationship of the Hebrew seer to the Mesopotamian diviner, but has exaggerated its significance.

[36] See S. Daiches in *Hilprecht Anniversary Volume* (Leipzig, 1909), pp. 60-70. A very interesting seal from the early second millennium, discovered in a thirteenth-century stratum at Beth-shan, bears the legend "Manum the *bârû*, the servant of Ea."

The current explanation of the word *nabhî'* "prophet," as "speaker, announcer," is almost certainly false. The correct etymological meaning of the word is rather "one who is called (by God), one who has a vocation (from God)," as appears from the fact that this is almost always the sense which the verb *nabû* "to call," has in Accadian, from the middle of the third millennium to the middle of the first. The king is repeatedly termed "the one whom the great gods (or a special high god) have called." Using a noun (*nibîtu*) derived from this verb, the king is styled "the one called by the great gods, etc." The verbal adjective *nabi'* means "called," in the Code of Hammurabi. All Hebrew verbal forms from this root are transparent denominatives from the noun *nabhî'*, and throw no light whatever on the derivation of the latter.[37] This interpretation of the word suits its meaning exactly; the prophet was a man who felt himself called by God for a special mission, in which his will was subordinated to the will of God, which was communicated to him by direct inspiration. The prophet was thus a charismatic spiritual leader, directly commissioned by Yahweh to warn the people of the perils of sin and to preach reform and revival of true religion and morality.

There are no clear traces of the prophetic movement as such in Israel before the end of the eleventh century.[38] The only apparent exception is that of Eldad and Medad (Num. 11:26 ff.), but the names are pagan and their

---

[37] The etymology is original with the writer (barring correction). For the latest statement of the usual etymology see Guillaume, *op. cit.*, pp. 112 f., but his formulation of the case does not strengthen it at all. There is no basis for E. Ebeling's rendering of *na-bit ilani^pl* as "Prophetin der Götter" (*Mitt. Vord. Ges.*, XXV [1918], p. 52, top of page [line 23]); the word *nabit* is clearly archaic for *nibit* (cf. the parallel *ba'it* "sought of"), "the one called (by the gods), (their) favorite." Four lines previously in the same text occurs the phrase *na-ba-at ta-bi-ni* "she who creates (lit. names) the multitude" (contrast Ebeling and for the meaning of *tabinu* see the material collected by Mullo Weir, *Lexicon of Accadian Prayers* [London, 1934], pp. 357 f.).

[38] With the following sketch compare the writer's fuller treatment, *Jour. Bib. Rel.*, VIII (1940), pp. 131-36.

rhyming assonance suggests the legendary character of their association. The first reference which is clearly authentic belongs to the beginning of Saul's reign, cir. 1020 B.C. However, the Report of Wen-amun, from the early eleventh century, describes a case of ecstatic trance at Byblus in Phoenicia, which obviously belongs to the same picture, though it was apparently a pathological condition rather than the result of group activity. It is significant that all early references are to a state of frenzy followed by trance, a fact which indicates that the movement was just commencing at that time. The correctness of this inference is supported by Mesopotamian parallels (there is none from Egypt, aside from the passage just cited, which refers to foreigners). In Assyrian inscriptions of the first millennium we frequently hear of a *makhkhû,* a kind of priest or diviner who did not belong to any of the regular categories of earlier times. The derived adverb *makhkhûtash* means "like a madman, in a state of madness." The words occur only rarely in documents antedating the first millennium. A collection of extremely interesting poetic oracles from the seventh century B.C. has been preserved on an Assyrian tablet in the British Museum, dating from the reign of Esarhaddon. All the oracles are attributed to different men and women of Arbela, who delivered them in the name of their goddess, Ishtar of Arbela. Most of these bearers of oracles were females, but there is not the slightest concrete basis for the usual assumption (e. g., Jastrow, Langdon, Guillaume) that they were priests.[39]

It has been suggested that the ecstatic movement from which Israelite prophetism arose, is somehow akin to Dionysiac frenzy and that there was a revival of it in Asia Minor about the end of the second millennium which swept over

[39] See especially Langdon, *Tammuz and Ishtar* (Oxford, 1914), pp. 128 ff. The word which appears as *še-lu-tu,* supposed to mean some kind of female priest, is otherwise unknown and is probably a mistake for *še-ib-tu* "old woman"; for old women as experts in Hittite ritual and divinatory lore see A. Goetze, *The Hittite Ritual of Tunnawi* (New Haven, 1938), and the writer's comments, *Jour. Bib. Lit.,* 1940, p. 316 (with regard to the "witch of Endor").

Greece in one direction and Syria-Palestine in another. The legendary Bacchantic irruption into Greece, of which Euripides wrote so eloquently, and the prophetic movement in Israel may then have a common historical source.[40] Since mass-movements of this type spread with infectious rapidity, this suggestion is not historically improbable, but it must certainly be modified in at least one respect. The ecstaticism of the prophets of the Tyrian Baal, described so vividly in I Kings 18, belongs to the Dionysiac type, while that of the early prophets of Yahweh as described in I Sam. 10 and 19 has nothing orgiastic about it, but rather reminds one of the activities of certain extreme Pentecostal groups of today. Perhaps the Yahwistic movement arose partly as a reaction against pagan ecstaticism, which must have threatened the religion of Israel as few other movements of history.

In keeping with the point which we made above, that the *nabhî* was primarily a man who felt himself specially called by God for a religious mission, are other facts.[41] The true prophet felt himself to be under a strong compulsion (Jeremiah) or was conscious of an experience which transformed his life (Hosea, Isaiah, Jeremiah, Ezekiel, etc.), i. e., a true conversion, as in the typical case of Saul (I Sam. 10:9).[41a] From David's time on, the prophetic mission was closely associated with moral and political reformation as well as purely religious revival, as is shown clearly by the rôle of Nathan. It can hardly be accidental that the flow of charismatic energy in Israel was diverted from military

---

[40] On the historical background of the Greek stories see now Dodds, *Harv. Theol. Rev.*, 1940, pp. 155-76. In culture there was so close a relationship between Macedonia and Thrace on the one hand, and Asia Minor on the other, that his emphasis on eventual Macedonian origin does not affect the validity of the Anatolian theory.

[41] This aspect of the prophetic experience has been correctly emphasized by J. Hempel in his essay "Berufung und Bekehrung" in *Beerfestschrift* (Stuttgart, 1935), pp. 41 ff.; cf. Hempel in *Der Alte Orient*, XXXVIII:1 (1938), p. 23.

[41a] See Albright, *Archaeology and the Religion of Israel*, pp. 24 f.

and political heroes and leaders to religious leaders almost immediately after the consolidation of the Monarchy. Seen in this light the establishment of the Monarchy seems to have been almost a prerequisite for spiritual revival, under the conditions which then prevailed.

References to prophetic activity increase in number after the time of Saul and the movement reached its climax in the ninth century under Elijah and Elisha, who founded schools of prophets whose members are called "the sons of the prophets," i. e., probably "the members of prophetic houses or groups," following widespread Semitic idiomatic usage in that period. At first sight it is curious that practically no oracles have survived; what we have belongs to the category of Deuteronomic sermon, though it presumably rests on a traditional nucleus. The prophets of the ecstatic period, including Elijah and Elisha, were men of deeds, not men of words, and the ecstatic tradition was still too strong to be broken. Except in very unusual cases, no prophet could emerge from an ecstatic experience to give a poetic address couched in such perfect literary form as are the best preserved oracles of Amos, Hosea, and Isaiah. In other words, we must differentiate sharply between the age of the great natural prophets, which came to an end in the ninth century B.C. and that of the literary prophets, which began several decades later.[42] But the latter carried on the religious movement which had been inaugurated by their forerunners, whose spiritual heirs they most certainly were. If we want to know how Elijah and Elisha reacted to the evils of the ninth century, we have only to read what Amos, Hosea, and Isaiah said in the eighth, though they may have expressed themselves differently.

Our most instructive historical document for the entire prophetic movement is the pericope of Elijah. In its present form it is obviously the product of oral tradition, which has seized on certain episodes and has developed their dramatic aspects. The Elijah stories cannot have been handed down

---

[42] Cf. the writer's observations about the historical background of the shift from ecstatic to rhapsodic prophetism in the article cited above, n. 38.

long by tradition, since they bear a very close relation to the facts of external history as we know them from other sources, and since they are written in the purest classical Hebrew, of a type which can hardly be later than the eighth century. At that time Israel was quivering under a religious invasion which threatened to crush the already seriously weakened body of Yahwism under its weight. Ahab's queen, Jezebel of Tyre, seems to have been an unusually ardent missionary of the cult of the Tyrian Baal, a god who was generally known in later times as Melcarth (literally, "King of the City," i. e., probably of the underworld, as in Ugaritic) and of his mother or wife, Asherah (I Kings 18: 19).[43] With its epidemic ecstaticism, its colorful ritual of fertility, and probably its picturesque initiations, it stood in sharp contrast to the sober hues and stern morality of Yahwism, even when the latter was made more palatable to the common man by sacrificial ritual and solemn chants. Elijah and Elisha threw themselves with unexampled ardor into the conflict and won a signal triumph. The menace of Melcarth was definitely exorcised, and with its elimination Yahwism triumphed at last over the direct onslaught of Baalism.

A vivid picture of Elijah's theological faith has been handed down in I Kings 19, which describes his pilgrimage to Horeb, the Mount of God, where Moses had received his first revelation more than four centuries earlier. The prophet stands on the craggy summit of the sacred mountain, face to face with his God. First comes a mighty wind-

[43] Eissfeldt's discussion of the Baal of Jezebel (*Zeits. Alttest. Wiss.*, LVII [1939], pp. 19 ff.) is correct in emphasizing the cosmic sweep and the prestige of this deity, but can hardly be correct in identifying it so specifically with Ba'al-shamem "the Lord of Heaven." That the Baal in question was identified with Ba'al-shamem may be considered as virtually certain, just as the Ishtar of Nineveh was identified with the Ishtar of Arbela. However, the dominating traits of Melcarth were probably chthonic; the Baal of Tyre was lord of the storm but he was also lord of the underworld and of its fertility-producing powers. It must be remembered that Baal spent some time every year in the underworld and that even such a chthonic divinity as Nergal was also originally a storm-god.

storm, which seems to split the mountains with its force—
but Yahweh is not in the wind. Then comes a terrifying
earthquake—but Yahweh is not in the earthquake. Then a
devastating fire—but Yahweh is not there. Finally comes a
gentle, murmuring whisper ("a still small voice")—and this
belongs to Yahweh, the God of Hosts. When we recall the
majestic theophany of Yahweh at Horeb, centuries before,
and the celebration of the power of God over the elements
in subsequent hymns, this complete reversal of tradition
might seem to belong to a different religion. Yet it is the
same religion, with a spiritual aspect which was latent from
the beginning and may have been as familiar to Moses as
it was to Elijah, though it could hardly have survived the
vicissitudes of the following three centuries of bitter struggle for existence on the part of a rugged but earthy people.
Yahweh remained a person, but His spiritual side was
henceforth increasingly stressed and the external character
of His theophany in nature was more and more restricted
to the sphere of poetic imagery.

At the same time that the very nature of spiritual communion[44] between the prophet and his God led to the spir-
itualization of His relationship to man in general, there was
no modification of the dominant concept of Yahweh as a
person—and as a person with human emotions, though on
a heroic scale and divested of the littleness of man's emo-

---

[44] We have carefully avoided the misleading term "mystical
communion"; see J. Lindblom for an exceedingly clear statement of the reasons why Israelite prophetic experience cannot
be identified with the *unio mystica* (*Zeits. Alttest. Wiss.*,
1940, pp. 65-74). On the other hand, such recent writers as
Hempel, Heschel, Tor Andrae, and others are fully justified in
recognizing a certain kinship to mysticism in the prophetic
experience. The Israelite prophet identified his utterance with
the command of Yahweh, much as the mediaeval Christian
mystic identified his sufferings with the sufferings of Christ
and received the impression of the stigmata on his own person.
The more extreme forms of mysticism among Christians, Jews,
Moslems, but especially among Brahmans and Buddhists of the
Middle East, where the mystic becomes one with God, have
no counterpart in Israelite religious experience, so far as we
know.

tional reactions. The Holy One of Israel could do nothing little or cheap; His sense of justice was a consuming fire which destroyed everything that violated it. The outstanding concept of God in the Prophetic Age was His character as a "jealous God" (*El qannô'*, later *El qannâ'*). Just what this expression means is clear from many passages in which the verb *qinne'* and the noun *qin'ah* occur. The basic sense of these words is both "to be jealous" and "to be zealous," and it is a good semantic illustration of the close affinity of these ideas that "jealous" and "zeal" come from the same Greek word, and that German *Eifer* "zeal," is the stem of *Eifersucht* "jealousy." Joshua is jealous for Moses' prestige; Saul is zealous to defend Israelite nationalism at the expense of the Gibeonites; Phinehas and Elijah are zealous to uphold the sole right of Yahweh to be worshipped in Israel. Similarly, Yahweh is zealous for the well-being of His people and jealous of His sovereignty and of the honor of His name. In the ninth century B.C. there was nothing soft or flabby about the worship of Yahweh. It might still be weak in certain deeper spiritual values and it might not be perfectly suited for an era of disillusionment, but for a people of extraordinary native vitality, which had not yet suffered seriously from the blows of Providence, but which had advanced rather steadily in number, in prosperity, and in culture for several centuries, a full-bodied religious faith was necessary, if the faith in question was to resist the seductive wooing of a religion of dramatic affective contrasts and lustful appeal to the senses.

2. *The Age of the Rhapsodist Prophets*

Between 842 and 836 B.C. the religious revolution inspired by Elijah was translated into political action in both the North and the South. With the accession of Jehu in Israel and Jehoash in Judah the way was clear for undisturbed worship of Yahweh, according to the ancient custom of Israel. But Baalism was too deeply rooted in tradition and custom to be so easily destroyed. The Canaanizing elements which had entered into official Yahwistic cult with

Solomon and Jeroboam were only the public recognition of an increasing tendency to adapt Baalistic practices to the local cult of Yahweh in open-air shrines and at rustic altars throughout the country. Our documentary sources list among such practices the planting of sacred trees called *asherah* and of altars of incense known as *ḥammân*. The former were called after the goddess of the name, but in one passage they are specifically referred to as "trees of Asherah," which are to be cut down, and elsewhere such terms as "plant," or "chop down" and "burn," are used of them, so their secondary nature is certain. From the connection in which they stand to the goddess of fertility it is clear that they were associated with pagan rites of fecundity and some idea of the license to which the periodical celebration of such rites gave rise may be obtained from the poetic addresses of Amos and Hosea. The meaning attached to the term *ḥammân* has been explained only recently by H. Ingholt (1940), who has discovered that the word meant "altar of incense" in Palmyrene.[45] This agrees with the etymology of the word, with such references as Hos. 4:13, and with archaeological finds of the past few years, which have brought to light numerous horned altars of incense in Israelite towns of the period between the tenth and the seventh century B.C.[46] For some reason, presumably because of its extremely close connection with licentious pagan ritual, the use of incense was opposed in early Israel, and there is no clear evidence for its official use that antedates the Priestly Code. We may suppose that it entered

[45] See his article in Vol. II of *Mélanges Dussaud* (Paris, 1939-40). For convenient reference to previous discussions see J. Lindblom, *Lunds Universitetes Årsskrift, N. F., Avd.* 1, Vol. XXXIV, No. 3 (1938), pp. 91-100, but he has certainly begun his reasoning at the wrong end, i. e., he should start with the altar of incense itself and not with theoretical considerations.

[46] The earliest now known altars of incense with four horns come from stratum V at Megiddo and must antedate the middle of the tenth century; cf. *Ill. London News*, June 20, 1936, pp. 1108-11 and *Am. Jour. Arch.*, XLI (1937), p. 148 a. On later altars of incense from Megiddo see May and Engberg, *Material Remains of the Megiddo Cult* (Chicago, 1935), pp. 12 f.

gradually with the Canaanizing of temple ritual. When it
finally came into general use in Yahwistic ritual it possessed
good traditional backing and had been effectively dissoci-
ated from pagan practices.[47]

In addition to these pagan cult-objects there were also
figurines of the goddess of fertility, which appear in definitely Israelite sites from the time of the Judges on. The
earliest ones, from Tell Beit Mirsim in the South, are simply
nude females represented as about to give birth, and there
is absolutely no indication of pagan symbolism about them,
so we may safely suppose that, whatever their origin, they
were considered as charms to aid expectant mothers.[48]
The characteristic later forms reflect known Canaanite
(Phoenician) prototypes of the Iron Age, such as standing
female figures, fully clothed and veiled with tambourines
pressed to their bosoms (representing the goddess as a musician), and as female busts whose prominent breasts are
supported by the hands, as if to suckle an infant (*dea
nutrix* type).[49] The former type is common in the North;
the latter is more characteristic of the South. At all events,
there is nothing either cultic or obscene about these figurines, though later biblical writers seem to have included
them under the general head of *teraphim* (literally, "vile
things").

Besides the cult-objects and amulets already described,
it is certain from many allusions in the Prophets and the
Books of Kings that there was constant percolation of different non-Yahwistic cults, in particular of novel religious systems and practices which can, as a rule, only be named
without being described. As Israel became more wealthy
and as more and more Israelites took an active part in commerce, the danger of such pagan intrusion became correspondingly greater. It was an age of very active syncretism
and new religious cults came into Palestine from all direc-

[47] Cf. the writer's observations on the monographs of Löhr
and Wiener, *Jour. Pal. Or. Soc.*, IX (1929), pp. 50-54.

[48] See *Mélanges Dussaud*, I (Paris, 1939), p. 119.

[49] *Ibid.*, p. 120; cf. Albright, *Arch. Pal. Bib.* (New York,
1932-35), pp. 121 f.

tions. Among the innovations were astral cults (Amos 5:
26) from Babylonia, and slightly later the vowing of sacred
horses and chariots to the sun-god in Assyrian fashion, and
the cult of Mesopotamian Tammuz and of Ishtar, the
Queen of Heaven.

About the middle of the eighth century Amos appears
on the scene, closely followed by Hosea and Isaiah.[50]
Their approach is dissimilar, as might be expected from
such different men: Amos was a poor peasant of Tekoa,
one of the poorest villages of Judah, who (like the modern
Arabs of the district) spent part of his time at home as a
shepherd and part of his time as a day-laborer working at
one of the most inferior tasks; Hosea was a man of higher
social position who had passed through bitter marital experiences; Isaiah was a high-born statesman and royal ad-
viser. But their point of view and their targets of attack are
virtually identical. To all three the wickedness of Israel was
comparable to that of the legendary Cities of the Plain.
They were profoundly moved by the decay of religion and
the spread of paganism, by the social corruption which existed on every side, and by the economic oppression which
accompanied increasing concentration of wealth in the
hands of a few.

Amos, the poor herdsman and laborer, inveighed against
the luxury of the rich and their oppression of the poor; in
unforgettable similes he draws a picture of Yahweh's anger
at the wickedness of the people and their rulers. Israel's sin
is just as heinous as the most notorious atrocities of Damas-
cus, of Ammon, and of Moab, which he names and because
of which he threatens dire punishment to these wicked
countries. But since Israel has been chosen by Yahweh from
all the peoples of the earth and has learned through a marvellous national history to rely upon Him, there is less ex-
cuse for its persistent wickedness than there is for the
sensational outrages of its neighbors. It has often been sup-

---

[50] For the most recent and in some respects the best general
account of the three great prophets of the eighth century see
Fleming James, *Personalities of the Old Testament* (New York,
1939), pp. 210-69.

posed by modern scholars that Amos was the first monotheist of recorded Israelite history, but there is not the
slightest hint of any such innovation in the poetic addresses
which bear his name. If we follow them without any pre-
conceived ideas, we see in Amos a worthy successor of
Elijah, a man on fire with zeal for a revival of religion and
of social morality, to whom the Canaanizing practices of
official Yahwism were almost as abhorrent as were specifically pagan rites, but he was no religious innovator, much
less the earliest monotheistic teacher of Israel.

Hosea was a man of deep emotional and spiritual life,
whose unhappy matrimonial experience, vividly pictured
in two successive passages, served to point his crushing
indictments of Israel. Hosea does not devote much time to
social injustice and oppression; for him the trouble lies
much deeper, in the increasing paganizing of Yahwism. His
rhapsodic sermons attack the cult of Yahweh Himself as
practiced in the Northern Kingdom; he excoriates the cult
of local shrines and central temples, the dead formalism of
sacrifices and offerings, and especially the rôle played by
the young bull (calf) of Yahweh, on which he heaps scorn.
Israel is a faithless wife, who has committed adultery and
has broken her solemn contract with Yahweh, by virtue of
which he espoused her and showered gifts and kindness
upon her. Hosea's ideal is a return to the simple semi-
nomadic life of antiquity, eschewing both the comforts and
the attendant evils of civilization.[51]

Isaiah, coming just when Israel was in the act of col-
lapsing under the blows of Assyria, and when Judah was
seriously imperilled, saw the Divine judgment in the very
process of fulfilment. His oracles and visions are full of the
majesty and awful holiness of Yahweh, and the eschatological element dominates all else. Isaiah's eschatology undoubtedly had an Oriental prehistory, certain glimpses of
which we get from time to time. It is probable that the

[51] For primitivism among the prophets see J. W. Flight,
Jour. Bib. Lit., XLII (1923), pp. 158-226, and the writer's
observations in Lovejoy and Boas, Primitivism and Related
Ideas in Antiquity (Baltimore, 1935), pp. 429-31.

eschatological framework of later prophecy was largely derived from him.[52]

D. CATHARSIS

Amos, Hosea, and Isaiah all share the concept of impending catastrophe, which they employ most effectively in their sermons. By the time of Hosea and Isaiah the Assyrian advance, which had been partly interrupted for half a century, had been resumed and the new policy of Tiglath-pileser III (745-727 B.C.), to conquer small states, deport their populations, and turn them into Assyrian provinces, was filling Syria and Palestine with justified foreboding. The security of immediately preceding centuries had been rudely broken; wickedness was on the increase, and the Day of the Lord was at hand. The Assyrian conquest of Gilead, Galilee, and Sharon in 733 B.C. was followed by the fall of Samaria in the first months of 721, and later rebellions proved futile; Samaria proper was settled by newcomers, themselves deported from Babylonia, Elam, and Syria by Sargon, Esarhaddon, and Sardanapalus of Assyria. Then came Judah's turn. After narrowly escaping in 701 Judah seems to have been invaded at least twice in the first half of the following century.[53] After 625 B.C. the rebellion of the Chaldaean Nabopolassar against his Assyrian suzerain gave new confidence to the land, and Josiah appears to have briefly reoccupied most of the former territory of Israel. However, the fall of Nineveh in 612 B.C. and of Harran about 609 B.C. only led to the substitu-

[52] After a period of extreme skepticism with regard to the authenticity of the ostensibly early Israelite eschatological predictions (mostly introduced by the words, "in that day") there has been a reaction, led by H. Gressmann in his *Ursprung der israelitisch-jüdischen Eschatologie* (1905), followed by T. H. Robinson and J. Hempel (see his discussion in *Gott und Mensch im Alten Testament* [second ed., 1936], pp. 27, 247 ff., etc.).

[53] The writer still believes in the "two-campaign" theory of Sennacherib's invasion of Judah; cf. *Jew. Quar. Rev.*, XXIV (1934), pp. 370 f.

tion of Egyptian sway for Assyrian. In 605 Nebuchadnezzar defeated the Egyptians at Carchemish and some two years later the Chaldaeans occupied Judah.[54] In fifteen years there were at least three major Chaldaean invasions of Judah,[55] which was finally brought to its knees by the destruction of Jerusalem in 587 and completely crushed by subsequent calamities.

It is not surprising that this age of growing insecurity, when the very foundations of life were trembling, should give rise to an earnest effort to find a cure for the increasing *malaise* of the social organism. Under such circumstances spirits turn with nostalgia to the past and endeavor to recapture the vital element underlying former prosperity and stability. So the men of Judah turned back to the Mosaic tradition, endeavoring to recover it as fully as possible and especially to reorganize the religion of the state on as pure a Mosaic basis as possible. The industrious work of the scribal groups to whom we owe the collection and the writing down of the matter of JE made it necessary for the Deuteronomic reformers to extend their investigations to more remote districts in the search for Mosaic traditions. Hence we find in Deuteronomy much material which has been correctly identified by Welch, Gressmann, and others as of Northern, Israelite provenience and as coming apparently from Shechem. This new matter (some of which was already found in substantially the same form in JE) became the nucleus of the Book of Deuteronomy. Characteristic of the preamble and of the other additions made in the late seventh century B.C. by the Deuteronomists is the disproportionate attention paid to antiquarian points, illustrated by numerous explanatory parentheses. It is very important to note that this nostalgic revival of interest in the past and this pronounced tendency to archaism, which are

[54] On the chronology of this period see the writer's observations, *Jour. Bib. Lit.*, LI (1932), pp. 84 ff., with which such dates as are given by S. Mowinckel in his monograph in *Acta Orientalia*, X (1932), pp. 161-277, *passim*, coincide.

[55] Cf. *Bull. Am. Sch. Or. Res.*, No. 47 (1932), pp. 12-14; No. 61 (1936), pp. 15 f.

otherwise unknown in biblical literature, have close parallels in contemporary Egypt and Western Asia. In other words, the Deuteronomic reaction was not an exclusively local phenomenon, but was part of a general tendency which extended to all lands of the ancient Near East. The sun of the ancient Orient was commencing to set and its peoples could not help but be obscurely and unhappily conscious of the approaching darkness. Since this important point has not hitherto been understood, we must devote some space to it.

In Egypt, after centuries of weakness, a revival of national spirit was inaugurated by the Libyan princes of Sais, who unified the country and made it independent in the second half of the seventh century B.C. Guided by priests and scribes, whose antiquarian interest had begun to exhibit itself under the later Bubastites and Ethiopians in the eighth century, the Saite kings of Dyn. XXVI (660-525 B.C.) deliberately tried to restore the Pyramid Age. Drawing and sculpture followed Old-Empire models so closely that we have examples of early mural paintings which had been covered by a grid of lines in the Saite age, for the purpose of assisting copyists to make exact duplicates of the scenes in question. Royal inscriptions imitated ancient prototypes; new scarabs bearing the names of pharaohs of the Old Empire were circulated. In religion an effort was made to revive ancient gods and forms of cult. In Assyria and Babylonia the same thing appears. Sargon II (722-705 B.C.) filled his inscriptions with archaisms and with reminiscences of the national epics, which had been composed in Old Babylonian times. Sardanapalus (669-633 B.C.) collected the greatest library of the ancient Orient and the first true library which was installed in a royal palace, so far as we now know. His scouts explored the magazines of Babylonian temples for lost documents and his scribes copied out thousands of old tablets in the beautiful chirography of the Sargonid age. His brother, Saosduchinus king of Babylonia, even had his official inscriptions written in the long extinct Sumerian tongue. Nebuchadnezzar, following the tradition of his immediate

Assyrian predecessors, also harked back to the past, ordering his scribes to compose a number of his royal inscriptions
in the long disused script and language of early Babylonia,
an undertaking which they carried out with notable lack of
success. Nabonidus (556-539) surpassed them all by his
zeal for antiquity, which led him to make excavations in
many of the then known temple-sites of Babylonia in order
to determine the name and date of the first builders. His
scholars were ordered to decipher all early inscriptions
which came to light and to date their authors (which they
were able to do with relative accuracy though not with
absolute precision). Moreover, he endeavored to revive ancient cults and rituals which had long since been abandoned, and he thus incurred the bitter enmity of the priests
of Marduk in Babylon, whose established prerogatives were
threatened by his innovations.[56]

It is highly probable that there was a similar revival of
interest in the past in Phoenicia at about the same time or
a little earlier. The discovery of the North-Canaanite mythological epics of Ugarit has demonstrated the genuinely
Canaanite origin (aside from Greek names) of the material
preserved by Philo Byblius (see above, pp. 230 f.). The
latter attributes the collection of this material to a certain
man of Berytus named Sanchuniathon, alleged to have
lived in the time of the Assyrian queen Semiramis (late
ninth century B.C.). Since the wildest fables about the latter
and about the date of her reign circulated in the Hellenistic
Near East, this proves nothing directly, except that Sanchuniathon was believed to be relatively ancient. However,
O. Eissfeldt has pointed out (1938) that other evidence
makes it difficult to date him later than the seventh century
B.C.[57] The name is found in Carthaginian inscriptions of

[56] See especially Landsberger and Bauer, *Zeits. f. Assyr.*,
XXXVII (1926), pp. 88-98, where previous literature is cited
and criticized. On the general situation see also the remarks
of W. von Soden in his paper, *Zeits. Alttest. Wiss.*, 1935, pp.
81-89.

[57] See *Forschungen und Fortschritte*, XIV, pp. 251 f. (reprinted in Eissfeldt, *Ras Schamra und Sanchunjaton* [Halle,
1939], pp. 67-71). A date in the sixth century is not, however,

the fourth or third century B.C. and the divine name *Sakkûn* first appears in Phoenician personal names of the fifth century B.C. Other onomastic evidence prohibits a date before about 1000 B.C. and makes one about the seventh century most probable. Now, it is very remarkable that there is a veritable flood of allusions to Canaanite (Phoenician) literature in Hebrew works composed between the seventh and the third century B.C.; illustrations, which are increasing constantly in number, abound in Job, Proverbs, Isaiah (the exilic sections and Deutero-Isaiah), Ezekiel, Habakkuk, the Song of Songs, Ecclesiastes, Jubilees, and parts of Daniel, all of which can be dated in their present form between cir. 600 and cir. 200 B.C. Many of the Psalms have been adapted from Canaanite prototypes, but here the question of date is more difficult and some of them may go back to the early Monarchy. This direct literary influence must be distinguished from the indirect influence on poetic style which we find from the earliest times, as in the Song of Deborah. The natural explanation is that there was a revival of Canaanite literature about the seventh century B.C., which brought with it not only a ren-

---

excluded. If Porphyry and his source, Philo Byblius, are correct in attributing also to Sanchuniathon the authorship of a history based on previous work by Hierombalos priest of the god Ieuo in the time of Abibalos king of Berytus, it may be observed that the latter name was particularly common among Phoenician kings of the tenth (Abibaal of Tyre and his namesake of Byblus) and of the seventh century (Abibaal of Arvad and his namesake of Shamshimoron [Samsimuruna in cuneiform]), and that the priest's name presumably reflects Phoenician *Yerem-baʿal* (*e* would then be a copyist's error for *o*). The latter name occurs in the hypocoristic form *Rmbʾl* in a Phoenician inscription from Abydos in Egypt, dating from about the fifth century B.C. (now republished by Lidzbarski, *Ephemeris*, III, p. 102); it is strictly parallel in form and meaning to Hebrew *°Yerem-yahu* (Jeremiah), on the etymology of which see the correct observations of M. Noth (*Die israelitischen Personennamen*, p. 201). The Hebrew name is common in biblical and extra-biblical occurrences from the seventh-fifth centuries B.C. Our date for Sanchuniathon in the seventh or sixth century B.C. thus becomes still more plausible.

aissance of the early epic literature, but also an unexampled diffusion of Phoenician writings. How this literature influenced the Jews of the Exilic Age is easy to understand, since Phoenician and Biblical Hebrew were only dialectically distinct, and there was little more difference between Phoenician and North Israelite than there was between the latter (which we know from the Ostraca of Samaria) and South Israelite (which we know from the Bible and from the inscriptions of Jerusalem and Lachish). In keeping with the literary revival to which we can point is also the fact that the Byblian inscriptions of the Persian period contain many archaisms which had disappeared in normal Phoenician long before the middle of the first millennium B.C.[58]

In the light of these extra-Palestinian parallels the Deuteronomic movement of the late seventh century appears somewhat differently from the interpretation given it by the school of Wellhausen. Instead of being a progressive reform based on an advance beyond previous levels of religion and cult, it was a conscious effort to recapture both the letter and the spirit of Mosaism which, the Deuteronomists believed, had been neglected or forgotten by the Israelites of the Monarchy. The theory of De Wette and his successors that Deuteronomy is "pious fraud" is contrary to ancient Oriental practice (see above, pp. 77 f.); the materials contained in the book were really believed to go back to Moses and probably do reflect, in general, a true Mosaic atmosphere. The first eleven chapters and some other insertions are written in an elaborate rhetorical style without counterpart in the classical Hebrew literature of the early Monarchy, but with good syntactic parallels in the Lachish Letters of 589 B.C.[59] Otherwise the contents are in large part considerably earlier, as has been increas-

[58] Cf. Z. Harris, *Development of the Canaanite Dialects* (New Haven, 1939), p. 97, n. 6. Archaizing is, however, seldom consistent, as may be seen by examining late Egyptian and Babylonian texts.

[59] See the provisional observations, *Bull. Am. Sch. Or. Res.*, No. 73 (1939), pp. 20 f., on the syntactic similarity of "Lachish" Hebrew to the language of the Deuteronomic literature, and on their relationship to Classical Hebrew.

ingly recognized by scholars. The Blessing of Moses seems to date from the tenth century and the legislative portions reflect a juristic phase prior to Jehoshaphat's reorganization of the judicial system of Judah, though details have been modernized.[60] The religious-ethical point of view is, however, definitely that of the seventh century B.C.; Deuteronomy clearly follows the direction of development already marked by J, which preceded the height of the prophetic movement in the ninth century B.C., and by E, which followed it. The Deuteronomist avoids the inconsistency into which J and even E sometimes fell by their use of pre-Mosaic or crude early Israelite matter. To him Yahweh is the sole God in heaven and earth, who must be worshipped as a spirit without any visible form (Deut. 4:12). He is absolutely pure and holy, and perfectly just; and He has shown unequalled kindness to His chosen people, Israel. The influence of Isaiah and his school comes to fruition in the Book of Deuteronomy, in which the concepts of Yahweh's sublime holiness and of His non-corporeal nature are strongly emphasized. This contrasts rather strikingly with the anthropomorphism of early Israelite language, though the difference was little felt, we may suppose, by contemporaries, who were so used to poetic imagery that they did not attempt to derive logical conclusions from it, as many modern scholars do. Deut. 4:19 is usually taken to mean that the sun, moon, and stars had been distributed by Yahweh to the nations as objects of their worship, and it was in fact so interpreted by most rabbinical commentators. This explanation is perfectly possible, but the text actually says only that the heavenly bodies have been assigned by Yahweh to all nations alike (and there is, accordingly, no reason why Israel should worship them), whereas Yahweh has chosen Israel as his own exclusive property. There can surely be no question but that the Israelites knew perfectly well that the visual distribution of the heavenly bodies was the same over surrounding lands as it was over Israel.

Deuteronomic literature is saturated with the concept of

[60] See provisionally Albright, *Arch. Pal. Bib.*, pp. 154 ff., and *Jour. Bib. Lit.*, LV, p. 168.

inevitable Divine justice, which is impartially visited upon
the individual evil-doer as well as upon the nation as a
whole. For the first time in the records of Israel, as far as
we possess them, the concept of theodicy is inextricably
interwoven with history. The narratives of Judges were
collected and edited, with recurring emphasis on the theme
that Divine punishment is always retribution for the sin
of the nation. Similarly the chronicles of Israel and Judah
were edited, every successive ruler of importance being
judged by his inferred attitude to the correct cult of
Yahweh as reconstructed for the Mosaic age by the Deuteronomic school. No similar works have been recovered
from Egypt, but several are known from later Babylonia,
the two clearest of which belong to the end of the second
millennium B.C., as is proved by language and contents. At
that time Babylonia had also passed through a shattering
series of invasions and civil disorders, which had aroused
thinking circles to raise the question of theodicy. In one of
them (published by E. Ebeling in 1923) an ostensibly
prophetic appraisal of successive late Cossaean and Babylonian kings from the twelfth century is given, each being
judged by his relation to the gods.[61] In contrast to the
Deuteronomists this text lacks any clear-cut sentiment of
the causal relation between sin and punishment. The other
document (found in the Spartoli tablets) is couched in
narrative form and pictures the disasters that come upon
the land and its kings for neglect of the cult of Marduk.
Here the most interesting point is that each invader comes
to a terrible end after serving as the instrument of Marduk,
thus being punished in turn for his own offense against the
chief god of Babylonia.[62]

[61] For a translation see Ebeling in *Altor. Texte* (Tübingen,
1926), pp. 283 f. The writer would identify the last three
kings of the middle column on the "first" side of the tablet with
the last three kings of the Third Dynasty of Babylon, since
regnal years and political events agree perfectly. The following restoration then refers to the Fourth Dynasty (Nebuchad-
rezzar I). The original text of these prophecies *ex eventu*
may then belong to the eleventh century B.C.

[62] For the latest translation of the Spartoli tablets see A.

The traditional interpretation of the Babylonian conquest of Judah as almost completely depopulating the country and as transferring the center of Jewish life and thought to Babylonia for nearly three generations, has been vigorously criticized by critical scholars, notably by S. A. Cook and C. C. Torrey. The latter has been extreme in his revulsion against the standard tradition, maintaining that Judah may have been decimated but was not depopulated, that the refugees returned to Jerusalem and other towns and reoccupied them soon after the catastrophe of 587, and that there was no true Babylonian captivity at all. The center of Jewish life remained, he supposes, in Palestine, where it had always been. The mission of the prophet Ezekiel, so far from having been carried out among the exiles in Babylonia, is entirely apocryphal. Since there was no "Captivity," he says, there could not have been a "Restoration"; the traditions preserved in Ezra are as apocryphal as are his memoirs, and all records of the Restoration except the Memoirs of Nehemiah are, he insists, historically worthless. The merited reputation of Torrey as a Semitic philologian has given these disconcerting views wide currency, but they are as totally devoid of historical foundation as they are of respect for ancient oriental records. Excavations in Judah since 1926 have shown with increasing weight of evidence that the Chaldaean destruction of Jewish towns was thorough-going and that few of them arose from their ruins. Until the excavations at Bethel (which was in the Assyro-Babylonian province of Samaria) in 1934, no remains of the sixth century which could be dated after cir. 587 B.C. were known; the land was an archaeological *tabula rasa* for that period. Work at Beth-zur (O. R. Sellers and the writer, 1931) and at Bethel (the writer and J. L. Kelso, 1934) has shown that Jewish revival was slow and that the first settlers were few and poor.[63] Innumerable detailed

---

Jeremias, *Mitt. Vord. Ges.*, XXI (1916), pp. 69-97, and for the most recent discussion of details see the writer, *Jour. Soc. Or. Res.*, X (1926), pp. 233 ff.

[63] See especially the writer's remarks, *Jour. Bib. Lit.*, LI (1932), pp. 77-106, 381 f.; *Arch. Pal. Bib.*, pp. 169 ff.; *Bull. Am. Sch. Or. Res.*, No. 56, p. 14.

finds, the most important of which have not yet been published, though familiar to the present writer from personal communications, disprove practically every one of Torrey's concrete arguments for his position. The facts are precisely the opposite of what they should be if Torrey's contentions were correct. We need only point to the work of E. Meyer, H. H. Schaeder, R. de Vaux, and the writer, who have marshalled the accessible material against Torrey.[64] In short, we are justified in rejecting his position completely, without any concessions—except that Torrey's searching criticisms of the sources and their interpretation have been of immense heuristic value.

The salient phases of Jewish history after the Exile may be briefly summarized as follows:—The final Chaldaean invasion of Judah almost completely denuded the central hill-country and the Shephelah of Judah, leaving Jewish settlers only in the Negeb (Neh. 11:25 ff.), which appears to have been separated from Judah at an earlier date, and in the district to the north of Jerusalem which was under the control of the Babylonian governor of Samaria. The southern hill-country, south of Beth-zur, was gradually occupied by the Edomites (Esdras 4:50), who had been pushed out of their home in Mt. Seir by Arab invasions. The northern hill-country of Judah was attached to the province of Samaria and the Jewish remnant gradually resettled it after a fashion, reoccupying a number of ruined villages south of Jerusalem (Neh. 7:26). The Jews still hoped for the restoration of the captive Jehoiachin, who was then residing with his family in Babylon, as we know from tablets which have just been published by E. F. Weidner (1940).[65] Jeremiah and Ezekiel pleaded with them to be content with their lot, which was only the deserved punishment for their sins. However, hope lingered and after Jehoiachin's death it was transferred to his grandson, Zerubbabel. The fall of Babylon in 539 B.C. and Cyrus' promises to the Jewish

[64] See especially H. H. Schaeder, *Esra der Schreiber* (Tübingen, 1930), and *Iranische Beiträge*, I (1931); R. de Vaux, *Rev. Bib.*, XLVI (1937), pp. 29-57.

[65] *Mélanges Dussaud*, II (1940), pp. 923-35.

exiles in Babylonia fanned their growing excitement and stimulated a vigorous proto-Zionist movement among the Jews of the Diaspora. Between 538 and 522 a considerable number of Jews had returned to Palestine, and the Temple was built in the years 520-515 B.C., but not until there had been an abortive revolutionary movement to make Zerubbabel king. The following years are obscure but the data in Ezra 4 make it clear that the young community in Jerusalem was constantly being hampered in its development by the authorities of the Persian province of Samaria, who then controlled it directly, as shown by A. Alt (1934).[66] Finally, in 444 B.C., Nehemiah, who had attained an important post in the royal household, obtained special authority from Artaxerxes I, came to Judaea as autonomous governor, built the city wall, and reorganized the administration of the new province. As a result of Nehemiah's efforts the official practice of the Temple in Jerusalem, embodied in the Priestly Code, was made standard for Judaism throughout the Persian Empire, as we know particularly from the Passover Letter of the year 419 B.C., discovered at Elephantine in Upper Egypt. Probably through Nehemiah's efforts came the priest and scribe, Ezra, who was armed with special royal authority to reorganize the ecclesiastical administration of Judaea. The traditional date for Ezra makes him prior to Nehemiah, but this is not only opposed to the indirect evidence of our sources, but is also in direct contradiction to the statements in Ezra 10:6; Neh. 12:23, 26. Since the distinguished Catholic scholar, A. van Hoonacker, first proposed this shifting of Ezra's date, it has been adopted by more and more scholars, and may now be said to be virtually certain.[67] Ezra's activity ushers in the period of the autonomous theocratic state of Judah, which in the fourth cen-

---

[66] *Festschrift Otto Procksch* (Leipzig, 1934), pp. 5-28.

[67] See the literature cited by the writer, *Arch. Pal. Bib.*, pp. 169 ff., and for more recent literature see Fleming James, *Personalities of the Old Testament* (New York, 1939), pp. 463 f. A date for Ezra toward the end of the reign of Artaxerxes I is even more probable.

tury B.C. struck its own silver coinage and controlled the administration of the Temple treasury for the benefit of the ecclesiastical authorities.[68]

The foremost spiritual figure of Judaism (as we must henceforth call Yahwism) during the Exile is indisputably the prophet Ezekiel. Influenced by Torrey's denial of the authenticity of Ezekiel, several recent writers, notably A. Bertholet and S. Spiegel, have plausibly suggested that the prophet may have uttered some of his earlier prophecies in Judah and some later ones in Babylonia.[69] The writer is not convinced and believes that R. Kittel's portrayal of Ezekiel's personality and career (1927)[70] is substantially correct. Ezekiel was one of the greatest spiritual figures of all time, in spite of his tendency to psychic abnormality—a tendency which he shares with many other spiritual leaders of mankind. A certain "abnormality" is required to divert a man's thoughts and his emotional experiences from the common treadmill of human thinking and feeling. While the individual is undoubtedly happiest when his personality is most fully integrated, the traditional motto, *mens sana in corpore sano*, is not well calculated for progress since it conduces rather to stagnation (see above, pp. 105 f.). Whether the dramatic scenes of life in Jerusalem which he saw in his visions were literally accurate or not is immaterial, since their deeper historical meaning can hardly be disputed. Until the possibility of true clairvoyance has been disproved—and it can not be disproved merely by justified criticisms of Rhine's cheap experiments or by unmasking such outstanding mediums as Palladino or Cranston—it would be rash to deny the possibility of Ezekiel's autoptic

[68] Cf. the writer's remarks, *Bull. Am. Sch. Or. Res.*, No. 53, pp. 20-22. S. A. Cook's observations, *Zeits. Alttest. Wiss.*, 1938, pp. 268 ff., are misleading.

[69] See especially A. Bertholet, *Hesekiel* (Tübingen, 1936), S. Spiegel, *Jour. Bib. Lit.*, LVI, pp. 403-8, and the latter's Hebrew article "When was Ezekiel exiled?" in the *Turov Volume* (New York, 1937/8).

[70] *Geschichte des Volkes Israel*, Vol. III (1927), pp. 144-80; cf. also the sympathetic treatment of the prophet by Fleming James, *op. cit.*, pp. 331-59.

visions. As a poet Ezekiel was even inferior to Jeremiah, and neither of them ever touch the lyric and dramatic heights reached almost casually by Amos, Hosea, and Isaiah; the strength of the great exilic prophet lay in his vivid imagination and profound moral earnestness, in both of which he is unsurpassed by any other rhapsodist prophet. The tendency of the latest commentators (especially of Bertholet and Galling) is to consider the book as essentially a unit, including the pericope of Gog and Magog, as well as the account of the future Temple. Most of the recent critical dissection of Ezekiel is unnecessary; it is clear, however, that the manuscript tradition must have been very corrupt, since the present massoretic text is full of doublets and conflate readings, many of which were not yet incorporated in the recension used by the Greek translators of the second century B.C.

Unlike his prophetic predecessors Ezekiel could not lay his principal emphasis on collective guilt, since Israel and Judah were no longer nations and every Israelite group had to fend for itself. It is not surprising, therefore, that the idea of individual responsibility, explicit in the apodictic law (above, p. 268) from the beginning of Yahwism in Israel and emphatically reiterated by the Deuteronomists, receives powerful expression in Ezekiel's words: "The soul that sinneth, it shall die. The son shall not be responsible for the iniquity of the father, neither shall the father be responsible for the iniquity of the son; the righteousness of the righteous shall be his (alone) and the wickedness of the wicked shall be his (alone)."

A generation after Ezekiel came the great unknown prophet whose collected poems were attached to the anthology of Isaiah—possibly because he bore the same name (which was common in that age, as shown by a number of other biblical and inscriptional occurrences). The exact extent of the writings of Deutero-Isaiah is uncertain; competent opinion ranges from Torrey's view that chapters 40-66 are substantially a unit to Duhm's complicated dissection. The general opinion of scholars is that Isa. 40-55 forms a unit, coming from the period just before and just after

Cyrus' victory over Nabonidus of Babylon (539 B.C.). In two respects Deutero-Isaiah marks the culmination of the Mosaic movement as such: in his clear-cut and sweeping definition of the concept of ethical monotheism and in his doctrine of vicarious suffering.

It is frequently asserted that true ethical monotheism does not appear in the Old Testament before Deutero-Isaiah. This statement is very misleading, as the reader may conveniently see for himself by examining the exhaustive classification of pertinent data made by Count Baudissin as long ago as 1876.[71] Unmistakable claims of world-power and uniqueness for Yahweh appear with the earliest known rhapsodist prophets, Amos and Hosea, and become frequent in Isaiah and Jeremiah. Along with them appears outspoken repudiation of pagan deities and their claims. For instance, Amos and Jeremiah call pagan deities "lies" and "falsehood"; Isaiah and Jeremiah call them "vanities" and "illusions"; Jeremiah and the Deuteronomic school call them "no-gods"; Ezekiel, the Deuteronomists, and Jeremiah call them *gillûlîm*, which seems to mean properly "pellets of dung." This list is surely opposed to the idea that pagan deities were conceded real existence by the prophets. If we had poems or sermons from the climax of the prophetic movement in the ninth century B.C., we should doubtless find the same attitude toward the claims of pagans for their deities. The words of Elijah in I Kings 18:27 or in II Kings 1:6 have a flavor of ironic pragmatism which is quite characteristic of early Israel (see above, p. 220); it was enough for the prophet to deny the pagan god any power, after which the question of his existence became an unimportant consideration. As a matter of fact there is no single utterance in preëxilic sources which sounds as polytheistic as the assertion of the Chronicler (II Chron. 2:5, which is not taken from Kings but is quite original with the Chronicler) that "our God is greater than all the gods." Yet few would claim that orthodox Jewry was polytheistic in the

---

[71] *Studien*, I, pp. 47-178. Contrast the latest formulation by Oesterley and Robinson, *Hebrew Religion* (second ed., 1937), pp. 299 ff.

fourth century B.C.¹ In the second century B.C. the Jewish author of Aristeas declares that the God of Israel is identical with the Greek Zeus and about the same time the translators of the Septuagint render various Hebrew terms for pagan gods as "demons" (*daimônia*). Moreover, the Book of Enoch says that the pagan cults were introduced by fallen angels and this conception was generally held both by rabbinical theologians and by the early Church Fathers. Philo Judaeus sees no harm in identifying the Hellenic gods and demons with Jewish angels and in regarding all of them as emanations of the divine essence, forming a bridge between God and man.

In order to understand the view-point of Yahwistic thinkers of the Prophetic Age (since we cannot directly control the ideas of their predecessors), we must bear in mind that they lived in an age of empirical logic, many generations before the dawn of systematic philosophical reasoning. Nowhere in the prophetic writings of preëxilic times is there any hint of cosmic speculation. The prophets were not interested, so far as we can tell, in how the world had come into existence or how the forces of nature operated; it was quite enough for them to know that God controlled them. They had a real moral interest in knowing why God did certain things, but the idea that any of God's actions were subject to general physical laws which man might discover by observation and reasoning was totally foreign to them, as it was to all pre-philosophical thought. Similarly it was enough for them to know that pagan deities had no real power and could be over-ruled at any time by Yahweh: whether their existence was real or only nominal, whether they were angels or demons or simple illusions mattered little, since they were in any event evil or powerless. By the middle of the sixth century B.C. all was changed for the orthodox Jews; they were now living in the Diaspora, among idolators, where it was increasingly difficult for worshippers of Yahweh to preserve their faith and that of their families. Compromise was no longer possible; either the pagan gods existed or they did not exist, and if they did not exist it was well to sweep away all other intermediaries between the invisible spiritual lord of the universe and His people Israel. The pure ethical monotheism of Deutero-Isaiah would have been too rarified a faith to have had permanent religious value if it were not for his doctrine of the infinite kindness and generosity of God, who feeds His flock like a shepherd, who carries the lamb in His bosom and gently leads pregnant ewes (Isa. 40:11).

In order to obtain a clear perspective for Deutero-Isaiah's concept of vicarious suffering, a brief survey of pertinent germinal conceptions and of the development of belief in theodicy is necessary. Among these germinal concepts may be noted in the first place the widespread primitive custom of charging some object, animal, or person with the sin or suffering of a group, after which the object, animal, or person is sacrificed or driven away in order to carry the sin and suffering of men away with it. Frazer has collected a mass of illustrative material in his book, *The Scapegoat* (1913). The Hebrew ceremony of the "scapegoat for Azazel" may perhaps have had a Canaanite origin. Sumerians and Babylonians also believed that man was created by the sacrifice of a god or gods, who were killed that man might live. This is attested by a Sumerian text according to which the Lamga-gods (the "carpenter" gods) were killed that man might be given life with their blood. In Accadian inscriptions this rôle falls to the cosmogonic deity Qingu.[72] Behind the gruesome mythology and human sacrifice of the Canaanites lay the same idea that life and fertility must come through death and sacrifice of fertility. The sufferings of Attis and of Bel-Marduk were in later times considered as vicarious.

It was hardly possible for such primitive conceptions to acquire any deeper religious value until they had been combined with a much more acute sense of the problem of divine justice than was possible for prelogical man. The question of theodicy always comes to the fore during prolonged times of crisis, when human emotions are winnowed and purified by a sustained catharsis. So it was in Egypt

[72] See now E. F. Weidner, *Arch. f. Orientf.*, XI (1936), pp. 72-74.

between 2200 and 2000 B.C., so it was in Babylonia after
1200 B.C., and so it was among the Jews between 700 and
500 B.C. In Egypt, however, the problem of theodicy was
not seriously ventilated—perhaps the time was not ripe. The
first clear and detailed treatment of the problem appears
in two Babylonian texts written probably between 1200 and
800 B.C.[73] The older one is well known as the "Babylonian
Job," and was entitled "Let me Praise the Lord of Wisdom,"
from its opening lines. A man, who seems to have been
originally rich and powerful, complains bitterly that all his
past piety and attention to the service of the gods have
been in vain; he has been overtaken by the most grievous
illness and misfortune, until his whole life is utterly miserable. No amount of prayer and sacrifice, no efforts of priests
or magicians are of any avail. He concludes that the will
of the gods is inscrutable and that divine justice follows
different ways from its human counterpart. At last, after
all hope has been given up, Marduk suddenly turns and
rewards him for his persistent virtue by freeing him from
his ban and restoring his health. The text ends in a burst
of praise to Marduk, who must be adored by men wherever
they live, "as far as the earth extends and heaven spreads
and the sun shines and fire glows and water flows and the
wind blows." The other, later composition was first adequately published by E. Ebeling in 1922, but was not fully
understood until B. Landsberger's treatment in 1936.[74] It
is a very remarkable dialogue between two men, one of
whom is a poor wretch who has never had anything but
suffering and who does not believe in the existence of divine justice, a view which he illustrates by many examples.
The other is a pious man who unceasingly preaches humble
acquiescence in the will of the gods, together with unremit-
ting attention to their cult; after long effort he finally suc-
ceeds in converting his skeptical antagonist. Here also is
stressed the inscrutability of divine justice and the need of

---

[73] See W. von Soden, *Zeits. Deutsch. Morg. Ges.*, LXXXIX
(1935), pp. 164 ff.

[74] *Zeits. f. Assyr.*, XLIII, pp. 32-76.

the most complete humility and abnegation of self in one's relation to the gods.

In the history of thought, though probably not in time, Job is intermediate between these Babylonian texts and Deutero-Isaiah. This book, which seems to have been written in the fifth (or the sixth) century B.C., is built around the story of an ancient West-Semitic wise man, who must have been well known since Ezekiel brackets him with Noah and Daniel (the Dan'el of Canaanite legend, who becomes the father-in-law of the wise Enoch in the book of Jubilees, written about the third century B.C.). The name "Job" first appears in an Egyptian list of Palestinian chieftains from about 2000 B.C., and also occurs once in the 14th century B.C.[75] The prose introduction to the book, as we have it, is written in very late Hebrew and the poetic part is saturated with allusions to lost Northwest Semitic literature. In character it bears an extremely close relation to the Babylonian works which we have listed and they may have been known indirectly to the author of Job in some Aramaic adaptation, just as Accadian gnomic texts passed into contemporary Aramaic literature in the form of the Akhiqar Romance. The Hebrew author comes to a conclusion which superficially resembles that of his Babylonian precursors, though after a vastly superior literary effort. Job rises to the heights of unquestioning faith and plumbs the depths of disillusionment and skepticism, while his friends reiterate all the shop-worn arguments for the existence of a direct relationship between suffering and sin. Job has the last word after silencing his friends (the Elihu speech is generally recognized as secondary), but God Himself replies to him and proclaims His tremendous superiority to man so eloquently that Job repents his rebellious spirit and is suitably rewarded. The conclusion of the author of Job is profounder than that of the Babylonians: suffering is not necessarily a result of sin, but may be inflicted by the Almighty for the purpose of testing and tempering man. In other words, human suffering may be part of God's purifying process. The

[75] *Jour. Pal. Or. Soc.*, VIII (1928), p. 239.

combination of these two concepts, vicarious suffering and purification through suffering, lies behind Deutero-Isaiah's doctrine of salvation.

The most obvious characteristic of the Servant of Yahweh in Deutero-Isaiah is his humility and meekness in the presence of his tormentors. Humility, silence, and meekness became increasingly characteristic of ancient oriental piety after the late second millennium B.C. The inscriptions of the Neo-Babylonian kings (sixth century B.C.) often begin with the words (following the titulary), "the meek and humble one." The words "I am a humble man" appear at the commencement of an inscription of a king of Hamath about 800 B.C.[76] Humility is also a characteristic of the worshipper in late Egyptian and Assyrian prayers to the gods. It is, therefore, entirely in order when we find the pious worshipper of the Psalms frequently called *'anaw* "humble." This concept can hardly antedate the Exile in its present form, and we may attribute its increasing popularity to the influence of Deutero-Isaiah and his followers.

After many efforts by Old Testament scholars to interpret the Servant of Yahweh as the people Israel itself, or as some historical character such as Jeremiah, Jehoiachin, Zerubbabel, Cyrus—or even Moses (E. Sellin)—there has been a pronounced reaction.[77] The figure changes so frequently and so disconcertingly as we endeavor to fix it that we must regard it in all probability (unless we wish to resort to subjective and futile surgical operations on the text) as a standing theme which is differently treated in different poems. In other words, the concept is presumably older than Deutero-Isaiah and it so impressed itself upon his sensitive spirit or seemed so ideally suited to his religious message that he utilized it in various ways. All of these varying applications have a common theme: it is the humble Is-

[76] Line 2 of the Zakir inscription: *'iš 'ânê 'anâ;* contrast the writer's interpretation of these words, *Jour. Pal. Or. Soc.,* VI, pp. 86 f., which can no longer be defended.

[77] On the Servant in Deutero-Isaiah see now H. H. Rowley, *Israel's Mission to the World* (London, 1939), pp. 10-25; Fleming James, *op. cit.,* pp. 383 ff.

raelite worshipper of God through whom the people must be saved. Only by submitting to the severest tests without losing faith or showing a rebellious spirit, only by being ready to undergo the most brutal martyrdom can the Servant of Yahweh do his divinely imposed duty. The experience of Jeremiah and Ezekiel, to say nothing of their prophetic predecessors, many of whom had suffered cruelly or had even been put to death, was sufficient to indicate what the true servant of Yahweh must be like in order to serve his God to the fullest effect. When not only the leaders themselves, but also every pious Israelite is ready to give himself as a vicarious victim for his people, then God will restore Israel and will give it a glorious future. In this interpretation the different aspects of the Servant of Yahweh receive due consideration. The Servant is the people of Israel, which suffers poignantly in exile and affliction; he is also the pious individual who atones for the sins of the many by his uncomplaining agony; he is finally the coming Savior of Israel:

My righteous servant shall justify many
    And their guilt shall he bear . . .
And he shall bear the sin of many
    And intercede for transgressors   (Isa. 53:11-12).

Chapter VI

IN THE FULNESS OF TIME . . .

(Galatians 4:4)

A. The Rise and Diffusion of Hellenic Culture

When we move from Judah of the fifth century B.C. into contemporary Attica we seem to enter a different world. In Greece at that time there was a new spirit abroad; men found that the human mind possessed hitherto unimagined potentialities, and there seemed no limit to the beauty that man might create or to the profound truths that his reason might deduce by introspection and observation. In the fifth century B.C. Israel had reached the summit of its spiritual evolution and like its Egyptian, Phoenician, and Aramaean (Mesopotamian) neighbors, it looked back into the past, seeking the source of life there and endeavoring to preserve that past and thus to avert disintegrating change. This awareness of a rich tradition and consciousness of national dignity gave a certain moral grandeur even to late Egyptian and Babylonian literature, but they were fatal to progress. The Near East had reached the term of its development and there was little hope of any significant forward movement without powerful outside intervention. The imposition by the Persians of a common government on most of the known world, accompanied by the diffusion of a common material civilization and of a common Aramaic language of communication, brought with it countless benefits, but it also brought inevitable stagnation, just as it did in the Roman Empire some five centuries later.

In the Greek world, especially in its cultural center, Attica, new life was stirring. Though a rarely endowed people, the Greeks had not emerged from the age of barbarism that followed the collapse of the aristocratic culture of the Mycenaean Age until the eighth century B.C. Then they awoke with startling suddenness and reacted to the advanced civilization of their Near-Eastern neighbors, among whom the Canaanite Phoenicians undoubtedly played the most important rôle. The Greeks of Ionia and the Islands led the way by shifting from piracy to commerce and colonization, by imitating Phoenician artistic models, by borrowing the Phoenician alphabet and adapting it to Hellenic use. About 776 B.C. national events began to be systematically recorded in writing and a century later arose Hesiod, the first Greek writer whose work and personality are at all tangible. It is very significant that the literary aspect of higher culture preceded the artistic aspect in its development. When the Homeric epics were put into approximately their present form Greece was in the artistic barbarism of the early Geometric Age. Hesiod wrote when Greek art was just beginning to free itself from its swaddling clothes. The greatest of early Hellenic lyric poets, Archilochus, Alcaeus, and Sappho, wrote during the century beginning about 650 B.C., when sculpture was still unbelievably stiff and crude in comparison with its later development. While Thales was inaugurating Greek philosophical thought about 600 B.C., art still remained oriental and archaic in character. Then, after 500 B.C., came a burst of cultural progress unexampled in history, which in half a century brought Attica to the age of Pericles, to the drama of Aeschylus, Sophocles, and Euripides, the sculpture of Phidias, and the painting of Polygnotus. Greece had now far surpassed the best artistic and literary productions of the ancient Near East; it was about to reach heights of philosophical and scientific thought which were to usher in a new era in human history, the age of logical thinking and philosophical speculation. There is less intellectual difference, in consequence, between the modern thinking man and his Hellenic precursor, some 2300 years ago, than there

336 FROM THE STONE AGE TO CHRISTIANITY

was between the educated Greek of the fourth century B.C. and the learned Near-Eastern scribe of the same period.

The beginnings of Greek philosophical speculation under the influence of the Milesian school of the sixth century were modest enough. What we know of Thales, Anaximander, and Anaximenes does not suggest that they had even reached, much less surpassed, the empirical knowledge of science and mathematics already possessed by the Babylonians and Egyptians. The cosmogony of Thales attributed the origin of everything to water, just as was true of Egyptian and Babylonian mythology, as well as of the Priestly Code in Israel. Thales borrowed his first notions of geometry and surveying from sources going back to Egypt and his ability to predict eclipses came from Babylonia, where it was still a comparatively recent discovery (going back probably to the eighth century B.C.). It is hardly likely that his actual knowledge of empirical mathematics and astronomy could compare with that of the most learned Egyptians and Babylonians of his time. On the other hand, he possessed something which they lacked: intellectual curiosity. Instead of being contented with empirical knowledge he wished to understand the facts which he had learned; he wanted to know why things happened and how they happened. For the first time the Ionic Greeks realized that Nature is one and that her manifestations follow definite laws, which man can discover by sufficient effort of his intellect. Thales' successor Anaximander was able to discard mythology completely and to erect a logical system of cosmogony which was entirely free of mythological connotations. When the European Greeks took up the torch laid down by the Ionians, they made such rapid strides that philosophical speculation was fully developed and elaborately ramified by the middle of the fifth century B.C. However, this speculation was generally (except in the work of Pythagoras and his disciples) devoted to the service of skepticism in religion and its scientific results were much more valuable than its achievements in the social and ethical field. In the realm of practical morality and of loyalty to accepted values it was, indeed, so destructive of convention and so generally demoralizing that a powerful reaction developed.

It is not our purpose to dwell on the great work of Socrates, of Plato, or of Aristotle, since they have become part of our inherited intellectual tradition and there is no question of vital importance to us here which remains to be solved, thanks to the wealth of literary sources and to the devoted research of several generations of modern Hellenists and philosophers. Socrates polished the dialectic method of the Sophists until it became an instrument which skilfully combined analysis with deduction; he applied this powerful new tool primarily to the purpose of ethics and social morality. To Socrates religion was not less real because he conceived of the divine in immaterial form. . . . The majestic edifice of philosophical idealism which Plato built and the vast structure of encyclopaedic science which Aristotle erected on a solid foundation of observation and logical reasoning were already standing when Alexander conquered Asia and reduced it to the rank of a great province of Hellenistic culture.

The idea that Greece and Hellenic culture were little known in Western Asia before Alexander the Great is difficult to eradicate. Actually, as we know from recent archaeological discoveries, there was not a century of the Iron Age during which objects of Greek origin, mostly ceramic in character, were not being brought into Syria and Palestine. Greek traders and mercenaries were familiar in Egypt and throughout Western Asia from the early seventh century on, if not earlier. As early as the sixth century B.C. the coasts of Syria and Palestine were dotted with Greek ports and trading emporia, several of which have been discovered during the past five years. None of these could begin to approach the prosperity of the great Hellenic harbors of Naucratis and Daphne in Egypt. There were Greek mercenaries in the armies of Egypt and Babylonia, of Psammetichus II and Nebuchadnezzar. About 500 B.C., a recently discovered inscription of Darius Hystaspes tells us, Ionian, Carian, and Lydian craftsmen were summoned to Susa (Shushan) to help decorate the royal palace. In the fifth century, as we know from Greek sources, the Near East was flooded with Greek adventurers, among whom were such learned men as Hecataeus, Herodotus, Ctesias, and Xenophon. Archaeological research in the past generation has shown that Greek art was by this time highly prized in Western Asia and there is no excavation of any extent in a fifth-century site which does not yield Greek pottery and other objects. The wealthy Phoenicians buried their dead in marble sarcophagi which had been carved by Greek craftsmen. The commercial influence of Greece became so great that the Attic standard of coinage began to displace older media of exchange even before 450 B.C. and by the middle of the fourth century Greek coins were being imitated by the Persian satraps and local rulers of Cilicia, Syria, and Palestine. Even the South Arabians then fashioned crude local imitations of Attic coins for their purposes. The little priestly state of Judaea received permission to strike its own silver coins, which imitated Attic issues but added the inscription *Yehûd* "Judaea," as E. L. Sukenik has recently discovered.[1] From the standpoint of material civilization Alexander's conquest only intensified and organized a movement which was already well under way.

With this preparation, it is not surprising that Alexander's triumph found the Greeks amply prepared to take advantage of it. The Macedonian colonies which he scattered lavishly over Western Asia and Egypt became the centers of an exceedingly rapid process of Hellenization. The following century must have witnessed a mass emigration of Greeks and Anatolians (for every Mysian and Pamphylian was now a Hellene) comparable only to what has happened in Europe during the past century of migration to America. From Epirus to Pontus and from Sicily to Cyprus, the world of the Northern Mediterranean disgorged its swarms of traders and mercenaries into the Near East. The Phoenicians had become so Hellenized in the preceding centuries that their cities rapidly became foci of Hellenization. One of the most instructive illustrations of what hap-

[1] See Chap. V, n. 68.

pened is the story of the Sidonian colony founded by Apol-
lophanes at Marisa (Mareshah) in the low hill-country of
Judaea about 250 B.C.[2] The Phoenician origin of the colony
is established by the numerous Phoenician names which appear in its tombs during the first two or three generations
after its foundation. But it speedily became so Hellenized
in language that all the tomb inscriptions of the second century B.C. are in Greek and there is even a neatly written
interchange of Greek notes by a lover and his mistress, written on the wall of one of the tombs early in the second
century. In the ruins of the town of Marisa was found a
quantity of Greek magical curses on tablets of soft limestone, dating from the second century B.C. A further example of the intensity of Greek influence is the mass of papyri
from the Ptolemaic age which have been discovered in
Egypt. Among the most important of them for our purposes
are the archives of Zeno found at Gerzeh in the Faiyum and
published since the War. Some of them refer to conditions
in Palestine, throwing considerable light on the process of
Hellenization in the third century B.C.

Soon after Alexander's conquest of Egypt the cultural
center of the Hellenic world was shifted to Alexandria
by the prolonged efforts of two unusually enlightened
monarchs, Ptolemy Lagi (323-285) and his son, Ptolemy
Philadelphus (285-247 B.C.). In the third century B.C.
Alexandrian culture reached hitherto unequalled heights,
stimulated by the presence or the visits of the leading philosophers and scientists of the age. How brilliant an age it
was may be illustrated by the simple enumeration of a few
great names of that century: the Cypro-Phoenician Zeno
(cir. 360-263 B.C.), who founded the Stoic school of philosophy, and his most distinguished pupils, Cleanthes of
Assos, Chrysippus the Cilician, Diogenes the Babylonian,
and Antipater of Tarsus; the Athenian Epicurus (cir. 341-
270 B.C.), who founded the Epicurean school; the geome-
trician Euclid, who flourished at Alexandria about the beginning of the third century; the geographer Eratosthenes;

[2] See Vincent, *Rev. Bib.*, 1920, pp. 176 ff., and V. Tscheri-
kower, *Mizraim*, IV-V (1937), pp. 9 ff.

the mathematician and engineer Archimedes, who discovered the first principles of differential calculus in the late third century (not rediscovered for nearly 2000 years); Aristarchus of Samos, who discovered the heliocentric principle of astronomy in the late third century B.C., and his pupil(?), Seleucus the Babylonian. Such a list as this shows both how active intellectual life then was and how international its scope had become.

Many non-Hellenic natives of the Near East caught the Greek spirit and pursued historical, philosophical, and scientific studies in Greek fashion. Among the earliest of them were the Egyptian historian Manetho and the Babylonian Berossus,[3] who put the native chronicles and king-lists into Greek early in the third century B.C.; the investigations of the past few decades have increasingly demonstrated the faithfulness with which they reproduced their sources. Babylonian astronomers, who had for several centuries devoted painstaking attention to astronomy and in the service of astrology had accumulated impressive records of their observations, were drawn into the current of international science. They alone among Near-Eastern scholars had continued to develop the empiric science of the ancient Orient. This unexpected vitality of the Babylonian mind, which had slumbered in most respects since the age of Hammurabi, seems to have been partly due to the influx of new blood which came into Babylonia with the Chaldaean and Aramaean tribes from the tenth century B.C. on. By the eighth century Babylonia was largely Chaldaean in blood, and the vigorous new settlers soon became thoroughly Babylonian in culture. In 747 B.C. a new system of keeping systematic records of astronomical observations seems to have been introduced, and before the seventh century the art of predicting lunar and solar eclipses by use of empirically discovered cycles had been developed. As P. Schnabel has demonstrated (first in 1923, corrected in 1926, accepted by Fotheringham and Schaumberger), the two greatest advances in Babylonian astronomy were made by

[3] See P. Schnabel, *Berossos und die babylonisch-hellenistische Literatur* (Leipzig, 1923).

two Chaldaean scholars, Naburianus (Nabu-rimani), who
flourished about 508 B.C., and Cidenas, about 379 B.C.
Through the study devoted by the latter to the older records
of solar and lunar observations, with the aid of his own precision and insight, he was able to discover the fact of the
precession of the equinoxes nearly 250 years before it was
scientifically explained by Hipparchus (cir. 130 B.C.), and
to develop the calculation of lunar movements to a degree
of precision which was not surpassed until the eighteenth
century A.D., as has recently been shown by J. Schaumberger (1935).[4] The rediscovered Chaldaean observations
of the moon have enabled European astronomers to introduce important corrections into their tables. It is very
possible that Cidenas was already under indirect Greek influence. At all events, the scientific importance of the Chaldaean astronomical records was well known to Aristotle,
who commissioned his pupil Callisthenes to investigate
them, which he did in the year 331 B.C.[5] In the following
decades the Babylonian scholar Berossus, who founded a
Greek astrological school at Cos about 280 B.C., made
the first translations of Babylonian astronomical texts into
Greek, followed probably by others, since it has been lately
shown by Schnabel and Schaumberger that Geminus (of
Tyre?), the pupil of Posidonius, published Greek versions
of Babylonian astronomical tables in the early first century
B.C.[6] About 250 B.C. a distinguished Chaldaean astrologist
and writer, named Sudines (Shum-iddin), was active at
Pergamum. Apparently Chaldaean astrology was favorably
received from the outset in most Greek philosophical circles, and even Hipparchus became an adept. The first
Greek to popularize it in Egypt may have been Critodemus,
and it was embraced there with such extraordinary ardor

---

[4] P. Schnabel, *Zeits. f. Assyr.*, XXXVII (1926), pp. 1-60;
Kugler-Schaumberger, *Sternkunde und Sterndienst in Babel, 3.
Ergänzungsheft* (Münster, 1935), pp. 376-91.

[5] On the earliest traces of Asiatic astrological influence on
the Greeks in the fourth century B.C. see M. Nilsson, *Harv.
Theol. Rev.*, XXXII (1940), pp. 1-8.

[6] Schnabel, *op. cit.*, p. 35; Schaumberger, *op. cit.*, p. 378.

that Egypt became the classical land of astrological "research" in the second century B.C. (Cumont, 1937),[7] thanks to the activity of two native Egyptians, Nechepso and Petosiris (cir. 150 B.C.). It is quite possible that these Egyptian astrologers simply took advantage of the situation to popularize an Egypto-Chaldaean astrology dating back to the Persian period, to which the legendary Ostanes must have belonged.[8]

The Stoic philosophers took up astrology with such enthusiasm that it became an integral part of the Stoic system in the later Hellenistic period, as illustrated especially by three successive generations of philosophers, all of Near-Eastern origin: Boethus of Sidon in the second century, Posidonius of Apameia in Syria (cir. 135-50 B.C.), Geminus (of Tyre?), in the early first century. Posidonius in particular, with his encyclopaedic learning and his facile combination of Stoic with Platonic and Aristotelian views, exercised a tremendous, though somewhat obscure influence over his contemporaries.[9] The Stoic doctrine of the *heimarménē* ("allotted destiny") and of the essential harmony of the world of nature with the divine was so perfectly congruent with the principles of Babylonian astrology that they were practically fused. Outside of philosophical circles astrology was everywhere received with open arms, so it may be said to have become the fashionable creed of the Hellenistic world in the second century B.C.

Theologically Stoic doctrine varied from essentially materialistic pantheism to true theism or polytheism. Above the unchanging destiny of nature the Stoics set the free divine element which created it and which could rise above it. This divine element has its origin, they taught, in pure

---

[7] *L'Egypte des astrologues* (Brussels, 1937).

[8] J. Bidez and F. Cumont, *Les mages hellénisés: Zoroastre, Ostanes et Hystaspe d'après la tradition grecque* (Paris, 1938).

[9] The forthcoming elaborate study of Posidonius by Ludwig Edelstein of the Johns Hopkins University will clarify the activity of Posidonius in many respects, though Edelstein's negative attitude toward later classical tradition, as well as his reaction against the combinatory structures of modern scholars, is perhaps carried to an extreme.

fire, from which the world came and to which it will ultimately return. This divine fire they identified with creative reason (*lógos spermatikós*), which embraced a multitude of embryonic forms, called "creative reasoning bodies" (*lógoi spermatikoí*). Since the divine must be good and must therefore prevail over evil, the Stoics built up a theocentric system of ethics, which considered the eternal laws of destiny as essentially good and maintained that what seems evil and unjust to man, with his limited knowledge, would really appear good and just to him if he possessed divine knowledge. This form of theodicy enjoyed exceedingly great popularity in the Near East in later times and is still the dominant type today in Islam. The Stoic system could be adapted to any religion, since the Stoics developed an elaborate method by which they explained all the crudities of Greek and Oriental religion allegorically, treating them as examples of profound insight into the laws of nature, couched in sensuous dress. Thanks to this elastic quality which it possessed, to the large part which was taken by Orientals in propagating it, and to its intimate association with astrology and other forms of divination, Stoicism was able to color practically all subsequent pagan thought and to form the philosophical basis for Gnosticism.

Over against the Stoic system stood the Epicurean, which developed almost *pari passu* with the former and in constant opposition to it. The Epicureans held in theory precisely opposite positions to those which we have just outlined. Where the Stoics saw the operation of eternal divine law the Epicureans recognized the sway of chance (*tychê*), which was, however, considerably limited in their expanded system. Where the Stoics considered doing one's duty as the principal function of man the Epicureans believed that man's obligation is to enjoy life to the fullest, since the gods either do not exist or will not interfere and man has no destiny to support. To be sure, the sounder Epicureans did not maintain for a moment that the enjoyment of life permitted all sorts of excesses; their contention was that reasonable virtue and especially philosophic detachment from the storms of life are essential to the greatest measure of human happiness. To the orthodox Epicurean, astrology and all forms of divination belonged to the same limbo of superstition to which he attributed religious observances and beliefs. Epicureanism was thus essentially anthropocentric, again in opposition to the Stoics. However, many Epicureans, especially among later eclectic circles, recognized the existence of a god or of many gods, but did not think that they took an active interest in man. Epicureanism was more in keeping with the traditions of Hellenism than with those of the Near East, yet we find ample evidence that the East participated in its development. The best known early Epicurean scholar, Philodemus (cir. 150-75 B.C.), whose writings have been recovered in part from the ruins of Herculaneum, probably came from Gezer in Palestine,[10] and Zeno the Epicurean was a native of Sidon. In this connection it may be noted that the Platonist Antiochus (cir. 125-67 B.C.) was born at Ascalon. Even the ruling Epicurean principle of chance, which seems so foreign to Oriental religion, was actually harmonized with the latter, and the Greek Good Fortune (*agathê tychê*) became in Aramaic dress *naḥshâ ṭâbhâ,* a popular object of worship,[11] while every Syrian town had its Tyche (*Gaddâ*), identified with the local divinity. It must be admitted that neither the Oriental nor the average Greek saw a clear distinction between "fortune" and "fate."

[10] According to Strabo (XVI. 2. 29) Philodemus was one of several distinguished literary figures who came from "Gadara near Ascalon." Since the Gadara of the Decapolis (Muqeis) is far from Ascalon beyond Jordan, there has obviously been confusion of Gazara (Gezer) with Gadara. This confusion is very natural, since Heb. *Gezer* received the Aramaizing form *Gedar* (occurring as *Gadara* several times in Josephus, as pointed out by Schürer, *Geschichte des jüdischen Volkes* [3-5], p. 339, n. 5) by a common back-formation (cf. Bib. Achzib, Gr. Ekdippa, now ez-Zib). Of course, Philodemus may have come from the other Gadara, but Gezer was still a flourishing town in the second century B.C., as we know from excavations.

[11] Cf. Ingholt, *Berytus,* II, p. 92, and the writer, *Bull. Am. Sch. Or. Res.,* No. 66, p. 31. Aram. *naḥšâ,* Syr. *neḥšâ* meant properly "omen, augury."

B. JUDAISM AND THE RELIGIOUS LIFE OF THE HELLENISTIC AGE

The fourth century B.C. marks a major interruption in the continuity of Jewish evolution. Until then neither the normative theology nor the basic legal system of Judaism was fixed. It is certain from the literary and historical analysis of the pentateuchal documents that the Priestly Code, in spite of the relative antiquity of most of its contents, does not antedate the beginning of the sixth century B.C. It is equally clear that the four documents were not put together into the present form of the Torah before the Babylonian Exile. Many scholars follow the Wellhausen school and insist that the Priestly Code circulated in separate form down into the middle of the fifth century or even into the fourth, but there is no concrete basis for this view. The Passover Letter of the year 419 B.C. only proves that the Jewish colony at Elephantine was considered as heterodox and was probably still in a "pre-Deuteronomic" stage of religious development. Since there is not a single passage in the whole Pentateuch which can be seriously considered as showing post-exilic influence either in form or in content, it is likely that the entire Pentateuch was compiled in substantially its present form before 522 B.C. However, this does not mean that its form was already fixed according to the standards prevailing in the time of the Septuagintal translation (cir. 250 B.C.) or in that of the Samaritan recension (which Samaritan palaeography practically compels us to place between cir. 100 and cir. 63 B.C.),[12] to say nothing of mas-

---

[12] Such recent discoveries as the Lachish Ostraca and miscellaneous seal-impressions, etc., from the Persian period make it clear that the revival of preëxilic script in Maccabaean coins after 135 B.C. (there were no bronze coins struck under Simon as formerly thought; see Sellers and the writer, *Bull. Am. Sch. Or. Res.*, No. 43, p. 13, and H. Willrich, *Zeits. Alttest. Wiss.*, LI [1933], pp. 78-79) was purely archaizing and does not represent a continued evolution of the current script, as in the case of Aramaic (for which see the writer's paper on the Nash Papyrus, *Jour. Bib. Lit.*, LVI [1937], pp. 145-72). If

soretic standards more than a millennium later. G. von Rad has demonstrated (1930) that the Chronicler (who must be dated about 400 B.C. according to recent research) possessed a Torah which must have been substantially like ours, but which contained a few laws which are not found in the Pentateuch as we have it.[13] At the same time, the Chronicler went considerably beyond the pentateuchal law in insisting on the mandatory character of numerous regulations which he regarded as of Davidic origin; so he must have been well on the way to creating a kind of super-Torah. In other words, the Pentateuch had long been completed by 400 B.C., but there was no standard recension of it as yet, and different copies contained slightly varying collections of traditional material. This reminds one somewhat of the relation between different recensions of the Egyptian Book of the Dead, but especially of that between the massoretic Hebrew recensions of Jeremiah or Ezekiel and the forms underlying the Greek translations of the second century B.C.

The oldest extra-biblical Jewish work is almost certainly the book of Jubilees, preserved mainly in an Ethiopic translation of a lost Greek version of the original Hebrew. The latter was probably not written in the late second century B.C., as supposed by nearly all recent authorities, including R. H. Charles and E. Schürer. Ed. Meyer (1921) was the first to see that the book must be a century older and that

---

we compare the oldest lapidary examples of Samaritan writing with the coins of the Hasmonaeans (for which see the convenient table in Narkiss, *Coins of Palestine* [Hebrew; Jerusalem, 1936]), dated between 135 and 37 B.C., a relatively late date for the origin of the Samaritan script as such seems highly probable. Moreover, since Shechem and Samaria were conquered by the Jews between 128 and 110 B.C. and were lost to the Romans in 63 B.C., it would be only natural to date the final schism between the sects somewhere in the early first century B.C. It was presumably then or somewhat later that the entire Samaritan Pentateuch was retranscribed into the archaizing "Samaritan" script, which symbolized the refusal of the Samaritans to follow the "modernists" of Jerusalem.

[13] See the discussion at the end of his monograph, *Das Geschichtsbild der Chronistischen Werke* (Stuttgart, 1930).

the book of Enoch to which it refers must have been a precursor of the extant book of that name.[14] S. Zeitlin has now
(1939) published a strong argument for a still earlier date
and has even suggested that it might belong to the early
post-exilic age.[15] While this date is demonstrably much too
high, he shows that the book is older than the time of the
disputes between the Pharisees and Sadducees, which began about the middle of the second century B.C., and that
it even opposes many pentateuchal laws and traditions. If
we bear in mind that its historical and geographical point
of view is essentially pre-Hellenistic, that its angelology is
on a par with that of Job and earlier than that of Daniel and
Enoch, that it contains several clear allusions to Canaanite
(Phoenician) mythology and legend,[16] and that all the
arguments for a Maccabaean date are feeble, we may attribute it to the early third century B.C. (possibly even to
the late fourth century). An earlier date is rendered virtually impossible by the presence of numerous Greek geographical names and by the fact that the war between Esau
and Jacob takes place in Idumaea (southern Judah), not
in Seir, and that Esau is said to have been buried at Adoraim, which was the commercial center of Idumaea in the
early third century B.C., as we learn from the Zeno Papyri.
Since the Idumaeans had only occupied the southern hill-
country of Judah in the sixth century B.C. (see above,
p. 323), sufficient time must be allowed to establish the
tradition that Esau was buried in Adoraim.

The book of Jubilees is not only interesting because it
shows that the canonic form of our Pentateuch can hardly
be earlier than about 300 B.C. and was presumably fixed by

---

[14] *Ursprung und Anfänge des Christentums*, II (Stuttgart,
1921), pp. 45 ff.

[15] *Jew. Quar. Rev.*, XXX (1939), pp. 1-31.

[16] E. g., Enoch is said to have married Edni (or Edna),
daughter of Dan'el, who can only be the Dan'el or Dani'el of
Ugarit and Ezekiel, chap. 14. In a similar way Tobit was
made the uncle of the wise Akhiqar in the Book of Tobit. The
Elyo (Eleyo) of Jub. 7:22 may be the ʿElyon (Eliun) of Philo
Byblius 10. 14 f.

the scholars of the "Great Synagogue";[17] it also illustrates the advance of Jewish theological ideas at the beginning of the Greek period, before Hellenism had begun to make any inroads into Jewish thought. The author of the book repeatedly eliminates or refines passages and concepts which he considers as too crude. God remains personally aloof from contact with humanity and His transactions with man are usually carried on through angels. For instance, the angels, not God, bring the animals to Adam in order that he may name them; the Presence of God, not God Himself, issues the order to destroy the children of the fallen angels; the angel of God often takes God's place in His dealings with the Patriarchs, etc. In the story of the sacrifice of Isaac, the tempter becomes the head of the evil spirits (Mastema = Satan), whereas in the original God Himself is represented as testing Abraham. While this advance in the idealization of God was strictly in keeping with the tendency of prior centuries which reached a climax in Deutero-Isaiah, it nevertheless represented increasing spiritual danger, especially in circles where interest in the letter of the Torah eclipsed attention to the spirit underlying it. It is also characteristic of the times that astrology, not idol-worship, serves as the principal target for the author's attacks.

The most important step toward the Hellenization of Jewry after Alexander's Conquest was taken during the reign of Ptolemy Lagi, about 300 B.C., when many thousands of Jews came to Egypt, either as voluntary immigrants and mercenaries (according to Hecataeus of Abdera, who was a contemporary) or as slaves (according to Pseudo-Aristeas, who wrote in the second third of the second century B.C., as recently shown by E. Bickermann).[18]

---

[17] See S. Zeitlin, *Proc. Am. Acad. Jew. Res.*, III (1932), pp. 155 f.

[18] *Zeits. Neutest. Wiss.*, XXIX (1930), pp. 280-98. R. Tramontano's date at the end of the third century B.C. (*La lettera di Aristea a Filocrate* [Napoli, 1931]; cf. A. Barrois, *Rev. Bib.*, 1932, pp. 104-12) is too high, but is excused by the fact that Pseudo-Aristeas employed older materials; cf. L. H. Vincent, *Rev. Bib.*, 1908, pp. 520 ff., and 1909, pp. 555 ff. (on the topography of Jerusalem) and A. T. Olmstead, *Jour. Am. Or.*

The substantial historicity of the former statement has been confirmed by O. R. Sellers' discovery at Beth-zur (1931) of a coin bearing the name of Hezekiah, who seems to be the priest mentioned by Hecataeus in this connection.[19] It is likely enough that Ptolemy carried many Jews as slaves to Egypt after his capture of Jerusalem. At all events, epigraphic data make it certain that thousands of Jews settled in Egypt in the third century B.C. and that they were in the main fresh immigrants, not descendants of the Jewish colonists of the Persian period. Two Jewish-Aramaic papyri and at least eight ostraca from Tbo, now Edfu in Upper Egypt, and Zawiyet el-Meitin have recently been discovered, all dating from the third century B.C.; their evidence is supplemented by that of the Zeno Papyri, which contain a number of Jewish names, as well as by that of Aramaic tomb inscriptions from Alexandria itself and of Aramaic graffiti on coins from Demanhur. The personal names of the new Jewish colonists do not carry on the preëxilic onomastic tradition, like the Elephantine Papyri, but belong to three main types: familiar biblical names like Abram, Judah, Joseph, Simeon (Simon); Aramaic names not found in the Old Testament but common later; Greek names. It is curious enough that the list of seventy-two Jewish translators of the Septuagint, as given by Pseudo-Aristeas, though hardly quite authentic, reads like a list of contemporary names from the newly discovered inscriptions! Among the Jewish immigrants were men of distinguished ancestry, like Akabiah son of Elioenai, a namesake of the Davidic prince mentioned in I Chron. 3:24, and perhaps his grandson. In view of this great influx of Jews, it is not surprising that it became necessary to translate the

Soc., LVI (1936), pp. 243 f., _Bull. Am. Sch. Or. Res._, No. 63 (1936), p. 6. Note also the present writer's observation that the list of Jewish names given by Pseudo-Aristeas in connection with the translation of the Septuagint contains authentic personal names of the third century and so may conceivably reproduce the membership of a real advisory body after all.

[19] Olmstead, _loc. cit._; cf. F. M. Abel, _Rev. Bib._, 1935, pp. 577 f.

Torah into Greek within half a century (about 250 B.C.).
That there were still Jews in Egypt who read Hebrew in the
late second century B.C. is shown by the Nash Papyrus,
containing the Decalogue and the Shema, evidently for
ritual purposes; its date, hitherto obscure, has lately been
approximately fixed by the writer.[20]

The first certain traces of the impact of Greek thought on
Jewish theology appear in the late third century B.C. One
is recorded by the Jewish treatise Pirqe Abhoth, a very reliable work dating from the third century A.D. According
to the tradition which it preserves, Antigonus of Socho, who
followed Simon the Just and probably flourished in the second half of the third century B.C., taught: "Be not like
slaves who serve the master on condition that they receive
a reward, but be like slaves who serve the master on condition that they receive no reward; and let the fear of Heaven
be incumbent upon you." The meaning of this passage is
generally watered down by translators, but the Hebrew is
clear. Antigonus, whose Greek name betrays the Hellenistic influence under which he had been reared, here ex-
presses the lofty sentiments which animated the best of the
proto-Sadducean school, who opposed the growing popular
belief in a blissful future life, as well as the traditional view
according to which the soul continues indeed to exist, but
in a shadowy, inactive state. The authors of Isa. 29:19
(sixth century B.C.?) and of Job already seem to react
against the pallid traditional view of Israel, which was no
longer enough for an age which had removed God so far
from the world and from contact with mankind. In Jubilees
(third century B.C.?) we find an interesting intermediate
position: the dead rest in the earth and there is no resurrection of the body, but their souls rejoice in their knowledge of God's vindication of justice. Ben Sira, however, at
the beginning of the second century, states explicitly on
several occasions that there is no resurrection; death is the
destiny of all mankind, and when a man dies he becomes
the prey of worms. And yet, the book of Daniel, the book

[20] *Jour. Bib. Lit.*, LVI (1937), pp. 145-76.

of Enoch, and other works of the same general age show that a positive doctrine of the after-life had already gained the upper hand as early as 165 B.C., so we may safely suppose that it had been current for a long time in certain circles.

The teachings of Antigonus and of Ben Sira, from which later Sadduceanism derived its conceptions regarding immortality, are not simply a continuation of earlier Jewish views, but represent a definitely new stand on a question which had always previously remained unsettled, so far as we know. Pre-philosophical Jewish thought was content to know that the dead still existed and that their continued existence was in some way the reflection of their life on earth; it did not ask, so far as we know, for a precise definition of what constituted the future life nor did it enquire how we know that the human spirit continues to exist. But as post-exilic Jewish circles developed increasingly concrete ideas on the nature of the future life, on the coming of a divine judgment followed by a sharp separation between the righteous and the wicked—probably under indirect Iranian influence (see below)—more conservative groups found it necessary to clarify their opinions. The Greek dialectic spirit was abroad; debates between adherents of the two influential new schools, the Stoic and the Epicurean, could be heard on all sides. Antigonus of Socho was evidently influenced by the Stoic position that the foremost obligation of man was to do his duty, regardless of what might come. Both orthodox Stoics and Epicureans denied the existence of conscious after-life and the latter rejected belief in any kind of immortality. The impersonal "Heaven" of Antigonus sounds suspiciously like the Stoic *heimarmênê*, though in itself it is simply a euphemism for the Tetragrammaton, *YHWH*, which was no longer pronounced after the fourth century B.C.

Over against the Stoic tinge of Antigonus we may set the equally clear eclectic coloring of the book of Ecclesiastes, whose author was probably nearly contemporary with him. The title applied to himself by its author, *Qohéleth*, is still enigmatic; it may contain some Aramaic literary allusion

which escapes us. Efforts made to find specific Greek influence in the book have consistently failed; it is likely that
it reflects the general impression made by Greek dialectic
methods and philosophical attitudes on a highly intelligent
Jew who did not read Greek.[21] Ecclesiastes agrees with
Epicurean ideas in his view that reasonable and virtuous
enjoyment of life is man's highest good and in his firm belief
that there is no future life at all (3:19 ff., etc.). On the
the other hand he approaches Stoic teaching in his emphasis
on man's duty to "fear God and keep His commandments,
for this is all of man." Moreover, his statement, "Then shall
the dust return to the earth as it was, but the spirit shall return to God who made it" (12:7) is certainly not Epicurean
but distinctly Stoic, since the latter school taught that human souls were offshoots of the world-soul, to which they
returned after death. Furthermore, Ecclesiastes' doctrine
of the cyclic recurrence of natural phenomena (1:5 ff.) is
rather Stoic than Epicurean, though it probably arose from
still earlier sources; but his statements with reference to
chance and destiny are clearly tinged with Epicureanism.
The effect of Ecclesiastes' teachings on the young would
be definitely Epicurean, since it is precisely in those views
where he approaches Epicurus most closely that he diverges
farthest from traditional Jewish ideas. Though the misunderstood attribution of the authorship of Ecclesiastes to Solomon and its extremely pious interludes and finale assured
the book an ultimate place in the Canon, Epicureanism as
such was banned by orthodox Jewry and the name of its
founder became synonymous with "unbeliever" in the
period of the Mishnah, and has kept this meaning in Hebrew ever since.

The opposition between the more aristocratic conserva-
tives who believed in maintaining old Jewish religious
beliefs as they were stated in the Law and the Prophets,
and the representatives of the masses, who attributed equal
practical value to later literature and traditions, must have

[21] See the well-balanced statement of the problem and its
solution by H. W. Hertzberg in his commentary on Ecclesiastes
(Leipzig, 1932), pp. 47 ff.

continued to grow in intensity during the early second century, but it was over-shadowed by the far greater actuality of the conflict between Judaism as a whole and Greek paganism. As has recently been shown by E. Bickermann (1937) the cult of Zeus Olympius introduced into the Temple in Jerusalem at the same time that the cult of Zeus Xenius was imposed on the Samaritans, was actually liberal Judaism in a Hellenized form.[22] In other words, the Hellenizing high priests Jason and Menelaus (cir. 175-165) went so far in their efforts to win the support of the new Seleucid overlords of Palestine that they actually proposed or accepted the reorganization of Judaism as a Syro-Hellenic religion. In the face of such a menace as this there was no longer any major significance in the fight against astrology or in the debate between those who defended belief in the future life and those who opposed it. All pious Jews, regardless of party and creed, now rallied to the support of the Maccabaean patriots, who struggled with an energy and a zeal seldom approached and perhaps never surpassed in history, until under Simon (143-135 B.C.) they attained their goal, the autonomy of Judaea and the purification of Jerusalem. Hardly had this been accomplished when strife broke out between the Sadducees and the Pharisees, as the two chief parties were thenceforth entitled. For two full centuries, from cir. 130 B.C. to 70 A.D., Jewish religious life was characterized by this party conflict, in which the Pharisees gained ground steadily at the expense of their more aristocratic brethren.

Thanks to repeated statements of Josephus, supplemented and confirmed by other Jewish and Christian data, we know the essential differences between the Sadducees and the Pharisees. It is very interesting to note that these differences were basically due to the different ways in which Jewish groups reacted to the challenge of Hellenic ways of thinking. Their conservative insistence on restricting the

[22] *Der Gott der Makkabäer* (Berlin, 1937). See also the favorable reviews by F. M. Abel, *Rev. Bib.*, 1938, pp. 441-46; K. Galling, *Or. Lit.-zeit.*, 1939, cols. 225-28; J. A. Montgomery, *Jour. Bib. Lit.*, 1940, pp. 308 f.

scope of canonical Hebrew literature had confirmed the Sadducees in their conviction that belief in a future life, in a divine judgment, in bodily resurrection, and in an angelic hierarchy were unscriptural and therefore contrary to the religion of the fathers. The thinking of their predecessors, such as Antigonus of Socho and Ben Sira, who had developed their beliefs under the irresistible pressure of new Greek ways of thinking, enabled them to buttress these instinctive reactions with a philosophical scaffolding. The Sadducees, probably reacting against the Stoic attitude of some of their precursors, insisted on freedom of the human will and opposed the Stoic doctrine of predestination (*heimarménē*) with the utmost vigor. Ben Sira, who may be considered as the prototype of the Sadducees, again and again declares that man, not God, is responsible for sin. The Pharisees, on the other hand, allowed for a duality of factors in human life: the predestination or providence of God and the free action of man's will. In this respect it was the Pharisees who carried on the Old Testament tradition and who marked out the delicate but fundamental line which orthodox Christianity was to take.[23]

In spite of the fact that it was the Sadducees who first came under strong Hellenistic influence because of their patrician connections, it was the Pharisees who eventually became more thoroughly Hellenized. In fact, we are hardly going too far if we say that the Pharisaic movement represents the Hellenization of the normative Jewish tradition. This fact seems to have been first pointed out by E. Bickermann (1935),[24] but he did not go nearly far enough, since he overlooked the most important aspect of this Hellenizing process, that of the exegetic and dialectic methods employed by the Pharisees in developing the ritual law. The

[23] On the Pharisees and their movement see especially L. Finkelstein, *The Pharisees* (two vols.; Philadelphia, 1938), where full bibliographies will be found. Cf. also the reviews of Finkelstein by the writer, *Menorah Journal*, 1939, pp. 232-34, by S. Baron, *Jour. Bib. Lit.*, 1940, pp. 60-67; P. Benoit, *Rev. Bib.*, 1939, pp. 280-85; S. Zeitlin, *Horeb* (Hebrew), 1938/9, pp. 27-42.

[24] *Die Makkabäer* (Berlin, 1935), pp. 58 ff.

Pharisees, first of all, laid extraordinary emphasis on study of the law and the formation of schools of disciples. Ben Sira had snobbishly restricted the professional study of the Torah to patricians with background and leisure. According to Ben Sira no craftsman or peasant could hope to become a sage. On the other hand, the Pharisees believed that the poorest man might aspire to become a great scholar if he had enough ability and industry. All this emphasis on the value of systematic study and on the widest possible scope of education was foreign to early Israel and to the ancient Orient in general, but was part and parcel of the liberal Hellenistic ideal.[25] Again, Pharisaic insistence on the need of extending the operation of the Law to suit new conditions and to cover all possible eventualities was thoroughly Hellenistic. The Pharisees took up a slogan which may once have served as a rallying cry for the members of the traditional Great Synagogue, "Make a fence for the Torah," since it is attributed to them by the Pirqe Abhoth, composed several centuries later. Instead of limiting the scope of canonical legislation it now extended its scope by hedging the rules of the Torah around with new regulations which protected the observance of the original rules. For instance, in order to ensure proper Sabbath observance they introduced many rules defining what constitutes work, even including under this head many harmless acts such as carrying a shawl or picking up a towel. In order to ensure that a kid was never cooked in milk (Ex. 23:19) they set up an elaborate system of differentiation between milk-foods and meat-foods, though fish and locusts were neutral. However, these distinctions were only carried out in detail in tannaitic times, after the fall of Jerusalem in 70 A.D. We mention them here in order to illustrate the tendency of the Pharisaic *halakha*. Louis Finkelstein has shown in his recent work on the Pharisees (1938) that many of the differences between the *halakhôth* (rules) of the Sadducees and the Pharisees as well as of the two principal Pharisaic schools

[25] Cf. C. F. Angus, *Cambridge Ancient History*, Vol. VII, pp. 224 ff.

were based on the needs of life in different parts of the country or in different classes of society.

The best illustration of the thoroughly Hellenistic framework of Pharisaic thought (we are not speaking of the content of their teaching!) is found in the oldest exegetical and hermeneutic rules which were employed by the Pharisees in order to build up their system. Seven of these rules are attributed to Hillel, who was a contemporary of Herod the Great, but these rules must have been already in use, since nothing is said by tradition about any opposition between the school of Hillel and its bitter adversary, the school of Shammai, with regard to them. Briefly stated these norms of Hillel include inferences *a minori ad maius* and *a fortiori*; argument from analogy; "the construction of a family (of biblical passages) from one passage" (i. e., an inference as to the connotation of several passages from that of one of them); "the construction of a family from two passages"; argument from the general to the particular and from the particular to the general; exposition by inference from a parallel passage; deduction from the context of a passage. Over a century after Hillel a much longer list of exegetical norms was drawn up by Rabbi Ishmael, an older contemporary of Aqiba, and further additions were made in later times. It is only necessary to quote the original list to show that Pharisaic reasoning, though often forced, was far from being illogical. Hillel's principles of interpretation have no more in common with the ancient Near East than they have with Mayan civilization but they are characteristically Hellenistic in concept and even in form.[26] S. Rosenblatt's careful inductive study of *The Interpretation of the Bible*

---

[26] See A. Kaminka, *Encyclopaedia Judaica*, IV, p. 623; Jew. *Quar. Rev.*, XXX (1939), pp. 121 f. The application of Aristotelian methods to exegesis and hermeneutics was largely the work of Aristarchus of Samothrace (cir. 215-145 B.C.), who reached the summit of his reputation at Alexandria cir. 150 B.C.; he correctly stressed the importance of analogy in philology. The most important of his pupils and successors were the authors of the first Greek grammar, Dionysius Thrax (cir. 166 B.C.–) and Didymus (cir. 65 B.C.-10 A.D.), a contemporary of Hillel.

in the Mishnah (1935) confirms the impression given by the examination of Hillel's norms. The exegetes of the Mishnah laid great stress on literal, grammatically exact, and legally sound exegesis, using methods parallel in fundamental respects to those of the Alexandrian philologians of the Ptolemaic age, to whom we owe so much of our knowledge of Greek grammar and literature. The far-fetched exegesis of Egyptian and cuneiform scribes, where methods of interpretation swing violently from mechanical collocation to wild combination, without any logical basis, has nothing in common with the sober logic of the Pharisees. It may be added that another almost equally wide gulf separates the latter from the midrashic interpretations which became increasingly popular after the third century A.D.

There were still other Jewish groups and individuals which stood apart from the main current and which presumably exerted little or no influence on later Judaism, but which helped to form the background of Christianity. The philosopher and historian Aristobulus, who flourished shortly after the middle of the second century B.C., the author of the book of Wisdom, who probably wrote in the first half of the first century B.C.,[27] and Philo Judaeus, who was a contemporary of Christ and the Apostles,[28] illustrate a progress which eventually led to complete Hellenization and which could not, therefore, have much direct effect on the main stream of Jewish life, though the latter two are significant for the beginnings of Christianity, as we shall see.[28a]

[27] See now J. Fichtner, *Zeits. Neutest. Wiss.*, XXXVI (1937), pp. 113-31.

[28] The study of Philo has now been greatly advanced and facilitated by the work of E. R. Goodenough, especially in his *By Light, Light* (New Haven, 1935) and *Politics of Philo Judaeus* (New Haven, 1938), to which an elaborate bibliography is appended. His contention that Philo was actually a member of a Jewish mystery-cult goes too far, and has not hitherto found any adherents in the ranks of specialists.

[28a] These are not, of course, the only works of this age important for the understanding of Hellenistic Judaism, but they

C. NON-HELLENIC CURRENTS IN HELLENISTIC
JUDAISM

Besides influences from Greek life and thought upon Hellenistic Judaism, there are other more obscure effects created by the impact on the Jewish Diaspora of many centuries of close association with Oriental peoples. Some of these effects may be demonstrated from contemporary texts; others may be inferred from their presence in documents of *both* earlier and later age. Great caution must be exercised in order not to push back unduly the time at which a given influence began to be exerted. Since scholars have sinned greatly in this respect, it will be necessary to devote a few words to two outstanding cases, Mandaeanism and Hermeticism. We shall take up successively influences from Iranian religion, proto-Gnostic currents, and the Logos conception.

While it is hard to exaggerate the importance of Iranian religious influences on the paganism of the Roman Empire, as well as upon later Gnosticism, their value for our understanding of Judaism and early Christianity has been greatly over-estimated. Some scholars have gone so far as to connect the emergence of pure monotheism among the Jews with the victory of the Achaemenian dynasty! R. Reitzenstein has derived the idea of the "Son of Man" from Iranian sources. The whole question is immensely complicated by the fact that the data for the history of Mazdayasnianism (the religion of Zoroaster) are very obscure and conflicting. In fact no two specialists agree in their interpretation of the evidence, as is particularly clear if we compare the views of the latest competent writers on the subject, such as A. Christensen (1931–), G. Messina (1930–), E. Herzfeld (1930–), E. Benveniste (1929–),

---

are the most important for our present purpose. For an interesting recent treatment of the bearing of the Sibylline Oracles on the ideology of the Jewish diaspora just before the time of Christ see J. Klausner, *From Jesus to Paul* (Hebrew; Tel-Aviv, 1939-40), I, pp. 131-65.

and especially H. S. Nyberg whose recent work, *Die Religionen des alten Iran* (1938), is revolutionary in its significance.[29] The following sketch will limit itself strictly to what has been demonstrated or at least recognized as probable by the consensus of recent opinion.

Early Iranian religion was substantially identical in general character and even in detail with the Aryan faith of the Rig Veda; it was a naturalistic polytheism essentially like Homeric Greek religion. At the head of the pantheon stood Ahura Mazda, "the Lord of Wisdom" (cf. Sumerian Zen, the god of the moon, whose name has the same meaning); among the most important deities were Mithra, the god of light, and the goddess of fertility, Ardvisura Anahita, "the Great Stream, the Unblemished One." This period of Iranian religion is reflected by some of the Yashts of the Avesta, which have been only lightly worked over by later Zoroastrian editors; their constant references to chariot-warriors show that their original composition must antedate the ninth century B.C. at the latest, since cavalry had replaced chariotry by that time. Somewhere in the ninth (or an earlier) century B.C. arose Spitama Zarathushtra (Zoroaster), member of an Iranian agricultural and cattle-breeding community in the far northeastern marches of Transoxiana (so Nyberg), who preached a new gospel, the general nature of which is clear from the Gathas of the Avesta. It is true that the latter do not appear to have been reduced to canonical form until about the third century A.D., but they seem to have been put into writing under the Parthian kings, probably in the first century A.D. Judging from linguistic and palaeographic evidence, they were transmitted orally for not less than 800, and perhaps for

---

[29] On the revolutionary character of Nyberg's book cf. the review by Zaehner, himself a first-class authority in the field, *Jour. Roy. Asiat. Soc.,* 1940, pp. 210 ff. The book was translated from Swedish by one of the most eminent specialists in the Iranian field, H. H. Schaeder, and as Zaehner observes, even if many of the author's somewhat paradoxical conclusions rest on slender foundations, his work retains its fundamental value as a reconsideration of the entire subject by a very brilliant and learned scholar.

over 1100 years. Zoroaster taught that there was only one supreme being, the good and bright Ahura Mazda, against whom stood the independent representative of the evil and dark forces of nature, Angra Mainyu (Ahriman). Ahura Mazda created five or six (later increased to seven) minor deities, called "the Beneficent Immortals" (Amesha Spentas), all of whom bore abstract names: Good Thought, Best Order (Truth), Desirable Domination, Beneficent Devotion, Holiness, Immortality, to whom a seventh, Beneficent Spirit, was later added. To oppose these, Angra Mainyu also created evil deities or spirits. Zoroaster seems to have simplified the native religious cult of the Iranians by emphasizing the sacredness of fire, of the cow, and of the haoma plant, which was used to make a fermented sacred drink. According to Zoroaster the good Ahura Mazda will ultimately prevail over the forces of evil. The old Iranian gods were in general relegated to the rank of demons (*daivas*). There must have been some form of belief in the divine judgment and the separation between the good and the evil in the next world, but it cannot be traced with certainty back to the Achaemenian period.

Epigraphic discoveries have made it quite certain that Darius and his immediate successors (cir. 522-405?) were the only Achaemenian kings who can safely be called Mazdayasnians, and some eminent authorities are inclined to deny that even *they* were true Zoroastrians. And yet, the inscriptions of Darius and Xerxes, especially those published by E. Herzfeld in the past few years, contain nothing which is definitely anti-Zoroastrian, and the references to "Ahura Mazda, the great god who has created heaven, earth, mankind" and to the sway of the Lie (*drauja*), etc., suggest that they were followers of Zoroaster. However, the Magian priests against whom Darius fought and the Persians whose religion is described by Herodotus about 450 B.C. were certainly not Zoroastrians but rather Iranian polytheists (Magians). Moreover, about 400 B.C. the inscriptions of Artaxerxes II abandon Mazdayasnian phraseology and frankly list the chief gods of the pantheon as Ahura Mazda, Mithra, and Anahita. About the same time, according to Berossus, as cited by Clement of Alexandria, supported by a passage in the Avesta, the Iranian gods were first represented in the form of images.[30] That Magianism was the form of Iranian religion which continued to hold sway over the western half of the old Achaemenian Empire, is perfectly clear from the present evidence. In Hellenistic times Magianism was combined on the one hand with Greek paganism (Mithra became Helius, etc.) and on the other with astrology, as is evident from the rock inscription of Antiochus of Commagene in the first century B.C. It also became strangely fused with Orphism (Cumont, 1934), and the Orphic "Ageless Time" became identified with the non-Zoroastrian Iranian "Unending Time" (Zervan Akarana).[31] In the late first century A.D. Mithraism emerged as a rival of Christianity, especially in military circles.

There is no clear trace of Iranian influence on Judaism before the second century B.C., though the beginnings of this influence may well go back a century or two earlier. In the form which Iranian religion takes in all inscriptions and literary sources of the last four centuries B.C. it can hardly have possessed any appeal to the Jews as a monotheistic or aniconic system. Even in the Gathas, Ahura Mazda is only the mighty head of a hierarchy of good minor deities, against whom are arrayed Angra Mainyu and his evil followers. Iranian influences must have entered into Judaism first as a result of certain features which reminded the Jews of corresponding elements in their religion. These common features may be identified in Judaism with ease: a tendency toward dualism and to the creation of a personal antagonist to God; a tendency toward the formation of an organized angelic hierarchy; developing belief in the last judgment and in rewards and punishments after death. In a number of passages in Jewish literature dating from cir. 400-165 B.C. we find the idea of a personal Satan developing from the original sense of an angelic plaintiff in the celestial court, where the Almighty was allegorically repre-

[30] Cf. A. Christensen, *Acta Orientalia,* IV (1926), pp. 113 ff.
[31] *Rev. Hist. Rel.,* CIX, pp. 63-72.

sented as sitting in judgment over the deeds of men (Zech. 3; Job 1; cf. for still older conceptions I Kings 22:19 ff.), to its final sense of the chief of the invisible powers opposed to God (so partly in Jubliees). But it is not until the late second century B.C., in the Testaments of the Twelve Patriarchs, that we find characteristically dualistic conceptions: e. g., the spirit of error is set against the spirit of truth (Test. Jud., 20) and Beliar (Belial) is set against God (*passim*), light is opposed to darkness (*passim*), and the seven evil spirits are arrayed against the seven good spirits. This type of dualism decreased greatly in importance in later Judaism and seems, in fact, to have been rejected by orthodox rabbinic circles, though it obtained considerable popular support in still later times. In Christianity, on the other hand, the modified dualism of the Testaments of the Twelve Patriarchs achieved a signal triumph, since it offers a simpler and more intelligible solution of the problem of evil than any other ever proposed. The very fact that it was rejected by normative Judaism shows that it was foreign to Jewish tradition, and Iranian influence can hardly be denied, especially in view of the parallels which will be described in the next two paragraphs.

It is highly probable that the idea of seven archangels was taken from Iranian sources. In the earlier books of the Old Testament and the earliest apocryphal and pseudepigraphical literature there is nowhere any suggestion that certain angels formed a specially privileged group in the celestial hierarchy, nor do any angels receive personal names identical with those of human beings. In Daniel (cir. 165 B.C.) Michael and Gabriel appear, and in Enoch Uriel (Ôrî'el "God is my Light") and Raphael, as well as many other names, are added. The number of the principal angels (archangels) varies from four to seven, the latter being distinctly later than the former, as is clear not only from their literary age but also from the fact that only these four have genuinely early Israelite (or Canaanite) names, after which all others have obviously been modelled. It is curious to note that all four names belong to a type which was in most active use before the tenth century B.C. and which became archaistic after the Exile. There can, therefore, be little doubt that these angelic figures have a prehistory (Israelite or pagan?) which escapes us entirely.[32] In any case only the *idea* of seven chief angels and of their relative station was taken from Iranian sources, since the names are absolutely different in character.

The idea of the Last Judgment also has strong Jewish roots, though Iranian conceptions appear to have influenced details. Since God was believed to sit in judgment on the deeds of all mankind (see above), and since the last Day of the Lord was an old eschatological concept in Israel, it was a natural transition to the Last Judgment. In the form in which it appears in Daniel (7:9-12) Iranian influence is most unlikely, but in Enoch (41:1 and *passim*) and elsewhere in the last century and a half before our era, we find such distinctively Iranian details as the use of the balance to weigh the deeds of men.[33] The apocalyptic picture of the end of the world (e. g., Rev. 8 ff.) calls to mind many Iranian parallels, though in view of the obscurity of Zoroastrian literary chronology, it cannot be definitely shown that they antedate Sassanian times (third-seventh centuries A.D.). The idea of the destruction of the world by fire is much more likely to be derived from the astrological interpretation of the Stoic *ekpýrôsis*, the conflagration which follows a cosmic cycle, since P. Schnabel's studies (1923) have shown that this theory goes back to the last two centuries B.C.[34]

From the foregoing paragraphs it appears that Iranian

---

[32] The writer indulged once in some rather rash speculations on this subject (*Am. Jour. Sem. Lang.*, XLIII [1926], pp. 234 ff.), comparing Michael, Gabriel and Raphael with Enoch, Moses, and Elijah, respectively.

[33] Egyptian influence has also been suggested, and later Asiatic use of the motif may go back ultimately to Egypt. The balance was also known in Babylonian and Elamite religion, where it played a similar part; cf. Meissner, *Babylonien und Assyrien*, II (1926), pp. 146 f. (the deity who presides over the balance is not "Shugurnak" but Shushinak, the chief god of Susa).

[34] *Berossos* (Leipzig, 1923), pp. 182 ff.

conceptions did not begin to influence Judaism until the last two pre-Christian centuries, and even then exerted no effect except where the ground was already fully prepared for them. When we turn to the sphere of influence which we shall term "proto-Gnostic," for lack of a better expression, the situation changes materially. Here, however, even greater caution is needed than in dealing with Iranian influences, since we are largely dependent upon fragmentary bits of information and indirect inferences. First we must dispose of the alleged antiquity of the Mandaean and Hermetic literatures, both of which have been erroneously traced back to pre-Christian times by eminent scholars.

In his *Poimandres* (1904) Reitzenstein traced the curious documents of pagan mysticism which are known as the Hermetic Corpus back to the work of the astrologers Nechepso and Petosiris (see above), now known to have flourished in the second century B.C. Subsequent research has, however, made it increasingly clear that he was entirely wrong and that the literature in question must be in the main posterior to the rise of Neo-Platonism about the middle of the third century A.D., though its roots are undoubtedly older. Hermeticism thus drops out of consideration as a source for any phase of early Christianity.[35]

The Mandaean situation is much more complex and elusive, but general agreement seems now to have been reached by competent scholars on certain basic points.[36] Since John the Baptist (Yohanna) is the central figure of the Mandaean system and baptism in the (symbolic) Jordan plays the principal rôle in their ritual, it is only natural to look for traces of very early religious ideas in their elaborate literature. Until recently, however, Man-

[35] See W. Scott, *Hermetica*, I-IV (Oxford, 1924-36) and especially the notes by A. S. Ferguson in the *Introduction* to Vol. IV.

[36] There is now a vast literature dealing with the Mandaeans, which has been listed (up to 1930) by S. A. Pallis, *Essay on Mandaean Bibliography* (Copenhagen, 1933). The soundest recent treatment of the subject is to be found in J. Thomas, *Le mouvement baptiste en Palestine et Syrie* (Gembloux, Belgium, 1935), pp. 186-267.

daean literature remained virtually inaccessible, because of the peculiar script and dialect of Aramaic in which it was written, to say nothing of a still more obscure theological and ceremonial terminology and of almost hopeless corruption of the text in many places. These difficulties were removed by the brilliant work of M. Lidzbarski in editing, translating, and explaining the principal religious works of the Mandaeans (1905-25). Since 1937 Mrs. E. S. Drower has begun the publication of her rich folkloristic and mythico-magical data on the Mandaeans of modern Iraq. Lidzbarski himself inaugurated a period of exaggerated respect for the antiquity of Mandaean literature, in which he was eagerly followed by such scholars as R. Reitzenstein (1921–) and R. Bultmann (1923–), and numerous others, all of whom endeavored to demonstrate Mandaean influence on early Christianity, especially on the Gospel of John. W. Bauer incorporated the new parallels into the second edition of his standard commentary on John (1925).[37] Meanwhile, however, E. Peterson (1923–), M. J. Lagrange (1927-37), F. C. Burkitt (1928), and H. Lietzmann (1930) headed a reaction against these extreme views. The criticisms and warnings of these scholars

[37] In his valuable study, *Untersuchungen über den Ursprung der johanneischen Theologie* (Lund, 1939), E. Percy has attacked Bultmann and Bauer with great vigor and success; cf. P. Benoit, *Rev. Bib.*, 1940, pp. 259-64 and W. L. Knox, *Jour. Theol. Stud.*, XLI (1940), pp. 66-68. Bultmann has replied to Percy's criticisms with equal vigor in *Orient. Lit.-zeit.*, 1940, cols. 150-75. The writer's reaction may be briefly stated as follows. Mandaeanism is definitely post-Gnostic, reflecting an advanced form of dualism which is more Iranian than anything comparable in the Western forms of Gnosis. The Gospel of John reflects certain concepts which must have been current in proto-Gnosticism but, as Percy makes clear, without attaching to them dualistic connotations of Iranian character; i. e., light and darkness, truth and lie are contrasted ideas in John and these ideas possess dualistic potentialities, but they are in no sense cosmological and metaphysical entities as assumed by Bultmann. On the other hand, Bultmann is right in objecting to Percy's arbitrary exegesis of John and to his constant denial of soteriological implications to the Mandaean conceptions under discussion.

were so obviously sound that they had great effect; and the sensational discovery of the long-lost original Manichaean literature (in Coptic translations from the fourth century A.D.), followed promptly by its publication (since 1933), has almost completely killed the Mandaean fashion, since this system is obviously later than the Manichaean (third century A.D.). The prevailing view today is probably that of Burkitt, whose philological arguments are decisive: the Mandaean system arose in southern Iraq about the fifth century A.D., under the influence of Dosithaean, Marcionite, and Manichaean teachings. There is probably nothing in their literature which antedates the fifth century A.D. in its extant form, and most of it does not antedate the seventh century A.D.[38] Yet the explicit statements of Theodore bar Koni in the eighth century and of an-Nadim in the tenth indicate that the Mandaean sect was only a derivative of older groups, among which the Baptist Dosithaeans may be considered as the oldest. Of real importance is the increasing mass of evidence showing that the Mandaeans inherited the debris of Canaanite and Aramaean mythology, on the one hand, and of Babylonian mythology and folklore, on the other.[39] While nothing in Mandaean literature can be di-

---

[38] It must be emphasized that, though Mandaean is very closely related to Babylonian Aramaic, as was recognized by Nöldeke in his epoch-making *Mandäische Grammatik* (1875), its orthography is considerably later in type and the laryngals are thrown together. Even in the oldest amulets the confusion of laryngals is already evident, though the system of vowel-letters is still comparatively undeveloped. Now the orthography of Babylonian Aramaic was presumably fixed during the Amoraic period of the Talmud, i. e., between 300 and 500 A.D. It follows that the oldest Mandaean inscriptions can hardly antedate the sixth century. Lidzbarski's dating of a lead amulet about 400 A.D. was thus highly improbable (contrast J. Thomas, *op. cit.*, p. 214, n. 3) and a date a century or more later is probable.

[39] For references to Lidzbarski and H. Bauer and for additions to their material see the writer, *Am. Jour. Sem. Lang.*, LIII (1936), pp. 11 f. For Babylonian survivals cf. (in addition to the material collected previously by Anz and Zimmern) the writer's suggestions and observations, *Am. Jour. Sem. Lang.*, XXXVI (1920), pp. 265 f., 291 ff., now in part superseded.

rectly employed to demonstrate the existence of a given conception in the first century A.D. or earlier, Mandaean names, ideas, and practices which can be proved to go back to pre-Christian paganism often possess exceptional value for the historian of Christian and Gnostic beginnings.

Few problems in the history of religion are so elusive as the question of Proto-Gnosticism and Judaeo-Gnosticism. Since the earliest literary remains of Gnosticism proper do not antedate the second century A.D. and since the earliest Gnostic known to Irenaeus and Hippolytus was Simon Magus (cf. Acts 8:9 ff.) it is obvious that we cannot use Gnostic data directly in any reconstruction of Hellenistic Jewish currents of thought. However, there is now direct evidence that some of the central ideas of the Gnostic system go back into the ancient Orient. We shall, accordingly, discuss this evidence briefly, after which we shall characterize Proto-Gnosticism as a movement and point out its relation to Judaism and Christianity.

The central figure of Gnostic mythology is that of Sophia "Wisdom." It is true that the Sophia appears in very different rôles in different Gnostic systems and that her figure is split into two, but the standard form is that of the Lesser Sophia, who descends from the world of spirit and light into the sphere of matter, where she becomes besmirched and cannot rise. She is then raised by God or by a special emanation from Him (generally identified by the Christian Gnostics with Christ) and returns to her original place in heaven. The Lesser Sophia also received the name *Achamoth* "Wisdom," which identified her with the Canaanite-Hebrew hypostatized Wisdom. The latter first appears in a remarkable gnomic document which has been incorporated into the Book of Proverbs (chaps. 8-9), but

---

At an early opportunity the writer hopes to describe a number of unrecognized Babylonian elements in Mandaeanism, some of them very striking (the figure of Miryai, the Virgin Mary, has, for example, been assimilated to the Babylonian Sabitu-Sambethe). None of these pagan elements proves that the Mandaean system is particularly ancient: they only show that it has inherited much pagan material from earlier syncretistic sects.

which is now known to be of Canaanite origin, since it
swarms with words and expressions otherwise found only
in such Canaanite texts as the Ugaritic tablets and the
Phoenician inscriptions.[40] In this document, whose rich
pagan imagery offered no stumbling-block to orthodox Judaism, since it was interpreted quite symbolically, Wisdom
is called both *Hokhmah* and *Hakhamôth* (*Hokhmôth*), the
latter being a form of probable Phoenician origin. Wisdom
here appears as the first creation of Yahweh, who was emanated (lit. "poured out") by Him before the beginning of
creation;[41] she also appears as owning a temple with seven
pillars, the cosmic significance of which is clear.[42] The original Canaanite text of Prov. 8-9 can hardly be later than
the seventh century B.C., but the glorification of wisdom
has much earlier roots in Canaanite, since we read in the
epic of Baal from Ugarit (cir. 15th century B.C.): "And the
lady Asherah of the Sea (consort of El) answered, 'The
wise El has attributed to thee (O Baal) wisdom (*hkmt*),
together with eternity of life and good fortune.'"[43] In the
recently discovered Aramaic Proverbs of Akhiqar, from
about the sixth century B.C., we read: "(Wi)sdom is (from)
the gods, and to the gods is she precious; for(ever) her
kingdom is fixed in heav(en), for the lord of the holy ones
(i. e., the gods of heaven) hath raised her."[44] A Jewish
counterpart to this is found in Enoch 42:1-2 (second cen-

[40] See provisionally *Jour. Pal. Or. Soc.*, XIV (1934), p. 134,
n. 175.

[41] See *Am. Jour. Sem. Lang.*, XXXVI, p. 286.

[42] Cf. W. Staerk, *Zeits. Neutest. Wiss.*, XXXV (1936), pp.
234 ff.

[43] See the writer's translation and commentary, *Jour. Pal.
Or. Soc.*, XIV, p. 122. W. L. Knox's interesting treatment of
"The Divine Wisdom" (*Jour. Theol. Stud.*, 1937, pp. 230-37)
omits so much vital evidence that his chronology becomes entirely misleading and he actually dates the origin of the Jewish
figure of Wisdom in the third century B.C.

[44] *Am. Jour. Sem. Lang.*, XXXVI, p. 285. There can be no
doubt that Wisdom (*Hokhmethâ*) is referred to in the last part
of Pl. 44, line 16, as will be seen by comparing the traces
with the writing of the same word at the beginning of the
line; the letters [(w)H]kmth are very clear.

tury B.C.): "Since Wisdom found no place to dwell, she received an abode in heaven; when Wisdom came to dwell among men and found no abode, she returned to her place and dwelt among the angels." Ben Sira (early second century B.C.) makes Wisdom similarly say: "I came forth from the mouth of the Highest, and like vapor I have covered the earth; I have made my abode in the heights, and my throne on a pillar of cloud (24:3-4)." Here Wisdom is poetically likened to a breath issuing from the mouth of God and spreading until it penetrates into all recesses. In the Wisdom of Solomon (7:25) Wisdom is called "a breath of the power of God and an emanation (outflowing) of the pure effulgence of the Almighty." Finally in Philo Judaeus we find that Wisdom (Sophia or Episteme) was the first emanation of God, who created the world and became the mother of the Logos, remaining herself a virgin, since God does not generate in human fashion.

These passages, which may easily be increased in number, prove conclusively that the central concept and myth of the Lesser Sophia is of Canaanite-Aramaean origin, going back at least to the seventh century B.C. Sophia evidently replaces an older Canaanite goddess of wisdom, like the Mesopotamian Siduri Sabitu, who is called in a text of the late second millennium, "goddess of wisdom, genius of life," and who is undoubtedly the prototype of the sibyl Sambethe, later identified with the Lesser Sophia.[45] There is nothing essentially Hellenic about either the idea of pre-existence, which was characteristic of the gods in general, or the idea of emanation, since the latter is simply a euphemistic substitute for the basic idea of creation by sexual act. All figures of early Near-Eastern and Hellenic theogonies, both concrete deities and abstractions, were created by the outpouring of semen; and the concept was so simple and so capable of receiving philosophical interpretation that it was seized upon by the early Greek cos-

---

[45] See the writer's treatment of this material, *Am. Jour. Sem. Lang.*, XXXVI, pp. 260 ff., 287 ff., approved by Gressmann, *The Tower of Babel* (New York, 1928), pp. 29, 71 f., as well as in personal letters to the writer.

mologists, from Thales on. The idea of the descent of Wisdom to earth is probably connected with the myth of the descent of Ishtar or Anath to Hades, as clearly illustrated by later Gnostic mythology. The myth of her elevation to heaven is again transparently connected with that of the exaltation of Ishtar or Anath to be queen of heaven.[46] Gnostic thinkers had merely to identify the eternal Wisdom with the Iranian world of good and light, and with the Stoic divine fire and creative reason. Since the author of the Wisdom of Solomon already places God over against matter in essentially Gnostic fashion, and since he considers the body as the prison of the soul, which exists before and after life, it is safe to assume that the decisive step toward a Jewish Gnosis had already been taken in the first century B.C.[47] At all events, the elements were at hand, and by the

---

[46] Cf. the Sumerian poem celebrating the exaltation of Ishtar (Innini) which has been published by F. Thureau-Dangin, *Rev. Assyr.*, XI (1914), pp. 141-58. Both the descent and the exaltation of Ishtar are connected with the vicissitudes of the planet Venus.

[47] The problem of Judaeo-Gnosticism is exceptionally difficult, because orthodox Judaism consistently suppressed it and because the chronology of later Jewish works with Gnostic tendencies is extremely elusive. M. Friedländer (*Der vorchristliche jüdische Gnosticismus* [Göttingen, 1898], and subsequently) carried his conclusions so far that a reaction set in and respectable scholars stopped mentioning its possible existence (cf. Moore's *Judaism* [1927], and Bousset-Gressmann, *Die Religion des Judentums* [1926]). The soundest treatment of the subject by a friendly Jewish scholar up to recently was L. Blau's article, "Gnosticism," in the *Jewish Encyclopedia* (V, 1903, pp. 681-86). In recent years the situation has changed, owing to new materials and methods being employed by competent scholars. H. Odeberg's publication of "Third Enoch" (*The Hebrew Book of Enoch* [Cambridge, 1928]; cf. Lagrange's review, *Rev. Bib.*, 1930, pp. 452-55) has brought to light a Hebrew work with definitely Gnostic tendencies, dating from the second or third century A.D. This confirms the views of G. Scholem, the foremost living authority on the Qabbala, who has maintained a much higher antiquity for the principal ideas of the Zohar than hitherto supposed by critical students; cf. especially his article "Kabbala" in *Encyclopaedia Judaica*, IX (1932), pp. 630-732, and *Die Geheimnisse der*

middle of the first century A.D. they had already been fitted into the first known Gnostic system by Simon Magus. Since the latter was a younger contemporary of Philo but does not seem to have borrowed anything directly from him, we may safely suppose that both drew inspiration from a common proto-Gnostic background.

The concept of Sophia completely overshadowed that of the Logos in Jewish as well as in Gnostic thought. In early Christian thought the Logos displaced Sophia, as we know especially from the prologue to the Gospel of John. The Christian Logos concept has generally been considered to be specifically Greek, but a brilliant recent study by the Catholic theologian, L. Dürr (1938), has effectively demonstrated that it is really of Oriental origin.[48] The idea goes back to a dynamistic conception of the third millennium B.C. (see above, pp. 195 f.), which makes the voice of a god act as a distinct entity with power of its own. Sumerian and Canaanite texts show that the divine voice or command was concretely represented by the mighty sound of thunder. Later, in Egyptian, cuneiform, and biblical literature, we find many passages where the command of a god, the word issuing from his mouth, is virtually hypostatized. For example, in Deutero-Isaiah 40:8 we read, "But the word of our God will exist for ever." In the Wisdom of Solomon, some four centuries or more later, occurs the remarkable passage (18:15): "Thy almighty Word (Logos) sprang from heaven, from the royal throne, a stern warrior, into the land devoted to destruction, bearing Thy unchanging command as a sharp sword." As Dürr has shown, with a wealth of illustration, this idea is Semitic, not Hellenic; in the Proverbs of Akhiqar from Elephantine

---

Schöpfung (Berlin, 1935). In this connection it may be mentioned that Scholem has pointed out probable dependence of the palmistry of the Qabbala on lost cuneiform prototypes, in which the lines of the hand were compared to cuneiform characters. The earliest Jewish scholar with Gnostic tendencies who is mentioned in the Talmud is Johanan ben Zakkai, a contemporary of St. Paul and the first "Christian" Gnostic, Simon Magus.

[48] See Chap. III, n. 64.

(see above), the word of an earthly monarch is described
in terms which closely resemble the passage just quoted
from the Wisdom of Solomon: "Mild is the word (*millethâ*)
of a king, but sharper and more cutting than a two-edged
sword. . . . Gentle is the tongue of a king, yet it breaks
the ribs of a dragon (*tannîn*)."

In the Judaeo-Hellenistic literature outside of Philo there
is no clear evidence that the "Word" or "Command" of God
was substituted for the Divine Name. However, in the Targums there are numerous examples of this development,
which have recently been collected and critically discussed by G. F. Moore (1922) and by Strack-Billerbeck
(1924).[49] The term used is *mêmrâ* "word, command,"
which is frequently substituted for the name of God in passages which were considered as likely to be misinterpreted
and thus had to be protected against further misconstruc-
tion. In Deut. 3:22, for example, it is not God but his
Mêmrâ which fights for the Israelites (cf. also Ex. 3:12;
Gen. 21:20). In Deut. 4:24 it is not God Himself but His
Mêmrâ which is a consuming fire; in Deut. 9:3 His *Mêmrâ*
is a consuming fire which goes before Israel. In the light of
the entire rabbinic material, Moore was perfectly justified
in insisting that *Mêmrâ* is a "verbal buffer to keep God from
seeming to come to too close quarters with men and things."
However, in view of the extraordinarily close parallelism between such uses of *Mêmrâ* in the Targums and the examples
from Aramaic and Judaeo-Hellenistic literature which have
been cited above, it is perfectly clear that the targumic
Mêmrâ is simply a fossilized expression surviving from a
period when influential Jewish groups were engaged in
"building a fence" around the holiness of God, by substituting words denoting aspects or qualities of Him, such as
Divine Wisdom, the Divine Word, the Divine Presence

---

[49] See also the important study of V. Hamp, *Der Begriff
"Wort" in den aramäischen Bibelübersetzungen* (Munich,
1938). Hamp comes to the same conclusion as Moore after an
exhaustive analysis of the relevant targumic material; he also
goes a shade too far in treating *mêmrâ* as exclusively a "translation phenomenon"; cf. P. Benoit, *Rev. Bib.*, 1939, pp. 617 ff.

(*Panîm* in earlier times, *Yeqârâ* in later), for His Divine Name. It is still uncertain whether Philo's combination of Wisdom with the Logos by considering the latter as son of the former (in other passages this idea is variously modified) was original with him or was derived from older sources.

If the writer is correct in explaining the divine names of the Jewish pantheon at Elephantine in the fifth century B.C. as hypostatized aspects of Yahweh, we should have a paganizing prototype of Philonic hypostatic speculation, completely stripped of its philosophical trappings, at least a century before Alexander the Great.[50] According to this view, the three divine names *Eshem-bêth'el*, *Ḥerem-bêth'el*, *'Anath-bêth'el* (= *'Anath-Yahu*), meaning respectively "Name of the House of God" (= God), "Sacredness of the House of God," and "Sign(?)[51] of the House of God" would reflect pure hypostatizations of deity, probably influenced by contemporary Canaanite-Aramaean theological speculation, in which *Bêth'el* frequently appears as the name of a god (from the seventh to the fourth century B.C.).[52] However this may be, it is clear that pagan theological conceptions had entered into post-exilic Jewry through the circles to which these Jews belonged, and through heretical groups like the Phrygian Jews who identified Sabazius with Hebrew

---

[50] Cf. *Am. Jour. Sem. Lang.*, XLI (1925), pp. 92-98, 284; XLIII, pp. 233 ff. The usual view is that these figures are polytheistic borrowings from Aramaean paganism; see for elaborate discussion and full bibliographic references A. Vincent, *La religion des Judéo-Araméens d'Eléphantine* (Paris, 1937), pp. 562-680, and the observations of E. Dhorme, *Rev. Hist. Rel.*, CXVII, pp. 112 ff. (Dhorme misrepresents the writer's view rather drastically on p. 113.)

[51] See the writer, *Jour. Pal. Or. Soc.*, XII (1932), pp. 193 f. and n. 24; *Jewish Social Studies*, 1939, p. 128. In a very ancient psalm, Ps. 18:36 = II Sam. 22:36, we find the word *'anath* or *'anôth* used as a surrogate for *YHWH*. The Accadian *ettu* "sign," is the same word originally as Heb. *'eth* "sign, time"; for the Semitic cognates see the writer's discussion cited in n. 50.

[52] In addition to the material collected by Vincent see J. P. Hyatt, *Jour. Bib. Lit.*, 1937, pp. 387 ff.

Sebaoth.[53] Of course, all such divagations were vigorously repulsed by orthodox Judaism, but as in most such cases the very intensity of the reaction produced somewhat analogous phenomena in reverse. Just as the Church Fathers, from the second century A.D. on, found it increasingly necessary to employ Greek philosophical methods and terminology to explain their views to non-Christians as well as to defend them from heretics, so Jewish thinkers of the Hellenistic age were compelled to adapt the methods and the terminology of their pagan antagonists to their own purposes, both in order to combat the latter and in order to distinguish between orthodox Judaism and the vagaries of such groups as the Essenes and the Therapeutae. Moreover, the direct evidence of Jewish writings from the period 600-200 B.C. proves that pagan Phoenician literature was then exerting a very considerable direct and indirect influence on Jewish thought, and the evidence of the Elephantine Papyri and of Tobit demonstrates that pagan Aramaic literature also began to exercise similar influence after the sixth century B.C.

It is increasingly clear that indirect pagan influences entered mainly through the compositions of eschatologists, who swarmed in Jewry during the period which began with Daniel and Enoch and which ended with the Apocalypse and IV Esdras. The eschatologists were pneumatic souls who saw visions of the future while they were in ecstatic condition, and translated them into words with which they stirred men's imaginations and whipped them up to action. Without unfairly identifying the phenomena of ecstatic vision with ordinary dream-life, there can be no doubt that they both exhibit a divorce between conscious will and involuntary imagination, a separation which leads to unusual and often fantastic associations of ideas. At the same time, the spiritual exaltation of the visionary is undoubtedly transferred to his subconscious mental life, where it is translated into grandiose and often majestic imagery,

---

[53] For the latest discussion of the subject, with fairly adequate bibliography, see W. O. E. Oesterley, *The Labyrinth* (London, 1935), pp. 115-58.

drawn from many different sources and often quite desti-
tute of any logical connection, though all the more powerful in its emotional effect. In practice, conventional ideas
and patterns of imagery would prevent the visions of an
ecstatic from assuming the pathologically bizarre forms
illustrated by De Quincey and Baudelaire. Through the
eschatologists innumerable elements of pagan imagery and
even entire myths entered into the literature of Judaism and
Christianity, though it is safe to say that only an infinitesi-
mal amount of the original mass has actually survived, since
visionary excesses invariably repel sober scribes and theologians. The admission of Daniel and the Apocalypse to the
Christian canon has immeasurably enriched the affective
and aesthetic life of Christianity, without in the least demoralizing its theology (except in the case of certain
chiliastic sects).

Among the eschatological groups we may count the
enigmatic Essenes, who already formed a distinctive Jewish sect in the second century B.C. Since we possess none
of their writings but only descriptions of their tenets and
their organization given by Philo and Josephus (who had
spent some time with them in his youth), it is difficult to
place them in the religious history of the time. None of the
alleged Hellenistic elements of their system can stand serious criticism, in view of our lack of first-hand documentary
sources, since Philo and Josephus were both given to Hellenizing Jewish phenomena which they described. They
rejected marriage and lived in semi-monastic communities,
owning everything jointly. They also rejected bloody sacrifices, though they still revered the Torah and the Temple.
In place of the sacrificial system they introduced an elaborate system of sacramental meals and of lustration with
water. They further possessed an extensive esoteric literature, access to which was only allowed members of the
order. According to Josephus, they were interested in the
virtues of plants and stones, they possessed an elaborate
angelography, knowledge of which was incumbent upon
the neophyte, they were rigid predestinarians, and they attached great importance to the art of predicting the future,

in which they seldom made mistakes. The last three statements are particularly significant, since we can only infer from them that the Essenes, in opposition to virtually all pre-cabalistic Jews, were believers in astrology, which harmonized just as well with their strict predestinarianism as it did with the Stoic *heimarménê*. It is hardly likely that any extant Jewish esoteric works, from Enoch to the Qabbala, can be attributed to the Essenes, at least in their present form. It seems probable that the Essenes represent a sectarian Jewish group which had migrated from Mesopotamia to Palestine after the victory of the Maccabees.[54] This theory would explain their interest in the virtues of plants and stones (Berossus is said to have composed a treatise on the latter subject), their attention to divination and astrology, their frequent lustrations (hygienically necessary in Iraq, but not in Palestine), as well as their prayer to God for sunrise, performed daily before dawn, facing eastward, since all of these points were characteristic of Mesopotamian practice. Moreover, it is easier to explain their refusal to take part in sacrificial ritual if they had come from a region so far from Jerusalem that performance of sacrifices was physically impossible at the time when their beliefs were crystallized. The relatively great ceremonial significance of lustration with water in Mesopotamian ritual has been repeatedly emphasized; and it is now known that the Euphrates was the center of a cult of water traceable in the upper Euphrates Valley from about 2800 B.C. to the third century A.D., when we have a mosaic showing the river-god Euphrates with an accompanying bilingual caption in Greek and Syriac: "King (river) Euphrates." In the second century A.D. there was a Baptist sect of Gnostics whose cult of the living water of the Euphrates is thus illustrated by Hippolytus: "We are the chosen pneumatics from the living Euphrates which flows through the midst of Babylon"—"Mesopotamia is the stream of great Ocean flowing from the midst of the perfect man." As has been

[54] On the relative antiquity of Mesopotamian proto-Baptist ideas and practices see the writer, *Am. Jour. Sem. Lang.*, XXXVI (1920), p. 293 (cf. J. Thomas, *op. cit.*, pp. 307 f.).

shown by the writer, on the basis of Mesopotamian iconography (1919-24), the concept of the water of baptism
as "a fountain of water gushing forth to eternal life" (John
4:14), whose effect on the believer is such that "rivers of
living water shall flow from his belly" (John 7:38) is not
only genuinely Oriental but is specifically Mesopotamian
in origin.[55] It is significant that the second citation is
quoted by St. John from an otherwise unknown written
source, which at least proves that there was a proto-Baptist
literature which was definitely tinged with proto-Gnostic
ideas.

In this milieu John the Baptist must certainly be placed,
since he combined the zeal of an Israelite prophet with a
true soteriological passion for saving souls from the wrath
to come (Mat. 3:7), and since he united an unusually
pronounced asceticism with the practice of initiating converts into the kingdom of God by baptism in the Jordan.
Unfortunately, we know next to nothing of his own doctrine; and that of his alleged pupil and successor, Dositheus
of Samaria, is even more obscure, though Simon Magus is
said to have emerged from his school. Since John the Baptist was a prophetic evangelist who taught that repentance,
confession, and baptism must precede remission of sins, it
is most unlikely that John's system was itself proto-Gnostic.
However, it is generally recognized that John forms the
most important channel through which eschatological and
soteriological ideas and practices passed from Essene or
proto-Gnostic sources into Christianity. The speculations of
R. Reitzenstein with regard to the origin of Christian
baptism (1929) have been effectively refuted by H. H.
Schaeder and others,[56] and may now be considered as antiquated. The view that Christian baptism originated in the

[55] See the writer's discussion, *Harv. Theol. Rev.*, XVII
(1924), pp. 190 ff.— Contrast Torrey's interpretation, slightly
modified by de Zwaan, *Jour. Bib. Lit.*, LVII, pp. 165 f. Even
if they are correct in principle, the Greek of John reflects a
very early exegetical interpretation for which there is no Hebrew
scriptural warrant.

[56] See Schaeder, *Gnomon*, V (1929), pp. 353-70; J.
Thomas, *op. cit., passim* (especially pp. 415 ff.).

Jewish baptism of gentile proselytes, which is attested as early as the first century A.D. as shown by J. Jeremias (1929),[57] is possible, but it is perhaps more likely that both go back to a common source among the Essenes or a similar group.[58]

One of the most characteristic features of the eschatological pattern of this age is the doctrine of the divine Messiah who was to appear in human form and who was regularly entitled "the Son of Man." The latter feature of this belief has been referred by W. Bousset (1913), R. Reitzenstein (1921), and C. H. Kraeling (1927) to the Iranian myth of the archetype man, Gayomart, which undoubtedly did underlie some of the later Gnostic conceptions of the figure of Anthropos (Primal Man).[59] Not content with this hypothesis Mlle. Maryla Falk has recently (1937) tried to derive the complex Logos-Anthropos system (or rather its reconstructed form) from the Hindu figures of Purusha and Vac. Since both the systems which she compares must be reconstructed from disparate elements before they can be equated at all, and since the connecting links are missing, we can hardly treat her hypothesis seriously.[60]

Practically every detail of Jewish messianic expectation may be shown to be derived from the Old Testament, especially from Isaiah and Deutero-Isaiah. However, in the earliest apocalyptic literature, Dan. 7:9-14 and Enoch (*passim*), we encounter another belief: the Son of Man is represented as residing in heaven, where he was created by

[57] *Zeits. Neutest. Wiss.*, XXVIII (1929), pp. 312-20.

[58] On the ultimate origin of the idea see G. A. Barton, *Jour. Am. Or. Soc.*, LVI (1936), pp. 155-65. Barton's treatment is rather superficial and unnecessarily sensational in its statement, but may be partially correct; cf. the writer's observations, *Jour. Am. Or. Soc.*, XXXIX (1919), pp. 70 ff.; *Am. Jour. Sem. Lang.*, XXXV (1919), pp. 161-95; and especially *ibid.*, XXXVI, pp. 292 f.

[59] On this subject see C. H. Kraeling, *Anthropos and Son of Man* (*Columbia Univ. Orient. Stud.*, 25 [New York, 1927]).

[60] *Studi e Materiali di Storia delle Religioni*, XIII, pp. 166-214 (cf. the review by J. Przyluski in the *Polish Bulletin of Oriental Studies*, II [1939], pp. 7-12). In the work of this school chronology and documentation are of minor importance.

God before the creation of the world in order to appear as Messiah in the fulness of time. The ramifications of this Jewish belief in the preëxistence of the Messiah, traces of which survived into rabbinic times in the idea of the preexistence of the Messiah's *name*, have been discussed fully by W. Bousset, G. Dalman, and others, and need not concern us here. The meaning of the term "Son of Man" has been discussed so often in the past generation that all possibilities would seem to be exhausted. However, this is not quite true, since there is important cuneiform evidence which remains to be properly appraised, though attention has been called to it by H. Zimmern and other Assyriologists. We now have extensive remains of a Neo-Assyrian mythological epic which is generally called "Ea and Atrakhasis," the nature of which is elucidated by another Assyrian fragment and two long fragments in Old Babylonian, from the first quarter of the second millennium B.C.[61] These texts describe the beneficent intervention of Atrakhasis on behalf of mankind at least twice when it was threatened with complete destruction, once from a prolonged drought and once from the great Flood.[62] The standing appellation of Atrakhasis (lit. "the Very Wise One") in the Assyrian recension (seventh century B.C.) is "man" (*amêlu*). Similarly, in the Adapa myth, the hero is also called both "the Very Wise" (using the same expression) and "seed of mankind" (*zêr amêlûti*), i. e., "member of the human species." It is, in fact, very likely, though by no means certain, that *Adapa(d)* is the Sumerian name (meaning perhaps "chosen counsellor") of the figure which was commonly called *Atrakhasis*. Since Hebrew *ben 'adham* and Aramaic *bar nâshâ* both mean primarily "human being" in distinction to "man," as we know from a great

---

[61] On this material see Zimmern, *Zeits. f. Assyr.*, XIV (1899), pp. 277-92; S. H. Langdon, *The Sumerian Epic of Paradise, the Flood and the Fall of Man* (Philadelphia, 1915), pp. 24 ff.; E. Ebeling, *Tod und Leben nach den Vorstellungen der Babylonier* (Berlin, 1931), pp. 172 ff.

[62] A threefold destruction, once from pestilence, has often been assumed, but is not quite certain.

many occurrences and similar expressions in these languages, the expressions are all parallel. There are a number of points, into which we shall not enter here, which make it very probable that Atrakhasis, the recurrent Mesopotamian savior of mankind from catastrophe, son of the god Ea, yet explicitly called "man," was actually fused in Jewish-Aramaic tradition with the figure of the Messiah, as reconstructed from messianic prophecies in the Old Testament. On the basis of the attested Jewish belief and its probable prehistory it is, therefore, practically certain that Christian tradition was correct in recognizing the term "Son of Man" in the Gospels as explicitly stating the messianic rôle of Jesus.

D. JESUS THE CHRIST

1. *The Documentary Sources*

During the century that has elapsed since K. Lachmann made the revolutionary observation (1835) that the Gospel of Mark underlay both Matthew and Luke, New Testament scholars have labored very industriously to build up a logical system of historico-literary criticism, analogous to what was accomplished in the nineteenth century by Old Testament critics of the Pentateuch. By the World War there was general agreement with respect to two Gospel sources, Mark and Q, which included many sayings of Jesus found in both Matthew and Luke but not in Mark. Since Matthew and Luke often reproduce these sayings in the same order, Q was taken to be a real entity and not a hypothetical construction (see below). Beyond this point there was no agreement, and the residue of matter in Matthew and Luke which came neither from Mark nor from Q was sometimes explained in one way, sometimes in another. The Gospel of John was set apart from the Synoptic Gospels and was considered as much later in date. The usual chronological scheme was simple: Mark and Q were prior to the Fall of Jerusalem in 70 A.D.; Matthew and Luke were dated between 70 and 90 A.D.; John was

placed between 90 and 120 A.D. The radical members of
the Tübingen and the Dutch school thought that John was
even posterior to 150 A.D., but they had very few adherents in this extreme position. To maintain it they were
forced to perform the most remarkable somersaults in dealing with early Christian tradition and literature.

In 1919 M. Dibelius, followed closely by R. Bultmann
and others, introduced the new method of *Formgeschichte*,
usually called "form-criticism" in English. This may be defined as an effort to get behind the documents (Mark, Q,
etc.) to the oral sources, especially by grouping the latter
according to their form and their literary character, but
also by analyzing their "Sitz im Leben," i. e., the situation
in which they arose or through which they were modified.
Dibelius was at first strongly influenced by E. Norden, H.
Gunkel and others, but since material for the analysis of
form was too often lacking, he and his successors have
pushed their research out in increasingly subjective directions. As we have already pointed out with emphasis (see
above, pp. 70 f.), the principle of aetiology must be used
with great caution in fixing the historical content of oral
tradition, since it works both ways, i. e., aetiological explanations originate as a necessary didactic aid to memory and
the reversal of the process is a strictly secondary phenomenon. Moreover, Dibelius and Bultmann, together with
their followers, endeavor first to reconstruct the life of the
earliest Church, the methods of preaching and evangelizing
which it employed, and the development of Christian doctrine, after which they determine the hypothetical "Sitz im
Leben" of a given verse or passage, in order to judge its
historical value—or more usually to reconstruct its evolution as a literary entity. As E. Fascher has pointed out, the
leading exponents of the school disagree completely in their
theories as to the relation of the principal categories of
form-criticism to the life of the early Church, and vicious
circles are evident throughout their work.[63] The method
employed by form-critics is essentially an application of the

[63] E. Fascher, *Die formgeschichtliche Methode* (*Beih. Zeits.
Neutest. Wiss.*, No. 2 [Berlin, 1924]), especially pp. 156 ff.

"logico-meaningful" principle of Sorokin (see above, pp. 105 ff.), which is only a prolix statement of the familiar adage, "The proof of the pudding is the eating thereof." In practice it becomes a complex case of the logical fallacy known as *argumentum in circulo*, except where it can be controlled by entirely independent outside facts. In New Testament studies such outside facts are seldom available and many of those which have at one time or another been thought to exist, have been disproved by the progress of archaeological and papyrological research. From the standpoint of the objective historian data cannot be disproved by criticism of the accidental literary framework in which they occur, unless there are solid independent reasons for rejecting the historicity of an appreciable number of other data found in the same framework.

However, form-criticism has yielded some very valuable results, first by classifying the material found in the Synoptic Gospels under such heads as apothegm-stories (sayings of Jesus for which the rest of a narrative serves as a framework), miracle-stories, parables, and various types of *logia* (sayings), and secondly by pointing out a number of blocks of material which may be traced directly back to Jesus in their present form (e. g., Mat. 5:17-48; Mat. 6:25-32; Luke 6:27-38). A number of scholars, notably C. F. Burney and B. S. Easton, have discovered striking phenomena characteristic of Hebrew and Aramaic verse in some of these blocks, and have thus enhanced the probability that we are dealing with original matter.[64]

The next important recent advance in uncovering the sources of the Gospels has been made by C. C. Torrey, who published his first study, *The Translations Made from the Original Aramaic Gospels*, in 1912 and has recently followed it with two works (*The Four Gospels*, 1933; *Our Translated Gospels*, 1936), in which he has collected the results of a generation of work on the Aramaic sources of the four Gospels. In these and other studies along the same line Torrey undertakes to demonstrate that the whole of

[64] Cf. E. B. Redlich, *Form Criticism* (London, 1939), pp. 42-48.

Mark and Matthew, most of Luke, and the entire Gospel
of John were written in Aramaic, from which they were
translated into Greek. This sensational conclusion he
reaches by marshalling an impressive list of awkward translations from Aramaic into Greek, together with reproduction in Greek of syntactic and idiomatic peculiarities of the
supposed Aramaic original, as well as direct errors and mis-
interpretations. Torrey concludes that all the Gospels were
written before 70 A.D. and that there is nothing in them
which could not have been written within twenty years of
the Crucifixion. It is difficult to imagine a more complete
volte-face than would be necessary for New Testament
criticism if Torrey's views were proved correct. He has consequently been attacked with the greatest vigor by many
New Testament scholars, led by E. J. Goodspeed and D.
W. Riddle. Other scholars, few of whom are specialists in
the New Testament, have rallied to his support, but the
majority remains on the side-lines, equally awed by Torrey's
learning and impressed by the authority of his antagonists.[65] The present writer holds an intermediate position,
as will become evident in the following brief discussion.

To begin with, there can be no doubt whatever, in spite
of various innuendoes, that Torrey is thoroughly competent
as an Aramaic scholar and that he is at home in all the
Aramaic dialects of importance for this type of research.
Quite aside from his personal record as an Aramaic philologian is the endorsement of his competence by such authorities as T. Nöldeke and E. Littmann.[66] Moreover, it
must be said emphatically that his basic method is sound:
first, the analysis of types of translation Greek and the systematic comparison of them with standard Greek prose of
the Hellenistic period; secondly, an exhaustive search for
phenomena in the Greek of the Gospels which are hard to

---

[65] Cf. Ralph Marcus, *Harv. Theol. Rev.*, XXVII (1934), pp.
211-39 (and Torrey's reply, *Jour. Bib. Lit.*, LIV [1935], pp. 17-
28); J. de Zwaan, *Jour. Bib. Lit.*, LVII (1938), pp. 155-71;
and against Torrey cf. D. W. Riddle, *Jour. Bib. Lit.*, LIV,
pp. 127-38.

[66] See *Zeits. Neutest. Wiss.*, XXXIV (1935), pp. 20-34.

explain except as evidence of translation from Aramaic. Every philologist who is familiar with languages can immediately detect the original tongue from which a given translation was made, if he knows both the original language and the one into which the translation was made. There are many amusing and instructive illustrations of linguistic phenomena peculiar to translations. Judged by the severest standards, it must be said that Torrey has proved a respectable proportion of his examples. On the other hand, there are difficulties which Torrey has not surmounted. There is no literary Greek of precisely comparable type, since the *Koinê,* or vulgar Greek of the time, was not used for literary purposes and the examples from contemporary papyri, though extremely valuable for grammar and vocabulary, are yet very different in subject, style, and atmosphere, as pointed out effectively by A. D. Nock, who writes (1933): "Any man who knows his classical Greek authors and reads the New Testament and then looks into the papyri is astonished at the similarities which he finds. Any man who knows the papyri first and then turns to Paul is astonished at the differences. There has been much exaggeration of the Koine element in the New Testament."[67] Much more serious than the lack of comparable Greek is the absence of any satisfactory examples of Palestinian Aramaic from the period 50 B.C.-70 A.D., aside from over two hundred inscriptions, the majority of which consist only of one or two names each.[68] The inscriptions prove, moreover, that the Jewish Aramaic of the first century A.D. was different in detail from the official Aramaic of the Persian Empire (which continued in use for a century or two after Alexander as a literary tongue), from the contemporary Aramaic of the Nabataean and Palmyrene inscriptions (which was much like the literary Aramaic of the Persian period), from the Mesopotamian Aramaic of the Peshitta, from the Jewish Aramaic of the Targums and the Jerusalem Talmud (which belongs mainly to the period

[67] *Jour. Bib. Lit.,* LII, p. 138.
[68] For a sketch of this material see the writer, *Jour. Bib. Lit.,* LVI, pp. 157 ff.

300-600 A.D., as we know from contemporary synagogal inscriptions), and from Christian Palestinian Aramaic (which seems to belong to the seventh century A.D. and later).[69] To be sure, there were many elements common to all these dialects, and a trained linguist is generally safe in inferring the existence of a word or a form at a given period from earlier and later occurrences of it. In addition to these linguistic sources of error is the fact that Torrey, Burney, and others often base their theories on arbitrary judgments as to what the original text should have said. Moreover, Torrey neglects many of the assured as well as the probable results of New Testament criticism, both textual and literary—and no amount of clever improvisation can replace sound philological method.

The present writer believes that Torrey has demonstrated the existence of a much more important and much more far-reaching Aramaic substratum of our Greek Gospels than had been believed previously by any first-class scholar. On the other hand, not a single case of alleged scribal error adduced by Torrey is convincing. The most plausible examples can just as well be explained as failure to hear correctly or to understand the precise sense of a recited Aramaic word or form. For instance, it would be a simple matter for a listener to confuse the passive plural participle 'Abhîdhîn "(they) are done," with the active 'âbhedhîn "(they) are doing," since the accent was on the last syllable in both cases. In other words, the Aramaic substratum may be entirely, or almost wholly, oral. The significance of this observation appears from the demonstrated fact that the teachings of contemporary Jewish scholars were handed down mainly by tradition. It has already been emphasized

[69] A good illustration of the situation is provided by the "Uzziah" inscription, discovered and published by E. L. Sukenik; cf. the writer's observations, *Bull. Am. Sch. Or. Res.*, No. 44 (1931), pp. 8 ff. When the inscription was first examined, there were two words in it which defied Jewish scholars: the second, which is found in Biblical Aramaic but not in Jewish Aramaic; the third, which is not known from any Jewish Aramaic dialect but appears in Samaritan. Two such words out of eight is a rather high proportion!

(see above, pp. 64 ff.) that oral composition and transmission of literature played a far greater rôle in antiquity than is generally supposed. As is well known, even Graeco-Roman writers generally composed and polished their work orally before reducing it to writing. This had always been the custom and writing materials were too expensive to be wasted on tentative efforts. Even today the old-fashioned Jewish or Moslem scholar never dreams of looking up passages in the Bible, Talmud, or Qur'an, but depends on his memory for citations. It follows that we should not expect to find the words and acts of Jesus put into writing until the expansion of missionary activity, the flood of new gentile converts, and the menace of heretical teachings made it practically impossible to continue without written documentation.

J. Jeremias has recently (1930) pointed out, following T. Soiron, that the sayings of Jesus common to both Matthew and Luke are not only often arranged according to a common word or idea, which serves as a connecting link, but often differ in their order because of the selection of different words or ideas to serve as a bond.[70] He has correctly observed that this phenomenon is so characteristic of oral transmission, which is accustomed to utilize similar mnemotechnic devices, that one can only conclude that the first and third Gospels drew their "Q" matter from related oral sources. The efforts so far made to weaken the force of this argument are extremely feeble, and the observation must stand. However, Jeremias goes unnecessarily far in using it to prove that the supposed source Q never existed. We must rather admit the existence of oral collections of material, which assumed slightly differing forms as they were circulated among early Christian communities. With our present evidence it seems rather hopeless to try to reconstruct the exact development of the Synoptic Gospels from the Aramaic form in which substantially all of the pericopes and categories which have been isolated by form-critics must once have circulated, to the final form which

---

[70] *Zeits. Neutest. Wiss.*, XXIX, pp. 147 ff.

they assumed not later than about 80 A.D. All we can say is that a period of between twenty and fifty years is too slight to permit of any appreciable corruption of the essential content and even of the specific wording of the sayings of Jesus. When we compare this interval with the centuries of oral transmission between Moses and the reduction of JEP to writing, or between Zoroaster and the final codification of the Avesta under the Sassanian kings, or between Rabbi Aqiba, for example, and the writing down of the traditions which circulated about him, it hardly seems possible that there was any serious modification of the historical tradition. We have mentioned the case of Rabbi Aqiba because of the reconstruction of his career published by L. Finkelstein in 1936, an account which is almost entirely based on Jewish tradition, some of it not put into writing for at least four centuries after his death. Of course, Finkelstein's portrait is not necessarily correct in detail, but it is very interesting to see that a satisfying reconstruction can be presented on the basis of such data. The characteristics of oral transmission which we have repeatedly emphasized above appear clearly in the Synoptic Gospels: tradition has exercised its selective and refining influence, eliminating sayings and stories which did not suit the idea of Christ which the early Christians acquired from the mass of first-hand tradition about Him as well as from their vital religious experience of conversion through faith in Him. In some respects tradition may have idealized; in other respects it just as certainly failed to grasp the true stature of Jesus. The beneficial effect of oral transmission more than outweighs the slight historical loss through refraction, combination, and formation of doublets. However, only modern scholars who lack both historical method and perspective can spin such a web of speculation as that with which form-critics have surrounded the Gospel tradition. The sureness with which early Christian leaders distinguished between normative and aberrant sayings of Jesus becomes very clear when we analyze the so-called *agrapha,* or apocryphal *logia,* collected from extant and from recently excavated documents. The *agrapha* generally express Gnostic or anti-

nomian ideas which are foreign to the Gospels (for an illustration cf. above, p. 137).[71]

The Book of John stands apart from the Synoptic Gospels,
as recognized since the time of Origen (third century A.D.).
In view of the extremely late date to which it has often
been assigned, Torrey's demonstration that it rests on an
Aramaic substratum has been peculiarly resented by many
New Testament scholars, though it has been enthusiasti-
cally accepted in principle by men of the standing of J. de
Zwaan (1938).[72] Meanwhile the sensational publication of
a fragment of the Gospel from the early second century
(C. H. Roberts, 1935) and of a roughly contemporary fragment of an apocryphal gospel dependent on John (H. I.
Bell, 1935) has dealt the *coup de grâce* to all radically late
dating of John and has proved that the Gospel cannot be
later than the first century A.D. There can be no doubt that
John is the latest of the Gospels, but it is hard to accept
the usual critical view that it mainly reproduces ideas of
its author and cannot claim to reflect the thought of Jesus.
As has been repeatedly stressed in recent years, the personal allusions in the Book are so intimate and express so
sensitive and delicate a spirit on the part of the author that
pious fiction is psychologically almost unthinkable. At this
period we cannot, it is true, urge the relatively complete
absence of pious fraud from contemporary literature as an
argument for authenticity (see above, pp. 44 ff.), but we
can effectively stress the psychological argument, as emphasized by F. Torm (1913) and others.[73] Moreover, the objections to the authenticity of the Book because of its
alleged ignorance of history and geography have been con-

---

[71] Cf. the striking parallel demonstration of J. Fück, who
deals with the Islamic *ḥadîth* (*Zeits. Deutsch. Morg. Ges.*, XCIII
[1939], pp. 1-32); cf. above, Chap. IV, n. 81.

[72] Cf. above, n. 65.

[73] *Zeits. Neutest. Wiss.*, XXX (1931), pp. 124-44. In this
connection attention may be called to the admirable brief statement of the question and equally sympathetic resolution of it
by J. A. Montgomery, *The Origin of the Gospel according to
St. John* (Philadelphia, 1923).

siderably reduced in recent years.[74] One cannot, of course, place John on the same level with the Synoptic Gospels as a historical source, but one is quite justified in maintaining that it does reflect a side of Jesus which was too mystical for the ordinary man of that day to understand and which He presumably held in reserve for a few intimates. The authors of Hebrews (5:12 f.) and I Peter (2:2) recognized the difference between teachings suitable for neophytes and for advanced disciples, and St. Paul takes this point repeatedly for granted. It would be rather strange, to say the least, if the apostolic recognition of the difference between simple teachings which could be understood by all and more profound intellectual or mystic doctrines which could only be understood by a limited number did not go back to the example of Jesus Himself. That the Apostles actually followed His example is proved by the references to Jesus' messianic secret in the Synoptic Gospels. The advanced teachings of Jesus as transmitted by the Gospel of John contain nothing that can be reasonably adduced as evidence of late origin. The slight dualistic element was already present in Judaeo-Hellenistic literature as a legacy from Iranian religion. The so-called Gnostic elements have little in common with later Gnosticism and are rather proto-Gnostic; they consist mainly in a revival of dynamistic concepts and metaphors, such as identification of Jesus' person with abstractions (the way, the truth, and the life) and with concrete entities (light, bread, vine). Since these ideas strike deep into the psychic inheritance of mankind, and since they do not form the basis of any mythology, as with the Gnostics, their tremendous affective and emotional value is evident, and has been demonstrated by two millennia of Christian believers and mystics. Practically every motif in the Gospel of John can be paralleled in the Synoptic Gospels; it is only the rich accumulation and development of ideas which is different.

In dealing with the Gospels the historian cannot but see

[74] Cf. the writer, *Harv. Theol. Rev.*, XVII (1924), pp. 193 ff.; M. J. Lagrange, *Rev. Bib.*, 1937, pp. 321-41; and contrast C. C. McCown, *Jour. Bib. Lit.*, LIX (1940), p. 120, n. 10.

a profound difference between their contents and typical examples elsewhere of matter which has been long transmitted by oral tradition. What we have in them is rather a reflection of reports of eye-witnesses who were overwhelmed by the profound experiences and the extreme tension of mind and body through which they had passed. Men who see the boundary between conventional experience and the transcendental world dissolving before their very eyes are not going to distinguish clearly between things seen in the plane of nature and things seen in the world of spirit. To speak of the latter as "hallucinations" is quite misleading, since nothing like them is otherwise known either to historians or to psychologists. Here the historian has no right to deny what he cannot disprove. He has a perfect right to unveil clear examples of charlatanry, of credulity, or of folklore, but in the presence of authentic mysteries his duty is to stop and not attempt to cross the threshold into a world where he has no right of citizenship.

2. The Religion of Jesus

During the past thirty years the work of C. Montefiore, I. Abrahams, J. Klausner, L. Finkelstein, and other Jewish scholars, ably seconded by such Christian specialists as H. L. Strack and P. Billerbeck, P. Fiebig, J. Jeremias, R. T. Herford, G. F. Moore, H. Danby, has succeeded in revolutionizing our conception of the character and the development of the Pharisaic movement. It is true that most of these scholars represent the Pharisees of the time of Christ as prototypes of the rabbis of the second century A.D., thus failing to allow for such factors as a pronounced change in the relative place allowed to eschatology by the Pharisees. It is probable that the first-hand epistles of St. Paul present a more accurate reflection of certain aspects of the Hillelite school in which Paul was educated than do the tannaitic traditions of the second century A.D.[75] Yet we may

[75] It is often assumed or deduced that Paul had not been trained in Jewish law "at the feet of Gamaliel," or at least not for long (cf., e. g., A. D. Nock, St. Paul [1938], pp. 27-33). On

whole-heartedly accept the rehabilitation of the Pharisees, who were God-fearing men with views which closely approximated standard Christian theological positions with respect to the attributes of God, the question of predestination and free will, and the problem of the after-life. On the other hand, the Pharisees were rigorous legalists and their great aim was to perpetuate the Jewish Torah in the purest possible form, in order to maintain Israel's privileged place as the chosen people of God. This aim was in itself a noble one and it has proved astonishingly successful in keeping Judaism and the Jewish people intact until our day, in which they are making contributions to Western civilization which would not have been possible if they had been assimilated into the gentile world many centuries ago. For this great achievement we may thank the Pharisees without reservation.[76]

But the teaching of the Pharisees was not at all suited to become the vehicle of a great evangelistic movement, which was to embrace all mankind in its parish and was to transform Jewish doctrines of man's relation to God into a new religion of incomparable vitality. So reaction against the Pharisees had to come. With Jesus this reaction assumed the only form it could effectively take, that of a sweeping religious reformation, in some respects following the lines of the prophetic movement some nine centuries previously, in some ways prefiguring the Franciscan movement of the thirteenth century and in other ways the Wesleyan revival of the eighteenth. Again and again Jesus insisted that He

---

the other hand, J. Klausner, From Jesus to Paul (Hebrew; Tel-Aviv, 1939-40), II, pp. 9-12 and passim, protests vigorously against the views of Grätz and other Jewish and Christian scholars who insist that Paul was only an "'am ha'ares," a man ignorant of Jewish law. On the resemblance between Pauline and rabbinic methods of exegesis see P. Bonsirven, Exégèse rabbinique et exégèse paulinienne (Paris, 1939), who devotes more than 400 pages to a careful analysis of the question (cf. the review by P. Benoit, Rev. Bib., 1940, pp. 288 ff.).

[76] To this extent the writer agrees with the interesting remarks of J. Klausner at the end of Vol. II of the work cited above.

came to fulfil the Torah and the Prophets, not to destroy them. In order to fulfil them, however, He rejected the increasing mass of secondary regulations and restrictions, to some extent following precedents set by the Samaritans, the Sadducees, and the Essenes, but adopting a consistently spiritual attitude to ritual which was foreign to any of these groups. His hostility to the Pharisees as a body was based mainly on His profound sympathy for the poor and suffering, to whom the Pharisees as a group showed charity but scant sympathy, feeling in typically puritanic fashion that their misery must somehow be the result of sin. Jesus' attitude toward the "under-privileged" was in no sense comparable to that of modern exponents of the "social gospel," and it was still less like that of Marxian socialists. He fully recognized the close relation between sin (i. e., violation of natural and moral law) and suffering, but to Him suffering was not only the normal divine punishment of sin but a potent requisite for salvation, putting the unhappy and disoriented soul into a state of receptivity to Divine grace. Suffering was thus a blessing, or it was at least capable of yielding a blessing to the receptive sufferer. Through Jesus' exaltation of suffering the old problem of theodicy received a powerful new solution, one which had been at best only adumbrated in the Old Testament and which seems to have been quite foreign to Greek thought. This exaltation of the value of suffering had no ultra-ascetic nor encratic aspect, since Jesus did everything possible to alleviate the suffering of others, at the same time that He showed His own willingness to eat and drink with friends and hosts. In this respect as in others, we can only admire the exquisite balance of Jesus' ethical teachings and the success with which He could state them so dramatically and categorically that none could miss their meaning, yet without failing to correct over-emphasis whenever it became necessary. In the fine balance and the universality of His ethics we may detect Hellenistic influence (see below).   4

It cannot be emphasized too strongly that the true greatness of Jesus' ministry does not lie in His ethical teachings. The ethics of Jesus agree strikingly, if compared in detail, with contemporary Jewish ethical teaching, as may be seen by reading the exhaustive collection of early rabbinic parallels given by Strack and Billerbeck. Moreover, even the Golden Rule, which is nowhere adequately stated in rabbinic sources, has an excellent Assyrian parallel from the seventh century B.C. (at the latest): "As for him who doeth evil to thee, requite him with good";[77] the connecting link is perhaps furnished in part by several passages in Judaeo-Hellenistic literature. It is, however, true that in no pre-Christian or Jewish source do we find the same accumulation of lofty ethical injunctions in brief compass. Nor do we find elsewhere that astonishing balance with regard to fundamentally non-religious and societal questions such as the relation of master and servant, of state and subject, and such as the place for resistance and non-resistance, etc. Jesus has been turned into a social revolutionary, a pacifist, a prohibitionist, a royalist, a republican, a Y.M.C.A. secretary, an anti-Semite, but every effort of this kind has been accompanied by flagrant disregard of the material as a whole. On the other hand his ethico-religious doctrine has been considered by Christian theologians as too exacting for normal human life and has accordingly been labelled "interim ethics," i. e., ethics to be practiced only during the brief period of waiting for the end of the world and the last judgment. This view seems to be correct so far as expectation of the imminent end of the world is concerned (see below), but since Jesus is never represented as basing His ethical code on the nearness of the last judgment, it is far more reasonable to assume that He meant people to live on just as high a moral plane as they would if the end were expected at any moment. That this interpretation is correct would follow logically if one of the Oxyrhynchus logia which makes Him bid His disciples live as though every day were Sabbath, is authentic. Lofty as the ethical teachings of Jesus are, they might not be considered quite so impossible to carry out in life if would-be followers were

[77] S. H. Langdon, *Babylonian Wisdom* (London, 1923), p. 90, line 6.

not inclined to make their own eclectic selection and exegesis of injunctions to be followed.

The idea of God in the Gospels is no longer restricted to the lofty, but rarified ethical monotheism of Deutero-Isaiah. A nearly complete cycle separated the beginnings of Israel from the beginnings of Christianity, and the anthropomorphic concept of God in early Israel returned at the end of this cycle to the center of our field of vision—but the human form and emotions of Yahweh had become spiritualized in the process. God still loves and hates in the New Testament, but His love has far wider and deeper connotations. There is still only one God, as in Israel, but the acute danger of polytheism is over and He appears in three complementary hypostases. In one hypostasis He has drawn even closer to man than Yahweh could in earliest Israel, when He was still father and brother and kindred to His own (see above, p. 246). In another hypostasis He is the one eternal Creator and Lord of the universe, as He was to Deutero-Isaiah. In still another He is the Holy Spirit, alternately conceived as the Divine Wisdom or as the Paraclete. It should hardly be necessary to add that the trinitarian idea of God has immeasurably enriched the concept of monotheism, without in the least detracting from its unified character.

Even though we deny the substantial influence of Hellenism on Jesus' idea of God and admit it only in the Patristic Age, we cannot fail to recognize the profound effect of Hellenism in the formation of Jesus' other religious ideas. In them there is a fine Hellenic sense of balance and of proportion which are foreign to contemporary Judaism. Even in reacting against the exaggerated emphasis laid by the Pharisees on the Torah and against their essentially Hellenistic dialectic (see above), Jesus replaced this form of Hellenism with a far wider and deeper one: Hellenistic universalism and philanthropy, which underlie the whole subsequent history of Christianity.[78] It has often been stressed

[78] Cf. H. Preisker, *Arch. Rel.*, XXXV (1938), pp. 93-114. The Pharisees had, however, begun the movement toward Hellenistic universalism which reached its culmination with

of late that He was born and reared in a land (Galilee) where Jews, Syro-Phoenicians, and Greeks rubbed shoulder to shoulder, and where cosmopolitan influences were stronger than anywhere else in Jewish Palestine.

Vital to all understanding of the teachings of Jesus, as well as of the faith of the earliest Church, is the problem of His messianic consciousness and eschatological doctrine. This important question has been brought into the foreground of discussion again after several generations during which theologians and New Testament scholars did their best to evade it or to maintain that Jesus was either not conscious of being the Messiah or first reached this conclusion toward the end of His ministry. The messianic framework of the Gospels was regarded by most up-to-date scholars as quite a secondary thing, imported into the primitive Church long after the Crucifixion. However, increased realization of the antiquity and the inescapably messianic connotation of the expression "Son of Man" (see above) has of late brought increasing recognition that Jesus' messianic consciousness was the central fact of His life. No treatment of the subject which tries to evade or to deny this fact can hope to do justice to it. Jesus was the spiritual heir of a long line of Jewish eschatologists (see above), who had developed an elaborate doctrine, part of which is clearly documented in the Gospels. The messianic framework of the Gospels cannot, indeed, be proved to reflect the beliefs of Jesus throughout, but its central features clearly antedate the Crucifixion. And these central features are the belief that the Messiah is both Son of Man and Son of God (created according to Enoch before the beginning of the creation of the world), and that He is to suffer abasement and eventual death at the hands of His own people, for whom He will shed His blood as a vicarious and expiatory sacrifice.

It is true that most New Testament scholars have tried to date the introduction of these basic features of Christol-

---

Jesus and Paul; cf. above, n. 24. On the relation between Jesus and the Pharisees see also S. Zeitlin, *Essays and Studies in Memory of Linda R. Miller* (New York, 1938), pp. 235-86.

ogy (i. e., messianic doctrine, since Greek *christos* is simply
a literal translation of Hebrew *mashîah*) to the Apostolic
Age, between 30 and 50 A.D. or even later. Against this,
however, is the whole weight of early Christian literature,
combined with the difficulty of positing a situation where
the scattered and often opposed groups of apostolic Christians could agree on such startling innovations. Paul and
Peter fought bitterly over the question of the extension of
ancient Jewish ritual to gentile converts; they would certainly have fought much more bitterly over any supposed
innovations with respect to the person of their Lord. This
dilemma has been felt by the exponents of the "Christ-
myth" hypothesis, notably by its most recent advocate, P.
L. Couchoud, whose historical extravagances would otherwise merit no attention whatever. To this school there never
was a historical Jesus but only a savior-god, Christ the Lord,
who was originally worshipped by a pre-Christian sect resembling the Roman mystery-religions. Opponents of this
school have no trouble in pointing out the total lack of any
real parallel for such a sect or for its alleged teachings—
quite aside from the incredible hypothesis that there is no
historical basis for the Gospels or for the teaching of St.
Paul. It is historically dangerous to adduce parallels from
Gnosticism in its manifold forms, from Mithraism, from
Isiac, Neo-Pythagorean, and Hermetic systems, or from Ap-
ollonius of Tyana, since most of these parallels cannot
be shown to antedate the second or even the third century
A.D. The first known Gnostic, Simon Magus, was for a time
in intimate contact with Christianity (see above). All that
can be proved from a detailed study of the mystery-religions of the Roman Empire is that there was widespread
spiritual discontent and deep-seated yearning for salvation
in the first century A.D.,[79] and that St. Paul seems to have
adopted a number of expressions and points of view which
had originated with adepts of the mysteries.[80]

---

[79] See A. D. Nock, *Conversion* (Oxford, 1933).

[80] For the most exhaustive and also the most extreme statement of the theory of Pauline dependence on Hellenistic
mystery-cults see R. Reitzenstein, *Die hellenistischen Mysterien-*

On the other hand there are many striking parallels with more ancient Near-Eastern religious ideas, such as the virgin-birth of a god, his astral associations, birth among cattle, imprisonment, death, descent to the underworld, disappearance for three days, resurrection, exaltation to heaven, etc.[81] It is true that some of these parallels can be shown at once to be probably secondary: e. g., there is no mention of the descent to the underworld in the Gospels (though it already appears in I Peter 3:19) and the three-day interval in the tomb is actually reckoned as two. However, a sufficient number of direct parallels remain to indicate a relationship of some kind. What that relationship may have been, we cannot determine by historical methods, but a reasonable explanation for part of it is at hand, though

---

religionen, ihre Grundgedanken und Wirkungen (third ed.; Leipzig, 1927). For a much more sober verdict by a first-class scholar see A. D. Nock, *St. Paul* (London, 1938; it is characteristic that the word "mystery" does not appear in his index), especially pp. 77 ff.

[81] The most thorough and critical treatment of these matters remains that of C. Clemen, *Religionsgeschichtliche Erklärung des Neuen Testaments* (Giessen, 1934), pp. 62 ff., 192 ff. There is, of course, a vast literature on the subject including, on the liberal side, the works of A. Loisy (e. g., *Histoire et mythe à propos de Jesus-Christ* [Paris, 1938]) and, on the conservative side, the voluminous writings of M. J. Lagrange. New material from the ancient Near East continues to make its appearance. On the "virginity" of the Canaanite deities Anath and Astarte see especially the writer, *Jour. Pal. Or. Soc.*, XII (1932), p. 193; on the probable "virginity" of the mother of Tammuz, Zertur-Siduri, see *Am. Jour. Sem. Lang.*, XXXVI, p. 262. For the three days spent by a god of fertility in the underworld see *Jour. Am. Or. Soc.*, XXXIX, pp. 89 f., where the lunar and agricultural basis of the number is shown. S. Kramer has just discovered and translated a new fragment of the Sumerian original of the Descent of Ishtar in which the goddess Innini is explicitly said to remain three days and three nights in the underworld (*Bull. Am. Sch. Or. Res.*, No. 79, Oct., 1940). It must be remembered that the three days spent by Christ in Hades is a *theologumenon* from the Old Testament and does not correspond to the chronology of the Gospels, where a day and two nights seem to elapse between the crucifixion and the resurrection.

it must remain theoretical. We have in the Gospels a great many allusions to messianic predictions in the Old Testament. Rendel Harris and others have suggested that the first written document of Christianity consisted of a collection of these messianic passages, in the form of "Testimonies." However this may be, there can be no doubt whatever that Jewish eschatologists of the last two pre-Christian centuries had combed the Old Testament for messianic prophecies, and every messianic detail in the New Testament has its correspondence somewhere in the Old. With these texts from the Old Testament they combined (as in Enoch and later apocalypses) miscellaneous matter drawn from apocalyptic visions which were considered authoritative. As we have indicated above (pp. 374 f.), examination of Jewish eschatological literature discloses many reminiscences of pagan Near-Eastern literature through which apocalyptic imagery was greatly embellished and as a result of which Christian affective and mystic life has been immensely enriched. It is, we maintain, through the channel of Jewish eschatological literature, most of which has inevitably perished, that the field of messianic prophecy was extended to cover many verses which were not recognized as properly messianic by orthodox Jewish tradition. This principle would both explain how many passages of the Old Testament which have no original messianic application were so interpreted and how the messianic framework of the Gospels came to bear such a striking, though quite superficial, resemblance in details to the corresponding framework of the cycles of Tammuz, Adonis, Attis, Osiris, etc. The affective religious value to early Christianity of these superficial resemblances must have been very great, since the cycles to which we have referred had been gradually put into extraordinarily effective dramatic forms, all essentially alike in principle (see above, pp. 193 f.). The underlying dramatic forms which had swayed the religious emotions and impulses of the Near East for three millennia made the same psychological appeal to the multitudes of the first century A.D. as they had to their forefathers—and they still exert as powerful an effect today. The new religious content of this ancient framework was, however, as different as light is from darkness. The Church Fathers saw truly when they represented these aspects of paganism as part of the divine preparation for Christianity. We can never know to just what extent details of the messianic framework of the Gospels are *literally* true. Because of their highly intimate and personal character some of them are set forever beyond the reach of the critical historian, within whose epistemological range they can not be drawn (see above, pp. 112 ff.). In other words, the historian cannot control the details of Jesus' birth and resurrection and thus has no right to pass judgment on their historicity. On the other hand the historian is qualified to estimate the historical significance of the pattern and its vital importance for the nascent Christian movement as embodied in the person of its Master. A number of coincidences between a literal sequence of events and a traditional pattern are necessary before the former can be appropriated and modified by the latter (see above, pp. 67 ff.). It follows that the historian must recognize the presence of an important factual element in the Christian adaptation of the messianic tradition. Since, accordingly, there can be no complete factual judgment and since the historian cannot settle questions which are outside of his jurisdiction, the decision must be left to the Church and to the individual believer, who are historically warranted in accepting the whole of the messianic framework of the Gospels or in regarding it as partly true literally and as partly true spiritually—which is far more important in the region of spirit with which the Christian faith must primarily deal. The historian, *quâ* historian, must stop at the threshold, unable to enter the shrine of the Christian *mystêria* without removing his shoes, conscious that there are realms where history and nature are inadequate, and where God reigns over them in eternal majesty.

EPILOGUE

The task which we have set ourselves is completed; the reader must decide whether we have succeeded in executing it. In covering a field of such extent, both chronologically and geographically, the underlying historical pattern may sometimes have been obscured by unconscious selection of data. At other times the fragmentary nature of available material has made it hard to discern the texture of the pattern. Throughout we have resisted the temptation to modify our statement of historical fact in order to produce a simpler—but less objective—picture. We have endeavored to make the facts speak for themselves, though our care to state them fairly and to provide evidence to support them, where necessary, may sometimes have made it difficult for the reader to follow the unfolding scroll of history.

How does the picture of the history of monotheism which emerges from our study compare with the picture which has been handed down by biblical tradition? The tradition of Israel represents Moses as a monotheist; the evidence of ancient Oriental religious history, combined with the most rigorous critical treatment of Israelite literary sources, points in exactly the same direction. The tradition of Israel represents the Prophets as preachers and reformers, not as religious innovators; rigid historical and philological exegesis of our sources agrees with tradition. Christian tradition represents Jesus of Nazareth as the Christ of faith; historical and literary criticism, assisted by the evidence of Near-Eastern religious history, finds that there is nothing against the tradition—except prejudice. Mosaism is a living tradition, an integrated organismic pattern, which did not change in fundamentals from the time of Moses until the time of Christ; Moses was as much a monotheist as was Hillel, though his point of view may have been very different in detail. Christianity is also an integrated organismic pattern; it arose with Jesus of Nazareth, not with Paul or John, and its orthodox branches have modified their basic faith only in detail.

A double strand runs through our treatment: first, the ascending curve of human evolution, a curve which now rises, now falls, now moves in cycles, and now oscillates, but which has always *hitherto* recovered itself and continued to ascend; second, the development of individual historical patterns or configurations, each with its own organismic life, which rises, reaches a climax, and declines. The picture as a whole warrants the most sanguine faith in God and in His purpose for man. In detail it does not justify either fatuous optimism or humanistic meliorism. Contrary to the favorite assertion of the late J. H. Breasted, man has *not* raised himself by his own bootstraps.[1] Every human

---

[1] For detailed exposition of Breasted's humanistic philosophy of religious evolution see *The Dawn of Conscience* (New York, 1933), especially pp. 411-20. Cf. also *Time*, XVIII:24, pp. 23 f. (Dec. 14, 1931); the writer, *The American Scholar*, 1936, pp. 295 ff. For a discussion of the historical significance of Judaeo-Christianity from a theistic point of view, paralleling and supplementing the treatment here, see the writer's paper "Archaeology and Religion," presented at the Conference on Science, Philosophy, and Religion in New York City, September, 1940 (to appear in the publications of the Conference). It may be observed in this connection that it is singularly one-sided to recognize that man's physical constitution is an elaborately designed structure which will at best require a vast amount of research to understand, but at the same time to insist that the emotional, aesthetic, and religious ideas and aspirations of man are idle vestiges of a savage past or are mere puerile superstitions. It is far more "reasonable" to recognize that, just as man is a being evolved by the eternal spirit of the Universe, so his religious life is the result of stimuli coming from the same source and progressing toward a definite goal. In other words, the evolution of man's religious life is guided by divine revelation. Since, moreover, the affective religious life of man has a much more complex and elusive

culture has risen and has fallen in its turn; every human pattern has faded out after its brief season of success. It is only when the historian compares successive configurations of society that the fact of real progress makes itself apparent.

Nothing could be farther from the truth than the facile belief that God only manifests Himself in progress, in the improvement of standards of living, in the spread of medicine and the reform of abuses, in the diffusion of organized Christianity. The reaction from this type of theistic meliorism, which a few years ago had almost completely supplanted the faith of Moses, Elijah, and Jesus among modern Christians, both Protestant and Catholic, is now sweeping multitudes from their religious moorings. Real spiritual progress can only be achieved through catastrophe and suffering, reaching new levels after the profound catharsis which accompanies major upheavals. Every such period of mental and physical agony, while the old is being swept away and the new is still unborn, yields different social patterns and deeper spiritual insights. Our own age is witnessing a true catharsis which will, we believe, bring profound spiritual rebirth and will prevent man from destroying himself, as man has every apparent intention of doing.

Several hundred thousand years after primitive man had begun to make his first artifacts, and a little over two thousand years ago, Greek civilization reached its climax. Between 450 and 100 B.C. Hellenic thinkers formulated all the elements of modern science, philosophy, and art, and Jewish thinkers plumbed the depths of human relationship to God. However, just before man's fumbling hands could make use of the powerful new tools which were now at his disposal—and just when he should have entered a new era of progress, original intellectual activity practically ceased

---

structure, composed of psychological and historical elements, than the body of man, how much more research will at best be required to comprehend it! Yet the positivistic rationalist and the religious humanist claim in their *hybris* to understand enough of it to be able to direct man's ethical and social aspirations, often in serene disregard of our religious heritage.

and further progress was delayed for a millennium and a half. Meanwhile the civilized world had achieved unity and prosperity under Graeco-Roman culture and Roman domination, only to discover that its material and intellectual life was so far ahead of its spiritual development that the lack of integration became too great to permit further progress on the old lines. Jesus Christ appeared on the scene just when Occidental civilization had reached a fatal impasse.

The civilization of that day was in many respects comparable to what it is today. Philosophy ranged over just as wide fields of speculation; men's religious attitudes varied from the loftiest ethical monotheism to the most benighted superstition, just as today. Moreover, the modern world had, a quarter of a century ago, almost achieved comparable unity under the sway of a culture which was the lineal offspring of Graeco-Roman civilization; a few years later the same world achieved partial unity of political life under the League of Nations; there seemed to be no end to mechanical progress or to the advance of knowledge, employing the tools which had been forged so successfully by the Greeks. Yet today we see Occidental civilization tottering; we see intellectual activity declining with unexampled speed over a large part of the globe; we see a sensational revival of such pseudo-sciences as astrology (Babylonian in origin), Neo-Gnosticism ("New Thought" in all its varied forms), racial mysticism, etc.; we see scientific methods and discoveries judged by Marxist and racist gauges instead of by independent scientific standards. In short, we are in a world which is strangely like the Graeco-Roman world of the first century B.C. We need reawakening of faith in the God of the majestic theophany on Mount Sinai, in the God of Elijah's vision at Horeb, in the God of the Jewish exiles in Babylonia, in the God of the Agony at Gethsemane . . .

CHRONOLOGICAL TABLE*

Early Palaeolithic (Chellean, Acheulian): began at least 100,000 B.C.
Middle Palaeolithic (Levalloisian, Mousterian): at least 30,000 B.C.
Upper Palaeolithic (Aurignacian, Lower Capsian): at least 15,000 B.C.
Mesolithic (Natufian, etc.): at least 8000 B.C.
Neolithic: at least 5000 B.C.

CHRON-OLOGY B.C.	PALESTINE (including Syria)	EGYPT	BABYLONIA	NORTH MESOPOTAMIA (including Assyria)
About 3800......	Jerichoan (Jericho VIII)	Badarian		Halafian
About 3700......	Ghassulian		Proto-Obeidian	
About 3500......	Esdraelon	Amratian	Obeidian	
About 3200......	Early Bronze I	Gerzean	Warka period	Obeidian
About 3000......	Early Bronze II	First Dynasty	Jemdet Nasr period	
2800.............	Early Bronze III	Third Dynasty (Pyramid Age)	Early Dynastic I	
2600.............			Early Dynastic II	Gawra VIII
			Early Dynastic III	
			Empire of Accad (Sargon I, Naram-Sin) [c. 2360–2180]	
2300.............	Early Bronze IV (or III B)	Sixth Dynasty		
		First Intermediate		

* Reprinted from "Recent Discoveries in Bible Lands," the supplement to Young's Analytical Concordance to the Bible, copyrighted by Funk & Wagnalls in 1936 and 1955.

Date	Palestine	Egypt	Babylonia	Assyria / Hatti
2100	MIDDLE BRONZE I	TWELFTH DYNASTY	THIRD DYNASTY OF UR (Shulgi) [c. 2060-1950]	
2000				ASSUR INDEPENDENT
1900	MIDDLE BRONZE II A			CAPPADOCIAN COLONIES
1800			DYNASTIES OF ISIN AND LARSA — DYN. I of Babylon [c. 1830-1530] (Hammurabi) [c. 1728-1686]	
1700	MIDDLE BRONZE II B	SECOND INTERMEDIATE (Hyksos Period) [1710-1550]		EARLY HITTITE EMPIRE
1600	MIDDLE BRONZE II C	EIGHTEENTH DYNASTY [1570-1310]	COSSAEAN DYNASTY [c. 1600?-1150]	MITANNIAN EMPIRE [16th-14th cent.]
1500	LATE BRONZE I	(Tuthmosis III) [1490-1435]		
1400-1350	(AMARNA PERIOD)	(Amenophis III) [1406-1370]		NEW HITTITE EMPIRE
Late 14th cent.	LATE BRONZE II	NINETEENTH DYNASTY [1310-1200]		REVIVAL OF ASSYRIA (Asshur-uballit) [1354-1318]
Late 13th cent.	*Israelite occupation*	(Ramesses II) [1290-1224]		
1200	IRON I A	TWENTIETH DYNASTY [1200-1065]		(Tukulti-Ninurta I) [1234-1197]

CHRONOLOGY B.C.	PALESTINE (including Syria)	EGYPT	BABYLONIA	NORTH MESOPOTAMIA (including Assyria)
Late 12th cent....	Iron I B (Philistines)	(Ramesses III) [c. 1175-1144]	Fourth Dynasty of Babylon	(Asshur-dan I) [1179-1133]
1100.........	Gideon	Dynasty XXI (Tanis) [1065-935]		(Tiglathpileser I) [1115-1076]
1050....	*Fall of Shiloh*			
Late 11th cent....	Iron I C		Dynasty of Sea-Lands	Asshur-rabi II [1012]
c. 1020....	Saul			
c. 1000.......	David			Asshur-resh-ishi II [972]
c. 961........	Solomon	Dynasty XXII	Dynasty VIII	Tiglathpileser II [967]
c. 922....	*Division of Monarchy*	Shishak I [935]		Asshur-dan II [935]
c. 913....	Asa in Judah	Osorkon I [914]		Adad-nirari II [912]
c. 876....	Omri in Israel	Takelot I [874]		Asshur-nasir-apal II [884]
c. 873....	Jehoshaphat (Judah)	Osorkon II [860]		Shalmaneser III [859]
c. 842....	Jehu (Israel)			Shamshi-Adad V [824]
c. 800....	Amaziah (Judah)			Adad-nirari III [811]
c. 786....	Jeroboam II			Shalmaneser IV [783]

Date	Palestine	Egypt	Assyria / Babylonia / Persia
			Asshur-dan III [773]
c. 783	Uzziah (Judah)		Tiglathpileser III [745]
c. 745	Menahem (Israel)		Nabonassar [747]
c. 735	Ahaz (Judah)		Shalmaneser V [727]
722-1	Fall of Samaria	END OF DYNASTY XXII *Ethiopian conquest* [c. 720]	Sargon II [722]
715	Hezekiah (Judah)	Taharko [689]	Sennacherib [705]
687	Manasseh	*Assyrian conquest* [671]	Esarhaddon [681]
			Asshur-ban-apal [669]
			Fall of Nineveh [612]
640	Josiah		Nabopolassar [625]
609	Jehoiakim	Necho [609]	Nebuchadnezzar [605]
587	Fall of Jerusalem	Apries (Hophra) [588]	
		Amasis [569]	Cyrus of Persia conquers Astyages
549			*Cyrus conquers Babylon* [539]
538	Edict of Cyrus	*Persian conquest* [525]	Cambyses of Persia [530]
			Darius I (Hystaspes) [522]
515	Temple finished		Xerxes (Ahasuerus) [486]
458	Ezra's mission ?		Artaxerxes II (Longimanus) [464]

CHRONOLOGY B.C.	PALESTINE (including Syria)	EGYPT	BABYLONIA	NORTH MESOPTAMIA (including Assyria)
445	Nehemiah arrives		Darius II (Nothus) [423]	
c. 428	Ezra's mission ?		Artaxerxes II (Mnemon) [404]	
....	Jaddua high priest		Artaxerxes III (Ochus) [359]	
330	Macedonian conquest		Alexander the Great conquers Asia [334-323]	
....	Egyptian occupation	Ptolemy I [323]		Seleucus I [312] (Syria & Mesopotamia)
....		Ptolemy II [285]		Antiochus I [280]
....		Ptolemy III [246]		Antiochus II [261]
....		Ptolemy IV [221]		Seleucus II [246]
....		Ptolemy V [203]		Antiochus III [223]
200	Simon the Just / Syrian conquest	Ptolemy VI [181]		Seleucus IV [187]
167	Maccabaean revolt			Antiochus IV [175]
160	Jonathan high priest			Demetrius [162]
143	Simon high priest	Ptolemy VII [146]		Alexander Balas [150]
134	John Hyrcanus			Antiochus VII [138]

104........... Alexander Jannaeus

63........... Pompey takes Jerusalem

Roman conquest [30]

Augustus (first Roman emperor) [30]

37........... Herod the Great

4 B.C.,........... Archelaus

Tiberius [A.D. 14]

Caligula [A.D. 37]

Claudius [A.D. 41]

A.D. 37........... Herod Agrippa

Nero [A.D. 54]

Vespasian [A.D. 70]

A.D. 70........... Fall of Jerusalem

Roman occupation of Syria [63]

INDEX